Publications on Ocean Development

A SERIES OF STUDIES ON THE INTERNATIONAL, LEGAL, INSTITUTIONAL AND POLICY ASPECTS OF OCEAN DEVELOPMENT

General Editors

Robin Churchill
Alex Oude Elferink

VOLUME 100

The titles published in this series are listed at *brill.com/pood*

Marine Scientific Research and the Regulation of Modern Ocean Data Collection Activities under UNCLOS

The Library of Congress Cataloging-in-Publication Data is available online at https://catalog.loc.gov
LC record available at https://lccn.loc.gov/2022028528

Typeface for the Latin, Greek, and Cyrillic scripts: "Brill". See and download: brill.com/brill-typeface.

ISSN 0924-1922
ISBN 978-90-04-50858-3 (hardback)
ISBN 978-90-04-50859-0 (e-book)

This book is printed on acid-free paper and produced in a sustainable manner.

Marine Scientific Research and the Regulation of Modern Ocean Data Collection Activities under UNCLOS

By

Chuxiao Yu

BRILL
NIJHOFF

LEIDEN | BOSTON

Contents

Acknowledgement

This book is a slightly revised version of my PhD thesis, which was submitted in October 2020, and defended in February 2021 at Utrecht University. It would not have been possible for this book to come to fruition without the generous support and guidance of many people.

First and foremost, I would like to express my profound gratitude to my supervisors Prof. Dr. Alex G. Oude Elferink and Dr. Lan Nguyen. Thank you both for your infinite patience and enlightening supervision. I learnt a lot from your professional advice, the invaluable discussions we had, and the insightful comments you provided to my drafts. Beyond being witty mentors, you also set up role models for me and make me think about what kind of researcher I want to be in my future career. Special thanks are reserved for Prof. Dr. Otto Spijkers, who has acted as my daily supervisor for three years and is now a colleague of mine at Wuhan University. Thank you, Otto, for providing me with thoughtful guidance and constructive criticism during the PhD process.

Apart from my supervisors, I would like to sincerely thank the members of the Reading Committee, Prof. Dr. Alfred H.A. Soons, Prof. Dr. Şeline Trevisanut, Prof. Dr. Joanna Mossop, Prof. Dr. Keyuan Zou, and Prof. Dr. Erik Franckx, for the constructive and thought-provoking comments which helped me prepare the version for publication.

Special mention also goes to Prof. Dr. Ted McDorman of University of Victoria, Mr. Roland Rogers of National Oceanography Centre, Mr. Andrea Stefanus of Utrecht University, and other experts who prefer to remain anonymous for their valuable feedback on State practice concerning the regulation of foreign marine scientific research activities.

Of course, I would not have been able to initiate this work in Utrecht without the financial support provided by the China Scholarship Council (CSC). I am also most grateful to Prof. Dr. Tianbao Qin of Wuhan University, who always believes in me, gives me unconditional support and inspiring suggestion. I would not have had the courage to pursue a doctoral degree abroad without your guidance and help. I am extremely lucky to meet Prof. Dr. Marleen van Rijswick, who visited Wuhan in 2015 and planted the seed of my dream of becoming a PhD researcher at Utrecht University.

I am also appreciative of the stimulating academic platform provided by the Utrecht Centre for Water, Oceans and Sustainability Law (UCWOSL) and the Netherlands Institute for the Law of the Sea (NILOS). Great appreciation goes to my colleagues and friends at Utrecht, who make my stay in Europe an unforgettable experience. Thank you, Liping, Catherine, Tong, Chenyu, Yen,

Solène, Danae, Nikolas, Rozemarijn, Minh. I will always remember the great times that we shared and the joyful academic and non-academic chats that we had. Special thanks go to my paranymphs, Wen and Xuexia, for standing by my side not only at my online defense but also all the time when I need your advice in the past years. It has always been a pleasure to dive into the law of the sea with you with endless talks and to share with you the ups and downs of this PhD journey.

I also would like to thank the editors of the series on Publications on Ocean Development of Brill and the two anonymous reviewers for their invaluable feedback and comments. My gratitude also goes to Savitha, Kelley, Beth, and Marie from Brill for their help and understanding throughout the process of preparing this work for publication, and to Junrong and Zixuan for their patience in proofreading earlier versions of this manuscript.

Finally, and most importantly, I owe my deepest gratitude to my family for their enduring love and support. Several months after the defense of this work, my lovely daughter Amy came to this world. She is the most precious gift of my life and thus I dedicate this book to her.

August 2022, Wuhan

Abbreviations

ASAP	Automated Shipboard Areological Program
BBNJ	Biological Diversity of Areas Beyond National Jurisdiction
CBD	Convention on Biological Diversity
CEOS	Committee on Earth Observation Satellites
CGMS	Coordination Group for Meteorological Satellites
CLIVAR	Climate and Ocean: Variability, Predictability and Change
COP	Conference of the Parties
DBCP	Data Buoy Cooperation Panel
DOALOS	Division for Ocean Affairs and the Law of the Sea
ECVs	Essential Climate Variables
EEZ	Exclusive Economic Zone
EOVs	Essential Ocean Variables
EU	European Union
EuroGOOS	European Global Ocean Observing System
FAO	Food and Agricultural Organization
GCOS	Global Climate Observing System
GDP	Global Drifter Program
GLOSS	Global Sea Level Observing System
GODAE	Global Ocean Data Assimilation Experiment
GO-SHIP	The Global Ocean Ship-Based Hydrographic Investigations Program
GOOS	The Global Ocean Observing System
IAMC	The Integrated Assessment Modelling Consortium
ICRW	International Convention on the Regulation of Whaling
ICJ	International Court of Justice
ICNT	Informal Composite Negotiating Text
ICP	Informal Consultative Process
I-GOOS	Intergovernmental IOC-WMO-UNEP Committee for GOOS
IGC	Intergovernmental Conference
IHO	International Hydrographic Organization
ILBI	International Legally Binding Instrument
ILC	International Law Commission
IMO	International Maritime Organization
IOC	Intergovernmental Oceanographic Commission
IOC/ABE-LOS	IOC Advisory Body of Experts of the Law of the Sea
IPCC	Intergovernmental Panel on Climate Change
ISA	International Seabed Authority
ISNT	Informal Single Negotiating Text

ISOM	The International Research Ship Operators' Meeting
ITLOS	International Tribunal for the Law of the Sea
ITP	International Tsunameter Partnership
IUCN	International Union for Conservation of Nature
IWC	International Whaling Commission
JCOMM	The WMO-IOC Joint Committee for Oceanography and Marine Meteorology
LC	Convention on the Prevention of Marine Pollution by Dumping of Wastes and Other Matter (London Convention)
LICG	Legal Intersessional Correspondence Group
LP	Protocol to the Convention on the Prevention of Marine Pollution by Dumping of Waste and Matters (London Protocol)
MEOP	Marine Mammals Exploring the Oceans Pole to Pole
MPA	Marine Protected Area
MSR	Marine Scientific Research
OceanSITES	Ocean Sustained Interdisciplinary Timeseries Environment Observation System
PCA	Permanent Court of Arbitration
PrepCom	Preparatory Committee
RSNT	Revised Single Negotiating Text
SOT	Ship Observations Team
SOOP	Ship-of-Opportunity Program
SPLOS	Meeting of States Parties to the United Nations Convention on the Law of the Sea
TIP	Tropical Moored Buoy Implementation Panel
UK	United Kingdom
UN	United Nations
UNCLOS	United Nations Convention on the Law of the Sea
UNCLOS III	The Third United Nations Conference on the Law of the Sea
UNEP	United Nations Environment Programme
UNESCO	United Nations Educational, Scientific and Cultural Organization
UNFCCC	United Nations Framework Convention on Climate Change
UNGA	General Assembly of the United Nations
US	United States
VCLT	Vienna Convention on the Law of Treaties
VOS	Voluntary Observing Ship
WCRP	World Climate Research Programme
WIGOS	WMO Integrated Global Observing System
WMO	World Meteorological Organization
WTO	World Trade Organization
XBTS	Expendable Bathythermographs

Figures and Table

Figures

Table

CHAPTER 1

Introduction

1.1 The Impetus for the Current Research

It is often said that humanity knows less about the oceans than the heavens.[1] To fill this knowledge gap, increasing availability of data collected in the marine environment is inevitably in huge demand. Marine scientific research is seen as an essential activity that contributes to such an end.[2] The general regime regarding marine scientific research is contained in the United Nations Convention on the Law of the Sea ("UNCLOS" or "the Convention"),[3] especially in Part XIII of the Convention. The Convention divides the sea into several maritime zones, in which the coastal State and user States exercise rights and duties of a different scope. Part XIII of UNCLOS provides that in its internal waters and territorial sea, the coastal State has the exclusive right to regulate, authorize and conduct marine scientific research and that foreign research may be conducted "only with the express consent of and under the conditions set forth by the coastal State".[4] In the exclusive economic zone (EEZ) and on the continental shelf, the Convention similarly provides the coastal State with the right to regulate, authorize, and conduct marine scientific research.[5] Consent from the coastal State shall be obtained before engaging in marine scientific research in its EEZ or on its continental shelf.[6]

Although the Convention includes a whole part on marine scientific research, it does not contain a definition of the term "marine scientific research". As a result, the scope of activities covered by the term "marine scientific research", and hence the scope of regulation of the UNCLOS marine scientific research regime,

1 Tim Stephens and Donald Rothwell, "Marine Scientific Research", in *The Oxford Handbook of the Law of the Sea*, edited by Donald Rothwell, et al. (Oxford University Press, 2015), 559.

2 Alexander Proelss, ed. *United Nations Convention on the Law of the Sea: A Commentary* (C.H. Beck; Hart; Nomos, 2017), 1608. For a further discussion on the needs for marine scientific research, see Alfred H. A. Soons, *Marine Scientific Research and the Law of the Sea* (Kluwer Law and Taxation Publishers, 1982), 14–16.

3 United Nations Convention on the Law of the Sea, 1982.

4 Ibid., Article 245.

5 Ibid., Article 246(1).

6 Ibid., Article 246(2).

 | DOI:10.1163/9789004508590_002

remain unclear or controversial.[7] This has led to different opinions on the relationship between some specific ocean data collection activities and marine scientific research. One example is provided by survey activities. In practice, the United States has expressed that it does not consider survey activities as falling within the requirements of Part XIII of UNCLOS.[8] However, several States disagree with this interpretation, most notably India and China, both of which have lodged a series of protests over the survey activities undertaken by the United States and the United Kingdom in their EEZs.[9]

Besides, scientific advances and technological developments have driven transformative changes in how, where, and by whom ocean data collection activities can be conducted. These advances present opportunities to enhance knowledge and deliver benefits. However, they also bring new challenges for legal regulation, particularly where the legal classification of the activities at issue is unclear or controversial.[10] An example of such activities is operational oceanography that uses modern methods and means.[11] States have taken

7 Aldo Chircop, "Advances in Ocean Knowledge and Skill: Implications for the MSR Regime", in *Law, Science & Ocean Management*, edited by Myron Nordquist, et al. (Brill, 2007), 597; Montserrat Gorina-Ysern, *An International Regime for Marine Scientific Research* (Brill-Nijhoff, 2003), 181.

8 "The United States has identified some marine data collection activities that are not marine scientific research. These include prospecting for and exploration of natural resources; hydrographic surveys (for enhancing the safety of navigation); military activities including military surveys; activities related to the laying and operation of submarine cables [...]". See the official website of the US Department of State, "Marine Scientific Research Consent Overview", available at https://www.state.gov/marine-scientific-research-consent-overview/.

9 See, for instance, Kamlesh Kumar Agnihotri and Sunil Kumar Agarwal, "Legal Aspects of Marine Scientific Research in Exclusive Economic Zones: Implications of the Impeccable Incident", *Maritime Affairs: Journal of the National Maritime Foundation of India* 5, no. 2 (2009): 357; Donald R. Rothwell and Tim Stephens, *The International Law of the Sea (2nd edition)* (Hart Publishing, 2016).

10 Harriet Harden-Davies, "The Regulation of Marine Scientific Research: Addressing Challenges, Advancing Knowledge", in *Routledge Handbook of Maritime Regulation and Enforcement*, edited by Robin M Warner and Stuart Kaye (Routledge, 2016), 212.

11 The term "operational oceanography" is not used in UNCLOS or any other international legal document. Until now, there is no generally accepted definition of this term. See "Technical Workshop Enhancing Ocean Observations and Research, and the Free Exchange of Data, to Foster Services for the Safety of Life and Property: Final Report", Geneva, Switzerland, 2019, at p. 30. In its report submitted to the First Meeting of IOC/ABE-LOS, the GOOS Project Office (GPO) defined operational oceanography as: "the activity of routinely making, disseminating, and interpreting measurements of the seas and oceans and atmosphere, so as to: (i) provide continuous forecasts of the future condition of the sea as far ahead as possible; (ii) provide a description of the present state of the sea including living resources, with optimal accuracy; (iii) assemble long term climatic data

different views as to the legal classification of this kind of activities and the relationship between such activities and marine scientific research.[12] The introduction of such modern methods and means has dramatically changed the nature of ocean data collection activities, which significantly changes the situation that led to the negotiation and then the conclusion of relevant provisions contained in UNCLOS. Soons has submitted that "the current international legal regime for marine scientific research, as reflected in Part XIII of UNCLOS, was developed in the mid-1970s. It was mainly based on the classical mode of conducting [marine scientific research], by means of vessels engaged in cruises to obtain data in the marine environment".[13] Similarly, Bork *et al.* have observed Part XIII of UNCLOS was drafted on the basis of the specific understanding that marine scientific research involves "sampling data in a certain area within a limited time frame as well as in a foreseeable manner and with enough time for advance planning",[14] which is inconsistent with some new kinds of research methods adopted nowadays, such as floats[15] and gliders[16]. The question that arises is whether the UNCLOS marine scientific

---

sets to describe past states, and time series showing trends and changes". "Report by GPO on "the Argo Project" Developments", Doc. IOC/ABE-LOS I/10, 2001, pp. 4–5. A further discussion on the notion of operational oceanography and its relationship with marine scientific research will be included in Chapter 7 of this study.

12 Tullio Treves, "Marine Scientific Research", in *Max Planck Encyclopedia of Public International Law* [*MPEPIL*] (2008), para.2; Tim Stephens and Donald Rothwell, "Marine Scientific Research", 574–575; Philomène A Verlaan, "Current Legal Developments: Intergovernmental Oceanographic Commission of the United Nations Educational, Scientific and Cultural Organization (IOC/UNESCO)", *The International Journal of Marine and Coastal Law* 24 (2009): 177.

13 Alfred H. A. Soons, "The Impact of Technological Developments on the International Legal Regime of Marine Scientific Research", in *30 Years after the Signature of the United Nations Convention on the Law of the Sea: the Protection of the Environment and the Future of the Law of the Sea*, ed. Marta Ribeiro (Coimbra Editora, 2014), 329–330.

14 Katharina Bork et al., "The Legal Regulation of Floats and Gliders - In Quest of a New Regime?", *Ocean Development & International Law* 39, no. 3 (2008): 312.

15 A float is defined as "an autonomous vehicle used for collection of [...] data [...] and floating passively at a preprogrammed pressure level until at predetermined time intervals rising to the ocean surface to broadcast its position and, as the case may be, collected data to a satellite". See Draft [Practical] Guidelines of IOC, within the Context of UNCLOS, for the Collection of Oceanographic Data by Specific Means, 2007, IOC/ABE-LOS VII/7, http://unesdoc.unesco.org/Ulis/cgi-bin/ulis.pl?catno=218771&set=0057FC2FCE_3_441&gp=0&lin=1&ll=s, para.7(II).

16 Gliders are autonomous submersible vehicles, which can be pre-programmed or controlled from shore to navigate to designated waypoints in order to collect data not only at various depths but over a wide geographical area. See Tim Stephens and Donald Rothwell, "Marine Scientific Research", 575.

research regime covers these uses, *i.e.,* whether the activities involving these uses constitute marine scientific research in the context of UNCLOS or are regulated in some other ways by UNCLOS.

To the extent that the activities involving these new uses qualify as marine scientific research, it might be improper to put them under the same regulatory requirements and conditions as "traditional" marine scientific research. This can be illustrated by the introduction of bio-logging technology, which refers to the use of miniaturized animal-attached tags for logging and relaying of data about an animal's movements, behavior, physiology and environment.[17] In ocean data collection, when the devices are attached to marine animals, which may migrate into the territorial sea or the EEZ of the coastal State, the devices will record certain kinds of oceanographic data therein. The highly variable and hardly predictable behavior of marine animals makes it impracticable to accurately forecast the precise route that individual animals may travel. There is no efficient and acceptable way to direct or interfere with the movements of these animals either.[18] In this regard, the implementation of the consent regime set out in UNCLOS is problematic. It would be difficult to argue that, for a research project using bio-logging technology, the researching State has to fully comply with the requirements of obtaining the consent from the coastal State before the commencement of the project.

Another example is ocean data collection activities involving marine genetic resources. It is argued that if and to the extent that such activities belong to the category of marine scientific research, certain problems will occur when implementing relevant provisions of the Convention. For instance, when such activities are conducted in the Area, the conditions enumerated in Part XI of the Convention apply, and the researching State shall cooperate with the International Seabed Authority (ISA) in disseminating the results of the research and developing training programs for developing countries.[19] Many of these

17 Christian Rutz and Graeme C Hays, "New Frontiers in Biologging Science", (The Royal Society London, 2009), 289.

18 Richard J. McLaughlin, "UNCLOS and the Growing Use of Electronic Tagged Marine Animals as Autonomous Ocean Profilers", in *Governing Ocean Resources - New Challenges and Emerging Regimes: A Tribute to Judge Choon-Ho Park,* edited by Jon M. Dyke, et al. (Leiden, The Netherlands Martinus Nijhoff Publishers, 2013), 496; James Kraska, Guillermo Ortuño Crespo, and David W Johnston, "Bio-logging of marine migratory species in the law of the sea", *Marine Policy* 51(2015): 395–396; Richard J. McLaughlin, "Bio-Logging as Marine Scientific Research Under the Law of the Sea: A Commentary Responding to James Kraska, Guillermo Ortuño Crespo, David W. Johnston, Bio-Logging of Marine Migratory Species in the Law of the Sea, Marine Policy 51-(2015) 394–400", *Marine Policy* 60(2015): 180.

19 UNCLOS, Article 143.

conditions may be incompatible with the nature of some of these activities which require that sampling results need to be kept confidential.[20]

As "a constitution for the oceans",[21] UNCLOS aims at settling "all issues relating to the law of the sea".[22] Accordingly, it is submitted that the Convention also covers ocean data collection activities that do not qualify as marine scientific research and provides guidance for their regulation. For instance, in cases where an ocean data collection activity is carried out in the EEZ, it may amount to the exploration or exploitation of natural resources,[23] or "other internationally lawful uses of the sea related to" the freedoms of navigation, overflight, and of the laying of submarine cables and pipelines.[24] It may also be the case that the undertaking of an ocean data collection activity falls within the scope of Article 59 of the Convention concerning unattributed rights and jurisdiction in the EEZ of a coastal State. These provisions provide the basis for identifying the appropriate legal framework(s) for certain types of ocean data collection activities.

Nevertheless, it is also recognized that, in some instances, the Convention does not set out sufficiently detailed rules for some newly emerged activities, either because its provisions treat the subject too summarily or because they do not address it at all.[25] Additionally, to ensure contemporary relevancy, the Convention contains various options for using its flexibility to adapt to new circumstances, which have emerged since its adoption. Some of these options are provided by the Convention itself, while others are found outside the framework of the Convention.[26] Because some options are found

20 See Salvatore Arico and Charlotte Salpin, "Bioprospecting of Genetic Resources in the Deep Seabed: Scientific, Legal and Policy Aspects", (2005), para.5.1.5; Robin M Warner, "Protecting the Diversity of the Depths: Environmental Regulation of Bioprospecting and Marine Scientific Research beyond National Jurisdiction", *Ocean Yearbook*, no. 22 (2008): 411–443.

21 The expression was firstly coined by Tommy T.B. Koh and repeatedly echoed in the international legal literature, see "A Constitution for the Oceans", Remarks by Tommy T.B. Koh, President of the Third United Nations C-onference on the Law of the Sea, available at http://www.un.org/depts/los/convention_agreements/texts/koh_english.pdf.

22 UNCLOS, Preamble, 1st preambular Paragraph.

23 Ibid., Article 56(1)(a).

24 Ibid., Article 58(1).

25 Tullio Treves, "The Development of the Law of the Sea since the Adoption of the UN Convention on the Law of the Sea: Achievements and Challenges for the Future", in *Law, Technology and Science for Oceans in Globalisation: IUU Fishing, Oil Pollution, Bioprospecting, Outer Continental Shelf*, edited by Davor Vidas (Brill Nijhoff, 2010), 53.

26 Although such options are found outside UNCLOS, they maintain a strong link with it. Ibid., 49–51. See also Alan Boyle, "Further Development of the Law of the Sea Convention: Mechanisms for Change", *International & Comparative Law Quarterly* 54, no. 3 (2005).

outside the framework of UNCLOS, it is becoming increasingly apparent that issues of law of the sea cannot be considered in isolation.[27] UNCLOS is not the sole regime governing the conduct of ocean data collection activities. Other pertinent international legal instruments include the Convention on Biological Diversity (CBD)[28] and the Nagoya Protocol on Access to Genetic Resources and the Fair and Equitable Sharing of Benefits Arising from Their Utilization to the Convention on Biological Diversity (hereinafter Nagoya Protocol),[29] the United Nations Framework Convention on Climate Change (UNFCCC),[30] the Convention on the Prevention of Marine Pollution by Dumping of Wastes and Other Matter (hereinafter London Convention),[31] the Protocol to the Convention on the Prevention of Marine Pollution by Dumping of Waste and Matters (hereinafter London Protocol),[32] and the International Convention on the Regulation of Whaling (ICRW).[33] Presumably, these instruments serve as a good starting point for identifying the appropriate legal framework for certain ocean data collection activities, even if the relationship between the activities concerned and marine scientific research is not clearly addressed. In addition, they may be relevant in shedding light on understanding legal terms that are pertinent to the regulation of ocean data collection activities, such as the "due regard" provision contained in UNCLOS.[34]

Against this backdrop, the present research aims to examine the relevant provisions of UNCLOS, subsequent practice of States, and rules of other relevant international conventions pertaining to ocean data collection in light of current technological developments. On the basis of such an examination, this research will discern the legal classification of ocean data collection activities that have emerged as a result of technological developments after the adoption of UNCLOS (hereinafter "modern" ocean data collection activities) and accordingly consider the appropriate legal framework(s) for their regulation.

---

27 Tullio Treves, "The Development of the Law of the Sea since the Adoption of the UN Convention on the Law of the Sea: Achievements and Challenges for the Future", 55.

28 Convention on Biological Diversity, 1992.

29 Nagoya Protocol on Access to Genetic Resources and the Fair and Equitable Sharing of Benefits Arising from Their Utilization to the Convention on Biological Diversity, 2010.

30 United Nations Framework Convention on Climate Change, 1992.

31 Convention on the Prevention of Marine Pollution by Dumping of Wastes and Other Matter, 1972.

32 Protocol to the Convention on the Prevention of Marine Pollution by Dumping of Wastes and Other Matter, 1996.

33 International Convention on the Regulation of Whaling, 1946.

34 UNCLOS, Articles 56(2), 58(3).

1.2 Research Questions

The ultimate goal of this research is to identify the appropriate legal framework(s) for "modern" ocean data collection activities in the context of UNCLOS. Based on the above discussion, the main research question of this research is formulated as follows:

> To what extent do UNCLOS and its marine scientific research regime regulate "modern" ocean data collection activities, and through which regulatory arrangements might any gaps for regulation in the Convention be filled?

This research question results in several sub-questions:

1. What is the scope of regulation of the UNCLOS marine scientific research regime, *i.e.* what is the meaning of the term "marine scientific research" in the context of UNCLOS?
2. What are the rules that apply to different types of ocean data collection activities under UNCLOS in light of current developments, and how are they implemented in practice?
3. What are the limits and strengths of UNCLOS and its marine scientific research regime in regulating different types of "modern" ocean data collection activities?
   3.1 Are there any regulatory gaps for UNCLOS and its marine scientific research regime in regulating different types of "modern" ocean data collection activities?
   3.2 What options exist within UNCLOS to fill such regulatory gaps, and what are the implications of these options? Do relevant subsequent practice of States and rules contained in other international conventions provide any guidance in this respect?

1.3 Structure of the Book

Considering the purpose of the present research, that is, to analyze and understand the implications of new developments on the interpretation and application of UNCLOS, the method adopted is to interpret relevant UNCLOS provisions – the nature of the present research is legal positivism. The interpretation of such positive law in the present research will follow the rules of international law governing treaty interpretation found in Articles 31–33 of the

Vienna Convention on the Law of Treaties (VCLT).[35] Notably, in the interpretation of pertinent provisions of UNCLOS, sources including "subsequent agreements between the parties", "subsequent practice [...] which establishes the agreement of the parties" and "other relevant rules of international law applicable in the relations between the parties" would be taken into consideration.[36]

Following the rules of international law governing treaty interpretation under Articles 31–33 of VCLT, it is noted that some uncertainties exist about the reach of some canons of interpretation contained in the provisions. For instance, Article 31(1) states that "[a] treaty shall be interpreted [...] in accordance with the ordinary meaning [...]".[37] However, it is unclear whether it is "the ordinary meaning" at the time of concluding the treaty or "the ordinary meaning" at the time of interpretation that shall be consulted.[38] The same question applies to Article 31(3)(c), which stipulates that together with the context, "[a]ny relevant rules of international law applicable in the relations between the parties" shall be taken into account in the interpretation.[39] It remains an open question whether such "relevant rules of international law" are those that exist at the time of the conclusion of the convention being interpreted or at the time of interpretation.[40] The International Law Commission

35 Vienna Convention on the Law of Treaties, 1969.

36 Ibid., Article 31(3). This provision (Article 31(3), VCLT) ensures that "every treaty provision [...] be read not only in its context, but in the wider context of general international law". Ian McTaggart Sinclair, *The Vienna Convention on the Law of Treaties* (Manchester University Press, 1984), 138.

37 VCLT, Article 31(1).

38 Ulf Linderfalk, "Doing the Right Thing for the Right Reason – Why Dynamic or Static Approaches Should be Taken in the Interpretation of Treaties", *International Community Law Review* 10, no. 2 (2008): 111; Paolo Palchetti, "Interpreting "Generic Terms": Between Respect for the Parties' Original Intention and the Identification of the Ordinary Meaning", in *International Courts and the Development of International Law*, edited by Nerina Boschiero, et al. (Springer, 2013); Sondre Torp Helmersen, "Evolutive Treaty Interpretation: Legality, Semantics and Distinctions", *European Journal of Legal Studies* 6(2013): 166; Panos Merkouris, "(Inter)Temporal Considerations in the Interpretative Process of the VCLT: Do Treaties Endure, Perdure or Exdure?", *Netherlands Yearbook of International Law* 45(2015).

39 VCLT, Article 31(3)(c).

40 Eduardo Jimenez De Arechaga, *International Law in the Past Third of a Century* (Martinus Nijhoff, 1978), 49; Rosalyn Higgins, "Time and the Law: International Perspectives on An Old Problem", *International & Comparative Law Quarterly* 46, no. 3 (1997): 519; Campbell McLachlan, "The Principle of Systemic Integration and Article 31(3)(c) of the Vienna Convention", *International & Comparative Law Quarterly* 54, no. 2 (2005): 279; Duncan French, "Treaty Interpretation and the Incorporation of Extraneous Legal Rules", *International & Comparative Law Quarterly* 55, no. 2 (2006): 281; Ulf Linderfalk, "Doing the Right Thing for the Right Reason – Why Dynamic or Static Approaches Should be Taken in the

(ILC) has commented that "in any event, the relevance of rules of international law for the interpretation of treaties in any given case was dependent on the intentions of the parties".[41] Therefore, before commencing the interpretation of substantive rules governing ocean data collection, the present research will first ascertain if it is the intention of the parties to UNCLOS to refer to the "ordinary meaning" of a treaty term and "relevant rules of international law" at the time of concluding UNCLOS or at the time of interpretation (Chapter 2). This will inform the types of interpretative material that will be considered in the subsequent chapters for the interpretation of UNCLOS.

Chapters 3 to 5 will set out the current legal framework for the regulation of ocean data collection activities under UNCLOS (Chapter 3) and assess how stakeholders have implemented the relevant provisions within that framework (Chapters 4 and 5). Pursuant to the general rule of treaty interpretation contained in VCLT, these chapters respectively look at the text of UNCLOS pertaining to the regulation of ocean data collection activities in light of current developments with a focus on issues of marine scientific research (Chapter 3), subsequent practice of States in the application of relevant UNCLOS provisions (Chapter 4), and other relevant rules of international law in the field of ocean data collection (Chapter 5).[42]

After setting out the legal framework for the regulation of ocean data collection activities and options for using the flexibility provided by UNCLOS to cope with new developments in ocean data collection (Chapters 3 to 5), the present study will illustrate the strengths and limits of UNCLOS and its marine scientific research regime in regulating "modern" ocean data collection activities, through two specific case studies (Chapters 6 and 7).[43]

Interpretation of Treaties", 111–112; Panos Merkouris, "(Inter)Temporal Considerations in the Interpretative Process of the VCLT: Do Treaties Endure, Perdure or Exdure?"; Sondre Torp Helmersen, "Evolutive Treaty Interpretation: Legality, Semantics and Distinctions", 166; Panos Merkouris, *Article 31(3)(c) VCLT and the Principle of Systemic Integration: Normative Shadows in Plato's Cave* (Brill, 2015).

41 "Report of the International Law Commission on the second part of its seventeenth session and on its eighteenth session", Doc. A/CN.4/SER.A/1966/Add.1, 1967, 222.

42 Although VCLT does not require the interpretation to be processed in the order listed in Articles 31–32, it has been submitted that the order "is intuitively likely to represent an effective sequence in which to approach the task". Martti Koskenniemi, "Fragmentation of International Law: Difficulties Arising from the Diversification and Expansion of International Law (Report of the Study Group of the International Law Commission)", UN Doc. A/CN.4/L.682, 2006, para.428.

43 Case study research "involves the study of an issue explored through one or more cases within a bounded system (a setting, a context)". John W. Creswell, *Qualitative Inquiry and Research Design: Choosing Among Five Approaches* (Sage Publications, 2007), 73.

The present research takes the topics of access to marine genetic resources (Chapter 6) and operational oceanography (Chapter 7) as examples to assess the strengths and limits of the current legal framework in regulating new uses in ocean data collection. These activities are selected because relevant discussions in international fora suggest that they have raised the most controversial legal issues, particularly in relation to the applicability of the UNCLOS marine scientific research regime and the appropriate legal framework for their regulation. On the basis of the conclusions drawn in the previous chapters, Chapters 6 and 7 will discern the legal classification of these two types of "modern" ocean data collection activities and consider the appropriate legal framework(s) for their regulation. The chapters will identify where gaps remain in UNCLOS in regulating these ocean data collection activities and examine whether the gaps can be filled by resorting to the insights gained from relevant practice or other conventions.

The concluding chapter (Chapter 8) draws together the conclusions arrived at in the previous chapters and presents the fundamental conclusions of this study.

1.4 Delineation of the Research and Use of Terminology

It is noted that there are generally two types of methods for ocean data collection activities: ground-based and remote sensing methods – the former mainly refers to *in situ* measurements, surveys or observations, that is, a sensor is at the immediate location of or in contact with the object in question; while the latter operates on the basis of image data acquired by a sensor from some distance.[44] Since it has been generally acknowledged that space activities fall outside the scope of UNCLOS – they are covered by a separate international legal regime[45] – the present research will only address the legal issues arising from ocean data collection activities that are conducted *in situ* in the marine environment. The term "marine environment" is not defined in the Convention. As is commonly understood, this term covers "the water column, the seabed and subsoil, and the atmosphere immediately above the sea".[46] Research activities

44 Florian H.Th. Wegelein, *Marine Scientific Research: The Operation and Status of Research Vessels and Other Platforms in International Law* (Martinus Nijhoff Publishers, 2005), 37.

45 Myron H. Nordquist et al., eds., *United Nations Convention on the Law of the Sea, 1982: A Commentary (Vol. IV)* (Dordrecht: Martinus Nijhoff Publishers, 1991), 532; Alfred H. A. Soons, *Marine Scientific Research and the Law of the Sea*, 5.

46 Alfred H. A. Soons, *Marine Scientific Research and the Law of the Sea*, 124.

that are carried out on land (in the laboratories) concerning objects that have been collected from the marine environment also fall outside the scope of this study.[47]

This research was primarily undertaken up to June 2020. Therefore, the relevant research materials, including State practice and international legal instruments, that are examined in the present research are those that have come to the attention of the author by this time.

To delineate the scope of the present research, some preliminary points need to be made regarding the use of terminology in the following chapters.

Marine Scientific Research and Ocean Data Collection: The term "marine scientific research" is not defined by UNCLOS. Under UNCLOS, the term "marine scientific research" only refers to the activities to be regulated by the Part XIII regime of the Convention.[48] It has been pointed out that on some occasions this term has been used loosely to denote all "activities undertaken at sea to gather/obtain knowledge", and marine scientific research in a strictly legal sense is only one category of such activities.[49] In order to avoid confusion, the term "marine scientific research" will only be used when the activity can be "legally" interpreted and classified as marine scientific research. In other cases, a more general term – "ocean data collection activity" – will be used. This term refers to an activity that on face value seems to be marine scientific research, but its legal classification remains undefined. It is noted that some activities that do not directly collect data, but rather samples (for example marine genetic resources), may also qualify as marine scientific research under UNCLOS. However, if the samples are collected for the purpose of collecting the samples *per se*, the activity at issue cannot be classified as marine scientific research – it is exploration or exploitation if the samples are natural resources. For marine scientific research or like activities, samples are collected for the purpose of extracting valuable data therefrom for the purpose of research and analysis.

Researching State: This term refers to the State that conducts marine scientific research. Under Part XIII of UNCLOS, apart from States, competent

---

47 Soons has observed that although the Part XIII regime is mainly concerned with marine scientific research undertaken in the marine environment, some provisions also cover marine scientific research activities conducted in laboratories on land. See ibid. For a further discussion on this point, see Chapter 3.2.2 of this book.

48 See ibid., 124–125.

49 Alfred H. A. Soons, "Marine Scientific Research Provisions in the Convention on the Law of the Sea: Issues of Interpretation", in *The UN Convention on the Law of the Sea: Impact and Implementation*, edited by ED Brown and RR Churchill (Honolulu: The Law of the Sea Institute, William S. Richardson School of Law, University of Hawaii, 1987), 366–367.

international organizations also have the right to conduct marine scientific research.[50] In this respect, in order to make the text of the present research more concise, the terms "researching States" and "the researching State" will be used to refer to the State(s) and/or the competent international organization(s) that conduct(s) marine scientific research, unless expressly stated otherwise.

Foreign Marine Scientific Research: This term refers to the marine scientific research project undertaken by a researching State or a competent international organization in maritime areas under the sovereignty or jurisdiction of other States.

50 UNCLOS, Article 238.

CHAPTER 2

An Analysis of the Approach to Interpreting Pertinent UNCLOS Provisions

2.1 Introduction

As indicated Chapter 1.3 of this book, the current chapter aims to identify the appropriate approach to interpreting relevant UNCLOS provisions on ocean data collection. To be more specific, this chapter addresses the question of whether said provisions should be interpreted against the background of the legal and factual circumstances at the time of the conclusion of UNCLOS, or at the time of interpretation. In the process, a focus will be placed on the interpretation of the term "marine scientific research", since discerning the scope of activities covered by this term is one of the fundamental questions to be answered in this book.

Although different opinions exist as to the objective of treaty interpretation,[1] it appears to be the mainstream viewpoint that the aim of interpretation is to unveil "the meaning which the parties may have intended to attach to the expressions that they employed in a document".[2] Accordingly, when addressing the question of whether the interpretation of the relevant UNCLOS provisions should follow the developments that occurred after the adoption of the Convention, it is necessary to determine the intention of the parties concerning this matter. Wyatt has termed this use of the term "intention" as "temporal sense-intention", which refers to "the particular problem of whether to give a treaty term its original or later-emerging meaning".[3]

---

1 There are mainly two schools of thoughts as to the purpose of treaty interpretation, one being the "assessment of the subjective intention of the parties", and the other being the "analysis of that intention as embodied by the objective text of a treaty". See Clément Marquet, "Prospective Linguistics and Trade: The Art of the Deal", in *Evolutionary Interpretation and International Law*, edited by Georges Abi-Saab, et al. (Bloomsbury Publishing, 2019), 196.

2 See, for instance, "Report of the International Law Commission on the second part of its seventeenth session and on its eighteenth session", Doc. A/CN.4/SER.A/1966/Add.1, 218; Robert Jennings and Arthur Watts, eds., *Oppenheim's International Law: Volume 1 Peace (9th Edition)* (Oxford University Press, 2008), 1267.

3 Julian Wyatt, "Using Intertemporal Linguistics to Resolve the Problem at the Origin and Core of the Evolutionary Interpretation Debate", in *Evolutionary Interpretation and International Law*, edited by Georges Abi-Saab, et al. (Bloomsbury Publishing, 2019), 54. Similarly, Merkouris adopts the term "time-will" referring to "the intention of the parties that determines

 | DOI:10.1163/9789004508590_003

Following this introductory section, Section 2.2 will set out the elements to be considered for determining the "temporal sense-intention" of the parties. The subsequent sections (Sections 2.3 to 2.6) address consecutively the elements identified in Section 2.2 and their implications for assessing the temporal sense-intention of the parties to UNCLOS. Section 2.7 concludes the chapter and presents some observations on the implications of the temporal sense-intention of the parties for interpreting relevant UNCLOS provisions.

2.2 Elements to Be Considered in the Assessment Process

The issues related to the temporal sense-intention have been addressed both in relevant international case law and legal literature. An overview of these sources indicates that the determination of the temporal sense-intention of the parties needs to consider the following elements.

2.2.1 *The Use of a Generic Term*

The first element is whether the concept or term at issue is a "generic term", or in other words, whether its meaning is either open-ended or evolving.[4] The International Court of Justice (ICJ) stated in the *Namibia* Advisory Opinion that concepts of "the strenuous conditions of the modern world", "the well-being and development", and "sacred trust" "were not static, but were by definition evolutionary".[5] It further considered that "the parties to the Covenant must consequently be deemed to have accepted them as such".[6] As a result, "the Court must take into consideration the changes which have occurred in the supervening half-century, and its interpretation cannot remain unaffected by the subsequent development of law".[7]

Later, in the *Aegean Sea Continental Shelf* case, the ICJ again noted that:

> Once it is established that the expression 'the territorial status of Greece' was used in Greece's instrument of accession as a generic term denoting

the temporal destiny of a particular term". See, Panos Merkouris, "(Inter)Temporal Considerations in the Interpretative Process of the VCLT: Do Treaties Endure, Perdure or Exdure?", 144.

4 The concept of "generic terms" will be further discussed in Section 2.4.1 of the current chapter.

5 ICJ, *Legal Consequences for States of the Continued Presence of South Africa in Namibia (South West Africa) notwithstanding Security Council Resolution 276-(1970)*, Advisory Opinion of 21 June 1971, para.53.

6 Ibid.

7 Ibid.

> any matters comprised within the concept of territorial status under general international law, the presumption necessarily arises that its meaning was intended to follow the evolution of the law and to correspond with the meaning attached to the expression by the law in force at any given time.[8]

The effect of the use of generic terms was affirmed again by the ICJ in its Judgment on *Dispute regarding Navigational and Related Rights* in 2009, in which the Court further stressed, "where the parties have used generic terms in a treaty, the parties necessarily having been aware that the meaning of the terms was likely to evolve over time".[9]

This approach is endorsed by the Conclusions adopted by International Law Commission (ILC) on Fragmentation of International Law, which state that "rules of international law subsequent to the treaty to be interpreted may be taken into account especially where the concepts used in the treaty are open or evolving".[10]

2.2.2 *The Nature of the Treaty*

A second element that plays a vital role in assessing the temporal sense-intention, as suggested by case law, is the nature or the intended lifespan of the treaty at issue. Both in the *Aegean Sea Continental Shelf* case and *Dispute regarding Navigational and Related Rights* case, in addition to considering the effect of the use of generic terms, the Court referred to the nature of the legal document at issue to confirm the presumption that the parties must have intended to give the relevant treaty terms an evolving meaning.[11] In its Judgment on the *Aegean Sea Continental Shelf* case, the Court considered that the presumption of the parties' intention to give the relevant treaty terms an evolving meaning:

> is even more compelling when it is recalled that the 1928 Act was a convention for the pacific settlement of disputes designed to be of the

8 ICJ, *Aegean Sea Continental Shelf* (*Greece v. Turkey*), Judgment of 19 December 1978, para.77.

9 ICJ, *Dispute Regarding Navigational and Related Rights* (*Costa Rica v. Nicaragua*), Judgment of 13 July 2009, para.66.

10 "Report of the International Law Commission (Fifty-eighth session)", Doc. A/61/10, 2006, at pp. 415–416.

11 ICJ, *Aegean Sea Continental Shelf* (*Greece v. Turkey*), Judgment of 19 December 1978, para.77; ICJ, *Dispute Regarding Navigational and Related Rights* (*Costa Rica v. Nicaragua*), Judgment of 13 July 2009, para.66.

> most general kind and of continuing duration, for it hardly seems conceivable that in such a convention terms like 'domestic jurisdiction' and 'territorial status' were intended to have a fixed content regardless of the subsequent evolution of international law.[12]

Later, in *Dispute regarding Navigational and Related Rights* case, the Court further stressed:

> where the treaty has been entered into for a very long period or is 'of continuing duration', the parties must be presumed, as a general rule, to have intended those terms to have an evolving meaning.[13]

According to the ICJ, the use of generic terms and the intended lifespan of a treaty are constituent elements of "a general rule" which allows subsequent developments to be taken into consideration of when interpreting the treaty terms at issue.

Broad support can be found in the literature for this approach – that the nature of a legal document constitutes a significant part in identifying whether the parties intend to give the term at issue an evolving meaning. As commented by ILC, "the character of a treaty may affect the question whether the application of a particular principle, maxim or method of interpretation is suitable in a particular case".[14] It has also been submitted that for treaties which are constitutional or which can be considered as living instruments, based on "the nature of the treaty" that the parties agreed to, the intention can be presumed that the interpretation of relevant treaty norms needs to bear in mind subsequent developments.[15]

---

12 ICJ, *Aegean Sea Continental Shelf* (*Greece v. Turkey*), Judgment of 19 December 1978, para.77.

13 ICJ, *Dispute Regarding Navigational and Related Rights* (*Costa Rica v. Nicaragua*), Judgment of 13 July 2009, para.66.

14 "Report of the International Law Commission on the second part of its seventeenth session and on its eighteenth session", Doc. A/CN.4/SER.A/1966/Add.1, 219.

15 See, for instance, Rosalyn Higgins, "A Babel of Judicial Voices? Ruminations from the Bench", *International & Comparative Law Quarterly* 55, no. 4 (2006): 797–798; Malgosia Fitzmaurice, "The Practical Working of the Law of Treaties", in *International law* (*Fourth Edition*), edited by Malcolm D. Evans (Oxford University Press, 2014), 183; Malgosia Fitzmaurice, "Interpretation of Human Rights Treaties", in *The Oxford Handbook of International Human Rights Law*, edited by Dinah Shelton (Oxford University Press, 2013), 759; Andrea Bianchi, "The Game of Interpretation in International Law", in *Interpretation in International Law*, edited by Andrea Bianchi, Daniel Peat, and Matthew Windsor (Oxford University Press, 2015), 44.

2.2.3 *The Drafting History of Relevant Treaty Terms*

It is noted that the approach adopted by the ICJ in the *Namibia* case and the *Aegean Sea* case – relying mostly on the use of generic terms to justify the presumed intention of the parties – has given rise to some debates. According to Thirlway, the Court failed to provide enough evidence to establish that it has been the *actual intention* of the parties to give a treaty term evolving meaning.[16] He further noted that in the particular case of the *Namibia* Advisory Opinion, nothing had been offered to show that the concepts were *at the time* regarded as evolutionary.[17] In order to convince its readers, "the concept of terminology capable of giving rise to an 'intertemporal-*renvoi*'" must refer to "the actual or legitimately deduced intention of the author or authors of the relevant text".[18] The emphasis placed on "the actual or legitimately deduced intention of the author or authors" seems to imply that the drafting history (the preparatory work and the circumstances of the conclusion) of the treaty text at issue should be given a certain weight in the process of assessment.

As regards the relevant drafting history of a treaty, it is noted that this element only serves as a supplementary means of interpretation under VCLT.[19] However, arguably, to ascertain the temporal sense-intention of the parties, it is important to refer to the subjective intention of the drafters of the legal document at the time of its conclusion. Therefore, more weight should be attached to the preparatory work of the treaty and the circumstances of the conclusion. As such, the relevant drafting history will be the third element for ascertaining the temporal sense-intention of the parties in the current research.

2.2.4 *The Object and Purpose of the Treaty*

Fourthly, according to some authors, the temporal sense-intention of the parties can also be deduced from the object and purpose of the agreement at issue.[20] It is submitted that if it is the object and purpose of a treaty to create

16 According to Thirlway, "there must be a danger, when applying this line of approach, of confusing what, on the basis of the available evidence, may be found to have been the actual intention of the parties concerned, and what is judged, with the benefit of hindsight, to be what *ought* to have been their intention". [emphasis in original] Hugh Thirlway, "The Law and Procedure of the International Court of Justice 1960–1989: Part One", *British Yearbook of International Law* 60, no. 1 (1989): 136–137.

17 Ibid., 137.

18 Ibid., 143.

19 VCLT, Article 32.

20 Rosalyn Higgins, "Time and the Law: International Perspectives on An Old Problem", 519. See also, Ulf Linderfalk, "Doing the Right Thing for the Right Reason – Why Dynamic or Static Approaches Should be Taken in the Interpretation of Treaties"; Ulf Linderfalk, "Discussing the Evolutionary Interpretation of Treaties", *EJIL:Talk!* (December 16, 2014),

long-lasting and solid relations between the parties, "it is hardly compatible with this purpose to eliminate new developments in the process of treaty interpretation".[21] Such viewpoints also find support in international judicial practice. The ICJ stated in the *Gabčíkovo-Nagymaros Project* case that,

> [w]hat is essential, therefore, is that the factual situation as it has developed since 1989 shall be placed within the context of the preserved and developing treaty relationship, in order to achieve its object and purpose in so far as that is feasible.[22]

In the *Iron Rhine Railway* case, the Arbitral Tribunal took into consideration of "new technical developments relating to the operation and capacity of the railway" to "ensure an application of the treaty that would be effective in terms of its object and purpose".[23] The same approach has been adopted by the WTO Appellate Body. In its report on the *US-Shrimp* case, the WTO Appellate Body made an explicit reference to "the objective of sustainable development in the preamble of the WTO Agreement" to justify the adoption of a modern-day meaning of the term "exhaustible natural resource".[24] In the case concerning *China – Publications and Audiovisual Product*, the Appellate Body again considered the object and purpose of the treaty at issue when assessing whether to interpret the term "sound recording distribution services" according to the meaning at the time of interpretation.[25]

It is noted that in some cases, the element of the object and purpose of a treaty may coincide or overlap with the nature or the intended lifespan of a treaty – the object and purpose of a treaty are to create lasting and solid relations

---

https://www.ejiltalk.org/discussing-the-evolutionary-interpretation-of-treaties/; Julian Arato, "Subsequent Practice and Evolutive Interpretation: Techniques of Treaty Interpretation over Time and Their Diverse Consequences", *The Law & Practice of International Courts and Tribunals* 9, no. 3 (2010); Paolo Palchetti, "Interpreting "Generic Terms": Between Respect for the Parties' Original Intention and the Identification of the Ordinary Meaning".

21 Rudolf Bernhardt, "Evolutive Treaty Interpretation, Especially of the European Convention on Human Rights", *German YB Int'l L.* 42(1999): 16–17.

22 ICJ, *Gabčíkovo-Nagymaros Project* (*Hungary/Slovakia*), Judgment of 25 September 1997, para.133.

23 PCA, *Iron Rhine Arbitration* (*Belgium/Netherlands*), Award of 24 May 2005, para.80.

24 Appellate Body of the WTO, *United States - Import Prohibition of Certain Shrimp and Shrimp Products*, WT/DS58/AB/R, Appellate Body Report of 12 October 1998, para.131.

25 Appellate Body of the WTO, *China - Measures Affecting Trading Rights and Distribution Services for Certain Publications and Audiovisual Entertainment Products*, WT/DS363/AB/R, Appellate Body Report of 21 December 2009, para.395.

between the parties.[26] However, there are also other instances where the two elements are to be considered separately, as in the *Iron Rhine Arbitration*.[27] Therefore, in the present research, the two elements will be treated consecutively, in order to fully explore the effect of these elements in determining the temporal sense-intention of the parties to UNCLOS.

2.2.5 *Other Elements that Play a Role?*

Apart from the elements pointed out above, it has been proposed that other elements contained in the general rule of treaty interpretation under VCLT, for instance, subsequent agreements and subsequent practice, also need to be considered to determine the temporal sense-intention of the parties. At its seventieth session, ILC adopted a series of conclusions on subsequent agreements and subsequent practice in relation to the interpretation of treaties, among which Conclusion 8 states that,

> [s]ubsequent agreements and subsequent practice under articles 31 and 32 [of VCLT] may assist in determining whether or not the presumed intention of the parties upon the conclusion of the treaty was to give a term used a meaning which is capable of evolving over time.[28]

However, it is submitted that subsequent agreements and subsequent practice are indications of *whether and how* the meaning of a treaty term has evolved since the adoption of the legal document.[29] In other words, these are elements for assessing whether the parties, as a matter of *fact*, have opted for a different meaning of the treaty term from the one at the time of concluding the treaty. It would make more sense to suggest that subsequent agreement and subsequent practice may serve to confirm or reject a presumed temporal sense-intention of the parties, rather than assist the determination of such an intention.

---

26 For instance, it has been observed that "[i]f it is the purpose of a treaty to create longer lasting and solid relations between the parties..., it is hardly compatible with this purpose to eliminate new developments in the process of treaty interpretation". Rudolf Bernhardt, "Evolutive Treaty Interpretation, Especially of the European Convention on Human Rights", 16–17.

27 In the *Iron Rhine Arbitration*, the Tribunal pointed out that "[t]he Iron Rhine Treaty was not intended as a treaty of limited or fixed duration". See PCA, *Iron Rhine Arbitration* (*Belgium/Netherlands*), Award of 24 May 2005, para.82.

28 "Report of the International Law Commission (Seventieth session)", Doc. A/73/10, 2018, at p. 14, commentary on this conclusion at pp. 64–70.

29 See, for instance, Julian Arato, "Subsequent Practice and Evolutive Interpretation: Techniques of Treaty Interpretation over Time and Their Diverse Consequences", 443–494.

2.2.6 *Interim Conclusions*

In sum, this chapter will focus on the four elements identified above, which are 1) the use of a generic term, 2) the nature of the treaty, 3) the drafting history of relevant treaty terms, and 4) the object and purpose of the treaty, to assess the parties' temporal sense-intention. A more natural flow of analysis would commence with an examination of the drafting history of the definition of the term "marine scientific research" (Section 2.3), followed by the discussion on the linguistic nature of the term – whether it is a "generic term" (Section 2.4), the nature of UNCLOS (Section 2.5), and the object and purpose of UNCLOS (Section 2.6).

2.3 Drafting History of the Definition of the Term "Marine Scientific Research"

Before examining the drafting history of the definition of the term "marine scientific research", it is necessary to provide some background information on the Third United Nations Conference on the Law of the Sea ("UNCLOS III" or "the Conference") and some general characteristics of the Conference.

UNCLOS, and the marine scientific research regime as embodied in Part XIII, are the product of the extensive negotiations that took place during UNCLOS III. UNCLOS III was the first United Nations (UN) law-making conference which used consensus decision-making.[30] As matters concerning the oceans are all interrelated, in order to avoid selective ratification as in the case of the four conventions resulting from the First United Nations Conference on the Law of the Sea, it was decided to adopt a "package deal" approach.[31] Under such circumstances and in the face of the large number of and often conflicting proposals put forward by the delegations, it was realized that in order to obtain the greatest possible support, informal discussions could be more effective than formal negotiations. Indeed, decisions on many controversial issues were made during informal meetings, which are considered as one of the dominant features of UNCLOS III.[32] This approach, to a certain extent, expedited the progress of reaching agreements. Nevertheless, a major defect (for legal

30 Robin Churchill, "The 1982 United Nations Convention on the Law of the Sea", in *The Oxford Handbook of the Law of the Sea*, edited by Donald Rothwell, et al. (Oxford University Press, 2015), 26; James Harrison, *Making the Law of the Sea: A Study in the Development of International Law* (Cambridge: Cambridge University Press, 2011), 40–44.

31 James Harrison, *Making the Law of the Sea: A Study in the Development of International Law*, 44–46.

32 Alfred H. A. Soons, *Marine Scientific Research and the Law of the Sea*, 109.

researchers at least) is that no record of these informal meetings exists.[33] As a result, it is sometimes difficult to rely on the drafting history to discern the intention of the parties and in some instances, the intention of the parties can only be inferred.

Turning back to the issue of the definition of the term "marine scientific research", during UNCLOS III, numerous proposals containing draft articles on the definition of the term were made.[34] During the Conference, several informal draft texts of the Convention were introduced. Some of the earlier versions of these draft texts included an article on the definition of the term "marine scientific research".[35] However, such an article was deleted in the Informal Composite Negotiating Text (ICNT) which was formulated in 1977 and the subsequent draft texts.[36] Since the negotiations leading to a deletion of the

---

33 Existing official records of UNCLOS III only concern formal meetings. Records of the meetings during UNCLO-S III can be found at the official website of UN Codification Division Publications, Diplomatic Conferences, "Thir-d United Nations Conference on the Law of the Sea", available at http://legal.un.org/diplomaticconferences/1973_los/.

34 For a further discussion on these proposed definitions, see Chapter 3. Official proposals containing a definition of the term "marine scientific research" made during UNCLOS III include, "Trinidad and Tobago: draft articles on marine scientific research" (1974), UN Doc. A/CONF.62/C.3/L.9, Article 1; "Austria, Belgium, Bolivia, Botswana, Denmark, Germany (Federal Republic of), Laos, Lesotho, Liberia, Luxembourg, Nepal, Netherlands, Paraguay, Singapore, Uganda, Upper Volta and Zambia: draft articles on marine scientific research" (1974), UN Doc. A/CONF.62/C.3/L.19, Article 1; "Bulgaria, Byelorussian Soviet Socialist Republic, Czechoslovakia, German Democratic Republic, Hungary, Mongolia, Poland, Ukrainian Soviet Socialist Republic and Union of Soviet Socialist Republics: draft articles on marine scientific research" (1975), UN Doc. A/CONF.62/C.3/L.26, Article 1; "Colombia, El Salvador, Mexico, Nigeria: draft articles on marine scientific research", UN Doc. A/CONF.62/C.3/L.29, Article 1. A comprehensive overview of these definitions has been provided by UN/DOALOS, "Marine Scientific Research: A Revised Guide to the Implementation of the Relevant Provisions of the United Nations Convention on the Law of the Sea", New York, 2010, paras.7–14; Myron H. Nordquist et al., eds., *United Nations Convention on the Law of the Sea, 1982: A Commentary (Vol. IV)*, 438–450; Alfred H. A. Soons, *Marine Scientific Research and the Law of the Sea*, 121–125.

35 Part III of the Informal Single Negotiating Text (ISNT), UN. Doc. A/CONF.62/WP.8/Part III, in its Part II contains an article on the definition of marine scientific research, which quotes as "[m]arine scientific research means any study or related experimental work designed to increase man's knowledge of the marine environment". This definition was incorporated in the Revised Single Negotiating Text (RSNT) with only one change of word - "man's" was replaced by "mankind's", UN. Doc. A/CONF.62/WP.8/Rev.1/Part III, Article 48.

36 Full text of the Informal Composite Negotiating Text and subsequent revisions and corrections can be found at the official website of UN Codification Division Publications, Diplomatic Conferences, "Third United Nations Co-nference on the Law of the Sea – Sixth session", http://legal.un.org/diplomaticconferences/1973_los/vol8.shtml.

definition occurred in an informal setting of which no official record is available, reasons for the deletion can only be inferred.[37]

At the resumed seventh session of the Conference (1978), the US proposed reinstating the definition of the term "marine scientific research" in future draft texts.[38] This proposal was based on the assumption that the article on the definition "was omitted, apparently inadvertently, during the drafting of ICNT when definitions were moved to article 1".[39] However, there was insufficient support for this proposal,[40] implying that the definition of the term was not omitted unintentionally.

The fact that States eventually decided to delete the article defining the term "marine scientific research" indicates that they, or at least some of them, at the time of UNCLOS III, did not agree on the definitions included in the proposals or the draft texts. As observed by the Virginia Commentary, the main divergence on this matter was the relationship between the so-called pure (or fundamental) marine scientific research and applied marine scientific research.[41] Delegations at the Conference could not reach an agreement on objective criteria to distinguish between the two.[42] Considering the persistent divergence on this matter, they decided to leave the term undefined, having the advantage of being able to incorporate divergent opinions, rather than to include a definition that would give rise to tensions. It turned out that the exclusion of the article concerning the definition of the term "marine scientific research" has indeed enabled delegations to reach consensus on the text of Part XIII.[43] In this sense, the deletion of the definition was a result of a

37 It has been noted that a consensus was reached during the informal discussions at the fourth session of UNCLOS III (1976) to abandon the definition of the term "marine scientific research", or at least not to consider this question for the time being. See Alfred H. A. Soons, *Marine Scientific Research and the Law of the Sea*, 123.

38 Myron H. Nordquist et al., eds., *United Nations Convention on the Law of the Sea, 1982: A Commentary* (*Vol. IV*), 448.

39 Ibid.

40 Ibid.

41 Ibid., 444. A further discussion on the notions of "pure" and "applied" marine scientific research is included in Section 3.2.4.1.

42 Ibid. See also the Summary Records of meetings of UNCLOS III, especially the summary records of meetings of the Second Committee during the Second Session and Third Session, available at the official website of UN Codification Division Publications, Diplomatic Conferences, "Third United Nations Conference on the Law of the Sea", http://legal.un.org/diplomaticconferences/1973_los/.

43 Aldo Chircop, "Advances in Ocean Knowledge and Skill: Implications for the MSR Regime", 97.

compromise among delegations since they "could do no better than reach[ing] a weak compromise".[44]

It is not hard to imagine that this would be a typical strategy for concluding "package deal" agreements such as UNCLOS, to win as much support as possible.[45] As commented by many scholars, being a "package deal" means that many provisions of UNCLOS are the result of compromises reached among States that held differing views.[46] Consequently, these provisions are ambiguously formulated and left for "future development through the interpretation or application of the Convention".[47]

Therefore, the reason for not including a definition of the term "marine scientific research" in the Convention is that there was no agreement among delegations on this matter. Admittedly, the absence of a definition causes controversies over the scope of regulation of the UNCLOS marine scientific research regime.[48] Nevertheless, what may be a weakness from one perspective can be a strength from another.[49] As indicated above, a major advantage

---

44 Robin Churchill, "The 1982 United Nations Convention on the Law of the Sea", 26.

45 The implications of the fact that UNCLOS is the outcome of a "package deal" for the present study will be addressed in Chapter 3 of this book.

46 See, for instance, Shunji Yanai, "The Contribution of the Tribunal to the Progressive Development of International Law", in *The Contribution of the International Tribunal for the Law of the Sea to the Rule of Law: 1996–2016*, edited by ITLOS (Brill-Nijhoff, 2018), 79; Richard Barnes, "The Continuing Vitality of UNCLOS", in *Law of the Sea: UNCLOS as a living treaty*, edited by Jill Barrett and Richard Barnes (London: The British Institute of International and Comparative Law, 2016), 483–84; James Harrison, "Judicial Law-Making and the Developing Order of the Oceans", *The International Journal of Marine and Coastal Law* 22, no. 2 (2007): 287.

47 See, for instance, Richard Barnes, "The Continuing Vitality of UNCLOS", 483–84; James Harrison, "Judicial Law-Making and the Developing Order of the Oceans", 287. The same viewpoint has been expressed by Shearer, who stated that "on certain critical points, disagreement was papered over by compromises or disguised by opaque texts that elude clear meaning". See Ivan Shearer, "Oceans Management Challenges for the Law of the Sea in the First Decade of the 21st Century", in *Ocean Management in the 21st Century: Institutional Frameworks and Responses*, edited by Alex Oude Elferink and Donald Rothwell (Brill, 2004), 4.

48 See Tullio Treves, "Marine Scientific Research", paras.1–4, 29; Alexander Proelss, ed. *United Nations Convention on the Law of the Sea: A Commentary*, 1609; Montserrat Gorina-Ysern, *An International Regime for Marine Scientific Research*, 181; Paul Gragl, "Marine Scientific Research", in *The IMLI Manual on International Maritime Law: Volume I: The Law of the Sea*, edited by David Attard, Malgosia Fitzmaurice, and Norman A Martínez Gutiérrez (OUP Oxford, 2014), 401; Harriet Harden-Davies, "The Regulation of Marine Scientific Research: Addressing Challenges, Advancing Knowledge", 212–213.

49 Shirley V. Scott, "The LOS Convention as A Constitutional Regime for the Oceans", in *Stability and Change in the Law of the Sea: The Role of the LOS Convention*, edited by Alex Oude Elferink (Martinus Nijhoff Publishers, 2005), 22.

of not including a definition is that it can incorporate divergent viewpoints, and stimulate the establishment of a compromised agreement. Besides, it enables the flexibility to adapt the spirit of Part XIII to new research frontiers.[50] Arguably, by omitting an article on the definition, States intended to leave the definitional issue to future developments.[51]

This observation is confirmed by Article 251 of the Convention, which requires States to "seek to promote [...] the establishment of general criteria and guidelines to assist States in ascertaining the nature and implications of marine scientific research".[52] This article creates an obligation for States to elaborate further the issue concerning the definition of the term "marine scientific research". If the meaning of the term "marine scientific research" was conceived as static, States would have needed to establish general criteria and guidelines concerning the nature and implications of marine scientific research that existed at the time of the negotiations. Most likely, this is not the case. Instead, by this provision, the drafters of the Convention seemed to advocate States to establish such criteria and guidelines based on their practical experiences accumulated since the adoption of the Convention at a time when they have a better comprehension of this kind of activities and at a time when there is a consensus on what the term "marine scientific research" should mean. Therefore, it is argued that this provision reinforces the argument that the parties intended to give the term "marine scientific research" an evolving meaning.

It is noted that no record of the meetings of UNCLOS III explicitly stated that the reason for omitting the definition of the term "marine scientific research" was to allow accommodating new developments. However, the absence of such a record does not reject the above observation either. Often, especially in the case of multilateral agreements, the preparatory work is not recorded in a

---

50 Aldo Chircop, "Advances in Ocean Knowledge and Skill: Implications for the MSR Regime", 599–600. The issue of definition arises not only in the context of marine scientific research, but also in the sphere of law in general. It relates to two essential functions of law: stability or adaptability. On the one hand, including a definition gives rise to legal certainty, and on the other, it presupposes adaptability to new circumstances, and therefore reduces the durability of the regime. See Pierre-Marie Dupuy, "Evolutionary Interpretation of Treaties: Between Memory and Prophecy", in *The Law of Treaties Beyond the Vienna Convention*, edited by Enzo Cannizzaro (Oxford University Press, 2011), 123; Ulf Linderfalk, "Doing the Right Thing for the Right Reason – Why Dynamic or Static Approaches Should be Taken in the Interpretation of Treaties", 109–110; Sondre Torp Helmersen, "Evolutive Treaty Interpretation: Legality, Semantics and Distinctions", 164.

51 In this connection, an analysis of subsequent practice and potential subsequent agreements on this matter will be provided in Chapter 4 of this book.

52 UNCLOS, Article 251.

reliable manner, and more often available records are incomplete or ambiguous.[53] As mentioned earlier, this is also the case for UNCLOS, because, for some essential meetings at UNCLOS III, the relevant discussion was not recorded. Therefore, it has been submitted that finding explicit evidence to support the presumption that certain treaty terms were meant to have meanings that are capable of evolving is not a prerequisite, as long as there is no evidence indicating the contrary.[54]

In sum, the relevant drafting history of the definition of the term "marine scientific research" and the reason of omitting an article on this matter in the Convention suggest that the parties to UNCLOS intended to give the term an evolving meaning. This is confirmed by the wording of Article 251 of the Convention. Bearing this observation in mind, the next section will address the issue of whether the term "marine scientific research" can be viewed as a generic term.

2.4 Can the Term "Marine Scientific Research" Be Viewed as a Generic Term?

In order to determine whether the term "marine scientific research" can be viewed as a generic term, it is necessary to introduce the notion of "generic term" and criteria to be deployed to assess whether a term is generic or not. In this section, relevant international judicial practice and literature will be presented to set a list of criteria for identifying generic terms (Section 2.4.1). After establishing the list, the discussion will shift towards the issue of whether the term "marine scientific research" can be viewed as a generic term (Section 2.4.2).

2.4.1 *What Is a "Generic Term"?*

Although various attempts have been made to define the concept of "generic term" in a legal context, there is no generally accepted definition of the

53 Gerald G. Fitzmaurice, "Law and Procedure of the International Court of Justice: Treaty Interpretation and Certain Other Treaty Points", *British Yearbook of International Law* 28(1951): 15; Rudolf Bernhardt, "Evolutive Treaty Interpretation, Especially of the European Convention on Human Rights", 14; Robert Jennings and Arthur Watts, eds., *Oppenheim's International Law: Volume 1 Peace (9th Edition)*, 1277–1278.

54 Paolo Palchetti, "Interpreting "Generic Terms": Between Respect for the Parties' Original Intention and the Identification of the Ordinary Meaning", 101–102.

concept.[55] The most often cited definition is that given by Judge Higgins in her Declaration attached to the Judgment of the *Kasikili/Sedudu Island* case, which referred to the concept of "generic term" as "a known legal term, whose content the parties expected would change through time".[56] According to this definition, the concept of "generic term" contains two levels of meaning. First, from a semantic perspective, the meaning of a generic term is capable of changing over time.[57] Second, from a legal perspective and in the context of treaty interpretation, an evolving meaning is given to a generic term only when it accords with the intention of the parties to a legal document. One can see that this intention is the same of what has been termed as "temporal sense-intention", which is at the core of determining whether new developments should be taken into account in the interpretation of treaty provisions. This section will address the first aspect – what is a generic term from a semantic perspective, and whether the term "marine scientific research" can be considered as such. The second aspect of Judge Higgin's definition of the concept of "generic term" concerning the temporal sense-intention of the parties is the theme of inquiry of this chapter in general.

2.4.1.1 Generic Terms as Identified by International Courts and Tribunals

As noted in Section 2.2.1 of the current chapter, the concept of "generic term" has appeared several times, implicitly or explicitly, in the Advisory Opinions and Judgments of the ICJ. For example, in the *Namibia* Advisory Opinion, the Court pointed out that terms "the strenuous conditions of the modern world", "the well-being and development", and "sacred trust" "were not static, but were

55 Panos Merkouris, "(Inter)Temporal Considerations in the Interpretative Process of the VCLT: Do Treaties Endure, Perdure or Exdure?", 141–142.

56 ICJ: *Kasikili/Sedudu Island* (Botswana v. Namibia), Judgment (13 December 1999), Declaration of Judge Higgins, para.2. The definition is echoed by many scholars. For example, Panos Merkouris, *Article 31(3)(c) VCLT and the Principle of Systemic Integration: Normative Shadows in Plato's Cave*, 124; Eduardo Jimenez De Arechaga, *International Law in the Past Third of a Century*, 49.

57 This perspective has been pointed out by Rosenne in 1969, which he termed as the problem of "intertemporal linguistics". See Max Sørensen, *Le problème dit du droit intertemporel dans l'ordre international* (1973), 80–81, (Observations de M. Shabtai Rosenne). Other authors have also written on this perspective. For instance, it has been submitted that, contrary to terms whose meanings were set at the time of concluding the treaty, generic terms have the capacity to evolve in harmony with the conditions and opinions prevailing from time to time, and that the linguistic character of a term as generic may lead its interpreter "in the direction of opting for an evolutive interpretation" of its meaning. See Eduardo Jimenez De Arechaga, *International Law in the Past Third of a Century*, 49; Panos Merkouris, "(Inter)Temporal Considerations in the Interpretative Process of the VCLT: Do Treaties Endure, Perdure or Exdure?", 141.

by definition evolutionary".[58] However, the Court did not provide any explanation of why it regarded those terms as such.

In *Aegean Sea Continental Shelf* case, the ICJ characterized the term "territorial status" as a "generic term denoting any matters properly to be considered as comprised within the concept of territorial status under general international law".[59] It considered that,

> as *the nature of the word* 'status' itself indicates, it was a generic term which in the practice of the time was understood as embracing the integrity and frontiers, as well as the legal régime, of the territory in question.[60]

The Court did not address in detail the criteria for determining whether a term is generic or not. What can be inferred from its line of reasoning is that a generic term may denote a group of things/matters comprised within a single concept.

Thereafter, in its Judgment on *Dispute regarding Navigational and Related Rights*, the Court identified "commerce" as a generic term, "referring to a class of activity".[61] Here, the Court confirms the assumption made above, that the reference to a group of things/matters is (one of) the characteristic(s) of being a generic term.

Other international courts and tribunals have also used the concept of "generic term" in their reasoning. For example, the WTO Appellate Body held that notions such as "natural resources",[62] "sound recording" and "distribution"[63] are generic terms. However, in none of these cases, explanations have been provided for the characterization.

Based on the available international case law that has used the concept of "generic term", arguably one criterion of this concept can be summarized

---

58 ICJ, *Legal Consequences for States of the Continued Presence of South Africa in Namibia (South West Africa) notwithstanding Security Council Resolution 276 (1970)*, Advisory Opinion of 21 June 1971, para.53.

59 ICJ, *Aegean Sea Continental Shelf (Greece v. Turkey)*, Judgment of 19 December 1978, para.76.

60 Emphasis added. Ibid., para.75.

61 ICJ, *Dispute Regarding Navigational and Related Rights (Costa Rica v. Nicaragua)*, Judgment 13 July 2009, para.67.

62 Appellate Body of the WTO, *United States - Import Prohibition of Certain Shrimp and Shrimp Products*, WT/DS58/AB/R, Appellate Body Report of 12 October 1998, para.130.

63 Appellate Body of the WTO, *China - Measures Affecting Trading Rights and Distribution Services for Certain Publications and Audiovisual Entertainment Products*, WT/DS363/AB/R, Appellate Body Report of 21 December 2009, para.396.

and that is that the concept of "generic term" refers to a class of activities or phenomena.

2.4.1.2 The Criteria for a Generic Term in the Literature

Since guidance offered by international courts and tribunals is relatively limited, the following sub-section will turn to the relevant discussion in the literature. As indicated above, determining whether a term is generic or not is not only a legal question but also a linguistic one. To better understand the issue, expertise needs to be borrowed from the discipline of linguistics.[64] Arguably, the general rule of treaty interpretation under Article 31 of VCLT already acknowledges the importance of linguistics. According to Article 31(1), the interpretation of a treaty shall be, among others, "in accordance with the ordinary meaning to be given to the terms of the treaty".[65] The process of identifying the ordinary meaning is an issue that falls, at least partly, within the discipline of linguistics.

The effort of borrowing expertise from the field of linguistics has been made by several legal scholars to understand the criteria for a generic term.[66] From the analysis provided by these scholars, one can note that the concept used both in the legal context (in international courts and tribunals as well as in the legal literature) and in the linguistic context – "generic term" – does not refer to the same thing. In a legal context, it refers to a term whose meaning is capable of changing and is highly likely to change over time. However, such a classification of words or expressions does not exist in a linguistic context.[67]

---

64 It is noted that the current study is of a legal nature; thus, one should be cautious when trying to step outside the field of law. However, as the fundamental aim of treaty interpretation is to ascertain the meaning of a treaty term following the parties' intention, and this aim cannot be accomplished without input from other disciplines including linguistics, the interconnection between law and linguistics cannot be ignored. For an in-depth discussion on the relationship between linguistics and international law (especially the interpretation of international law), see, for instance, Ingo Venzke, *How Interpretation Makes International Law: On Semantic Change and Normative Twists* (Oxford University Press, 2012); Julian Wyatt, *Intertemporal Linguistics in International Law: Beyond Contemporaneous and Evolutionary Treaty Interpretation* (Hart Publishing, 2019).

65 VCLT, Article 31(1).

66 See, for instance, Ulf Linderfalk, "Doing the Right Thing for the Right Reason – Why Dynamic or Static Approaches Should be Taken in the Interpretation of Treaties", 109–141; Sondre Torp Helmersen, "Evolutive Treaty Interpretation: Legality, Semantics and Distinctions", 161–188.

67 At this moment, there is no generally recognized theory of the evolution of language. However, some interesting approaches have been suggested. See Clément Marquet, "Prospective Linguistics and Trade: The Art of the Deal", 199–200.

Semantically, generic noun phrases refer to a category as an abstract whole (for example dogs as an entirety), not to any individual or group of individuals.[68]

Under this circumstance, Helmersen has proposed to make a distinction between "value driven" terms and "non-value driven" terms to assist the identification of generic terms in a legal context.[69] The former refers to terms whose meanings depend on values, while the latter does not.[70] Since values inevitably change over time, it makes sense to consider the meaning of "value driven" terms evolving as well, for example, "necessary measures", "inhuman punishment", "fair and equitable".[71]

The rationale of this approach is worth a closer examination. From the linguistic perspective, the meanings of any content words,[72] to which all nouns, most verbs, adjectives, and adverbs belong, have the potential of change. The focus of the current discussion is to address whether the meaning of some terms would have *greater* potential than others to evolve. If the content of a term can be related to an element which is widely acknowledged as being evolutive, such as value, the meaning of this term is more likely to evolve. This observation finds its basis in historical linguistics. It has been submitted that "language external factors" are common driving forces in meaning change.[73]

In Helmersen's analysis, the distinction between generic terms and non-generic terms is made on the basis of value. A pertinent question that arises is whether there are other elements, similar to value, that are generally recognized as being evolutive? Some examples of such elements can be found in the ILC Conclusions on Fragmentation of International Law ("the Fragmentation Conclusions"). In the Fragmentation Conclusions, a concept that is similar to "generic term" – open or evolving concepts – is used, which includes,

68 See Susan A. Gelman and Twila Tardif, "A Cross-Linguistic Comparison of Generic Noun Phrases in English and Mandarin", *Cognition* 66, no. 3 (1998): 216; John Lyons, *Semantics: I* (Cambridge University Press, 1977), 194; Nils Reiter and Anette Frank, "Identifying Generic Noun Phrases" (paper presented at the Proceedings of the 48th Annual Meeting of the Association for Computational Linguistics, 2010), 40.

69 Sondre Torp Helmersen, "Evolutive Treaty Interpretation: Legality, Semantics and Distinctions", 176.

70 Ibid. it is submitted that the term "values" in the current context refers to "[p]rinciples or standards of behaviour; one's judgement of what is important in life." See "value", Oxford Dictionary of English (Oxford Reference online version, 3rd edition, Oxford University Press, 2015).

71 Ibid.

72 In contrast to function words, content words are words that carry the content or the meaning of a sentence.

73 See Regine Eckardt, *Meaning Change in Grammaticalization: An Enquiry into Semantic Reanalysis* (Oxford University Press, 2006), 4.

a. the concept is one which implies taking into account subsequent technical, economic or legal developments;
b. the concept sets up an obligation for further progressive development for the parties; or
c. the concept has very general nature or is expressed in such general terms that it must take into account changing circumstances.[74]

The first category indicates that if a term is closely linked to inherently evolving elements, such as technical, economic and legal situations, its meaning is more likely to evolve.

It can be argued that all the terms characterized by international courts and tribunals as "generic" meet the criteria of ILC noted above. The concepts "the strenuous conditions of the modern world" and "territorial status" are time-related, since "conditions" and "status" inherently change alongside time. Other terms, such as "the well-being and development" and "sacred trust", are closely related to value as well as economy; "commerce" and "natural resources" to economy; and "sound recording" and "distribution" to technology.

2.4.2 *Is the Term "Marine Scientific Research" a "Generic Term"?*

Based on the foregoing analysis, two criteria can be applied in evaluating whether a term can be viewed as a generic term: 1) if the term refers to a category of activities, phenomena or subjects, and 2) if the content of the term is closely linked to an element that is widely recognized to be evolutive. Bearing in mind these criteria, this sub-section addresses whether the term "marine scientific research" can be considered as a generic term.

About the first criterion, it is noted that the term "marine scientific research" in the context of UNCLOS does not refer to a single activity or several activities, but rather a class of activities that have the same/similar trait(s). As will be further illustrated in the following chapters, this kind of activities can be undertaken using different tools and instruments, on various scales, and in differing forms and manners.[75] The working definitions of the term given by commentators also support the idea that the term "marine scientific research" denotes a category of activities. For example, Soons has submitted that the term "marine scientific research" as envisaged in UNCLOS "may be defined as any study or related experimental work designed to increase man's knowledge of the marine environment".[76]

---

74 "Report of the International Law Commission (Fifty-eighth session)", Doc. A/61/10, 415–416.
75 See, in particular, Chapter 7 of this study.
76 Alfred H. A. Soons, *Marine Scientific Research and the Law of the Sea*, 6. The definition has been echoed by a number of scholars, for example, Treves noted that marine scientific

As to the second criterion, the term "marine scientific research" is intimately related to several elements that are inherently evolutive over time, for example, technology, science, and economy. Evolution of these elements inevitably brings about changes to the methods, scale, and even purpose of undertaking marine scientific research activities. Thus, it is more than reasonable to argue that the term "marine scientific research", which refers to a kind of activities that are closely connected to technological developments and scientific advances, would have an evolving meaning that adapts to changing circumstances.

In sum, the above analysis leads to the conclusion that the term "marine scientific research" can be viewed as a "generic term", whose meaning is highly likely to evolve. However, it is noted that one cannot rely solely on the use of a generic term to ascertain the temporal sense-intention of the parties. Even if the meaning of the term *does* change over time (linguistically), its meaning within a legal context may remain static if that is the intention of the parties to the legal document. Several cases adjudicated by the ICJ support this argument.[77] Examples include the meaning of the term "dispute" in the context of a treaty concluded in 1836 in the case concerning *Rights of Nationals of the United States of America in Morocco*,[78] and the meaning of the terms "centre of the main channel" and "thalweg" under the Anglo-German Agreement of 1890 in the case concerning *Kasikili/Sedudu Island*.[79] In order to correctly determine the temporal sense-intention of the parties, the conclusions drawn on the assessment of the term "marine scientific research" as a generic term need

research "seems to include any study or related experimental work designed to increase knowledge of the marine environment". Tullio Treves, "Marine Scientific Research". Other similar definitions have been provided in Patricia Birnie, "Law of the Sea and Ocean Resources: Implications for Marine Scientific Research", *The International Journal of Marine and Coastal Law* 10(1995): 242; Yoshifumi Tanaka, "Obligation to Co-Operate in Marine Scientific Research and the Conservation of Marine Living Resources", *Zeitschrift fur Auslaendisches Oeffentliches Recht und Voelkerrecht* 65, no. 4 (2005): 938–939; Tim Stephens and Donald Rothwell, "Marine Scientific Research", 562.

77 As observed in the Judgment of the *Navigational and Related Rights* case:

> [t]he Court has so proceeded in certain cases requiring it to interpret a term whose meaning had evolved since the conclusion of the treaty at issue, and in those cases the Court adhered to the original meaning.

ICJ, *Dispute Regarding Navigational and Related Rights* (*Costa Rica v. Nicaragua*), Judgment of 13 July 2009, para.63.

78 ICJ, *Rights of Nationals of the United States of America in Morocco* (*France v. United States of America*), Judgment of 27 August 1952, at p. 189.

79 ICJ, *Kasikili/Sedudu Island* (*Botswana/Namibia*), Judgment of 13 December 1999, para.25.

to be complemented by the conclusions concerning the assessment of other elements identified in Section 2.2 of this chapter.

2.5 The Nature of UNCLOS and Its Implications for Ascertaining the Temporal Sense-Intention of the Parties

Many scholars have referred to UNCLOS as a "living instrument",[80] the meaning of which, among others, is that the provisions of the Convention were not set in stone at the time of its conclusion, and the Convention has the ability to evolve.[81] The role of UNCLOS as a living instrument was pointed out in a written statement and oral submissions to the International Tribunal for the Law of the Sea (ITLOS) in the *Sub-Regional Fisheries Commission Request for an Advisory Opinion*, and also in the Separate Opinion of Judge Lucky on this case.[82] According to Judge Lucky:

> The 1982 Convention and the Statute of the Tribunal are 'living instruments'. This means that they 'grow' and adapt to changing circumstances. An act/statute is always 'speaking'. The law of the sea is not static.[83]

80 See, for instance, Michael Wood, "Reflections on the United Nations Convention on the Law of the Sea: a Living Instrument", in *Law of the Sea: UNCLOS as a living treaty*, edited by Jill Barrett and Richard Barnes (London: British Institute of International and Comparative Law, 2016); Jill Barrett, "The UN Convention on the Law of the Sea: a "Living" Treaty?", in *Law of the Sea: UNCLOS as a living treaty*, edited by Jill Barrett and Richard Barnes (London: The British Institute of International and Comparative Law, 2016); Richard Barnes, "The Continuing Vitality of UNCLOS"; Alan Boyle, "Further Development of the Law of the Sea Convention: Mechanisms for Change".

81 Michael Wood, "Reflections on the United Nations Convention on the Law of the Sea: a Living Instrument", LXXVII; Richard Barnes, "The Continuing Vitality of UNCLOS", 459.

82 Germany raised this point in its written statement concerning the case (dated 18 November 2013), see "Written Statement by the Federal Republic of Germany", available at https://www.itlos.org/fileadmin/itlos/documents/cases/case_no.21/written_statements_round1/C21_3_Germany_orig_Eng.pdf, para.8. Subsequently, this idea was discussed in the oral proceedings, see the Verbatim Record of the public sitting held on Wednesday, 3 September 2014, at 10 a.m., Doc. ITLOS/PV.14/C21/2/Rev.1, at p. 14; the Verbatim Record of the public sitting held on Thursday, 4 September 2014, at 10 a.m., Doc. ITLOS/PV.14/C21/3/Rev.1, at p. 20.

83 ITLOS, *Request for an Advisory Opinion submitted by the Sub-Regional Fisheries Commission (SRFC)*, Advisory Opinion of 2 April 2015, Separate Opinion of Judge Lucky, para.18.

UNCLOS is living in a way that it evolves over time and has the capacity to adapt to changing circumstances.[84]

However, it has been observed that there are numerous ways to adapt the Convention to changing circumstances.[85] Interpreting a treaty term in an evolutive manner is but one of these ways to do so. Others include the "built-in" flexibility of the Convention, such as the meetings of State Parties (SPLOS),[86] the obligations set forth for relevant or competent international organizations to develop international rules and standards or guidelines,[87] the right or duty provided for States to cooperate on a bilateral, regional or global basis in implementing relevant provisions, its system of "rule of reference" to incorporate "decentralized administrative means",[88] its compulsory dispute settlement mechanism, the regulatory power given to the institutions it creates (e.g. the

---

84 Bernard H. Oxman, "Tools for Change: The Amendment Procedure" (paper presented at the Proceedings of the Twentieth Anniversary Commemoration of the Opening for Signature of the UNCLOS, New York, 2003), 199.

85 David Freestone and Alex Oude Elferink, "Flexibility and Innovation in the Law of the Sea: Will the LOS Convention Amendment Procedures Ever Be Used?", in *Stability and Change in the Law of the Sea: The Role of the LOS Convention*, edited by Alex Oude Elferink (Martinus Nijhoff Publishers, 2005); Bernard H. Oxman, "Tools for Change: The Amendment Procedure"; Alan Boyle, "Further Development of the Law of the Sea Convention: Mechanisms for Change"; Jill Barrett, "The UN Convention on the Law of the Sea: a "Living" Treaty?".

86 Article 319(2)(e) of UNCLOS requires the Secretary-General of the UN to "convene necessary meetings of States Parties in accordance with this Convention". UNCLOS, Article 319(2)(e). For more information on the role of SPLOS, see, for instance, Alex G. Oude Elferink, "Reviewing the Implementation of the LOS Convention: the Role of the United Nations Assembly and the Meeting of States Parties", in *Oceans Management in the 21st Century: Institutional Frameworks and Responses*, edited by Alex G. Oude Elferink and Donald R. Rothwell (Leiden: Martinus Nijhoff Publishers, 2004), 306–310; Tullio Treves, "The General Assembly and the Meeting of States Parties in the Implementation of the LOS Convention", in *Stability and Change in the Law of the Sea: The Role of the LOS Convention*, edited by Alex G. Oude Elferink (Leiden: Martinus Nijhoff Publishers, 2005), 68–73; James Harrison, *Making the Law of the Sea: A Study in the Development of International Law*, 70–83.

87 There are 91 provisions of UNCLOS where reference is made to one or more "competent or relevant international organizations". See David Freestone and Alex Oude Elferink, "Flexibility and Innovation in the Law of the Sea: Will the LOS Convention Amendment Procedures Ever Be Used?", 204.

88 Bernard H. Oxman, "Tools for Change: The Amendment Procedure", 202; Robin Churchill, "The 1982 United Nations Convention on the Law of the Sea", 31; Catherine Redgwell, "The Never Ending Story: the Role of GAIRS in UNCLOS Implementation in the Offshore Energy Sector", in *Law of the Sea: UNCLOS as a living treaty*, edited by Jill Barrett and Richard Barnes (London: British Institute of International and Comparative Law, 2016).

ISA),[89] and last but not least its amendment procedures.[90] Therefore, it seems that the nature of UNCLOS as a "living instrument" does not *in itself* lead to a firm conclusion for ascertaining the temporal sense-intention of the parties. However, the legal implications which such a nature entails, for instance, that there is the necessity to change and adapt to new circumstances, are relevant for the ascertainment. It is the viewpoint of the current author that such legal implications lend considerable support to the assumption that it accords with the intention of the parties to UNCLOS to refer to future developments to interpret provisions of the Convention, including the ones on marine scientific research. The following analysis will turn to another element – the object and purpose of UNCLOS – to see if it verifies or rejects this assumption.

2.6 Object and Purpose of UNCLOS and Its Implications for Ascertaining the Temporal Sense-Intention of the Parties

This section attempts to ascertain the object and purpose of UNCLOS and addresses its implications for the current discussion.

The first question that arises is how to determine the object and purpose of a treaty. International judicial practice is rich with examples of invoking the object and purpose of the instrument in question.[91] Nevertheless, the approaches employed for formulating the object and purpose are neither clear nor identical.[92] In some instances, the object and purpose of a treaty were found in the original intention of the drafters; while in others, international courts and tribunals adopted a more objective method – searching for the object and

89 The International Seabed Authority is an autonomous international organization established under UNCLOS and the 1994 Agreement relating to the Implementation of Part XI of the United Nations Convention on the Law of the Sea. The Authority is the organization through which States Parties to the Convention shall, in accordance with the regime for the seabed and ocean floor and subsoil thereof beyond the limits of national jurisdiction (the Area) established in Part XI and the Agreement, organize and control activities in the Area, particularly with a view to administering the resources of the Area. For more information, see its official website, https://www.isa.org.jm/authority.

90 Bernard H. Oxman, "Tools for Change: The Amendment Procedure," David Freestone and Alex Oude Elferink, "Flexibility and Innovation in the Law of the Sea: Will the LOS Convention Amendment Procedures Ever Be Used?."

91 Vesna Crnićgrotić, "Object and Purpose of Treaties in the Vienna Convention on the Law of Treaties", *Asian Yearbook of International Law* (1997): 160.

92 Isabelle Buffard and Karl Zemanek, "The "Object and Purpose" of a Treaty: An Enigma?", *Austrian Review of International and European Law* 3(1998): 317; Vesna Crnićgrotić, "Object and Purpose of Treaties in the Vienna Convention on the Law of Treaties", 160–161.

purpose of a treaty from its text, primarily from its preamble.[93] However, as indicated by international judicial practice and the literature, it seems to be the mainstream view that the preamble of a legal instrument is a significant place to look at to identify its object and purpose.[94]

In its Judgment on *Territorial and Maritime Dispute (Nicaragua v. Colombia)*, the ICJ noted that "[g]iven the object and purpose of UNCLOS, as stipulated in its Preamble, the fact that Colombia is not a party thereto does not relieve Nicaragua of its obligations under Article 76 of that Convention", and referred explicitly to the statement concerning the establishment of "a legal order for the seas and oceans [...]" contained in the fourth preambular paragraph[95] and the statement that "the problems of ocean space are closely interrelated and need to be considered as a whole" under the third preambular paragraph.[96] The object and purpose of the Convention identified in this case have been echoed by several leading law of the sea scholars. For example, Churchill refers to the settlement of "all issues relating to the law of the sea" as the broad aim of UNCLOS, and to the establishment of "a legal order for the seas and oceans [...]" as a particular aim.[97] The Virginia Commentary also submitted that the objective to establish "a legal order for the seas and oceans" contained in the fourth preambular paragraph is of particular importance for the interpretation of UNCLOS provisions.[98] The establishment of such a legal order is promoted by the desire to "settle, in a spirit of mutual understanding and cooperation, all issues relating to the law of the sea" as contained in the first preambular paragraph.[99]

---

93 Examples of the former include ICJ: *Reservations to the Convention on the Prevention and Punishment of the Crime of Genocide*, Advisory Opinion of 28 May 1951; examples of the latter include ICJ: *Fisheries Jurisdiction case* (UK v. Iceland), Judgment of 25 July 1974.

94 Vesna Crnićgrotić, "Object and Purpose of Treaties in the Vienna Convention on the Law of Treaties", 168.

95 This paragraph states that "[r]ecognizing the desirability of establishing through this Convention, with due regard for the sovereignty of all States, a legal order for the seas and oceans which will facilitate international communication, and will promote the peaceful uses of the seas and oceans, the equitable and efficient utilization of their resources, the conservation of their living resources, and the study, protection and preservation of the marine environment".

96 ICJ, *Territorial and Maritime Dispute* (*Nicaragua V. Colombia*), Judgment of 19 November 2012, para.126.

97 Robin Churchill, "The 1982 United Nations Convention on the Law of the Sea", 27.

98 Myron H. Nordquist et al., eds., *United Nations Convention on the Law of the Sea, 1982: A Commentary* (*Vol. III*) (Dordrecht: Martinus Nijhoff Publishers, 1991), 461. See also, Alexander Proelss, ed. *United Nations Convention on the Law of the Sea: A Commentary*, 9.

99 UNCLOS, Preamble.

If the object and purpose of UNCLOS are, as identified by the ICJ and the legal literature, to establish "a legal order for the seas and oceans" that contributes to the settlement of "all issues relating to the law of the sea", what are the implications for ascertaining the temporal sense-intention of the parties to UNCLOS in the current discussions?

The first implication would be that the provisions of the Convention need to provide flexibility, or in the words of President T. B. Koh, the Convention is to "stand the test of time".[100] It is fair to state that flexibility requires the ability of self-adaptation to new circumstances, thus avoiding frequent modifications or amendments. Likewise, in order to achieve the universal application of the legal order, the interpretation of UNCLOS provisions cannot be isolated from developments that have occurred or will occur after the conclusion of the Convention, since otherwise, the Convention would soon become outdated.

Secondly, another element of the object and purpose of the Convention – the "desire" of the Parties to settle "all issues relating to the law of the sea" – reflects that the Convention adopts "an integrated approach".[101] It has been commented that without a definitive list of such issues, the Convention is "accordingly open to future developments".[102] In most cases, to ensure contemporary relevancy, the provisions of UNCLOS are drafted in a way to encompass new problems not envisaged at the time of UNCLOS III.[103] As a result, the rules set out in the Convention may be interpreted in a way that encompasses an activity not considered by the drafters of the Convention.[104]

Some would argue that opening up UNCLOS provisions to future developments may lead to fragmentation both within the Convention and between the Convention and other rules of international law that would jeopardize "the coherence and uniformity of substance"[105] of UNCLOS. Nevertheless, the goal

---

100 "A Constitution for the Oceans", Remarks by Tommy T. B. Koh, President of the Third United Nations Confer-ence on the Law of the Sea, available at http://www.un.org/depts/los/convention_agreements/texts/koh_english.pdf.

101 ITLOS, *Case concerning Land Reclamation by Singapore in and around the Straits of Johor (Malaysia v. Singapore), Provisional Measures*, Verbatim Record of the Public Sitting held on Thursday, 25 September 2003, at 3.00 p.m., Doc. ITLOS/PV.03/02/Corr.1, p. 14.

102 Alexander Proelss, ed. *United Nations Convention on the Law of the Sea: A Commentary*, 7.

103 Tullio Treves, "The International Tribunal for the Law of the Sea and the Rule of Law", in *The Contribution of the International Tribunal for the Law of the Sea to the Rule of Law: 1996–2016*, edited by ITLOS (Brill-Nijhoff, 2018), 69.

104 Ibid. ITLOS, *The M/V Virginia G Case (Panama v. Guinea-Bissau)*, Judgment of 14 April 2014, paras.209–215.

105 According to Oxman, "if we want to maintain the uniformity reflected in the prohibition on reservations, then we should be cautious about actions that could fracture the Convention into a series of conflicting and competing instruments regarding basic rights and

of the coherence and uniformity of substance does not preclude progressive development that is allowed by the Convention itself. The Convention emphasizes uniformity by giving a definite and precise allocation of jurisdictions, but it still leaves the task of elaborating detailed standards to competent international organizations and State Parties.[106] In this sense, it seems that some of the provisions are precise and definite, so as to ensure the integrity and stability of the Convention, such as the provisions concerning the allocation of jurisdiction; while some other provisions are left open for future developments in order to fulfil the object and purpose of settling "all issues relating to the law of the sea". As will be discussed in Chapter 3 of this book, the drafters chose to leave some terms and phrases which play an essential role for the legal classification and the regulation of ocean data collection activities undefined, most notably the term "marine scientific research".[107] It seems that the interpretation of such terms and provisions falls into the second category and needs to incorporate subsequent developments.

In sum, in order to achieve the object and purpose of UNCLOS to establish "a legal order for the seas and oceans" that contributes to the settlement of "all issues relating to the law of the sea", the interpretation of certain treaty provisions of the Convention, including the term "marine scientific research" and the ones pertaining to the legal classification of ocean data collection activities, needs to take into account future developments. In this sense, it can be argued that, from the object and purpose of the Convention, one can gather that the parties to the Convention intend to subject the meaning of the term "marine scientific research" to change.

2.7 Conclusions and Implications for Analysis in the Subsequent Chapters

To conclude, the examination of the elements in the preceding discussions points to the conclusion that the parties to UNCLOS intend to refer the meaning of the term "marine scientific research" to future developments.

It is noted that there is no direct evidence indicating that the reason for not including a definition of the term "marine scientific research" was

---

duties and precise allocations of jurisdiction". Bernard H. Oxman, "Tools for Change: The Amendment Procedure", 197–198.

106 Ibid., 205.

107 Other terms or phrases include "other internationally lawful uses of the sea related to" the freedoms under Article 58(1), and "due regard".

to allow the regime to be adaptive to future development. Nevertheless, an examination of the relevant drafting history reveals that the delegations chose to omit the definition since they could not reach an agreement on this matter and had to leave it open for future development (Section 2.3). It is submitted that this assumption is confirmed by the creation of obligations, under Article 251 of the Convention, for States to seek to establish general criteria and guidelines in ascertaining the nature and implications of marine scientific research.

As to the nature of the term "marine scientific research" (whether it can be considered as a generic term or not), it is submitted that whether or not the meaning of the term *does* change is a linguistic problem. Yet, by applying the criteria for generic terms drawn from relevant international case law and the literature, it is concluded that highly likely the meaning of the term "marine scientific research" *may* change over time (Section 2.4.2).

International case law often combines the effect of using generic terms and the nature of the treaty at issue to ascertain the temporal sense-intention of the parties. Following this approach, the chapter also examines the nature of UNCLOS as a "living instrument" and its implications for the current discussion. In the viewpoint of the current author, the nature of UNCLOS itself does not suffice in ascertaining the temporal sense-intention of the parties. However, what the nature of UNCLOS entails – that the Convention needs to adapt to new circumstances – lends support to the argument that the parties to UNCLOS intend to refer treaty provisions, including the ones on marine scientific research, to future developments (Section 2.5).

In terms of the object and purpose of the Convention, on the basis of relevant case law and the observations made by some leading law of the sea scholars, this research considers the object and purpose of the Convention as the establishment of "a legal order for the seas and oceans" that contributes to the settlement of "all issues relating to the law of the sea". In order to fulfil that object and purpose, certain provisions of UNCLOS, arguably including the provisions relevant to the ascertainment of the regulatory scope of the marine scientific research regime and those concerning the regulation of ocean data collection activities in general, should be interpreted bearing in mind subsequent developments (Section 2.6).

After addressing the temporal sense-intention of the parties to the Convention, to fully solve the question concerning the interpretation of relevant UNCLOS provisions raised at the beginning of this chapter, it is necessary to point out the specific consequences of the temporal sense-intention of the parties for the current research.

As submitted by Thirlway:

> where it can be established that it was the intention of the parties that the meaning or scope of a term or expression used in the treaty should follow the development of the law, the treaty must be interpreted so as to give effect to that intention.[108]

In this light, the interpretation of relevant treaty provisions, particularly for ascertaining the nature of and criteria for the term "marine scientific research" in the context of UNCLOS, cannot be isolated from developments that occur after the adoption of the Convention. More specifically, when applying the general rule of treaty interpretation contained in Article 31 of VCLT to interpret relevant provisions of UNCLOS, the "ordinary meaning"[109] to be given to the term at issue should be the one existing at the time of interpretation taking into account all the relevant developments that contribute to the understanding of the term; and the "relevant rules of international law" under Article 31 shall include those adopted after the conclusion of UNCLOS.

Bearing in mind these observations, the subsequent chapters of this book will provide an interpretation of the substantive UNCLOS provisions on ocean data collection activities. Chapters 3 to 5 examine consecutively the text of UNCLOS concerning ocean data collection activities (Chapter 3), subsequent practice of States on the international regulation of ocean data collection activities (Chapter 4), and rules of other international treaties concerning the regulation of the said activities (Chapter 5).

---

108 Hugh Thirlway, "The Law and Procedure of the International Court of Justice 1960–1989: Part Three", *British Yearbook of International Law* 62, no. 1 (1991): 57.

109 It has been submitted that a treaty term "may have a number of ordinary meanings, which may even change over time". This intertemporal aspect is essentially dependent on the intention of the parties, in line with the requirement of interpreting treaty terms in "good faith". See, for instance, Mark Eugen Villiger, *Commentary on the 1969 Vienna Convention on the Law of Treaties* (Brill, 2008), 426.

CHAPTER 3

UNCLOS Provisions on Ocean Data Collection – with a Focus on the Marine Scientific Research Regime

3.1 Introduction

This chapter aims to examine UNCLOS provisions on the regulation of ocean data collection activities. An examination of these provisions serves two purposes. The first is to establish the criteria for the legal classification of an ocean data collection activity, especially in delineating its relationship with marine scientific research. The second purpose is to set out the framework for regulation, including in cases where the legal classification of the ocean data collection activity at issue remains undefined or controversial.

In terms of the first purpose, this chapter will answer two questions: 1) what is the nature of and criteria for marine scientific research in the context of UNCLOS, and 2) what are the boundaries of the UNCLOS marine scientific research regime, *i.e.*, what activities are not covered by the regime, and how do they differ from marine scientific research? These two questions are interrelated and at the same time independent. Understanding one of the questions would shed light on the other. To answer the latter question, one has to look beyond Part XIII of the Convention and discern from relevant provisions the relationship between marine scientific research and other similar activities. In contrast, the answer to the former question will be mainly provided by an interpretation of the provisions within Part XIII. In this regard, Section 3.2 of this chapter will examine the relevant provisions of Part XIII, whereas pertinent provisions beyond Part XIII will be examined in Section 3.3. Section 3.4 offers some concluding thoughts pertinent to subsequent chapters.

3.2 The Nature of and Criteria for Marine Scientific Research

This section focuses on the text of Part XIII of the Convention to ascertain the nature of and criteria for marine scientific research in the context of UNCLOS. Among the provisions contained in Part XIII, some articles are of particular relevance for said purposes. These articles include Article 240, which enumerates the general principles for the conduct of marine scientific research, Article

 | DOI:10.1163/9789004508590_004

244 on the publication and dissemination of information and knowledge, and Article 246 which provides detailed rights and obligations for the conduct of marine scientific research in the EEZ and on the continental shelf of a coastal State. These provisions will be addressed consecutively in the following discussions. Some provisions in Part XIII which do not inform the understanding of the scope of the term "marine scientific research" may, however, have implications for the implementation of the UNCLOS marine scientific research regime in light of new developments in ocean data collection. This concerns, for instance, Articles 242 and 243 on international cooperation and the creation of favorable conditions, Article 247 on marine scientific research projects undertaken by or under the auspices of international organizations, and Article 258 concerning the deployment and use of scientific research installations or equipment in the marine environment. These provisions are not the object of examination of this chapter. Their implications will be elaborated upon in the case studies included in Chapters 6 and 7 of this book.

Before examining the substantive provisions (Sections 3.2.2 to 3.2.4), this section will first look at the definition of the term "marine scientific research" offered by dictionaries, and the definitions contained in the official proposals put forward during UNCLOS III and relevant draft texts of the Convention (Section 3.2.1). Interim concluding remarks will be included in Section 3.2.5.

3.2.1 *Definitions of the Term "Marine Scientific Research"*

The Convention does not include a definition of the term "marine scientific research". The first step to establishing the "ordinary meaning" of this term would be to consult language dictionaries.[1] Because the term "marine scientific research" is not defined in any dictionary that was consulted, definitions of the terms "scientific research", "research", and "science" are looked at. Black's Law Dictionary defines the term "scientific research" as "the application of the scientific method to investigate any relationships amongst natural phenomena or to solve a technical or medical problem".[2] "Research" as a noun is defined as

1 VCLT, Article 31(1). The link between the "ordinary meaning" under Article 31(1) VCLT and the literal meaning contained in language dictionaries has been discussed by many scholars. See, for instance, Andrea Bianchi, "Textual Interpretation and (International) Law Reading: The Myth of (in)Determinacy and the Genealogy of Meaning", in *Making Transnational Law Work in the Global Economy: Essays in Honour of Detlev Vagts*, edited by Pieter H. F. Bekker, Rudolf Dolzer, and Michael Waibel (Cambridge University Press, 2010), 36–37; Oliver Dörr and Kirsten Schmalenbach, eds., *Vienna Convention on the Law of Treaties: A Commentary (Second Edition)* (Springer, 2018), 581.

2 "Scientific research", The Law Dictionary (Featuring Black's Law Dictionary Free Online Legal Dictionary 2nd Ed.), available at https://thelawdictionary.org/scientific-research/.

"the systematic investigation into and study of materials and sources in order to establish facts and reach new conclusions".[3] "Science" refers to "the intellectual and practical activity encompassing the systematic study of the structure and behavior of the physical and natural world through observation and experiment".[4] Based on these definitions, a conclusion can be warranted that activities falling under the term "marine scientific research" should have some scientific attributes. The ordinary meaning of the terms encompasses the idea of systematically studying the research object using scientific methods.

As mentioned in Chapter 2.3 of this book, some official proposals put forward during UNCLOS III and several informal draft texts of the Convention included draft articles on the definition of the term "marine scientific research". A list of definitions contained in these proposals and draft texts are provided in Table 1.[5]

It is noted that the definitions contained in the proposals and draft texts are mostly formulated in a general manner. Some differences are noticeable among these definitions. For instance, some definitions explicitly exclude activities that focus directly on the exploitation of marine resources.[6] In contrast, others indicate that it is impracticable to make a definite or precise distinction between pure scientific research and industrial or other research conducted with a view to commercial exploitation.[7] Besides, some definitions limit the scope of activities covered by the term "marine scientific research" to those conducted in the marine environment,[8] while others do not contain such a limit. This being said, these definitions share one commonality, that activities covered by the term "marine scientific research" should aim at furthering knowledge of the marine environment.

3 "Research", Oxford Dictionary of English (Oxford Reference online version, 3rd edition, Oxford University Press, 2015).

4 "Science", Oxford Dictionary of English (Oxford Reference online version, 3rd edition, Oxford University Press, 2015).

5 For a comprehensive introduction to the negotiations concerning the definition of the term "marine scientific research" during UNCLOS III, see, for instance, UN/DOALOS, "Marine Scientific Research: A Revised Guide to the Implementation of the Relevant Provisions of the United Nations Convention on the Law of the Sea", paras.7–14; Myron H. Nordquist et al., eds., *United Nations Convention on the Law of the Sea, 1982: A Commentary* (*Vol. IV*), 438–450; Alfred H. A. Soons, *Marine Scientific Research and the Law of the Sea*, 121–124; George K. Walker, *Definitions for the Law of the Sea: Terms Not Defined by the 1982 Convention* (Leiden: Brill, 2011), 241–243.

6 See, for instance, the definition included in Doc. A/CONF.62/C.3/L.19.

7 See, for instance, the definition included in Doc. O/CONF.62/C.3/L.9.

8 See, for instance, the definition included in Doc. A/CONF.62/C.3/L.29.

TABLE 1 Definitions of the term "marine scientific research" contained in official proposals put forward during UNCLOS III and informal draft texts of UNCLOS

Name of the document	Definition of the term "marine scientific research"
Trinidad and Tobago: draft articles on marine scientific research (Doc. A/CONF.62/C.3/L.9)	Article 1 (a) Marine scientific research is any study or investigation of the marine environment and experiments related thereto; (b) Marine scientific research is of such a nature as to preclude any clear or precise distinction between pure scientific research and industrial or other research conducted with a view to commercial exploitation or military use [...]
Austria, Belgium, Bolivia, Botswana, Denmark, Germany (Federal Republic of), Laos, Lesotho, Liberia, Luxembourg, Nepal, Netherlands, Paraguay, Singapore, Uganda, Upper Volta and Zambia: draft articles on marine scientific research (Doc. A/CONF.62/C.3/L.19)	Article 1 "Marine scientific research" means any study of and related experimental work in the marine environment, excluding industrial exploration and other activities aimed directly at the exploitation of marine resources, designed to increase man's knowledge and conducted for peaceful purposes.
Bulgaria, Byelorussian Soviet Socialist Republic, Czechoslovakia, German Democratic Republic, Hungary, Mongolia, Poland, Ukrainian Soviet Socialist Republic and Union of Soviet Socialist Republics: draft articles on marine scientific research (Doc. A/CONF.62/C.3/L.26)	Article 1 *Definition of marine scientific research* "Marine scientific research" means any study of, or related experimental work in, the marine environment that is designed to increase man's knowledge and is conducted for peaceful purposes.
Colombia, El Salvador, Mexico, Nigeria: draft articles on marine scientific research (Doc. A/CONF.62/C.3/L.29)	Article 1 *Definition of marine scientific research* For the purpose of this Convention "marine scientific research" means any study and related experimental work conducted in the marine environment designed to increase mankind's knowledge thereof.

TABLE 1 Definitions of the term "marine scientific research" contained in official proposals put forward during UNCLOS III and informal draft texts of UNCLOS (*cont.*)

Name of the document	Definition of the term "marine scientific research"
Informal single negotiating text, part III, Part II "Marine Scientific Research" (Doc. A/CONF.62/WP.8/Part III)	Article 1 Marine scientific research means any study or related experimental work designed to increase man's knowledge of the marine environment.
Revised single negotiating text (part III) (Doc. A/CONF.62/WP.8/Rev.1/Part III)	Article 48 For the purpose of this Convention, "marine scientific research" means any study or related experimental work designed to increase mankind's knowledge of the marine environment.

3.2.2 *Principles of Conducting Marine Scientific Research*

As a general provision, Article 240 of UNCLOS sets out the principles for the conduct of marine scientific research in all maritime zones:

a. marine scientific research shall be conducted exclusively for peaceful purposes;
b. marine scientific research shall be conducted with appropriate scientific methods and means compatible with this Convention;
c. marine scientific research shall not unjustifiably interfere with other legitimate uses of the sea compatible with this Convention and shall be duly respected in the course of such uses;
d. marine scientific research shall be conducted in compliance with all relevant regulations adopted in conformity with this Convention including those for the protection and preservation of the marine environment.[9]

Although this article deals with the issue of conducting marine scientific research in a legitimate manner, rather than the scope of marine scientific research, the relevant provisions under this article help understand the nature of and criteria for marine scientific research. Of relevance for the current study is the principle concerning the use of appropriate scientific methods and means.

9 UNCLOS, Article 240.

Article 240(b) requires all marine scientific research to be conducted with "appropriate scientific methods and means compatible with this Convention".[10] It has been submitted that presumably this paragraph is meant to prohibit the use of methods and means that are unnecessarily and unreasonably damaging the marine environment or interfering with other uses of the sea.[11] In this sense, this principle overlaps with the principles encapsulated in paragraphs (c) and (d) of this article. As to the requirement of "compatible with this Convention", the Convention itself does not place any explicit restrictions on the use of methods and means for marine scientific research activities. Therefore, it can be interpreted as including all means and methods which do not result in the breach of obligations established by the Convention.[12]

More specifically, this paragraph requires marine scientific research to be conducted with "scientific methods". As the ordinary meaning of the term "scientific method" suggests, under this requirement, marine scientific research shall follow a step-by-step approach to solving problems, *i.e.* "identify and define the problem, accumulate data, formulate a hypothesis, conduct experiments to prove hypothesis, interpret results in an objective manner and repeat".[13] This requirement suggests that to constitute marine scientific research, an ocean data collection activity needs to be carried out to confirm or disprove a hypothesis. It has been submitted by one author that the existence of "a hypothesis or attempt of explanation" is one of the elements that constitute the scientific attributes of a marine scientific research project.[14] This being said, the Convention does not provide any indication as to the requirement for the level of specificity of the hypothesis.[15]

It is increasingly common that ocean data are collected in large quantities and stored for future uses. It is unclear whether the use of data that have been already collected from the marine environment for the future use of verifying or falsifying a hypothesis can still be considered as marine scientific research. This question is valid since, as is observed by Soons, although the Part XIII regime

---

10 Ibid., Article 240(b).

11 Alfred H. A. Soons, *Marine Scientific Research and the Law of the Sea*, 136.

12 Alexander Proelss, ed. *United Nations Convention on the Law of the Sea: A Commentary*, 1621.

13 "Scientific method", The Law Dictionary (Featuring Black's Law Dictionary Free Online Legal Dictionary 2nd Edition), available at https://thelawdictionary.org/scientific-method/.

14 Florian H.Th. Wegelein, *Marine Scientific Research: The Operation and Status of Research Vessels and Other Platforms in International Law*, 90. Other elements include the existence of a natural phenomenon, an experiment or observation, and finally a conclusion.

15 This issue was discussed in the *Whaling in the Antarctic case*. See Chapter 5.5.2 of this study.

is mainly concerned with marine scientific research undertaken in the marine environment, some provisions also cover marine scientific research activities conducted in laboratories on land.[16] Article 243 of the Convention creates the obligation "to create favourable conditions for the conduct of marine scientific research *in the marine environment*".[17] The phrase "in the marine environment" is not included in other general provisions on marine scientific research, therefore indicating that not all stages of marine scientific research are necessarily conducted in the marine environment. However, as indicated in Chapter 1.4 of this book, such activities fall beyond the scope of this research as the present research only addresses the legal issues arising from ocean data collection activities that are conducted *in situ* in the marine environment. The question of legal classification would also arise for the activity that collected such data when the hypothesis has not been formulated at the time of ocean data collection. In other words, it remains to be discussed whether a hypothesis has to be formulated before the commencement of a marine scientific research project. The Convention does not provide any clear indication on this matter. The implications of the said activities and their appropriate framework for regulation are among the issues to be elaborated upon in Chapter 7 of this study.

3.2.3 *Obligation of Publication and Dissemination of Information and Knowledge*

Apart from the general principles for the conduct of marine scientific research, Article 244, which sets up the obligation to publish and disseminate information on and knowledge resulting from marine scientific research, is also relevant for the theme of this chapter. Article 244 provides that,

1. States and competent international organizations shall, in accordance with this Convention, make available by publication and dissemination through appropriate channels information on proposed major programmes and their objectives as well as knowledge resulting from marine scientific research.
2. For this purpose, States, both individually and in cooperation with other States and with competent international organizations, shall actively promote the flow of scientific data and information and the transfer of knowledge resulting from marine scientific research, especially to developing States, as well as the strengthening of the autonomous marine scientific research capabilities of developing States.[18]

16 Alfred H. A. Soons, *Marine Scientific Research and the Law of the Sea*, 124.

17 Emphasis added. UNCLOS, Article 243.

18 Ibid., Article 244. This article is subject to two potential exceptions. Firstly, according to Article 249(2), the open publication of research results of marine scientific research

This article contains two broad sets of obligations. The first is related to the publication and dissemination of information "on proposed major programmes and their objectives", and of knowledge "resulting from marine scientific research". The second is to promote "the flow of scientific data and information" and "the transfer of knowledge resulting from marine scientific research".

Under the first paragraph of this article, a distinction has been made between information "on proposed major programmes and their objectives", and knowledge "resulting from marine scientific research". It thus appears that knowledge resulting from all marine scientific research are to be published and disseminated, while advance information relating to proposed projects only needs to be provided concerning "major" projects.[19] It has been commented that, in this provision, "major programmes" would seem to refer to all marine scientific research programs which would involve conduct of research activities in areas that are not under the jurisdiction of the researching State itself, and which "are of more than purely local interest".[20]

Besides, the "knowledge" to be published under this paragraph is different from the "data and information" under Paragraph 2 of this article. The generation of knowledge would require some analysis and evaluation of the data and information collected through research.[21] In this regard, "knowledge" under this provision is somehow equivalent to "results" under Article 249(1)(d) and (e), which oblige the researching State to "provide the coastal State with an assessment of [...] data, samples [derived from marine scientific research project] and research results", and to "ensure, subject to [Article 249(2)], that the research results are made internationally available [...]".[22] The Convention

undertaken in the EEZ or on the continental shelf of a coastal State should be subject to "the laws and regulations of the coastal State for the exercise of its discretion to grant or withhold consent pursuant to article 246, paragraph 5, including requiring prior agreement for making internationally available the research results of a project of direct significance for the exploration and exploitation of natural resources." Secondly, Article 302 states that, "[w]ithout prejudice to the right of a State Party to resort to the procedures for the settlement of disputes provided for in this Convention, nothing in this Convention shall be deemed to require a State Party, in the fulfilment of its obligations under this Convention, to supply information the disclosure of which is contrary to the essential interests of its security".

19 Myron H. Nordquist et al., eds., *United Nations Convention on the Law of the Sea, 1982: A Commentary (Vol. IV)*, 486.

20 Alfred H. A. Soons, *Marine Scientific Research and the Law of the Sea*, 243; Alexander Proelss, ed. *United Nations Convention on the Law of the Sea: A Commentary*, 1461.

21 Alexander Proelss, ed. *United Nations Convention on the Law of the Sea: A Commentary*, 1642.

22 UNCLOS, Article 249(1)(d), (e).

does not provide any indication as to the requirement for the level of specificity or comprehensiveness of such knowledge or results. Therefore, the effective implementation of this article mainly depends on the researching State's good faith.[23] However, a pertinent implication of this article for the present research is that to fulfil the obligations under this Article, it is presumed that marine scientific research projects should lead to scientific data and information, and knowledge. This requirement can be considered as another indication of the existence of scientific attributes of marine scientific research projects.[24]

3.2.4 *The Regulation of Marine Scientific Research under Article 246*

It has been observed that the most essential article in the Part XIII regime is Article 246 of the Convention.[25] Although this article intends to set out the rights and obligations of the States concerned for the undertaking of marine scientific research projects, it provides several useful implications for ascertaining the nature of and criteria for marine scientific research. Of particular relevance are the provisions contained in Paragraphs (3) and (5) of this article, which state that:

> 3. Coastal States shall, in normal circumstances, grant their consent for marine scientific research projects by other States or competent international organizations in their exclusive economic zone or on their continental shelf to be carried out in accordance with this Convention exclusively for peaceful purposes and in order to increase scientific knowledge of the marine environment for the benefit of all mankind.
>
> [...]

---

23 However, for marine scientific research projects undertaken in areas under the jurisdiction of a coastal State, arguably the coastal State plays an essential role in shaping relevant practice on this matter. If the coastal State considers the researching State fails to fulfil the obligation under this provision, the coastal State may at its discretion withhold its consent to the conduct of future marine scientific research projects of the researching State under Article 246(5)(d). Besides, for ongoing marine scientific research projects in the EEZ or on the continental shelf of a coastal State, if the coastal State considers that the researching State fails to comply with the requirement on the publication of research results under Article 249(1)(e), the coastal State may require the suspension or cessation of the projects pursuant to Article 253.

24 The first indication is the use of "scientific methods", see Section 3.2.2 of this chapter.

25 As observed by the Chairman of the Third Committee of UNCLOS III, "[t]here was a generally shared understanding that the outcome of the negotiations on the whole chapter on marine scientific research depends on a satisfactory solution on the [earlier version of Article 246]", and it is "the core of the discussions on the item of marine scientific research". See Myron H. Nordquist et al., eds., *United Nations Convention on the Law of the Sea, 1982: A Commentary* (*Vol. IV*), 507.

5. Coastal States may however in their discretion withhold their consent to the conduct of a marine scientific research project of another State or competent international organization in the exclusive economic zone or on the continental shelf of the coastal State if that project:
   a. is of direct significance for the exploration and exploitation of natural resources, whether living or non-living;
   b. involves drilling into the continental shelf, the use of explosives or the introduction of harmful substances into the marine environment;
   c. involves the construction, operation or use of artificial islands, installations and structures referred to in articles 60 and 80;
   d. contains information communicated pursuant to article 248 regarding the nature and objectives of the project which is inaccurate or if the researching State or competent international organization has outstanding obligations to the coastal State from a prior research project.[26]

It has been submitted that research carried out "exclusively for peaceful purposes and in order to increase scientific knowledge of the marine environment for the benefit of all mankind" under Article 246(3) equates "pure" marine scientific research.[27] In contrast, those falling under Article 246(5)(a)–(c) are examples of applied marine scientific research.[28] To determine the indications provided by these provisions to discern the scope of marine scientific research under UNCLOS, the following discussion will commence with an analysis of the distinction between pure and applied marine scientific research, followed by an evaluation of whether such a distinction is preserved in Article 246 (Section 3.2.4.1). Sections 3.2.4.2 and 3.2.4.3 will sketch the implications of the findings of the previous section and of the substantive provisions under Paragraphs (3) and (5) of Article 246 for understanding the nature of and criteria for marine scientific research under UNCLOS.

3.2.4.1 Pure and Applied Marine Scientific Research

As discussed in Chapter 2.3 of this book, the significant divergence concerning the definition of the term "marine scientific research" during UNCLOS III involved the relationship between so-called pure (or fundamental) marine

---

26 UNCLOS, Article 246(3), (5).

27 See, for instance, R. R. Churchill and A. V. Lowe, *The Law of the Sea* (Manchester University Press, 1999), 405; Tullio Treves, "Marine Scientific Research", para.11; Yoshifumi Tanaka, *The International Law of the Sea*, Second ed. (Cambridge University Press, 2015), 361.

28 R. R. Churchill and A. V. Lowe, *The Law of the Sea*, 405–406.

scientific research and applied marine scientific research.[29] Presumably, a comprehension of the distinction between these two types of marine scientific research (pure and applied) would shed light on understanding the scope of marine scientific research.

The distinction between pure and applied marine scientific research dates back to the Convention on the Continental Shelf of 1958.[30] Article 5(1) of this convention stipulates that "fundamental oceanographic or other scientific research carried out with the intention of open publication" shall not be subject to interference by exploration and exploitation activities.[31] Paragraph 8 of the same article provides that,

> the coastal State shall not normally withhold its consent if the request is submitted by a qualified institution with a view to purely scientific research into the physical or biological characteristics of the continental shelf, [...] and that in any event the results shall be published.[32]

These provisions lay down the foundation for what is often termed as "pure" marine scientific research. Elements of such research include the intention of open publication[33] and the eventual outcome of the research purely serving scientific ends.

These provisions also provide a starting point for the negotiations during UNCLOS III concerning the consent regime for foreign marine scientific research undertaken in the EEZ or on the continental shelf of a coastal State.[34] During UNCLOS III, the distinction between pure and applied marine scientific

---

29 Myron H. Nordquist et al., eds., *United Nations Convention on the Law of the Sea, 1982: A Commentary* (*Vol. IV*), 444.

30 Convention on the Continental Shelf, 1958.

31 Ibid., Article 5(1).

32 Ibid., Article 5(8).

33 Under UNCLOS, Article 244 creates the obligation of publication and dissemination of information and knowledge. This provision applies to all marine scientific research, whether pure or applied. Notably, the *intention* of open publication is a subjective requirement, while the actual publication of information and knowledge is an objective requirement. However, given the difficulty of determining the existence of such an intention, and the vague formulation concerning the requirement of the intention of open publication (it remains unclear what will be published and where), practical implications of such a difference are limited. Therefore, this characteristic does not differentiate pure marine scientific research from applied marine scientific research.

34 Myron H. Nordquist et al., eds., *United Nations Convention on the Law of the Sea, 1982: A Commentary* (*Vol. IV*), 501. See also Alexander Proelss, ed. *United Nations Convention on the Law of the Sea: A Commentary*, 1652.

research was discussed intensively. Some States held the view that these two types of marine scientific research can be, or should be, distinguished from each other.[35] According to them, the main difference between the two types of activities is that applied marine scientific research is related to natural resources in the marine environment or is conducted with a view to subsequent applications, while pure marine scientific research is not.[36] The classification came under massive attack, mainly for the reason that it would be impracticable to draw such distinctions because any data acquired from scientific research could be used for commercial or other practical purposes.[37]

The debate concerning the distinction between pure and applied marine scientific research can be better understood when placed in the broader context of the negotiations concerning marine scientific research issues. Before the 1960s, marine scientific research could be carried out unimpededly beyond the territorial sea under the principle of the freedom of the high seas.[38] Even during UNCLOS III, the proposal of freedom of marine scientific research in the "to-be-established" EEZ was mooted several times and was supported by industrially advanced countries.[39] Confronted with heavy criticism

35 See, for example, the statement of France in the 7th meeting of the Third Committee (1974) in UNCLOS III, UN Doc. A/CONF.62/C.3/SR.7, in the Official Records of the Third United Nations Conference on the Law of the Sea, Volume II, 340, para.40; the statements of Finland and Senegal in the 9th meeting of the Third Committee (1974) in UNCLOS III, UN Doc. A/CONF.62/C.3/SR.9, in the Official Records of the Third United Nations Conference on the Law of the Sea, Volume II, 350, 353, 354, paras.40, 75. See also, "Bulgaria, Byelorussian Soviet Socialist Republic, Czechoslovakia, German Democratic Republic, Hungary, Mongolia, Poland, Ukrainian Soviet Socialist Republic and Union of Soviet Socialist Republics: draft articles on marine scientific research", UN Doc. A/CONF.62/C.3/L.26, Article 6; "Colombia, El Salvador, Mexico, Nigeria: draft articles on marine scientific research", UN Doc. A/CONF.62/C.3/L.29, Article 7.

36 Ibid.

37 Myron H. Nordquist et al., eds., *United Nations Convention on the Law of the Sea, 1982: A Commentary* (*Vol. IV*), 433. See also Lucius Caflisch and Jacques Piccard, "The Legal Regime of Marine Scientific Research and the Third United Nations Conference on the Law of the Sea", *Ocean Development & International Law* 4(1977): 850; Herman T Franssen, "Developing Country Views of Sea Law and Marine Science", in *Freedom of Oceanic Research: A Study Conducted by the Center for Marine Affairs of the Scripps Institute of Oceanography University of California, San Diego*, edited by Warren S. Wooster (New York: Crane, Russak & Company, Inc., 1973), 158.

38 Alfred H. A. Soons, *Marine Scientific Research and the Law of the Sea*, 1.

39 See the summary records of the plenary meetings and meetings of the Third Committee in UNCLOS III, especially in the second and third sessions of the Conference, available at the official website of UN Codification Division Publications, Diplomatic Conferences, "Third United Nations Conference on the Law of the Sea", http://legal.un.org/diplomaticconferences/1973_los/.

from coastal States, proposals on the notification regime and later the partial consent regime were put forward. Under the notification regime, foreign marine scientific research can be undertaken in areas under the jurisdiction of a coastal State after fulfilling a notification requirement.[40] Under the partial consent regime, in areas under the jurisdiction of a coastal State, marine scientific research projects related to the exploration and exploitation of natural resources shall be conducted with the prior consent of the coastal State, while projects that are not of such a nature can be conducted after advance notification.[41]

The debates concerning the distinction between pure and applied marine scientific research remained inconclusive after several rounds of negotiations. Delegations started to realize that a consent regime which is premised upon a purported distinction between these two types of research would not be accepted.[42] It was then decided to subject both pure and applied marine scientific research to a consent regime, which only distinguishes between marine scientific research projects to which the coastal State shall grant its consent "in normal circumstances", and those projects to which the coastal State may withhold its consent at its discretion.[43] Such a "partially absolute, partially qualified"[44] consent regime is included in Article 246 of UNCLOS, particularly in its Paragraphs (3) and (5). As a consequence, unlike the Convention on the Continental Shelf, which only deals explicitly with pure marine scientific research,[45] UNCLOS addresses both pure and applied marine scientific research. In other words, marine scientific research in the context of UNCLOS

40 "Austria, Belgium, Bolivia, Botswana, Denmark, Germany (Federal Republic of), Laos, Lesotho, Liberia, Luxembourg, Nepal, Netherlands, Paraguay, Singapore, Uganda, Upper Volta and Zambia: draft articles on marine scientific research", UN Doc. A/CONF.62/C.3/L.19.

41 See "Bulgaria, Byelorussian Soviet Socialist Republic, Czechoslovakia, German Democratic Republic, Hungary, Mongolia, Poland, Ukrainian Soviet Socialist Republic and Union of Soviet Socialist Republics: draft articles on marine scientific research", UN Doc. A/CONF.62/C.3/L.26.

42 See Myron H. Nordquist et al., eds., *United Nations Convention on the Law of the Sea, 1982: A Commentary (Vol. IV)*, 502–512; Alfred H. A. Soons, *Marine Scientific Research and the Law of the Sea*, 160–163.

43 For a comprehensive discussion about the development of the consent regime, see, for instance, Alfred H. A. Soons, *Marine Scientific Research and the Law of the Sea*, 160–163; UN/DOALOS, *Marine Scientific Research: Legislative History of Article 246 of the United Nations Convention on the Law of the Sea* (New York: United Nations Publication, 1994).

44 Alfred H. A. Soons, *Marine Scientific Research and the Law of the Sea*, 164.

45 Arguably, the Convention on the Continental Shelf also addresses applied marine scientific research, in only allowing pure marine scientific research to be carried out on the continental shelf of the coastal State without its consent. See Lucius Caflisch and Jacques

is not limited to pure marine scientific research.[46] Besides, as observed by the Virginia Commentary, the compromise embodied in Article 246 "leads to [...] the dropping of any attempt to base the regime on a purported differentiation between pure scientific research and scientific research of direct significance for the exploration and exploitation of natural resources".[47] Therefore, the distinction between pure and applied marine scientific research is not preserved in UNCLOS.

So, what are the implications of the above finding? Since Paragraphs (3) and (5) of Article 246 contain detailed provisions relating to the conduct of marine scientific research, one may inquire whether they provide any useful indications as to the nature of and criteria for marine scientific research. Specific questions in this regard include 1) whether the qualifications enumerated under Article 246(3) are the defining elements of the term "marine scientific research" under UNCLOS, and 2) what implications Article 246(5) provides for understanding the nature of and criteria for marine scientific research. The two questions will be addressed consecutively in the following analysis.

3.2.4.2 Qualifications in Article 246(3) as the Definition of the Term "Marine Scientific Research"?

Marine scientific research projects falling under Article 246(3) meet four qualifications, namely 1) carried out in accordance with the Convention,

---

Piccard, "The Legal Regime of Marine Scientific Research and the Third United Nations Conference on the Law of the Sea", 860–861.

46 This observation is supported by the fact that during UNCLOS III, due to the overlapping mandates of the Second and Third Committee of the Conference, both committees discussed different aspects of the issue of marine scientific research. As an outcome of the negotiations of the Second Committee, the relevant part on the EEZ of the ISNT included a provision on the consent regime for foreign marine scientific research in the EEZ, which only addressed the issue of pure marine scientific research, like in the case of the Convention on Continental Shelf. In his introduction to these provisions, the Chairman of the Second Committee recalled that the Third Committee was dealing with scientific research "in a wider context". Later, the attempts in the Second Committee to negotiate details of provisions on marine scientific research in the EEZ and on the continental shelf were ended. As explained by the Chairman of the Second Committee, he had "adopted suggestions based on the solutions being formulated in the Third Committee". See Myron H. Nordquist et al., eds., *United Nations Convention on the Law of the Sea, 1982: A Commentary (Vol. IV)*, 503–506.

47 See ibid., 518. The Virginia Commentary also observed that the ICNT, which contained a provision that was almost the same as Article 246 of UNCLOS, "departed significantly from the distinction between [pure and applied] scientific research as a basic premise for the regime of marine scientific research in the exclusive economic zone and on the continental shelf". Ibid., 434.

2) exclusively for peaceful purposes, 3) in order to increase scientific knowledge of the marine environment, and 4) for the benefit of all mankind.[48] The following analysis will discern whether these qualifications constitute the elements defining the term "marine scientific research" under UNCLOS. To address this question, it is necessary to examine the drafting history of Article 246(3) and this article as a whole, and the implications of the four qualifications.

3.2.4.2.1 *The Relevant Drafting History*

The qualifications under Article 246(3) were introduced by the Castañeda Group in 1977.[49] The Castañeda Group was established to resolve the considerable and persisting controversies among the delegations concerning the legal status of the EEZ, and the attribution of substantive rights and obligations to the coastal State or other States.[50] After several rounds of negotiations, the Group found new formulas that were acceptable (albeit with reluctance) to different delegations at the Conference. Among these formulas was a set of revised articles on marine scientific research.[51] Before the introduction of these revised articles, it had already been agreed to abandon the attempt to base the premise of the consent regime on the distinction between pure and applied marine scientific research.[52] The core of negotiations concerning the consent regime shifted to issues concerning the specific circumstances under which the coastal State should grant its consent in normal circumstances, and under which it might withhold its consent at its discretion.[53] Opinions on the scope of such circumstances varied.[54] It was in

---

48 UNCLOS, Article 246(3).

49 Myron H. Nordquist et al., eds., *United Nations Convention on the Law of the Sea, 1982: A Commentary* (*Vol. IV*), 509.

50 Jorge G Castañeda, "Negotiations on the Exclusive Economic Zone at the Third United Nations Conference on the Law of the Sea", in *Essays in International Law in Honour of Judge Manfred Lachs*, edited by Jerzy Makarczyk (Martinus Nijhoff Publishers, 1984), 619. See also Myron H. Nordquist et al., eds., *United Nations Convention on the Law of the Sea, 1982: A Commentary* (*Vol. IV*), 509–511. For further discussion on the legal issues of the EEZ, see Section 3.3.2 of this chapter.

51 Jorge G Castañeda, "Negotiations on the Exclusive Economic Zone at the Third United Nations Conference on the Law of the Sea", 622.

52 Myron H. Nordquist et al., eds., *United Nations Convention on the Law of the Sea, 1982: A Commentary* (*Vol. IV*), 507–509.

53 Ibid.

54 Ibid., 507–510. See also Alfred H. A. Soons, *Marine Scientific Research and the Law of the Sea*, 161–163.

such a setting that the four qualifications contained in Article 246(3) under UNCLOS were introduced. Apart from the qualifications under Article 246(3), the phrase "of direct significance for the exploration and exploitation of natural resources" under Article 246(5) which in effect circumscribed the coastal State's discretion to withhold its consent to foreign marine scientific research, also resulted from the negotiations in this Group.[55] In this regard, it is not hard to imagine that the qualifications under Article 246(3) were introduced as a compromise in the give-and-take negotiations to balance the interests of the coastal State and other States, especially regarding marine scientific research issues. To be more specific, Article 246(3) was meant to set out the criteria for marine scientific research projects to which the coastal State is obliged to grant its consent, instead of defining the term "marine scientific research" under UNCLOS.

3.2.4.2.2 *Implications of the Qualifications Contained in Article 246(3)*

This sub-section looks at the implications of the four qualifications under Article 246(3) and adjudges whether they can be considered as the elements defining the term "marine scientific research" under UNCLOS.

The first two qualifications do not shed much light on the current discussions. This is because the first one, "carried out in accordance with the Convention", concerns the legitimacy of the conduct of the research activity and applies to all ocean uses. The second qualification, "exclusively for peaceful purposes", is merely a repetition of the first principle contained in Article 240 of the Convention that applies to all marine scientific research.

The third qualification concerns the requirement to carry out marine scientific research "in order to increase scientific knowledge of the marine environment".[56] It is noted that most proposals mooted at UNCLOS III concerning the definition of the term "marine scientific research" referred to the furtherance of knowledge of the marine environment as the aim of this kind of activity.[57] However, none of these definitions required that this activity should aim at the furtherance of *scientific* knowledge of the marine environment. A pertinent question that arises is what the qualifier "scientific" implies.

55 See Myron H. Nordquist et al., eds., *United Nations Convention on the Law of the Sea, 1982: A Commentary (Vol. IV)*, 509. The implications of this phrase will be addressed in Section 3.2.4.3 of this chapter.

56 UNCLOS, Article 246(3).

57 See Section 3.2.1 of this chapter.

The term "scientific knowledge" is not defined by the Convention. Black's Law Dictionary defines this term as:

> [a] fact that has been acquired through the scientific method. Testing is rigorous and independent, needs peer review and subsequent publication, needs a measurement of potential or actual error and must gain a degree of acceptance from the scientific community.[58]

The term "knowledge" is defined as "[f]acts, information, and skills acquired through experience or education; the theoretical or practical understanding of a subject".[59] Arguably, the definition of the term "scientific knowledge", as compared to the definition of the term "knowledge", emphasizes two elements of relevance for the current analysis, being the use of scientific methods and the requirement of subsequent publication. The first element echoes the general principle enumerated in Article 240 that marine scientific research "shall be conducted with appropriate scientific methods [...]".[60] The second is closely linked to Article 244 of the Convention concerning the publication and dissemination of knowledge and information.[61] These two elements serve as reasonable indications of the existence of scientific attributes of a research project. Therefore, it is submitted that the qualifier "scientific" under Article 246(3) underpins the observation made in the preceding analysis that research projects under this provision should have certain scientific attributes.

One may inquire whether the qualifier "exclusively" applies both to the requirements of "for peaceful purposes" and "in order to increase scientific knowledge of the marine environment". In other words, the question arises whether Article 246(3) only covers marine scientific research that is carried out "exclusively [...] in order to increase scientific knowledge of the marine environment". Most likely, the answer is negative. Throughout the text of UNCLOS, the term "exclusively" seems to be a "fixed" qualifier for the requirement that the use of the oceans should be "for peaceful purposes". Apart from Article 246(3), the phrase "exclusively for peaceful purposes" is included in other provisions of the Convention, such as Article 240 which sets out the general principles for the conduct of marine scientific research, Article 141 concerning

58 "Scientific knowledge", The Law Dictionary (Featuring Black's Law Dictionary Free Online Legal Dictionary 2nd Ed.), available at https://thelawdictionary.org/scientific-knowledge/.

59 "Knowledge", Oxford Dictionary of English (Oxford Reference online version, 3rd edition, Oxford University Press, 2015).

60 UNCLOS, Article 240(b). See Section 3.2.2 of this chapter.

61 See Section 3.2.3 of this chapter.

the use of the Area "exclusively for peaceful purposes".[62] On the contrary, the Convention does not contain any provision explicitly referring to the requirement to carry out marine scientific research "exclusively in order to increase scientific knowledge of the marine environment". Besides, under Article 244, when setting out the obligation to publish and disseminate information and knowledge, references were made to "scientific data and information" and "knowledge" resulting from marine scientific research.[63] If the qualifier "exclusively" applies to "in order to increase scientific knowledge […]" and such a qualification defines the term "marine scientific research", all marine scientific research in Part XIII of UNCLOS should be conducted "exclusively" "in order to increase scientific knowledge". In this case, the term used under Article 244 would have been "scientific knowledge", rather than "knowledge".

As to the fourth qualification "for the benefit of all mankind", there is no definition provided in the Convention for this phrase. As opined by some scholars, it appears to require the general availability of scientific data and research results.[64] Public availability and free exchange add to the sum of human scientific knowledge on a particular subject; therefore, it can be presumed to benefit humankind.[65] In this sense, this qualification can be read in conjunction with Article 244 of the Convention concerning the obligation of publication and dissemination of information and knowledge.[66] Since Article 244 of the Convention applies to all marine scientific research, if one interprets "for the benefit of all mankind" as merely a requirement of making research information and knowledge available, this qualification does not add anything to the obligations contained in Article 244.

Besides, nowhere else does the Convention provide for the requirement that marine scientific research shall only be conducted "for the benefit of all mankind", except Article 143 which deals with marine scientific research in the Area.[67] However, as will be elaborated upon below, the obligation of carrying out marine scientific research in the Area "for the benefit of mankind as a whole" under Article 143 is one of the provisions that give effect to the common heritage of mankind principle contained in Article 136 of the

62 Other provisions include Articles 143(1), 147(2)(d), and 155(2).

63 UNCLOS, Article 244(2).

64 Alfred H. A. Soons, *Marine Scientific Research and the Law of the Sea*, 167; Florian H.Th. Wegelein, *Marine Scientific Research: The Operation and Status of Research Vessels and Other Platforms in International Law*, 300.

65 Alfred H. A. Soons, *Marine Scientific Research and the Law of the Sea*, 242–243; Lyle Glowka, "The Deepest of Ironies: Genetic Resources, Marine Scientific Research, and the Area", *Ocean Yearbook Online* 12, no. 1 (1996): 172.

66 UNCLOS, Article 244. This article has been examined in Section 3.2.3 of this chapter.

67 Ibid., Article 143.

Convention.[68] The fact that this requirement only applies to marine scientific research projects conducted in the Area and not to those conducted in other maritime areas attests that the qualification "for the benefit of all mankind" does not constitute a criterion defining the term "marine scientific research". This observation is again reinforced by the relevant drafting history. Among the officially proposed definitions of the term "marine scientific research" put forward during UNCLOS III, none of them referred to the requirement of "for the benefit of all mankind".[69]

3.2.4.2.3 *Interim Conclusions*

Based on the preceding analysis, it can be concluded that the qualifications under Article 246(3) do not define the term "marine scientific research" under UNCLOS. Instead, they were included in Article 246(3) to define the scope of research projects to which the coastal State is obliged to grant its consent "in normal circumstances". As a result, to constitute marine scientific research under UNCLOS, the ocean data collection activity concerned does not need to meet the requirements implied by the four qualifications. Most notably, a marine scientific research project does not necessarily have to be conducted "exclusively [...] in order to increase scientific knowledge of the marine environment for the benefit of all mankind". In other words, marine scientific research does not have to be conducted with the *sole* purpose of increasing scientific knowledge of the marine environment.

3.2.4.3 Article 246(5) and Its Implications for Understanding the Nature of and Criteria for Marine Scientific Research

Another provision that warrants a close examination for discerning the scope of marine scientific research is Article 246(5). This provision sets out the situations where the coastal State may, at its discretion, withhold its consent for foreign marine scientific research projects. Of particular relevance for the present study is the situation where the research project "is of direct significance for the exploration and exploitation of natural resources".[70]

68 Alex G. Oude Elferink, "The Regime of the Area: Delineating the Scope of Application of the Common Heritage Principle and Freedom of the High Seas", *The International Journal of Marine and Coastal Law* 22, no. 1 (2007): 156. See also Section 3.3.4.2 of this chapter.

69 See Section 3.2.1 of this chapter.

70 UNCLOS, Article 246(5)(a).

3.2.4.3.1 *Marine Scientific Research that Is "of Direct Significance for the Exploration and Exploitation of Natural Resources"*

The phrase "of direct significance for the exploration and exploitation of natural resources" is closely related to Article 251 of UNCLOS, which requires States to promote "the establishment of general criteria and guidelines to assist States in ascertaining the nature and implications of marine scientific research".[71] The link between the said phrase and Article 251 can be noted when looking at the evolution of Article 251 in the various drafting texts of the Convention produced at UNCLOS III. In particular, an earlier version of this article was placed under the same article as the consent regime for foreign marine scientific research in the EEZ or on the continental shelf of a coastal State.[72] This earlier version explicitly referred to

> the establishment of criteria and guidelines concerning the differentiation between research directly related to the exploration and exploitation of the living and non-living resources and fundamental research which is not directly related to exploration and exploitation of such resources.[73]

Since the adoption of UNCLOS, several efforts have been made to implement Article 251 and to ascertain the meaning of the phrase "of direct significance for the exploration and exploitation of natural resources". For instance, the UN/DOALOS guidelines on marine scientific research interpret the phrase as denoting projects which "can reasonably be expected to produce results enabling resources to be located, assessed and monitored with respect to their status and availability for commercial exploitation".[74] This interpretation emphasizes the idea that the outcome of research projects falling under this phrase should be "directly" related to the exploration and exploitation of natural resources.

This matter was also considered by the Intergovernmental Oceanographic Commission (IOC). In the first meeting of the IOC Advisory Body of Experts of the Law of the Sea (IOC/ABE-LOS), it was pointed out that the interpretation

---

71 Ibid., Article 251.

72 Informal single negotiating text, Part III, UN. Doc. A/CONF.62/WP.8/Part III, part II, Article 18.

73 Ibid., Article 18(2).

74 United Nations Office for Ocean Affairs and the Law of the Sea, "Marine Scientific Research: A Guide to the Implementation of the Relevant Provisions of the United Nations Convention on the Law of the Sea", New York, 1991, para.58; UN/DOALOS, "Marine Scientific Research: A Revised Guide to the Implementation of the Relevant Provisions of the United Nations Convention on the Law of the Sea", para.30.

of the single word "direct" is critical.[75] Too wide an interpretation of the word "direct" would make coastal States "feel obliged to reject" almost all applications for marine scientific research, "as all [marine scientific research] is in some way ultimately relevant [for] exploitation".[76]

To follow up on the observations made during the IOC/ABE-LOS meeting, since different elements of the marine environment are closely related, any kind of marine scientific research activity can lead to a result that is relevant or significant for the exploration and exploitation of natural resources. Such an inextricable link implies that even a research activity undertaken purely with a view to increasing human knowledge may also result in the discovery of commercially valuable information about natural resources. One example is the research that led to the discovery of manganese nodules, which turned out to be economically valuable after further study.[77] That research was conducted with a view to describing natural phenomena and increasing knowledge about the natural processes of the oceans, and happened to deliver economic benefits.[78] In this connection, it is submitted that, since all research may be relevant (of significance) for the exploration and exploitation of natural resources, it is the word "direct" that separates the marine scientific research projects under Article 246(5)(a) from other marine scientific research projects.[79] The Convention does not indicate what to be considered as "direct". The ordinary meaning of this qualifier is "immediate; operating by an immediate connection or relation, instead of operating through a medium".[80] Therefore, as commented by some scholars, to meet the qualification of "direct", there should be a certain degree of relevance, that is, results of the research in question must have their own, intrinsic value for exploration or exploitation and that it is not enough that the research results are only remotely significant.[81] A research project cannot be considered as "of direct significance for the exploration and exploitation of

---

75 David Pugh, "Criteria and Guidelines for Ascertaining the Nature and Implications of Marine Scientific Research (IOC/ABE-LOS I/7)", in *First Meeting of the Advisory Body of Experts on the Law of the Sea* (*ABE-LOS*) (Paris 2001), at p. 1.

76 Ibid., at pp. 1–2.

77 Joanna Mossop, *The Continental Shelf Beyond 200 Nautical Miles: Rights and Responsibilities* (Oxford University Press, 2016), 159.

78 Ibid.

79 Florian H.Th. Wegelein, *Marine Scientific Research: The Operation and Status of Research Vessels and Other Platforms in International Law*, 297.

80 "Direct", The Law Dictionary (Featuring Black's Law Dictionary Free Online Legal Dictionary 2nd Ed.), available at https://thelawdictionary.org/direct/.

81 Alfred H. A. Soons, *Marine Scientific Research and the Law of the Sea*, 171. See also Florian H.Th. Wegelein, *Marine Scientific Research: The Operation and Status of Research Vessels and Other Platforms in International Law*, 87.

natural resources" when it is carried out without a view to the commercial utilization of the research object.[82] Therefore, by including the phrase "of direct significance for the exploration and exploitation of natural resources" under Article 246(5), the Convention recognizes that marine scientific research under UNCLOS may be carried out with a view to the commercial utilization of the research object. This observation raises the question concerning the relationship between marine scientific research that "is of direct significance for the exploration and exploitation of natural resources" on the one hand and exploration and exploitation on the other. This question will be examined in Section 3.3.2.1.1 of this chapter. As will be concluded below, marine scientific research is distinct from exploration and exploitation. A pertinent implication of such a distinction is that too narrow an interpretation of the qualifier "direct" would lead to the confusion of the concepts of "marine scientific research that is of direct significance for the exploration and exploitation" and "exploration".

In practice, the right to determine whether a research project "is of direct significance for the exploration and exploitation of natural resources", according to UNCLOS, rests with the coastal State.[83] As it would be difficult, if not impossible, to agree on a general basis whether the results of the activities have that intrinsic value or not, the assessment can only be made in a case-by-case manner. Besides, the relevant provisions of UNCLOS indicate that the coastal State needs to determine whether the research project "is of direct significance for the exploration and exploitation of natural resources" several months before the commencement of the project.[84] At this stage, the coastal State cannot make the assessment based on the relevance of the research

82 Florian H.Th. Wegelein, *Marine Scientific Research: The Operation and Status of Research Vessels and Other Platforms in International Law*, 297. See also Alexander Proelss, ed. *United Nations Convention on the Law of the Sea: A Commentary*, 1662.

83 Myron H. Nordquist et al., eds., *United Nations Convention on the Law of the Sea, 1982: A Commentary* (*Vol. IV*), 518. Article 246(5) grants the coastal State the right to withhold its consent when it considers the research project "is of direct significance for the exploration and exploitation of natural resources". The coastal State's control over this matter is reinforced by Article 297(2)(a), which excludes any dispute arising out of "the exercise of the coastal State of a right or discretion in accordance with article 246" from the compulsory dispute settlement mechanism under section 2, Part XV, and by subsection (b) of the same paragraph, which provides that in the case of compulsory conciliation, the conciliation commission "shall not call in question the exercise by the coastal State [...] of its discretion to withhold consent in accordance with article 246, paragraph 5".

84 Article 248 obliges the research State to provide the coastal State with information about the research project "no less than six months in advance of the expected starting date of the marine scientific research project". Normally, the coastal State should respond to the researching State "within four months of the receipt of the communication containing such information". UNCLOS, Articles 248, 252.

results, because such results simply do not exist. The coastal State can only discern from the information provided by the researching State according to Article 248 of the Convention the possible relevance of the results for the exploration and exploitation of natural resources. Such information includes, among others, the nature and objectives of the project, research methods and means, the precise geographical areas in which the project is to be conducted and the name of the sponsoring institution.[85]

At the same time, relevant UNCLOS provisions require the determination to be made in an objective manner. For instance, Article 300 of the Convention states that the States Parties "shall exercise the rights, jurisdiction and freedoms recognized in this Convention in a manner which would not constitute an abuse of right".[86] This observation has been affirmed by the 1991 UN/DOALOS guidelines on marine scientific research, which stated that "this determination must be based on objective facts, viz., the information provided to the coastal State pursuant to article 248".[87]

The drafting history of Article 246(5)(a) also lends support to the observation made above. As can be noted in the earlier drafts of Article 246(5), in the beginning, the qualifier "direct" was not included.[88] In RSNT, a similar phrase – "bear substantially upon the exploration and exploitation"– was used.[89] The phrase "of direct significance for [...]" was introduced by the Castañeda Group in 1977.[90] The mandate of this Group and the context in which this phrase was introduced have been discussed in Section 3.2.4.2 of this chapter. As such, the term "direct", similar to the qualifications under Article 246(3), was introduced as a balancing element between the coastal State and other States. To be more specific, the term "direct" was inserted to avoid the coastal State from exercising its

85 Ibid., Article 248.

86 Ibid., Article 300.

87 United Nations Office for Ocean Affairs and the Law of the Sea, "Marine Scientific Research: A Guide to the Implementation of the Relevant Provisions of the United Nations Convention on the Law of the Sea", para.57. However, the statement was not contained in the UN/DOALOS Revised Guide issued in 2010. The reason for the omission remains unknown. See also Alexander Proelss, ed. *United Nations Convention on the Law of the Sea: A Commentary*, 1662.

88 The relevant terms that were used are "marine scientific research related to the exploration and exploitation [...]" and "any scientific research [...] bearing upon the exploration and exploitation [...]". See Myron H. Nordquist et al., eds., *United Nations Convention on the Law of the Sea, 1982: A Commentary* (Vol. IV), 504–505.

89 Revised single negotiating text, Part III, UN. Doc. A/CONF.62/WP.8/Rev.1/Part III, Article 60.

90 Myron H. Nordquist et al., eds., *United Nations Convention on the Law of the Sea, 1982: A Commentary* (Vol. IV), 509.

discretion to withhold consent for a research project too arbitrarily.[91] However, although the delegations agreed on a compromise, they did not agree on what connection could be considered as "direct". As argued above, it is for this reason that Article 251 was included to oblige States, through subsequent efforts, to seek to establish general criteria and guidelines for such purposes. In this regard, Chapters 4 and 5 of this book will look at relevant subsequent practice of States and rules of international treaties other than UNCLOS to discern whether States have established such criteria or guidelines.

3.2.5 *Interim Conclusions*

The above analysis leads to the following observations.

To constitute marine scientific research under UNCLOS, an ocean data collection activity has to contribute to the furtherance of knowledge of the marine environment. This observation is supported by the fact that all the definitions officially proposed during UNCLOS III refer to the requirement to "increase knowledge of the marine environment" (Section 3.2.1). At the same time, it needs to have some scientific attributes. The ordinary meaning of the term "marine scientific research" (Section 3.2.1) and relevant provisions of the Convention (Sections 3.2.2 and 3.2.3) provide indications for assessing the existence of scientific attributes of marine scientific research. For instance, the requirement of using scientific methods indicates that to constitute marine scientific research, there has to be a hypothesis. The obligation to share scientific data and information and knowledge arising from marine scientific research under Article 244 is another major aspect of determining the existence of scientific attributes of marine scientific research.

However, the Convention does not require marine scientific research to be conducted solely with a view to increasing scientific knowledge of the marine environment. Marine scientific research that solely contributes to the furtherance of scientific knowledge of the marine environment is usually termed "pure" marine scientific research, as opposed to applied marine scientific research. An investigation of the drafting history of Article 246 indicates that the distinction between pure and applied marine scientific research is not defined in UNCLOS, and marine scientific research under the Convention covers both kinds of research projects (Section 3.2.4.1).

A pertinent question arises whether the qualifications under Article 246(3) form the constituent elements defining the term "marine scientific research". The relevant drafting history of this paragraph points to a negative answer. The

91 See Alexander Proelss, ed. *United Nations Convention on the Law of the Sea: A Commentary*, 1662.

qualifications under Article 246(3) were introduced to define to the scope of research projects to which the coastal State is obliged to grant its consent "in normal circumstances", instead of serving as a definition of the term "marine scientific research" under UNCLOS. An examination of the implications of the substantive qualifications lends support to this argument (Section 3.2.4.2). Most notably, as a consequence of this finding, a marine scientific research project is not necessarily to be conducted "exclusively [...] in order to increase scientific knowledge of the marine environment for the benefit of all mankind". In other words, marine scientific research does not have to be conducted with the sole purpose of increasing scientific knowledge.

The phrase "of direct significance for the exploration and exploitation of natural resources" under Article 246(5)(a) also sheds light on understanding the scope of marine scientific research under UNCLOS. It is argued that by including this phrase, especially the qualifier "direct", under Article 246(5), the Convention recognizes that marine scientific research can be carried out with a view to the commercial utilization of the research objects (Section 3.2.4.3). This is because a marine scientific research project that is not conducted with such a view cannot be considered as being "of direct significance for the exploration and exploitation of natural resources". If all marine scientific research under UNCLOS must be carried out without a view to commercial gains, no research project may fall under Article 246(5)(a), and this provision will become obsolete.

Given the open-ended wording, this phrase gives rise to different interpretations. Article 251 of the Convention requires States to seek to promote the establishment of general criteria and guidelines for this matter. Relevant provisions of the Convention suggest that in practice, it is the coastal State that determines the nature of a marine scientific research project, *i.e.*, whether it falls under Article 246(5)(a). The determination should be made objectively in light of the information provided by the researching State pursuant to Article 248 (Section 3.2.4.3).

In sum, as minimum requirements, marine scientific research in the context of UNCLOS has to contribute to the furtherance of knowledge of the marine environment and display some scientific attributes. However, it can also contribute to commercial ends. In other words, marine scientific research can potentially serve multiple ends, and one of such ends shall be scientific.

3.3 Marine Scientific Research and Other Ocean Data Collection Activities

In different maritime zones, the Convention prescribes different sets of rules for different uses of the seas. An examination of the respective rules applicable to these uses in each of the maritime zones contained in UNCLOS would shed light on understanding the relationship between one activity and another.

The relevant UNCLOS provisions will be examined consecutively in this section: Section 3.3.1 on internal waters, territorial sea, and archipelagic waters; Section 3.3.2 on the EEZ; Section 3.3.3 on the continental shelf; Section 3.3.4 on the Area. The provisions on the high seas will not be addressed in detail in this section. This is because, under Article 87 of the Convention, nearly all uses of the high seas are governed by the principle of the freedom of the high seas.[92] Hence, the relevant provisions do not inform the understanding of the difference between various kinds of ocean data collection activities and thus are irrelevant for the analysis of this section. Likewise, provisions on contiguous zone will not be discussed further either. The contiguous zone is a zone contiguous to the territorial sea of a coastal State, in which the coastal State is entitled to exercise the control necessary to prevent and punish "infringement of its customs, fiscal, immigration or sanitary laws and regulations within its territory or territorial sea".[93] For a certain ocean data collection activity, regardless of its legal classification (be it marine scientific research or not), as long as it infringes the customs, fiscal, immigration or sanitary law and regulations of the coastal State, the coastal State may exercise the control to prevent and punish. On the contrary, since the provisions on the EEZ prescribe the most diversified rules for different ocean uses, which will likely inform the theme of this chapter, the relevant provisions on this area will be addressed in more details. In the substantive analysis, a comparison will be made between the rules applying to marine scientific research and those applying to other pertinent ocean data collection activities. However, because some of the provisions on marine scientific research have been addressed in the previous section, they will not be included in this section.

3.3.1 *Pertinent Provisions on Internal Waters, Territorial Sea and Archipelagic Waters*

In the internal waters, the territorial sea and archipelagic waters, as the coastal State enjoys sovereignty over these areas,[94] almost all activities can only be undertaken by other States in such areas with the express consent from the coastal State. One exception, though, is the right of innocent passage through the territorial sea, archipelagic waters, and under certain circumstances in the

---

92 UNCLOS, Article 87.

93 Ibid., Article 33(1).

94 Ibid., Article 2(1).

internal waters.[95] According to Article 19(2), the passage is no longer innocent if the foreign ship engages in any activity that does not have a direct bearing on passage.[96] Among others, research and survey activities are listed as examples of activities that are not allowed during such passage.[97] It has been submitted that "the collection of data by a ship in passage that are required for the safe passage of the ship in question [...] must be regarded a normal activity associated with the operation of ships".[98] As such, the ocean data collection involved in this situation, which only serves to ensure the safe navigation of the ship in question, cannot be considered as marine scientific research, because it is subject to different regulation.

3.3.2 *Pertinent Provisions on the EEZ*

The situation in the EEZ is less clear-cut than in the areas where the coastal State enjoys sovereignty. The approach adopted by the Convention to attributing rights and obligations in the EEZ is mainly included in Articles 56, 58 and 59. Article 56 specifies "rights, jurisdiction and duties" of the coastal State in its EEZ; Article 58 lists "rights and duties" of other States in the EEZ of the coastal State; and Article 59 provides a guideline for the resolution of conflict "where this Convention does not attribute rights or jurisdiction to the coastal State or other States" within the EEZ. Marine scientific research is among the activities over which the coastal State enjoys jurisdiction in its EEZ under Article 56.[99] Different allocations of rights and obligations are the results of parties' perception of the different nature of the activities concerned. An understanding of these provisions – how the rights and obligations are allocated, and why they are allocated as such – would inform the understanding of the relationship between marine scientific research and other activities alike.

Before commencing the analysis of the substantive provisions, it is necessary to look at the legal status of the EEZ in the Convention. This helps understand the attribution of rights and obligations in this area and the approach to resolving conflicts when the right pertinent to a certain activity has not been attributed to either the coastal State or other States by the Convention.

The concept of the EEZ was an innovation of UNCLOS III – it was introduced to resolve conflicts between two opposing principles that were proposed to

95 Ibid., Articles 8(2), 17, 52.

96 Ibid., Article 19(2). This provision also applies to the innocent passage of a foreign ship through archipelagic waters pursuant to Article 52(1) of UNCLOS.

97 Ibid.

98 Alfred H. A. Soons, *Marine Scientific Research and the Law of the Sea*, 149.

99 UNCLOS, Article 56(1)(b).

be applied in the area between the territorial sea and the high seas, which are territorial sovereignty and the freedom of the high seas.[100] After extensive negotiations, delegations realized that neither of these principles would achieve general acceptance.[101] As a result, a compromise was reached – the EEZ was subject to a *sui generis* legal regime that is established in Part V of UNCLOS.[102] The zone is neither under the sovereignty of the coastal State nor part of the high seas.[103]

Although a *sui generis* legal regime has been established for the EEZ, the interpretation and application of the regime are not free of problems. The most challenging question concerns the classification of a specific activity.[104] This question relates to determining whether a certain activity in the EEZ falls under the rights and jurisdiction of the coastal State (Article 56(1)), or the freedom of other States (Article 58(1)), or whether it is an activity that falls under the scope of Article 59 concerning unattributed rights and jurisdiction.[105] If an activity falls under the rights of either the coastal State or other States, the question at issue is to determine the content and extent of the right, taking into account the due regard obligation; if the Convention does not attribute the rights and jurisdiction concerning the activity, the question is then concerned with residual rights in the EEZ, to which Article 59 is to be applied.[106] Bearing this in mind,

100 ED Brown, "The Exclusive Economic Zone: Criteria and Machinery for the Resolution of International Conflicts between Different Users of the EEZ", *Maritime Policy and Management* 4, no. 6 (1977): 328. See also Francisco Orrego Vicuña, *The Exclusive Economic Zone: Regime and Legal Nature under International Law* (Cambridge University Press, 1989), 16–21.

101 See, for instance, Jorge G. Castañeda, "Negotiations on the Exclusive Economic Zone at the Third United Nations Conference on the Law of the Sea"; Francisco Orrego Vicuña, *The Exclusive Economic Zone: Regime and Legal Nature under International Law*; Dolliver Nelson, "Exclusive Economic Zone", in *Max Planck Encyclopedia of Public International Law* [*MPEPIL*] (2008); Robert Beckman and Tara Davenport, "The EEZ Regime: Reflections after 30 Years" (paper presented at the 2012 LOSI-KIOST Conference on Securing the Ocean for the Next Generation, 2012); Gemma Andreone, "The Exclusive Economic Zone", in *The Oxford Handbook of the Law of the Sea*, edited by Donald Rothwell, et al. (2015).

102 UNCLOS, Article 55.

103 Jorge G. Castañeda, "Negotiations on the Exclusive Economic Zone at the Third United Nations Conference on the Law of the Sea", 621; R. R. Churchill and A. V. Lowe, *The Law of the Sea*, 165–166; Robert Beckman and Tara Davenport, "The EEZ Regime: Reflections after 30 Years", 6; Donald R. Rothwell and Tim Stephens, *The International Law of the Sea (2nd edition)*, 87–88.

104 Tullio Treves, "Coastal States' Rights in the Maritime Areas under UNCLOS", *Brazilian Journal of International Law* 12(2015): 42–43.

105 UNCLOS, Articles 56(1), 58(1) and 59.

106 Camille Goodman, "Rights, Obligations, Prohibitions: A Practical Guide to Understanding Judicial Decisions on Coastal State Jurisdiction over Living Resources in the Exclusive

this section begins with an examination of the rights and jurisdiction of the coastal State in its EEZ (Section 3.3.2.1), followed by a discussion of the rights enjoyed by other States in the zone (Section 3.3.2.2). The due regard obligation, which needs to be fulfilled when exercising the rights, will be addressed in Section 3.3.2.3. Section 3.3.2.4 examines Article 59 that deals with residual rights in the EEZ. Section 3.3.2.5 presents some interim concluding remarks.

3.3.2.1 Rights and Jurisdiction of the Coastal State in Its EEZ

Rights and jurisdiction of the coastal State in its EEZ are provided for in Article 56(1). This provision categorizes the rights and jurisdiction of the coastal State into three kinds, which are:[107]

a. *sovereign rights* "for the purpose of exploring and exploiting, conserving and managing the natural resources, [...], and with regard to other activities for the economic exploitation and exploration of the zone, [...]";
b. *jurisdiction* with regard to "(i) the establishment and use of artificial islands, installations and structures; (ii) marine scientific research; (iii) the protection and preservation of the marine environment";
c. *other rights* "provided for in this Convention".

A distinction that is relevant to the current study is made between marine scientific research and activities over which the coastal State enjoys sovereign rights or "other rights". It has been submitted that "other rights" under Article 56(1)(c) include the rights that the coastal State has in the contiguous zone as contained in Article 33[108] and the right of hot pursuit under Article 111.[109] Since activities in relation to these rights rarely involve the collection of ocean data, the main focus of the following analysis will be on the distinction between marine scientific research and the activities over which the coastal State enjoys sovereign rights, especially activities for the purpose of exploring and exploiting the natural resources.

Economic Zone", *The International Journal of Marine and Coastal Law* 33, no. 3 (2018): 10; Francisco Orrego Vicuña, *The Exclusive Economic Zone: Regime and Legal Nature under International Law*, 39; ED Brown, "The Exclusive Economic Zone: Criteria and Machinery for the Resolution of International Conflicts between Different Users of the EEZ", 331.

107 UNCLOS, Article 56(1).

108 According to Article 33, the coastal State "may exercise the control necessary to: (a) prevent infringement of its customs, fiscal, immigration or sanitary laws and regulations within its territory or territorial sea; (b) punish infringement of the above laws and regulations committed within its territory or territorial sea."

109 R. R. Churchill and A. V. Lowe, *The Law of the Sea*, 169; Robert Beckman and Tara Davenport, "The EEZ Regime: Reflections after 30 Years", 10; Gemma Andreone, "The Exclusive Economic Zone", 165; Alexander Proelss, ed. *United Nations Convention on the Law of the Sea: A Commentary*, 430.

It has been a controversial issue whether "a difference in terms of quality" exists between sovereign rights under Article 56(1)(a) and jurisdiction under Article 56(1)(b).[110] Some authors take the view that "the change of terminology undoubtedly reflects a change in the balance of principles".[111] In contrast, others suggest that the different terms are only the result of compromises reached during UNCLOS III.[112] Relevant case law seems to lend support to the former view. In *M/V Virginia G*, ITLOS considers the term "sovereign rights" encompassing "all rights necessary for and connected with the exploration, exploitation, conservation and management of the natural resources".[113] In contrast, the coastal State only enjoys jurisdiction over the activities listed under Article 56(1)(b) to the extent "as provided for in the relevant provisions of [UNCLOS]".[114] This being said, as Treves commented, too much attention should not be placed on the different terms that have been used.[115] The content of the rights that the different terms entail are to be ascertained by an analysis of the specific articles of UNCLOS.[116]

3.3.2.1.1 *Exploration and Exploitation*

Different sets of substantive rules are formulated for the exploration and exploitation of natural resources (Articles 62–73, UNCLOS) and marine scientific research (Articles 246–254, UNCLOS) in the EEZ of a coastal State.

---

110 Alexander Proelss, ed. *United Nations Convention on the Law of the Sea: A Commentary*, 429; Tullio Treves, "Coastal States' Rights in the Maritime Areas under UNCLOS", 41.

111 ED Brown, "The Exclusive Economic Zone: Criteria and Machinery for the Resolution of International Conflicts between Different Users of the EEZ", 334; Francisco Orrego Vicuña, *The Exclusive Economic Zone: Regime and Legal Nature under International Law*, 26; R. R. Churchill and A. V. Lowe, *The Law of the Sea*, 167; Tullio Treves, "Coastal States' Rights in the Maritime Areas under UNCLOS", 41.

112 Alexander Proelss, ed. *United Nations Convention on the Law of the Sea: A Commentary*, 429; Alexander Proelss, "The Law on the Exclusive Economic Zone in Perspective: Legal Status and Resolution of User Conflicts Revisited", *Ocean Yearbook* 26(2012): 101–102.

113 ITLOS, *The M/V Virginia G Case (Panama v. Guinea-Bissau)*, Judgment of 14 April 2014, para.211. This statement finds its origin in the ILC's commentary on draft Article 68 (which became Article 2 of the 1958 Convention on the Continental Shelf) that dealt with the sovereign rights of the coastal State in relation to its continental shelf, which stated that "the text as now adopted leaves no doubt that the rights conferred upon the coastal State cover all rights necessary for the connected with the exploration and exploitation of the natural resources of the continental shelf". See "Report of the International Law Commission covering the work of its eighth session - Extract from the Yearbook of the International Law Commission: 1956, vol. II", Doc. A/3159, 1956, at p. 297.

114 UNCLOS, Article 56(1)(b).

115 Tullio Treves, "Coastal States' Rights in the Maritime Areas under UNCLOS", 41.

116 Ibid.

According to Article 62, the coastal State is obliged to give other States access to living resources in its EEZ only when it does not have the capacity to harvest the entire allowable catch.[117] In comparison, the coastal State shall "in normal circumstances, grant [its] consent for marine scientific research projects by other States or competent international organizations" if the projects meet the requirements under Article 246(3).[118] The different powers recognized for the coastal State for exploration and exploitation on the one hand, and marine scientific research on the other, indicate that parties to the Convention intend to make a distinction between the two kinds of activities. In this regard, since marine scientific research is to be distinguished from exploration and exploitation, the understanding of the criteria for the latter can help ascertain the scope of the former.

The Convention does not define the terms "exploration" or "exploitation". When interpreting these terms, references can be made to the Regulations adopted by the ISA with respect to the prospecting and exploration of mineral resources in the Area.[119] The definitions of the terms contained in these Regulations are nearly the same. The only difference is the type of mineral resources covered by each set of the Regulations. Generally, the term "exploitation" is defined as:

> the recovery *for commercial purposes* of [mineral resources] and the extraction of minerals therefrom, including the construction and operation of mining, processing and transportation systems, *for the production and marketing* of metals.[120]

The term "exploration" refers to:

> the searching for deposits of [mineral resources] *with exclusive rights*, the analysis of such deposits, the use and testing of recovery systems and equipment, processing facilities and transportation systems and the carrying out of studies of the environmental, technical, economic,

117 UNCLOS, Article 62(2).

118 Ibid., Article 246(3). These requirements have been discussed in Section 3.2.4.2 of this chapter.

119 These Regulations include, International Seabed Authority (ISA), Regulations on Prospecting and Exploration for Polymetallic Sulphides in the Area, 2010; International Seabed Authority (ISA), Regulations on Prospecting and Exploration for Cobalt-rich Ferromanganese Crusts in the Area, 2012; International Seabed Authority (ISA), Regulations on Prospecting and Exploration for Polymetallic Nodules in the Area, 2013.

120 Emphasis added. See, for instance, Regulations on Prospecting and Exploration for Polymetallic Sulphides in the Area, Regulation 1(3)(b).

commercial and other appropriate factors *that must be taken into account in exploitation*.[121]

Although the definitions apply specifically to mineral resources, some principles implied in the definitions can be applied more broadly.[122] From these definitions, it can be concluded that the term "exploitation" refers to the recovery of natural resources for commercial purposes and the production and marketing of certain products; "exploration" refers to research and analytical activities specifically contributing to the subsequent exploitation. The difference between the two is that while exploitation is carried out with a specific commercial purpose (for the production and marketing of goods), exploration is a vital step towards exploitation. Soons' seminal book lends support to this conclusion, which defined the term "exploration" as "data collecting activities concerning natural resources conducted specifically in view of the exploitation (*i.e.*, economic utilization) of those natural resources".[123] This definition is echoed by Wegelein, who defines "exploration" as "the collecting of data concerning natural resources with a view of using them economically", which should be carried out with "a clear view to subsequent exploitation (irrespective of whether or not this will take place)".[124]

Since marine scientific research is distinct from exploitation and exploration, a conclusion is warranted that marine scientific research activities are not conducted *solely* with a view to the commercial utilization of natural resources. In other words, if an ocean data collection activity is conducted solely in view of achieving commercial gains, the activity cannot be regarded as marine scientific research.

3.3.2.2 Rights of Other States in the EEZ of a Coastal State

Article 58(1) of the Convention lists the rights of other States in the EEZ of a coastal State. These rights include "the freedoms [...] of navigation and overflight and of the laying of submarine cables and pipelines", and "other internationally lawful uses of the sea related to these freedoms".[125] Neither marine scientific research nor other ocean data collection activities themselves can be considered as activities that amount to navigation, overflight or laying of

121 Emphasis added. See, for instance, ibid., Regulation 1(3)(c).

122 "Report of the Secretary-General on oceans and the law of the sea of 4 March 2004", UN Doc. A/59/62, para.262.

123 Alfred H. A. Soons, *Marine Scientific Research and the Law of the Sea*, 125, 170–171.

124 See Florian H.Th. Wegelein, *Marine Scientific Research: The Operation and Status of Research Vessels and Other Platforms in International Law*, 85.

125 UNCLOS, Article 58(1).

submarine cables and pipelines, notwithstanding the fact that they can be undertaken by means of navigation, overflight or laying of submarine cables and pipelines. Therefore, the pertinent question in the context of the current research is whether they can be classified as "other internationally lawful uses of the sea related to" these freedoms. Ocean data collection activities falling under this provision are not to be considered as marine scientific research, because different rules apply to them.

3.3.2.2.1 *Other Internationally Lawful Uses of the Sea Related to the Mentioned Freedoms*

Article 58(1) gives one example of "other internationally lawful uses of the sea related to" these freedoms, namely "those associated with the operation of ships, aircraft and submarine cables and pipelines".[126] The insertion of the phrase "such as" in the provision has given rise to different interpretations concerning the exact scope of such uses.[127] Unlike the freedoms explicitly listed in this provision, the identification of the uses falling under the phrase is subject to "a compatibility test".[128] Qualifications for the test include that such uses shall be 1) "related to" the three freedoms mentioned in Article 58(1), 2) "internationally lawful", and 3) "compatible with the other provisions of this Convention".[129]

For the first qualification, Article 58(1) does not indicate how close the relationship should be. One scholar has submitted that the phrase most likely includes support and maintenance activities, and that much will depend on whether the activity at issue is one that is a regular, common or even necessary requirement for the exercise of the freedoms of navigation, overflight and the laying of pipelines and cables.[130] Similarly, another author considers that there should be a "symbiotic link" between the activity at issue and the freedom referred to – they are "so integral to each other that either one would not and could not have taken place without the other".[131] On the face of it, such

126 Ibid., Articles 56(1)(a), 58(1).

127 Alexander Proelss, ed. *United Nations Convention on the Law of the Sea: A Commentary*, 445.

128 Bernard H. Oxman, "An Analysis of the Exclusive Economic Zone as Formulated in the Informal Composite Negotiating Text", in *Law of the Sea: State practice in Zones of Special Jurisdiction - proceedings [of the] Law of the Sea Institute [of the] thirteenth annual conference, co-sponsored by the Center for Economic and Social Studies of the Third World, Mexico City, October 15–18, 1979, Mexico City, Mexico*, edited by Thomas A. Clingan (1979), 69.

129 UNCLOS, Article 58(1).

130 Alexander Proelss, ed. *United Nations Convention on the Law of the Sea: A Commentary*, 452–453.

131 Kaiyan Homi Kaikobad, "Non Consensual Aerial Surveillance in the Airspace over the Exclusive Economic Zone for Military and Defence Purposes", in *International Law and*

interpretations seem to be imposing fairly strict requirements for "related to", edging closer to "necessary to". However, it is argued that these interpretations are in line with the drafting history of Article 58(1) and the general context of the EEZ regime. To be more specific, the inclusion in the Convention of the phrase "other internationally lawful uses of the sea related to these freedoms", rather than the wider formulation "other lawful uses of the sea" as favored by maritime powers at UNCLOS III, indicates that this phrase as now contained in the Convention cannot be interpreted too liberally.[132] Besides, the interpretation of the phrase "other internationally lawful uses of the sea related to these freedoms" raises the issue of the relationship between this provision and Article 59 which deals with residual rights in the EEZ. If the phrase is interpreted too liberally, nearly all kinds of oceanic activities conducted in the EEZ could in some way or other be subsumed under it.[133] This outcome would run contrary to the spirit of the EEZ regime to keep a balance between the interests of the coastal State and other States.

Apart from the first qualification, activities falling under the phrase "other internationally lawful uses of the sea related to these freedoms" also need to be "internationally lawful" and "compatible with the other provisions of the Convention". It has been submitted that these qualifications offer a legal basis to preclude certain kinds of activities undertaken in the EEZ of a coastal State, which are inconsistent with the other provisions of the Convention and other rules of international law even if they are "related to" the three freedoms.[134] In this sense, activities that, for instance, infringe the coastal State's sovereign rights and jurisdiction do not fall under Article 58(1).

Given the open-ended nature of the phrase "other internationally lawful uses of the sea related to these freedoms", it is impractical to list all of such uses. In the context of the present study, for a ship collecting ocean data that are required for the safe passage of the ship itself (such as water depth, wind

Power: Perspectives on Legal Order and Justice: Essays in Honour of Colin Warbrick, edited by Kaiyan Homi Kaikobad and Michael Bohlander (Brill Nijhoff, 2009), 521.

132 See Jorge G. Castañeda, "Negotiations on the Exclusive Economic Zone at the Third United Nations Conference on the Law of the Sea", 615. A comprehensive introduction to the drafting history of the phrase "other internationally lawful uses of the sea related to these freedoms" is provided by Kaikobad, see Kaiyan Homi Kaikobad, "Non Consensual Aerial Surveillance in the Airspace over the Exclusive Economic Zone for Military and Defence Purposes", 523–540.

133 David Testa, "Coastal State Regulation of Bunkering and Ship-to-Ship (STS) Oil Transfer Operations in the EEZ: An Analysis of State Practice and of Coastal State Jurisdiction Under the LOSC", *Ocean Development & International Law* 50, no. 4 (2019): 367.

134 Kaiyan Homi Kaikobad, "Non Consensual Aerial Surveillance in the Airspace over the Exclusive Economic Zone for Military and Defence Purposes", 533.

speed and direction), the ocean data collection activity involved is to be considered as "uses associated with the operation of ships", and thus falls under "other internationally lawful uses of the sea related to" navigation.[135] If such data are collected by the ship not (or not only) for its own safe navigation, but for the purposes of, for example, weather forecasting, "the situation becomes somewhat different".[136] It might, though, be *broadly* considered as "related to" the freedom of navigation.[137] A detailed analysis of the international regulation of such uses will be included in Chapter 7 of this study.

3.3.2.3 Reciprocal Obligations of "Due Regard" under Articles 56(2) and 58(3)

After listing the rights of the coastal State and other States in the EEZ, both Articles 56 and 58 set up an obligation of due regard – "[i]n exercising its rights and performing its duties under this Convention in the exclusive economic zone, the coastal State shall have due regard to the rights and duties of other States",[138] and *vice versa*.[139] Unlike the rules contained in Articles 56(1) and 58(1) which set up the rights of a State concerned, the due regard obligation is a rule that defines the ways such rights should be exercised.[140] This obligation can be invoked only when the existence of the right concerned is established in accordance with the Convention, and the right has been attributed to a State – either to the coastal State or a third State.[141] Once the activity at issue is considered as falling under the rights of either the coastal State or a third State, the due regard obligation can be invoked as a basis for assessing the

135 Alfred H. A. Soons, *Marine Scientific Research and the Law of the Sea*, 149.

136 Ibid.

137 Kaiyan Homi Kaikobad, "Non Consensual Aerial Surveillance in the Airspace over the Exclusive Economic Zone for Military and Defence Purposes", 538.

138 UNCLOS, Article 56(2).

139 Ibid., Article 58(3).

140 Ioannis Prezas, "Foreign Military Activities in the Exclusive Economic Zone: Remarks on the Applicability and Scope of the Reciprocal 'Due Regard' Duties of Coastal and Third States", *The International Journal of Marine and Coastal Law* 34, no. 1 (2019): 99. See also Rolf Einar Fife, "Obligations of 'Due Regard' in the Exclusive Economic Zone: Their Context, Purpose and State Practice", *The International Journal of Marine and Coastal Law* 34, no. 1: 45; Yurika Ishii, "The 'Due Regard' Obligation and the Peaceful and Economic Uses of the EEZ other than Fisheries", *The International Journal of Marine and Coastal Law* 34, no. 1 (2019): 74.

141 Ioannis Prezas, "Foreign Military Activities in the Exclusive Economic Zone: Remarks on the Applicability and Scope of the Reciprocal 'Due Regard' Duties of Coastal and Third States", 100.

reasonableness of the exercise of such rights.[142] The purpose of this obligation is to ensure conciliation between conflicting concurrent or overlapping rights and interests.[143]

Given the purpose of the due regard obligation, it presumably provides a good basis for resolving potential conflicts in ocean data collection activities by balancing rights and obligations involved. Therefore, the following analysis respectively examines the content of this obligation, rights and duties protected, and the mechanisms to implement this obligation, with a focus on the implications of this obligation for resolving conflicts arising from the exercise of rights concerning ocean data collection activities in the EEZ of a coastal State.

3.3.2.3.1 *The Content of the Due Regard Obligation in the EEZ*

The Convention does not define the term "due regard". As pointed out in *Enrica Lexie*, the ordinary meaning of the phrase "with due regard to" is "with the proper care or concern for", and "the ordinary meaning of 'due regard' does not contemplate priority for one activity over another".[144] The content of the due regard obligation has been addressed in detail in *Chagos Marine Protected Area Arbitration*.[145]

In examining the content of "due regard", the Tribunal considered that:

> the ordinary meaning of 'due regard' calls for the United Kingdom to have such regard for the rights of Mauritius as is called for by the circumstances and by the nature of those rights. The Tribunal declines to find in this formulation any universal rule of conduct. The Convention does not impose a uniform obligation to avoid any impairment of Mauritius' rights; nor does it uniformly permit the United Kingdom to proceed as it wishes, merely noting such rights. Rather, the extent of the regard required by the Convention will depend upon the nature of the rights held by Mauritius, their importance, the extent of the anticipated impairment, the nature and importance of the activities contemplated by the United Kingdom,

---

142 Yurika Ishii, "The 'Due Regard' Obligation and the Peaceful and Economic Uses of the EEZ other than Fisheries", 79.

143 Mathias Forteau, "The Legal Nature and Content of 'Due Regard' Obligations in Recent International Case Law", *The International Journal of Marine and Coastal Law* 34, no. 1 (2019): 25.

144 Annex VII Arbitral Tribunal of UNCLOS, *The 'Enrica Lexie' Incident* (*Italy v. India*), Award of 21 May 2020, para.973.

145 Annex VII Arbitral Tribunal of UNCLOS, *Chagos Marine Protected Area Arbitration* (*Mauritius v. United Kingdom*), Award of 18 March 2015.

> and the availability of alternative approaches. In the majority of cases, this assessment will necessarily involve at least some consultation with the rights-holding State.[146]

The Tribunal further stated that:

> the United Kingdom's obligation to act in good faith and to have 'due regard' to Mauritius' rights and interests [...] entails, at least, both consultation and a balancing exercise with its own rights and interests.[147]

Nonetheless, because the due regard obligation is included in the Convention to resolve potential conflicts, it is reasonable to argue that when there is no conflict arising from the exercise of rights under Article 56(1) or 58(1), and no conflict is likely to arise therefrom, the States concerned do not have to enter into consultation with each other.

For the obligation to consult, the Tribunal accepted the argument that "consultation need not continue indefinitely or 'until the other party is happy'".[148] However, the Tribunal stressed that,

> [t]he Tribunal's overall impression [...] was that there remained a number of issues unanswered, information that the United Kingdom promised to provide to Mauritius, and further work and consultations that would be jointly undertaken. It is difficult for the Tribunal to conclude, based on the foregoing, that this one meeting could satisfy the obligation to have 'due regard' or to consult.[149]

In contrast, the Tribunal considered,

> the United Kingdom's approach to consultations with the United States provides a practical example of due regard and a yardstick against which the communications with Mauritius can be measured. The record shows that the United States was consulted in a timely manner and provided with information, and that the United Kingdom was internally concerned with balancing the MPA with U.S. rights and interests.[150]

146 Ibid., para.519.
147 Ibid., para.534.
148 Ibid., para.531.
149 Ibid., para.530.
150 Ibid., para.528.

The Tribunal also concluded that the United Kingdom failed in its obligation to properly balance the interests involved.[151] It seems to be the view of the Tribunal that this obligation requires "a conscious balancing of rights and interests, suggestions of compromise and willingness to offer assurances [...], and an understanding of [the other State's] concerns in connection with the proposed activities".[152]

Elements that should be taken into account during the consultation and the balancing exercise include, as the Tribunal stated, "the nature of the rights held [...], their importance, the extent of the anticipated impairment, the nature and importance of the activities contemplated [...], and the availability of alternative approaches".[153] Concerning the criterion of the nature of the rights held, the Tribunal considered that when "significant" rights are at stake, they are "entitled, as a matter of good faith and the Convention, to a corresponding degree of regard".[154] In its assessment, the Tribunal also took into account the failure of the United Kingdom to "provide any convincing explanation for the urgency" with which it acted.[155] This element seems to be related to an evaluation of elements concerning "the nature and importance of the activities contemplated", and "the availability of alternative approaches".

Since the elements to be considered need to be assessed in a context-dependent manner, the outcome of the application of due regard obligations cannot be predetermined.[156] One can only give concreteness to the meaning of due regard obligations on a case-by-case basis.[157]

It is noted that according to relevant case law, the content of the due regard obligation is also concerned with a) a due diligence obligation to prevent the nationals of a third State from violating the coastal State's laws, b) a duty to protect the resources across the EEZ and the high seas, and c) a duty not to exercise the enforcement power excessively.[158] These elements are not addressed in this research, because they do not shed light on the central issues of this

151 Ibid., para.535.

152 Ibid.

153 Ibid., para.519.

154 Ibid., para.521.

155 Ibid., para.533.

156 Tullio Scovazzi, "'Due Regard' Obligations, with Particular Emphasis on Fisheries in the Exclusive Economic Zone", *The International Journal of Marine and Coastal Law* 34, no. 1 (2019): 63.

157 Ibid.; Yurika Ishii, "The 'Due Regard' Obligation and the Peaceful and Economic Uses of the EEZ other than Fisheries", 76.

158 See for instance, Yurika Ishii, "The 'Due Regard' Obligation and the Peaceful and Economic Uses of the EEZ other than Fisheries", 74; Mathias Forteau, "The Legal Nature and Content of 'Due Regard' Obligations in Recent International Case Law", 37–42.

study, which concern legal classification and the resolution of conflicts when the classification is unclear.

3.3.2.3.2 *"Rights and Duties" Protected by the Due Regard Obligation in the EEZ*

The Convention does not define the scope of "rights and duties" protected by the due regard obligation under Articles 56(2) and 58(3). Since the purpose of the due regard obligation is to reconcile rights and duties of different states, it is reasonable to consider that the rights and duties expressly mentioned in Article 56(1) and Article 58(1) are protected.

Apart from the rights and duties contained in Articles 56(1) and 58(1), in *Virginia G*, ITLOS stated that, the due regard obligation under Article 56(2),

> is to be interpreted to imply that in the exercise of its powers pursuant to article 73, paragraph 1, of the Convention, [...] the competent authorities of the coastal State shall proceed with all possible consideration.[159]

By using the phrase "all possible consideration", it seems that the Tribunal viewed that the scope of the rights and duties protected by the due regard obligation is broad – that such rights and duties are not limited to those mentioned in Articles 56(1) and 58(1).[160]

In the context of the present research, it could be argued that consideration concerning, for example, climate change mitigation, weather forecasts or the security of the States involved which are not explicitly contained in the Convention might be incorporated in the application of the due regard obligation. Implications of this observation will be further addressed in Chapter 7 of this book.

3.3.2.3.3 *How to Apply the Due Regard Obligation?*

With respect to how States may fulfil the due regard obligation, as indicated by relevant international case law, the States involved enjoy a wide margin of appreciation on this matter.[161] For example, ITLOS elaborated in *Bangladesh/Myanmar* case that,

---

159 ITLOS, *The M/V Virginia G Case (Panama v. Guinea-Bissau)*, Judgment of 14 April 2014, para.347.

160 Shotaro Hamamoto, "The Genesis of the 'Due Regard' Obligations in the United Nations Convention on the Law of the Sea", *The International Journal of Marine and Coastal Law* 34, no. 1 (2019): 7–24.

161 Mathias Forteau, "The Legal Nature and Content of 'Due Regard' Obligations in Recent International Case Law", 34.

> pursuant to the principle reflected in the provisions of articles 56, 58, 78 and 79 and in other provisions of the Convention, each coastal State must exercise its rights and perform its duties with due regard to the rights and duties of the other. There are many ways in which the Parties may ensure the discharge of their obligations in this respect, including the conclusion of specific agreements or the establishment of appropriate cooperative arrangements. It is for the Parties to determine the measures that they consider appropriate for this purpose.[162]

This approach was confirmed by the Annex VII Tribunal in *Bangladesh/India* case, where the Tribunal considered,

> [w]ithin the provisions of the Convention relating to the exclusive economic zone and continental shelf, articles 56, 58, 78, and 79 all call for States to exercise their rights and perform their duties with due regard to the rights and duties of other States. It is for the Parties to determine the measures they consider appropriate in this respect, including through the conclusion of further agreements or the creation of a cooperative arrangement.[163]

As can be noted, the Tribunals did not limit the ways in which the States concerned may comply with their due regard obligations. From the examples given, which are the conclusion of specific agreements or the establishment of appropriate cooperative arrangements, one can see that in any case, such obligations require negotiation and cooperation.[164]

3.3.2.4 Residual Rights in the EEZ

All the provisions considered above address rights that have been attributed to either the coastal State or a third State. For unattributed rights, pursuant to Article 59 of the Convention, in cases where a conflict arises between the interests of the coastal State and a third State, the conflict shall be resolved "on the basis of equity and in the light of all the relevant circumstances, taking

---

162 ITLOS, *Dispute concerning delimitation of the maritime boundary between Bangladesh and Myanmar in the Bay of Bengal* (*Bangladesh/Myanmar*), Judgment of 14 March 2012, paras.475–476.

163 Annex VII Arbitral Tribunal of UNCLOS, *Bay of Bengal Maritime Boundary Arbitration between Bangladesh and India*, Award of 7 July 2014, paras.507–508.

164 Mathias Forteau, "The Legal Nature and Content of 'Due Regard' Obligations in Recent International Case Law", 34.

into account the respective importance of the interests involved to the parties as well as to the international community as a whole".[165]

Because Article 59 deals with residual rights in the EEZ, it is to be considered as a supplementary provision to Articles 56 and 58. On the one hand, Article 59 should not be invoked without properly examining the applicability of Articles 56 and 58. On the other hand, as argued earlier, the inclusion of Article 59 in the Convention indicates that neither the scope of Article 56 nor Article 58 can be interpreted too broadly as covering all activities in the EEZ.[166]

Although Article 59 deals with the resolution of conflicts arising from unattributed rights in the EEZ, whereas the due regard obligations under Articles 56(2) and 58(3) address potential conflicts resulting from concurrent uses when the right concerned is already allocated, some similarities between these provisions can be identified.

First, one authority has observed that the underlying logic of Article 59 is identical to that of the due regard obligation.[167] Judge Laing also pointed out that both of them are norms and formulas created by the drafters of UNCLOS to address the diverse potential disputes and matters requiring resolution.[168] Because both the due regard obligation and Article 59 are incorporated in the Convention as a means to balance interests and to resolve conflicts, they require that when conflicts arise, there is no presumption in favor of either the coastal State or a third State and that such conflicts shall be resolved after a balancing test.

Second, both the due regard obligation and Article 59 are formulated in an open-ended fashion. Under Article 59, elements such as "equity" and "all the relevant circumstances" are so context-dependent that they can only be assessed on a case-by-case basis.[169] Therefore, the meaning of these provisions needs to be substantiated by concrete practice through the agreement between States, or through the decisions made by international courts and tribunals pursuant to Part XV of the Convention.[170] As of the time of writing, Article 59

165 UNCLOS, Article 59.

166 David Testa, "Coastal State Regulation of Bunkering and Ship-to-Ship (STS) Oil Transfer Operations in the EEZ: An Analysis of State Practice and of Coastal State Jurisdiction Under the LOSC", 368.

167 ED Brown, "The Exclusive Economic Zone: Criteria and Machinery for the Resolution of International Conflicts between Different Users of the EEZ", 344.

168 ITLOS, *The M/V "SAIGA" (No. 2) Case (Saint Vincent and the Grenadines v. Guinea)*, Separate Opinion of Judge Laing, para.55.

169 Alexander Proelss, ed. *United Nations Convention on the Law of the Sea: A Commentary*, 461.

170 Donald R Rothwell and Tim Stephens, *The International Law of the Sea (2nd edition)*, 91. See also Francisco Orrego Vicuña, *The Exclusive Economic Zone: Regime and Legal Nature*

has not been addressed in any of the *decisions* of international courts or tribunals. References to the article have appeared in the Declaration or Separate Opinion of some judges.[171] For instance, ITLOS in its Judgment on *M/V Virginia G case* concluded that bunkering to fishing vessels in the EEZ shall be subject to the sovereign right of the coastal State under Article 56(1)(a).[172] In contrast, Judge Nelson[173] and Judge *ad hoc* Treves[174] considered that Article 59 could also have been discussed in this case. However, they did not attempt to apply Article 59 in the case before them.

Third, neither Articles 56(2), 58(3) nor Article 59 define the scope of elements that should be considered in the balancing test. As noted above, Articles 56(2), 58(3) do not define "rights and duties" that are protected by the due regard obligation. Similarly, Article 59 only states that interests that shall be taken into account are the ones pertinent to 1) the coastal State, 2) the State entertaining a conflict with the coastal State, and 3) the international community as a whole. It does not mention the scope of interests that can be taken into account in the process – for instance, whether they are limited to the interests enshrined in Articles 56 and 58. This being said, because Article 59 is drafted to deal with situations which have not been addressed by the relevant provisions of the Convention, it can be reasonably argued that the interests that can be at play are not confined to the interests involved in Articles 56 or 58. This observation can be confirmed by the wording of Article 59, which requires the conflict to be resolved in the light of "all the relevant circumstances". The broad phrase "all the relevant circumstances" indicates that the scope of rights and interests that should be considered is very broad.

Therefore, it is argued that the observation made on the scope of "rights and duties" protected by the due regard obligation also applies here. Rights

---

under International Law, 36; Erik Franckx, ""Reasonable Bond" in the Practice of the International Tribunal for the Law of the Sea", *California Western International Law Journal* 32(2001): 309; Camille Goodman, "Rights, Obligations, Prohibitions: A Practical Guide to Understanding Judicial Decisions on Coastal State Jurisdiction over Living Resources in the Exclusive Economic Zone", 9.

171 See ITLOS, *The M/V Virginia G Case* (*Panama v. Guinea-Bissau*), Declaration of Judge Nelson, para.8; Declaration of Judge ad hoc Treves, para.8; ITLOS, *The M/V "SAIGA" (No. 2) Case* (*Saint Vincent and the Grenadines v. Guinea*), Separate Opinion of Judge Laing, paras.55–56; ITLOS, *The M/T "San Padre Pio" Case* (*Switzerland v. Nigeria*), *Provisional Measures*, Declaration of Judge Kittichaisaree, para.2.

172 ITLOS, *The M/V Virginia G Case* (*Panama v. Guinea-Bissau*), Judgment of 14 April 2014, para.211.

173 Ibid., Declaration of Judge Nelson, para.8.

174 Ibid., Declaration of Judge ad hoc Treves, para.8.

and interests that are not expressly listed under Articles 56(1) or 58(1) can be considered in the balancing test under Article 59.

As to the scope of ocean data collection activities that might fall under this article, it has been commented that operational oceanographic activities are covered by Article 59.[175] An analysis of this matter will be included in Chapter 7 of this book.

3.3.2.5 Interim Conclusions

From the above analysis, it can be concluded that in the EEZ the competence over a certain ocean use, including ocean data collection, needs to be determined mainly on the basis of the function or purpose of that use. To be more specific, if an ocean data collection activity is conducted purely with a view to commercial gains, it constitutes exploration or exploitation under Article 56(1)(a) of UNCLOS. Since marine scientific research is distinct from exploration and exploitation, a conclusion is warranted that marine scientific research is not conducted purely with a view to commercial gains.

If an ocean data collection activity is conducted to ensure the safe navigation, overflight, and the laying of submarine cables and pipelines, it can be considered as "other internationally lawful uses of the sea related to" the mentioned freedoms, and thus falls within the scope of rights of a third State under Article 58(1). Such an activity does not constitute marine scientific research either, because different sets of rules apply.

However, both Articles 56(1) and 58(1) and hence the scope of ocean data collection activities covered by them may be subject to different interpretations, mainly because of the vague phrases that are included. These open-ended phrases can be interpreted to tilt towards either the coastal State or a third State, depending on the political stand of the interpreter. However, it is important to recall the reason for incorporating these open-ended phrases – they were introduced as balancing elements between the interests of the coastal State and a third State.[176] As such, these phrases cannot be interpreted too expansively. When a careful assessment leads to the conclusion that the right over a certain ocean data collection activity is granted to either the coastal State or a third State, the exercise of such a right shall have due regard to the rights and duties of the other State concerned. As required by the due regard obligation, when a conflict arises or may arise, the States concerned shall engage in consultation with each other and properly balance the interests involved.

---

175 Alexander Proelss, ed. *United Nations Convention on the Law of the Sea: A Commentary*, 460–461.

176 Tullio Treves, "Coastal States' Rights in the Maritime Areas under UNCLOS", 43.

It is also possible that for a certain ocean data collection activity, the Convention does not attribute the rights to either the coastal State or a third State. In this scenario, when a conflict arises, the conflict should be resolved on the basis of the guideline contained in Article 59 of the Convention. This guideline requires that to solve the conflict, a balancing test should be carried out, taking into account all the relevant circumstances.

3.3.3 *Pertinent Provisions on the Continental Shelf*

Provisions concerning the continental shelf are contained in Part VI of the Convention. This section will look into the relevant provisions in this part and explore the implications for understanding the relationship between marine scientific research and other ocean data collection activities.

3.3.3.1 General Provisions on the Continental Shelf

After defining the concept of continental shelf in Article 76, the Convention addresses the rights of the coastal State over this area in Article 77.[177] According to this article, the coastal State "exercises over the continental shelf sovereign rights for the purpose of exploring it and exploiting its natural resources".[178] Other rights of the coastal State over its continental shelf include "the exclusive right to construct and to authorize and regulate the construction, operation and use of" artificial islands and installations and structures as indicated in Article 60(1),[179] and "the exclusive right to authorize and regulate drilling on the continental shelf for all purposes".[180]

Following these provisions, for an ocean data collection activity, irrespective of whether it constitutes marine scientific research or not, its conduct shall be subject to the sovereign/exclusive rights of the coastal State if the activity serves the purpose of exploring the continental shelf or exploiting the natural resources as defined in Article 77(4) of the Convention,[181] or if the activity involves the construction, operation and use of artificial islands or

177 UNCLOS, Articles 76–77.

178 Ibid., Article 77(1).

179 Ibid., Article 80.

180 Ibid., Article 81.

181 This is confirmed by ITLOS ruling on a request for provisional measures brought by Côte d'Ivoire against Ghana concerning oil exploration and exploitation in a disputed area of continental shelf. A Special Chamber of the Tribunal considered that:

> the rights of the coastal State over its continental shelf include all rights necessary for and connected with the exploration and exploitation of the natural resources of the continental shelf and that the exclusive right to access to information about the resources of the continental shelf is plausibly among those rights.

installations and structures indicated in Article 60(1), or if it involves drilling on the continental shelf.

Besides, the UNCLOS continental shelf regime also makes a distinction between exploration and exploitation on the one hand and marine scientific research on the other. Coastal States' rights to the exploration and exploitation of natural resources of the continental shelf are stipulated by Article 77 and are exclusive, while rights to regulate marine scientific research are set out in Article 246. Therefore, the analysis on such a distinction included in Section 3.3.2.1 of this chapter also applies to the situation on the continental shelf. In this sense, activities designed to collect data on the continental shelf specifically with a view to exploiting the natural resources, for instance, seismic surveying for the purpose of identifying commercial hydrocarbon resources on the continental shelf, is not considered as marine scientific research.[182]

3.3.3.2 Provisions on Marine Scientific Research on the Continental Shelf

Part VI does not contain an explicit reference to marine scientific research. However, as the title of Article 246 shows, this article applies to marine scientific research undertaken in the EEZ and on the continental shelf of a coastal State.[183] As such, the marine scientific research regime on the continental shelf is in principle the same as in the EEZ. Nonetheless, there are several issues specifically related to marine scientific research on the continental shelf.

Firstly, different interpretations exist as to the phrase marine scientific research "*on* the continental shelf". The phrase can have two different meanings, because of the use of the word "on".[184] If the preposition "on" is used to indicate the location of a research activity, the phrase must be interpreted as referring to marine scientific research involving physical contact with the continental shelf.[185] If it is used to indicate the object of the research, the phrase must be interpreted as referring to marine scientific research concerning the continental shelf. The distinction between these two interpretations is mostly

---

See ITLOS, *Dispute Concerning Delimitation of the Maritime Boundary between Ghana and Côte d'Ivoire in the Atlantic Ocean* (*Ghana/Côte d'Ivoire*), Order of 25 April 2015 (Provisional Measures), para.94.

182 Joanna Mossop, *The Continental Shelf Beyond 200 Nautical Miles: Rights and Responsibilities*, 153.

183 UNCLOS, Article 246.

184 Alfred H. A. Soons, *Marine Scientific Research and the Law of the Sea*, 215; Florian H.Th. Wegelein, *Marine Scientific Research: The Operation and Status of Research Vessels and Other Platforms in International Law*, 201.

185 The implications of the different language versions of the Convention will be discussed further below.

irrelevant in situations where the continental shelf overlaps with the seabed and subsoil of the EEZ of the coastal State because in this case, the coastal State has jurisdiction over research conducted both in the water column and on the seabed.[186] Whereas on the continental shelf areas beyond 200 nautical miles (hereinafter the outer continental shelf), the coastal State is only entitled to exercise its jurisdiction over marine scientific research on the seabed, because the suprajacent water column is the high seas, to which the principle of the freedom of the high seas applies.

Scholars have looked into other authentic texts of the Convention to ascertain the intention of the Parties when using the preposition "on".[187] However, it seems that no definitive answer can be obtained from this perspective because an analysis of these texts does not point in the same direction. Apart from the authentic texts of the Convention, focus has also been paid to the context of this article. Some scholars have examined, for example, the relationship between this article and Article 257 which deals with marine scientific research in the water column beyond the EEZ,[188] the drafting history of this provision,[189] the relevant State practice,[190] and relevant case law.[191] However, it seems that none of these elements suffices to provide a conclusive answer to the question whether the preposition "on" should be interpreted as "on top of" or "concerning". Therefore, it seems that this remains an open question. Nonetheless, Soons has observed that there is no indication that the States participating UNCLOS III intended to provide for a more limited coastal State jurisdiction over marine scientific research on its continental shelf than the then existing conventional or customary law.[192] Therefore, in the view of Soons, the most convincing interpretation of the phrase "on the continental shelf" would be "concerning the continental shelf".[193]

Secondly, according to Article 246(6), the coastal State is not entitled to withhold its consent for foreign marine scientific research undertaken on the

---

186 Joanna Mossop, *The Continental Shelf Beyond 200 Nautical Miles: Rights and Responsibilities*, 158.

187 Alfred H. A. Soons, *Marine Scientific Research and the Law of the Sea*, 216; Florian H.Th. Wegelein, *Marine Scientific Research: The Operation and Status of Research Vessels and Other Platforms in International Law*, 201–202.

188 See the overview provided by Mossop. Joanna Mossop, *The Continental Shelf Beyond 200 Nautical Miles: Rights and Responsibilities*, 162–163.

189 Alfred H. A. Soons, *Marine Scientific Research and the Law of the Sea*, 216.

190 See, for instance, Joanna Mossop, *The Continental Shelf Beyond 200 Nautical Miles: Rights and Responsibilities*, 163.

191 Ibid., 161–163.

192 Alfred H. A. Soons, *Marine Scientific Research and the Law of the Sea*, 216.

193 Ibid.

outer continental shelf if the project "is of direct significance for the exploration and exploitation of the natural resources".[194] This provision was a result of a compromise between major maritime powers and the coastal States with an outer continental shelf.[195] According to the resulting provisions, the researching State is still obliged to seek consent from the coastal State when it intends to undertake marine scientific research on its outer continental shelf. The coastal State shall grant its consent if the research project meets the conditions under Article 246(3) and at the same time does not fall under the situations in Article 246(5)(b)–(d).[196] Besides, the coastal State may withhold its consent when the project is to be undertaken in the areas for exploitation or detailed exploratory operations designated pursuant to Article 246(6).[197]

3.3.3.3 Interim Conclusions

The continental shelf regime does not shed much extra light (in addition to the conclusions drawn from the UNCLOS EEZ regime) on understanding the distinction between marine scientific research and other similar activities. The observations made concerning marine scientific research on the continental shelf may, however, have their implications in the actual implementation of relevant provisions in practice.

3.3.4 *Pertinent Provisions Applicable to the Area*

This section focuses on the relevant provisions of the UNCLOS Area regime. Section 3.3.4.1 addresses the general provisions on the Area, and Section 3.3.4.2 deals with provisions concerning the regulation of marine scientific research undertaken in the Area.

3.3.4.1 General Provisions on the Area

The regime concerning the Area is mainly provided for in Part XI of the Convention. Under Article 134(2) of the Convention, "activities in the Area shall be governed by the provisions of [Part XI]".[198] The term "activities in the Area" is defined by Article 1(1)(3) as "all activities of exploration for, and exploitation of, the resources of the Area".[199] Arguably, Article 134(2) does not purport to

---

194 UNCLOS, Article 246(6).

195 Alexander Proelss, ed. *United Nations Convention on the Law of the Sea: A Commentary*, 1663; Joanna Mossop, *The Continental Shelf Beyond 200 Nautical Miles: Rights and Responsibilities*, 157.

196 UNCLOS, Article 246.

197 Ibid., Article 246(6).

198 Ibid., Article 134(2).

199 Ibid., Article 1(1)(3).

list all the activities that are regulated by Part XI. As indicated earlier, marine scientific research is not exploration or exploitation.[200] The fact that Article 143 of the Convention explicitly addresses marine scientific research in the Area – an activity that is not included in "activities in the Area" as defined by Article 1(1)(3) – leads to the conclusion that the applicable scope of Part XI is not limited to "activities in the Area" as defined in Article 1(1)(3).

3.3.4.1.1 *Prospecting in the Area and Its Relationship with Marine Scientific Research*

Apart from marine scientific research, prospecting of mineral resources is another example of activities that are regulated by Part XI yet not included in the definition of "activities in the Area". This term is used several times in the Convention, especially in Annex III to the Convention which is titled "Basic Conditions for Prospecting, Exploration and Exploitation".[201] A definition of the term is provided by the ISA Regulations. According to the Regulations,

> prospecting means the search for deposits of [mineral resources] in the Area, including estimation of the composition, sizes and distributions of deposits of [mineral resources] and their economic values, without any exclusive rights.[202]

The Regulations also contain a definition of the term "exploration", which has been discussed in Section 3.3.2.1 of the current chapter. According to the Regulations, both prospecting and exploration can be used to denote activities involving the search for deposits of resources. Nevertheless, prospecting refers to the searching for deposits without any exclusive rights, while exploration refers to the search for deposits with exclusive rights.[203] Besides, according to relevant provisions of UNCLOS, there is no time limit for the conduct of prospecting activities. In contrast, the time for exploration is limited to that "of sufficient duration to permit a thorough survey of the specific area, the design and construction of mining equipment for the area and the design and construction of small and medium-size processing plants for the purpose of testing mining and processing systems".[204] The differences suggest a distinct

---

200 See Section 3.3.2.1 of this chapter.

201 UNCLOS, Articles 160(2), 162(2); Annex III to the Convention.

202 See, for instance, Regulations on Prospecting and Exploration for Polymetallic Sulphides in the Area, Regulation 1(3)(e).

203 Ibid., Regulation 1(3).

204 UNCLOS, Annex III "Basic Conditions of Prospecting, Exploration and Exploitation", Article 17(2)(b).

focus of the two activities. Arguably, prospecting means the searching starting from scratch, while exploration refers to the search based on certain previously gathered data and information or confirmed hypothesis.

While the Convention separates prospecting from exploration, it also separates prospecting from marine scientific research. This separation can be seen from the different sets of rules that have been established for the two activities.[205] For instance, prospecting in the Area can be commenced "only after the prospector has been informed by the Secretary-General [of the ISA] that its notification has been recorded pursuant to [the relevant provision]".[206] In contrast, such a requirement does not exist in the case of marine scientific research.[207] Because prospecting, like exploration, is an activity that mainly serves commercial purposes, the distinction made between prospecting and marine scientific research again reinforces the conclusion drawn earlier that if an activity is carried out specifically for commercial gains, it is not to be considered as marine scientific research in the context of UNCLOS.

The preceding observations, in particular, on the relationship between prospecting and exploration, and prospecting and marine scientific research, are of particular relevance for ascertaining the legal classification of ocean data collection activities involving access to marine genetic resources. The legal classification of this kind of activities, its relationship with marine scientific research and the appropriate legal framework for the regulation of such activities will be further examined in the case study contained in Chapter 6 of this book.

3.3.4.2 Provisions on Marine Scientific Research in the Area

Rights and obligations in relation to marine scientific research activities in the Area are mainly addressed by Articles 143 and 256 of the Convention, which provide that all States and competent international organizations have the right to conduct marine scientific research, and all marine scientific research activities in the Area shall be carried out "exclusively for peaceful purposes" and "for the benefit of mankind as a whole".[208] The requirement that marine

205 Prospecting in the Area is regulated by Part II of the ISA Regulations, while marine scientific research in the Area is regulated by Article 143 and Part XIII of UNCLOS.

206 Regulations on Prospecting and Exploration for Polymetallic Sulphides in the Area, Regulation 2(1).

207 UNCLOS, Article 143. See Ane Jørem and Morten Walløe Tvedt, "Bioprospecting in the High Seas: Existing Rights and Obligations in View of A New Legal Regime for Marine Areas Beyond National Jurisdiction", *The International Journal of Marine and Coastal Law* 29, no. 2 (2014): 329–330.

208 UNCLOS, Articles 143, 256.

scientific research shall be conducted "exclusively for peaceful purposes" is merely a repetition of the first general principle under Article 240 that applies equally to other ocean areas.[209] However, the second requirement, that marine scientific research in the Area shall be carried out "for the benefit of mankind as a whole" is an extra obligation for States and competent international organizations that conduct marine scientific research activities in the Area.[210]

Paragraphs 2 and 3 of Article 143 respectively provide for the duties of the ISA and States Parties.[211] The ISA's role is that it shall coordinate and disseminate the results and analysis of marine scientific research when available.[212] Under Paragraph 3, States Parties are obliged to promote international cooperation in marine scientific research in the Area by means including a) participating in international programs and encouraging cooperation by personnel, b) ensuring marine scientific research programs are developed through an international platform, and c) effectively disseminating the results of research and analysis when available.[213]

Similar obligations are provided for in Articles 242 and 244, which apply to marine scientific research conducted in all maritime zones. Article 242 requires States and competent international organizations to promote international cooperation in marine scientific research for peaceful purposes.[214] Cooperation is to be achieved through the conclusion of bilateral and multilateral agreements, in order to create favorable conditions for the conduct of marine scientific research and to integrate the efforts of scientists.[215] Article 244 concerns the obligations of States and competent international organizations to "make available by publication and dissemination through appropriate channels information on proposed major programmes and their objectives as well as knowledge resulting from marine scientific research", and for this purpose, special attention shall be paid to assisting developing States.[216]

---

209 Ibid., Article 240. A similar provision is contained in Article 301 of the Convention, which requires States Parties, when exercising their rights and performing their duties under the Convention, to "refrain from any threat or use of force against the territorial integrity or political independence of any State". This provision is applicable to all uses of the oceans.

210 See Section 3.2.4.2.2 of this chapter.

211 It is noted that the drafters use different wording in this article when referring to the duties of the ISA (the Authority may carry out marine scientific research *concerning* the Area and its resources) and States Parties (may carry out marine scientific research *in* the Area). The implication of the different wording will be elaborated upon further below.

212 UNCLOS, Article 143(2).

213 Ibid., Article 143(3).

214 Ibid., Article 242(1), (2).

215 Ibid., Article 243.

216 Ibid., Article 244.

The different wording of Article 143(3) and Articles 242 and 244 suggests that the obligations for researching States and international organizations in the Area are stronger and more concrete than those stated in Article 242 and 244. This finding, together with the extra obligation for marine scientific research in the Area to be conducted "for the benefit of mankind as a whole" noted above, implies a special status of marine scientific research activities in the Area. Given that Article 143 is placed in Part XI of the Convention, one may note that such a special status of marine scientific research is a result of the special status given by the drafters to the Area. Article 136 of the Convention expressly states the principle that the Area is the common heritage of mankind.[217] The obligation of "for the benefit of mankind as a whole", which appears in several provisions in Part XI, among others Article 143 on marine scientific research, is submitted to be one of the means to give expression to the common heritage of mankind principle that applies to the Area and its resources.[218]

Another issue concerns the scope of application of Article 143. Some scholars argue that this article only applies to marine scientific research with the Area and the mineral resources as the objects, since Article 133 of the Convention defines "resources" for the purposes of Part XI as mineral resources.[219] Some other scholars argue that the definitions given in Article 133 do not define the scope of application of the regime established for the Area.[220] The current author finds the latter view more convincing, because, as noted further by Oude Elferink, the drafting history of the Convention showed no indication of excluding living resources from the applicable scope of Part XI, and the exclusion of living resources would lead to a "curious result" as far as marine scientific research is concerned.[221] Besides, under Article 143, different phrases are used throughout this article. In Paragraphs 1 and 3, the Convention uses the phrase marine scientific research "in the Area" whereas in Paragraph 2, when establishing the rights and obligations of the ISA, the Convention uses

217 Ibid., Article 136.

218 Alex G. Oude Elferink, "The Regime of the Area: Delineating the Scope of Application of the Common Heritage Principle and Freedom of the High Seas", 156.

219 UNCLOS, Article 133. See, for instance, Craig H Allen, "Protecting the Oceanic Gardens of Eden: International Law Issues in Deep-Sea Vent Resource Conservation and Management", *Georgetown International Environmental Law Review* 13(2001): 630.

220 Alex G. Oude Elferink, "The Regime of the Area: Delineating the Scope of Application of the Common Heritage Principle and Freedom of the High Seas", 152–153.

221 Ibid. See also, Frida Armas Pfirter, "The Management of Seabed Living Resources in "the Area" under UNCLOS", *Revista electrónica de estudios internacionales* (*REEI*), no. 11 (2006): 7–9, 26–27.

the phrase marine scientific research "concerning the Area and its resources". This difference indicates that the scope of general provisions as provided in Paragraph 1 as well as in Paragraph 3 is broader than that of Paragraph 2.[222] It also reflects the intention that no limit has been attached to the objects of marine scientific research activities (living or non-living resources) in these provisions. In addition, the definition of "the Area" would also include natural resources contained therein. Article 1 of the Convention defines the "Area" as "the seabed and ocean floor and subsoil thereof, beyond the limits of national jurisdiction".[223] The ordinary meaning of the terms "seabed", "ocean floor" and "subsoil" would comprise the living and non-living resources that are found in those areas.[224] In this connection, the phrase "concerning the Area and its resources" would also cover living resources. Therefore, provisions contained in Article 143 are also applicable to research activities concerning marine living resources in the Area.

3.4 Concluding Remarks

In conclusion, although the Convention does not define the term "marine scientific research", pertinent provisions give useful indications for answering the two questions raised in the introduction of this chapter, which are concerned with 1) the nature of and criteria for marine scientific research, and 2) the boundaries of the UNCLOS marine scientific research regime, *i.e.*, what activities are not covered by the regime and how do they differ from marine scientific research?

In terms of the first question, as suggested by the ordinary meaning of the term "marine scientific research", the drafting history of the definition of this term and relevant UNCLOS provisions, there are some minimum requirements for constituting marine scientific research under the Convention. These requirements include 1) the activity at issue should contribute to the furtherance of knowledge of the marine environment, and 2) the activity should have some scientific attributes. The existence of a hypothesis

222 Soons observed that, the use of the preposition "in", which is clearly a *locativus*, indicated this provision covered research conducted physically on the seabed or in the subsoil. See Alfred H. A. Soons, *Marine Scientific Research and the Law of the Sea*, 227.

223 UNCLOS, Article 1(1)(1).

224 Alex G. Oude Elferink, "The Regime of the Area: Delineating the Scope of Application of the Common Heritage Principle and Freedom of the High Seas", 150. Oude Elferink further noted that the observation is "explicitly confirmed by the reference to 'the natural resources of the Area' in Article 145(b) of the Convention."

required by the principle of using scientific methods and the requirement that the research project should lead to scientific information, data and knowledge are the manifestations of the scientific attributes contained in the Convention.

However, the Convention does not require marine scientific research to be conducted solely with a view to or for the purpose of increasing knowledge of the marine environment. First, marine scientific research that solely contributes to the furtherance of scientific knowledge of the marine environment is usually termed as pure marine scientific research, as opposed to applied marine scientific research. An investigation of the drafting history of Article 246 indicates that the distinction between pure and applied marine scientific research is not preserved in UNCLOS, and marine scientific research in the context of the Convention covers both kinds of research projects.

Second, it is concluded that the qualifications under Article 246(3) do not purport to define the term "marine scientific research". This observation is supported by the relevant drafting history and an examination of the implications of the substantive qualifications. Most notably, as a consequence of this finding, a marine scientific research project is not necessarily conducted "exclusively [...] in order to increase scientific knowledge of the marine environment for the benefit of all mankind". In other words, marine scientific research does not have to be conducted with the sole purpose of increasing scientific knowledge.

Third, it is argued that by including the phrase "of direct significance for the exploration and exploitation of natural resources", especially the qualifier "direct", in Article 246(5), the Convention recognizes that marine scientific research can be carried out with a view to the commercial utilization of the research objects. This phrase excludes marine scientific research projects that are conducted without a view to the commercial utilization of the research objects. If all marine scientific research under UNCLOS must be carried out without a commercial view, no research project may fall under Article 246(5)(a), and this provision will become obsolete.

This being said, it is also acknowledged that the phrase "of direct significance for the exploration and exploitation of natural resources" gives rise to different interpretations. It is argued in this chapter that drafters included Article 251 in the Convention to oblige States to seek to establish general criteria and guidelines to assist States in clarifying the implications of this phrase and in ascertaining the nature and implications of marine scientific research through subsequent efforts. In this regard, Chapters 4 and 5 of this book will look at relevant State practice and international treaties other than UNCLOS to discern whether States have established, either explicitly or implicitly, such criteria or guidelines.

As to the second question, which is about the boundaries of the UNCLOS marine scientific research and the relationship between the activities concerned and marine scientific research (the legal classification of ocean data collection activities), it is concluded that the benchmark for the classification is the function or purpose of the activities.

To be more specific, pertinent provisions on the EEZ, the continental shelf, and the Area suggest if an ocean data collection activity is conducted purely with a view to commercial gains, it is to be considered as prospecting, exploration, or exploitation. Because marine scientific research is distinct from these activities and bearing in mind the preceding observation that marine scientific research may be conducted with a commercial view, a conclusion warranted is that marine scientific research is not conducted purely with a view to commercial gains.

If an ocean data collection activity is conducted to ensure safe navigation, it can be considered either as part of the innocent passage of the ship in the territorial sea or through the archipelagic waters of a coastal State or as "other internationally lawful uses of the sea related to" the freedom of navigation in the EEZ of a coastal State, depending on the use of the data collected and the location of the activity. Ocean data collection activities falling under "other internationally lawful uses of the sea related to" the freedoms mentioned in Article 58(1) also include those that form an integral part of navigation, overflight, and the laying of submarine cables and pipelines. Such activities do not constitute marine scientific research either, because different sets of rules apply.

It may also be the case that an ocean data collection activity, when carried out in the EEZ of a coastal State, falls under the meaning of Article 59 concerning unattributed rights and jurisdiction. The legal classification of such an activity is different from marine scientific research and the situations noted above.

This being said, the boundaries of the UNCLOS marine scientific research regime and hence the legal classification of ocean data collection activities may give rise to different opinions, considering the fact that many relevant provisions of the Convention have been drafted in an open-ended or ambiguous manner. The complexity of the legal classification can also be attributed to the fact that ocean data collection activities can be conducted for different purposes, serving various ends. As concluded in this chapter, the distinguishing benchmark for different kinds of ocean data collection activities is arguably the function or purpose of the activity. If an ocean data collection activity serves multiple purposes, its legal classification may be controversial or unclear. The problem of legal classification becomes the most acute for activities conducted in the EEZ of a coastal State, mainly because in this zone, the Convention prescribes the most diversified rights and obligations for the States concerned. It is argued that provisions under the UNCLOS EEZ regime provide a good basis for resolving the conflict that may arise from the legal classification and the regulation of ocean data collection activities. Most notably, when the rights over a certain ocean data collection activity are granted to either the coastal State or a third State, the exercise of such rights shall have due regard to the rights and duties of the other State concerned. Case law suggests that, under this obligation, when a conflict arises or may arise, the States concerned shall engage in consultation with each other and properly balance the interests that may be involved. The fulfilment of the due regard obligation can take various forms, including the conclusion of special agreements or the establishment of cooperative arrangements. For unattributed rights in the EEZ, when a conflict arises, the conflict shall be resolved according to the guideline contained in Article 59 of the Convention. This article also requires the conflict to be resolved after a balancing test taking into consideration all relevant circumstances. The implications of these observations will be further elaborated upon in the case studies to be included in Chapters 6 and 7 of this book.

CHAPTER 4

Subsequent Practice on Ocean Data Collection Activities

4.1 Introduction

Previous chapters have concluded that the interpretation of certain UNCLOS provisions pertinent to the legal classification and regulation of ocean data collection activities and particularly the term "marine scientific research" cannot be isolated from developments that have occurred after the adoption of the Convention (Chapter 2), and that although relevant provisions of UNCLOS on marine scientific research provide indications as to the scope of the term "marine scientific research" and the legal classification of an ocean data collection activity, they do not always suffice in differentiating one ocean data collection activity from another, primarily when the activity at issue serves multiple purposes (Chapter 3). In that light, an examination of subsequent practice concerning marine scientific research, and more broadly ocean data collection activities, mainly serves two purposes.

First, it serves to evaluate whether States have established an agreement on the scope of marine scientific research, or if there is a tendency to such an end. Article 31(3)(b) of VCLT requires that in the process of treaty interpretation, "[a]ny subsequent practice in the application of the treaty which establishes the agreement of the parties regarding its interpretation" shall be taken into account.[1] ILC has commented that subsequent practice may also be considered as a supplementary means of interpretation under Article 32 of VCLT.[2] This would be the case for subsequent practice that does not meet the criteria set out under Article 31(3)(b). The necessity of examining relevant subsequent practice can also be explained by the fact that relevant provisions of UNCLOS suggest that the parties to the Convention intend to subject the meaning of the term "marine scientific research" to subsequent developments.[3]

1 VCLT, Article 31(3)(b).

2 International Law Commission (ILC), "Draft conclusions on subsequent agreements and subsequent practice in relation to the interpretation of treaties and commentaries thereto", *Report of the International Law Commission, Seventieth session,* Doc. A/73/10, 2018, Conclusion 2(4), at p. 13.

3 See Chapter 2.3 of this book.

 | DOI:10.1163/9789004508590_005

Second, an examination of subsequent practice can reveal the state of implementation of the relevant UNCLOS provisions when the legal classification of an ocean data collection activity is unclear or controversial. As will be shown later, a preliminary examination of subsequent practice can already lead to the conclusion that there is no agreement among States concerning the definition of the term "marine scientific research". Against this background and bearing in mind the lack of a definition of the term in UNCLOS, an examination of relevant State practice serves to answer the questions of how the relevant UNCLOS provisions are implemented in practice, and how that practice has given consideration to the rights and obligations of coastal States and other States when undertaking ocean data collection activities. Attention will be mainly focused on the practice concerning the regulation of ocean data collection activities that serve multiple purposes.

Before setting out on the examination of subsequent practice, it is necessary to clarify the scope of the practice to be examined in this chapter and the criteria for identifying such practice.

4.1.1 *Scope of Examination*

As shown in the previous chapter, an interpretation of relevant UNCLOS provisions does not lead to a conclusive definition of the term "marine scientific research". Consequently, the substantive meaning of the term remains unclear. In this regard, one cannot ascertain for sure whether the practice concerned is related to marine scientific research or other ocean data collection activities. As the following analysis will demonstrate, the term "marine scientific research" has rarely been used in international legal instruments or domestic legislation. It is uncertain whether this is intentional or incidental, and if it is intentional, what the reasons are for adopting different terminologies.

These questions can only be answered after examining the content of the practice at issue. Therefore, the practice to be investigated in this chapter involves not only marine scientific research *per se*, but also ocean data collection activities whose legal classification remains unclear or has not been defined.

4.1.2 *Identification of Pertinent Subsequent Practice*

It remains controversial what types of practice can influence the interpretation of a treaty text, or in other words, can be considered as elements that fall within the scope of Articles 31–33 of VCLT.[4] For instance, although ILC

4 Irina Buga, *Modification of Treaties by Subsequent Practice* (Oxford University Press, 2018), 5.

has acknowledged that subsequent practice can play a role in treaty interpretation under Article 32 VCLT, different opinions exist as to the scope of such subsequent practice – for example, whether it shall be the practice "in the application of a treaty".[5]

Compared with formal amendment procedures, subsequent practice provides a more flexible mechanism through which treaties preserve their relevancy by adapting to factual changes. However, it is also because of its informal nature that the identification of subsequent practice is by no means an easy task. Subsequent practice can take various forms,[6] and oftentimes can be diffuse, ambiguous, and inconsistent.[7] Besides, due to the nature of the practice or confidentiality, most practice is invisible to the public.[8] Sometimes subsequent practice is not necessarily documented at the international level, and even more often, States are reluctant to publish their practice due to the concern that it may have unintended consequences or bind them to a specific interpretation.[9]

The same problem exists for the investigation and identification of subsequent practice on marine scientific research. The difficulty of looking into subsequent practice concerning marine scientific research was already pointed out by Leary in 2006. At the time, he was planning to obtain general

5 For instance, the ILC in its commentary to the Draft conclusions on subsequent agreements and subsequent practice in relation to the interpretation of treaties, states that subsequent practice under Article 32, 1) "does not require the agreement of all the parties", 2) "does not enunciate a requirement, like that in article 31, paragraph 3 (b), that the relevant practice be 'regarding the interpretation' of the treaty"; however, it still needs to be practice "in the application of a treaty". See International Law Commission (ILC), "Draft conclusions on subsequent agreements and subsequent practice in relation to the interpretation of treaties and commentaries thereto", Doc. A/73/10, Conclusion 4(3), at pp. 13, 33, 36. On the other hand, some scholars are of the view that the scope of Article 32 is wide, and it includes not only the elements mentioned in the ILC commentary, but also subsequent practice that is not "in the application of a treaty", and practice that is not of the parties. See Luigi Crema, "Subsequent Agreements and Subsequent Practice within and outside the Vienna Convention", in *Treaties and Subsequent Practice*, edited by Georg Nolte (Oxford University Press, 2013), 17; Irina Buga, *Modification of Treaties by Subsequent Practice*, 76.

6 International Law Commission (ILC), "Draft conclusions on subsequent agreements and subsequent practice in relation to the interpretation of treaties and commentaries thereto", Doc. A/73/10, Conclusions 5–6, at p. 14.

7 Irina Buga, *Modification of Treaties by Subsequent Practice*, 5.

8 Ibid. See also Daniel Bethlehem, "The Secret Life of International Law", *Cambridge Journal of International and Comparative Law* 1(2012): 24.

9 Georg Nolte, "Subsequent Agreements and Subsequent Practice of States Outside of Judicial or Quasi-judicial Proceedings - Report 3 for the ILC Study Group on Treaties over Time", in *Treaties and Subsequent Practice*, edited by Georg Nolte (Oxford University Press, 2013), 318; Irina Buga, *Modification of Treaties by Subsequent Practice*, 27.

background information on the nature of marine scientific research conducted at hydrothermal vents by interviewing scientists who had engaged in the related research projects.[10] It was only in the early stages of the interviews that Leary came to realize that the interviewees were either only able to provide information on general terms or unable to make comments at all.[11] The reasons include that interviewees were not involved in the clearance process concerning marine scientific research projects to be undertaken in the jurisdiction of foreign waters, or because of commercial confidentiality.[12]

Bearing in mind the preceding observations, this chapter adopts a flexible approach to identifying subsequent practice, to examine how subsequent practice operates in different contexts and to evaluate its full range of effect. For the current discussion, subsequent practice to be looked at in this chapter is not necessarily limited to the practice "in the application of" UNCLOS, or the practice that establishes the agreement of the parties to UNCLOS. This approach is adopted in this chapter so as not to limit the scope of relevant practice to be examined at the expense of the completeness of the analysis. The relevant analysis also contributes to the understanding of the general implementation or operation of relevant UNCLOS provisions when the legal classification of the ocean data collection activity at issue remains unclear or controversial.

4.1.3 *Structure of this Chapter*

To establish the structure of this chapter, it is necessary to delineate first the types of practice to be looked at. In this regard, ILC has commented that subsequent practice includes,

> not only official acts at the international or at the internal level [...], but also, *inter alia*, official statements regarding its interpretation, such as statements at a diplomatic conference, statements in the course of a legal dispute, or judgments of domestic courts; official communications to which the treaty gives rise; or the enactment of domestic legislation or the conclusion of international agreements for the purpose of implementing a treaty [...].[13]

10 David Kenneth Leary, *International Law and the Genetic Resources of the Deep Sea* (Brill, 2006), 184.

11 Ibid.

12 Ibid.

13 International Law Commission (ILC), "Draft conclusions on subsequent agreements and subsequent practice in relation to the interpretation of treaties and commentaries thereto", Doc. A/73/10, Commentary to Conclusion 4, para.18, see also paras.27, 28, 31, 35.

At the time of writing, there is no case before an international court or tribunal concerning the definition of the term "marine scientific research" under UNCLOS.[14] To the best of the current author's knowledge, there is no judgment of domestic courts which deals with the said matter either. Accordingly, in the field of marine scientific research, or more broadly of ocean data collection, subsequent practice of States can be classified into three main categories:

1. national legislation and policies on marine scientific research and similar activities;
2. the actual implementation of such legislation and policies, in particular, relevant information and data on the clearance procedure for foreign marine scientific research;
3. viewpoints expressed by States or the conduct of States at global fora.

As will be explained below, information on the first two categories either does not shed much light on answering the questions raised by this chapter, or information is generally lacking. Therefore, the relevant information on the first two categories will be merged and dealt with in Section 4.2. Section 4.3 will examine the relevant State practice in global fora. Section 4.4 concludes the chapter and presents some final observations.

4.2 National Legislation and Policies Concerning the Scope of Marine Scientific Research

This section will look at relevant national legislation and policies to find out States' perceptions of the scope of marine scientific research under UNCLOS, and the relationship between marine scientific research and other ocean data collection activities. However, it does not purport to investigate the legislation on marine scientific research of all the States around the globe. This is neither practical nor necessary. The reason is two-fold.

Firstly, there are many academic works dealing with the practice of States concerning marine scientific research.[15] Besides, the United Nations Office for

14 The ICJ in its Judgment on the *Whaling in the Antarctic case* addressed issues concerning the scope of activities "for purposes of scientific research" in the context of the 1946 International Convention for the Regulation of Whaling. Since this case is not adjudicated in the context of UNCLOS, it will not be included in this chapter. However, an analysis of this case and the Court's observations will be included in Chapter 5 of this book.

15 To name but a few, Montserrat Gorina-Ysern, *An International Regime for Marine Scientific Research*; Alfred H. A. Soons, "Regulation of Marine Scientific Research by the European Community and Its Member States", *Ocean Development & International Law* 23, no. 2–3 (1992); Alfred H. A. Soons, "The Developing Regime of Marine Scientific Research:

Ocean Affairs and the Law of the Sea published a book in 1989 compiling States' national legislation, regulations and supplementary documents on marine scientific research in areas under national jurisdiction.[16] More recently, IOC surveyed, via ABE-LOS Questionnaire No. 3, the practice of its Member States concerning marine scientific research and the transfer of marine technology and received 72 responses by 2009. Five analytical reports on the responses to ABE-LOS Questionnaire No. 3 have been issued by a sub-group under IOC/ABE-LOS in 2003, 2004, 2005, 2008 and 2009 respectively.[17] This survey is considered as one of "the most comprehensive primary sources of information" on State practice concerning marine scientific research.[18] Considering the efforts that have already been made, there is no need to conduct a thorough investigation again in the present research.

Secondly, national legislation shares one characteristic in common - it deals with its subject matters in a quite general manner. It has been observed that for States which have national legislation regarding marine scientific research, the relevant laws and regulations sometimes only simply replicate the provisions of UNCLOS without giving much additional guidance for researching States.[19] Besides, such laws and regulations rarely contain definitions for the

---

Recent European Experience and State Practice", in *New Developments in Marine Science and Technology: Economic, Legal and Political Aspects of Change*, edited by LM Alexander, S Allen, and LC Hanson (1988); Wolf Plesmann and Volker Röben, "Marine Scientific Research: State Practice versus Law of the Sea?", in *Law of the Sea at the Crossroads: The Continuing Search for a Universally Accepted Régime*, edited by Rüdiger Wolfrum (Berlin: Duncker & Humboldt, 1991); Kijun You, "The Law and Practice Relating to Marine Scientific Research in Northeast Asia", in *The Law of the Sea Convention: US Accession and Globalisation*, edited by Alfred H. A. Soons, et al. (Martinus Nijhoff Publishers, 2012); Stuart Kaye, "Marine Scientific Research and Military Survey: Law and State Practice", in *UN Convention on the Law of the Sea and the South China Sea*, edited by Shicun Wu, Mark Valencia, and Nong Hong (Ashgate Publishing, 2015); Charlotte Salpin et al., "Marine Scientific Research in Pacific Small Island Developing States", *Marine Policy* 95(2018).

16 United Nations Office for Ocean Affairs and the Law of the Sea, *National Legislation, Regulations and Supplementary Documents on Marine Scientific Research in Areas Under National Jurisdiction* (1989). Although this source is produced in 1989, it is submitted that it still has contemporary relevance. As will be shown later, the relevant laws and regulations on marine scientific research are very general and merely replicate the provisions of UNCLOS without giving much additional details.

17 All these reports are available at http://www.ioc-unesco.org/index.php?option=com_content&view=article&id=310&Itemid=100025.

18 Ronán Long, "Regulating Marine Scientific Research in the European Union: It Takes More Than Two to Tango", in *The Law of the Sea Convention: US Accession and Globalisation*, edited by Alfred H. A. Soons, et al. (Martinus Nijhoff Publishers, 2012), 462.

19 R. R. Churchill and A. V. Lowe, *The Law of the Sea*, 407–408; Wolf Plesmann and Volker Röben, "Marine Scientific Research: State Practice versus Law of the Sea?", 385; Paul Gragl,

term "marine scientific research". Among the 72 States that sent back their responses to ABE-LOS Questionnaire No. 3, 54% of them (39 States) adopted national legislation for marine scientific research, and 92% of them (66 States) had administrative procedures for marine scientific research.[20] However, only some of the States that have adopted such legislation and procedures have provided copies of these documents as requested by the Questionnaire.[21] Among these copies and from other online sources, the author managed to find the following national laws, regulations or policies which contain a definition of the term "marine scientific research".[22]

1. **Marine Scientific Research Act of the Republic of Korea** (amended by Act No. 12091, dated 13 August 2013) Article 2: "the term 'marine scientific research' means conducting research, exploration, etc. into the seabed, subsoil, superjacent waters, and lower atmosphere to study and discover the natural phenomena of the sea";[23]
2. **The Marine Scientific Research Regulations of 2014** (Cyprus, No. 577/2014) Article 2(1): "'marine scientific research' means any research activity, which is conducted for exclusively peaceful purposes, for the purpose of increasing scientific knowledge about the marine environment, including all natural resources, toward the benefit of mankind and according to [the United Nations Convention on the Law of the Sea of 1982]";[24]
3. **Foreign Scientific or Exploratory Expeditions in Canada** (Memorandum D2-1-2, dated 20 March 2017), **Guidelines and General Information** defines marine scientific research as "activities undertaken in the marine

"Marine Scientific Research", 425–426; Charlotte Salpin et al., "Marine Scientific Research in Pacific Small Island Developing States", 366.

20 "Practices of States in the Fields of Marine Scientific Research and Transfer of Marine Technology: An Analysis of Responses to ABE-LOS Questionnaire No. 3", 2009, http://www.ioc-unesco.org/index.php?option=com_oe&task=viewDocumentRecord&docID=3515.

21 Elizabeth J. Tirpak, "Practices of States in the Fields of Marine Scientific Research and Transfer of Marine Technology: An Update of the 2005 Analysis of Member State Responses to Questionnaire No. 3", Doc. IOC/ABE-LOS VIII/8, Paris, 2008, at p. 9. In this regard, the analysis of the responses could only be made in a general manner, lacking specific details on issues such as the definition of marine scientific research contained in the respective national legislation and/or administrative procedures.

22 List in a chronological order.

23 Marine Scientific Research Act of the Republic of Korea, full text available at the official website of FAO, http://extwprlegs1.fao.org/docs/pdf/kor52054.pdf.

24 The Marine Scientific Research Regulations of 2014, Cyprus, full text available at the UN official website of O-ceans and Law of the Sea, https://www.un.org/Depts/los/LEGISLATIONANDTREATIES/PDFFILES/Annex_I_MARINE_SCIENTIFIC_RESEARCH.pdf.

environment to enhance scientific knowledge regarding the nature and natural processes of the seas and oceans, the seabed and subsoil";[25]

4. **Maritime Zones (Conduct of Marine Scientific Research) Regulations of Mauritius** (GN No. 57 of 2017, dated 29 April 2017) Article 2: "'marine scientific research' or 'research' means any research or study, whether fundamental or applied, intended to increase knowledge about marine environment, including all its resources and living organisms and embraces all related scientific activity for the benefit of mankind and for peaceful purposes";[26]
5. **Décret n° 2017-956 du 10 mai 2017 fixant les conditions d'application des articles L. 251-1 et suivants du code de la recherche relatifs à la recherche scientifique marine** (France, dated 10 May 2017) Article 1(2): "for the purposes of this Decree, a marine scientific research activity is constituted by any campaign for the research, measurement or data collection relating to the marine environment conducted at sea from a ship, aircraft or by any other fixed, floating or drifting equipment, excluding: (1) activities governed by the mining code; (2) activities governed by the provisions of Articles 20 and 28 of Ordinance No. 2016–1687 of 8 December 2016; (3) underwater archeology research activities governed by Articles L. 532-1 et seq. of the French Heritage Code; (4) fishing activities subject to the fishing authorization scheme for scientific purposes provided for in Council Regulation (EC) No. 1224/2009 of 20 November 2009; (5) oceanographic research campaigns to estimate the abundance and distribution of fish stocks provided for in Council Regulation (EC) No 199/2008 of 25 February 2008; (6) equipment tests during the homologation, validation or certification phases of a ship or its gear that are authorized by the representative of the State at sea".[27]

From these definitions, one can see that States have different perceptions as to the scope of marine scientific research. For instance, one State, the Republic of Korea, includes exploration in the definition of the term "marine scientific

25 Foreign Scientific or Exploratory Expeditions in Canada (Memorandum D2-1-2), full text available at https://www.cbsa-asfc.gc.ca/publications/dm-md/d2/d2-1-2-eng.html.

26 Maritime Zones (Conduct of Marine Scientific Research) Regulations of Mauritius, full text available at the official website of FAO, http://extwprlegs1.fao.org/docs/pdf/mat166409.pdf.

27 Unofficial translation. Décret n° 2017–956 du 10 mai 2017 fixant les conditions d'application des articles L. 251-1 et suivants du code de la recherche relatifs à la recherche scientifique marine, full text (in French) available at https://www.legifrance.gouv.fr/affichTexte.do?cidTexte=JORFTEXT000034675364&categorieLien=id.

research". In contrast, some States (Cyprus and Canada) only regard activities undertaken to increase scientific knowledge about the marine environment as marine scientific research. This discrepancy indicates that States have not reached agreement on the definition of the term.

Apart from domestic legislation, the author also collected information on the clearance procedure for foreign marine scientific research.[28] Presumably, such information can best manifest what States consider as marine scientific research in practice. While UNCLOS obliges States and competent international organizations to "make available by publication and dissemination through appropriate channels information on proposed major programmes and their objectives [...]",[29] the vague wording of this provision seems to undermine its significance from a practical perspective. It remains largely unclear who should fulfil the obligation, for what kind of projects (what kind of projects qualify as "major programmes") and how to publicize and disseminate the information (what are the appropriate channels). As a result, information on marine scientific research programs is not readily available in the public domain in practice.[30]

To obtain relevant information, the author sent out e-mails to government officials working at the department responsible for the clearance procedure, scientists directly involved in foreign marine scientific research projects, and legal scholars with expertise in marine scientific research.[31] Questions asked

28 Admittedly, law enforcement and disputes also represent an important part of State practice. Such information is not addressed in this section mainly for two reasons: firstly, disputes arise and law enforcement is carried out primarily because the coastal State have different opinions concerning the legal classification of the activity at issue from the researching State, and this discrepancy can also be revealed by an examination of information concerning the clearance procedure; secondly, the former discussion already concluded that States have not reached agreement on the definition of the term "marine scientific research", and in that light, examining law enforcement and disputes in relation to marine scientific research would not shed much extra light on the current discussion.

29 UNCLOS, Article 244(1).

30 This issue has also been noted by other scholars, see, for instance, Charlotte Salpin, "The Law of the Sea: A before and an after Nagoya", in *The 2010 Nagoya Protocol on Access and Benefit-Sharing in Perspective: Implications for International Law and Implementation Challenges*, edited by Elisa Morgera, Matthias Buck, and Elsa Tsioumani (Brill Nijhoff, 2012), 161.

31 The current author sent out emails to government officials, scientists, and legal scholars of nearly 30 countries and received feedback from 13 persons respectively working at 11 countries respresenting different continents. Relevant data, including the name and affiliation of the recipients of the email (and the interviewees), text of the e-mails and messages exchanged with the recipients, notes taken during the subsequent interviews and the time and place of the interviews, are on file with the author.

in the e-mails and during the interviews conducted subsequently mainly included:

- From the perspective of researching States:
  1. What kinds of activities have been submitted for the application of consent from the coastal States under Article 246 of the Convention? (What kinds of activities are considered by researching States as marine scientific research and therefore are subject to the regulation of the coastal State?)
  2. Have all these activities been granted consent?
  3. If not, what are the reasons for denial (bearing in mind the provisions of Article 246(5))?
- From the perspective of coastal States:
  1. What kinds of activities have been submitted by the researching State for the grant of consent under Article 246?
  2. Have all these activities been granted consent?
  3. If not, what are the reasons for denial?

Through the exchange of e-mails, two interviewees agreed to do interviews in person or through a telephone call. Apart from that, eleven recipients of the e-mail mentioned above replied with relevant information. The replies received from the recipients and information gathered during the interviews are relatively general. There are not many specific details concerning what specific activities are considered as marine scientific research and what are not, and which factor(s) will lead to rejection by coastal States. The information gathered is inadequate for drawing any firm conclusions concerning the meaning of the term "marine scientific research". This being said, based on the information gathered, it seems that the UNCLOS marine scientific research regime works without severe problems in practice. This observation is consistent with the IOC report on the analysis of the responses received concerning ABE-LOS Questionnaire No. 3. Besides, States would conclude practical arrangements for certain ocean data collection activities even if the legal classification of the activities remains controversial, or if the activities amount to the exploration and exploitation of natural resources in areas under the jurisdiction of the coastal State. Whether or not States manage to conclude such arrangements depends in no small degree on the bilateral relationship between the researching State and the coastal State. It also depends on the nature of the ocean data collection activity at issue. For some States, a foreign marine scientific research project "that is of direct significance for the exploration and exploitation of natural resources" can only be undertaken in areas under the jurisdiction of the coastal State in cooperation with the coastal State. The relevant practice indicates that cooperation plays a significant role in the clearance procedure concerning foreign marine scientific research projects.

Apart from sending out e-mails, in 2019, the author attended a training program organized jointly by UN/DOALOS and OceanTeacher Global Academy on the "Conduct of Marine Scientific Research (MSR) under the United Nations Convention on the Law of the Sea (UNCLOS)".[32] Apart from the lectures given during the course, views expressed by 26 participants from about 20 countries during class discussion and individual presentations also provide useful insights for the current research.[33] Most of the participants work for their governments. Some of them are directly involved in or even responsible for the clearance procedure for foreign marine scientific research in their countries. A general impression of the presentations and relevant discussions during the lectures is that States often adopt quite general legislation on marine scientific research (for instance, by repeating the text of UNCLOS) or there is no relevant national legislation at all. Most conflicts between the coastal State and the researching State, including those concerning the nature of the research project at issue, and the area in which the project will take place, are resolved through diplomatic channels (by negotiation). Results of such negotiations might be that the consent is granted in the end, subject to the conditions set forth by the coastal State, including undertaking the project in cooperation with the coastal State.

In conclusion, although national legislation and policies are essential sources of subsequent practice, relevant information on these sources is generally lacking in the field of marine scientific research. From national legislation or policies which contain a definition of the term "marine scientific research", one can see that States have different perceptions of the scope of marine scientific research. However, despite the absence of a definition of the term in the Convention and the lack of subsequent agreement on this matter, the UNCLOS marine scientific research regime seems to work without serious problems in practice. When controversies arise, for example, when States involved disagree about the legal classification of an ocean data collection activity, they can either enter into negotiations or conclude practical arrangements. In both cases, cooperation plays a significant role.

Bearing in mind the above conclusions, the following section will turn to look at the official statements expressed by States in global fora.

---

32 For more information about the event, see https://www.oceanexpert.net/event/2141.

33 During the program, all participants were required to give a presentation on the implementation of the UNCLOS marine scientific research regime in their own country. The text of the presentations is on file with the author.

4.3 Subsequent Practice Concerning Ocean Data Collection Activities Manifested in Global Fora

When examining subsequent practice on marine scientific research or more broadly on ocean data collection activities, relevant information in global fora cannot be overlooked. International fora play an essential role in generating subsequent practice.[34] On the one hand, they provide valuable platforms for States to express their viewpoints concerning specific issues.[35] The summaries of these viewpoints, often contained in the reports of such fora, are valued materials for ascertaining the positions of States. Compared with national legislation and policies promulgated by States, such viewpoints are more targeted at specific kinds of ocean data collection activities. The viewpoints manifest more precisely States' perception of the legal classification of these ocean data collection activities and the appropriate regulation of them. On the other hand, international organizations which hold international meetings dealing with ocean data collection issues, are sometimes entrusted with the power to adopt resolutions or guidelines. Although such resolutions or guidelines may not qualify as a subsequent agreement under Article 31(3)(a) of VCLT, they are closely linked to the subsequent practice of States. Such resolutions and guidelines will not have been adopted by an international organization if there is no sufficient support from its member States. Therefore, to a certain extent, such resolutions and guidelines represent States' viewpoints on the relevant issues. Besides, nowadays, international oceanic activities are regulated to a significant extent by these soft law instruments. In this way, such instruments can influence the practice of States, and thus potentially contribute to shaping consistent or similar State practice.[36] In this light, this section begins with an identification of the relevant global fora to be addressed in this section (Section 4.3.1). The subsequent sub-sections (Sections 4.3.2 to 4.3.5) address the identified global fora consecutively.

4.3.1 *Identification of the Relevant Global Fora*

For global fora which manifest States' viewpoints on the interpretation and implementation of international conventions, one would first think of the

34 Georg Nolte, "Subsequent Agreements and Subsequent Practice of States Outside of Judicial or Quasi-judicial Proceedings - Report 3 for the ILC Study Group on Treaties over Time", 320.

35 James Harrison, *Making the Law of the Sea: A Study in the Development of International Law*, 23.

36 See Richard Barnes, "The Continuing Vitality of UNCLOS", 468–469.

review mechanisms of the treaties concerned that monitor the implementation of its provisions. However, UNCLOS does not explicitly provide for such review mechanisms. Unlike some other international agreements, especially in the field of international environmental law, the role of the Meeting of States Parties to UNCLOS (SPLOS) under the Convention is quite limited. Article 319(2)(e) requires the Secretary-General of the UN to "convene necessary meetings of States Parties in accordance with this Convention".[37] However, the Convention only explicitly accords SPLOS a mandate on administrative matters.[38] As of the time of writing, SPLOS has not generated any State practice pertinent to the theme of the present research.

In 1983, following the adoption of the Convention, the UN General Assembly (UNGA) adopted a resolution requiring the UN Secretary-General to report to UNGA on developments relating to the Convention.[39] Upon the entry into force of the Convention, UNGA adopted another resolution in which it decides to "undertake an annual review and evaluation of the implementation of the Convention and other developments relating to ocean affairs and the law of the sea".[40] In this way, UNGA has taken upon itself a task of reviewing and

37 UNCLOS, Article 319(2)(e).

38 See ibid., Annex II, Article 2(3) and Annex VI, Articles 4(4), 18 and 19. For more information on the role of SPLOS, see, for instance, Alex G. Oude Elferink, "Reviewing the Implementation of the LOS Convention: the Role of the United Nations Assembly and the Meeting of States Parties", 306–310; Tullio Treves, "The General Assembly and the Meeting of States Parties in the Implementation of the LOS Convention", 68–73; James Harrison, *Making the Law of the Sea: A Study in the Development of International Law*, 70–83.

39 "UNGA Resolution on "Third United Nations Conference on the Law of the Sea" of 14 December 1983", UN Doc. A/RES/38/59, para.8. In 1994, the General Assembly requested the Secretary-General to continue to carry out the responsibilities entrusted to him, in particular by preparing annually a comprehensive report, "for the consideration of the Assembly, on developments relating to the law of the sea, taking into account relevant scientific and technological developments, which could also serve as a basis for reports to all States parties to the Convention, the International Seabed Authority and competent international organizations, and which the Secretary-General is required to provide under the Convention". See "UNGA Resolution on the law of the sea of 19 December 1994", UN Doc. A/RES/49/28, para.15(a). The legal status of the reports prepared by the Secretary-General was under heated debate for several years, it was agreed on the fourteenth Meeting of States Parties to UNCLOS that the annual report of the Secretary-General on oceans and the law of the sea presented before the General Assembly should make reference to the fact that it is also presented to States parties pursuant to article 319 of the Convention. See "Report of the fourteenth Meeting of States Parties to UNCLOS", Doc. SPLOS/119, 2004, paras.78–89.

40 "UNGA Resolution on the law of the sea of 19 December 1994", UN Doc. A/RES/49/28, para.12. For a more detailed introduction to the background of this resolution, see Tullio

monitoring the implementation of UNCLOS.[41] It also provides a platform for States, including parties to the Convention and non-parties, "for announcing new developments, for expressing their views on them, and for obtaining information on what was happening in the multiple fora in which the law of the sea developed".[42] Nevertheless, the resolutions adopted by UNGA to date do not shed much light on the theme of the current discussion either. Therefore, these resolutions will not be dealt with in this chapter in detail.[43]

In the field of marine scientific research, it is widely acknowledged that IOC plays a significant role in generating State practice and formulating relevant guidelines. Since its inception in 1960, IOC has been promoting international collaboration in all aspects of marine scientific research.[44] In 1997, IOC established, pursuant to Resolution XIX-19 of the IOC Assembly, IOC/ABE-LOS to advise on issues of marine science and technology arising under UNCLOS and in particular Part XIII (Marine Scientific Research) and Part XIV (Development and Transfer of Marine Technology).[45] IOC/ABE-LOS is an intergovernmental

---

Treves, "The General Assembly and the Meeting of States Parties in the Implementation of the LOS Convention", 58–61.

41 Alex G. Oude Elferink, "Reviewing the Implementation of the LOS Convention: the Role of the United Nations Assembly and the Meeting of States Parties", 303–304. It is worth noting that the Convention does not provide any basis for the General Assembly to take an initiative role in reviewing the implementation of the Convention. As submitted by Treves, "[s]uch allocation of functions shows that the framers of the Convention wanted to avoid the establishment of a new institutional framework of general competence, or, if it had to be established, to make it as 'light' as possible, limiting to the maximum its functions". See Tullio Treves, "The General Assembly and the Meeting of States Parties in the Implementation of the LOS Convention", 57.

42 Tullio Treves, "The General Assembly and the Meeting of States Parties in the Implementation of the LOS Convention", 60.

43 Compared with the UNGA resolutions, the reports on the work of the Informal Consultative Process (ICP), which contain summaries of the deliberations during the ICP meetings, address issues on oceans and the law of the sea in a more detailed manner. ICP has been considered as "a unique forum for comprehensive discussions on issues related to oceans and the law of the sea". See, for example, "UNGA Resolution on oceans and the law of the sea of 17 March 2011", UN Doc. A/RES/65/37, para.331. In this regard, in the following analysis, references will be made to relevant viewpoints expressed during the ICP meetings.

44 UN/DOALOS, "Marine Scientific Research: A Revised Guide to the Implementation of the Relevant Provisions of the United Nations Convention on the Law of the Sea", para.92.

45 Philomène A Verlaan, "Current Legal Developments: Intergovernmental Oceanographic Commission of the United Nations Educational, Scientific and Cultural Organization (IOC/UNESCO)", 173. See also the official website of UNESCO/IOC, "IOC/ABE-LOS", available at http://ioc-unesco.org/index.php?option=com_content&view=article&id=364&Itemid=100047.

body composed of two national experts (one with training in the law of the sea and the other with training in marine science) designated by each of the IOC Member States.[46] Resolution XIX-19 does not mention the status of these experts – whether they attend IOC/ABE-LOS meetings in their own capacity or on behalf of their countries. However, the fact that these experts are designated by their countries indicates a close link between the experts and their governments.

Since its establishment, IOC/ABE-LOS has been working on four topics, on which four sub-groups have been set up respectively:[47]

1. the Practice of Member States in the application of Parts XIII (Marine Scientific Research) and XIV (Transfer of Marine Technology) of UNCLOS;
2. the Criteria and Guidelines on Transfer of Marine Technology;
3. the Procedure for the Application of Article 247 of UNCLOS (Marine scientific research projects undertaken by or under the auspices of international organizations) by IOC;
4. the Legal Framework, within the context of UNCLOS, which is applicable to the collection of oceanographic data.

The primary outcome of the sub-group on the first topic is the assessment reports of States' responses to Questionnaire No. 3, as discussed in Section 4.2 of this chapter. The second topic is mainly concerned with the interpretation and implementation of Part XIV of the Convention. The outcome of the third sub-group on the procedure for the application of Article 247 of UNCLOS provides a critical tool to promote international cooperation in the field of marine scientific research. Implications of this outcome will be addressed in subsequent chapters of this book, in particular Chapter 7.[48] Among the four sub-groups, the one that is the most relevant for the theme of the current chapter is the sub-group on the legal framework, within the context of UNCLOS, which is applicable to the collection of oceanographic data (hereinafter sub-group on the collection of oceanographic data).[49] Deliberations made during the IOC/ABE-LOS meetings under this sub-group and the relevant outcome of the meetings will be examined in Section 4.3.2.

As concluded in Chapter 3, it sometimes remains unclear what the appropriate regulation of ocean data collection activities that serve multiple purposes

---

46 For more information on IOC/ABE-LOS, see the official website of UNESCO/IOC, "IOC/ABE-LOS", available at http://ioc-unesco.org/index.php?option=com_content&view=article&id=364&Itemid=100047.

47 Ibid.

48 See in particular Chapter 7.4.1.2.3.

49 The sub-group on this topic was established by the IOC Assembly in 2003 by its Resolution XXII–12.

would be. The most contentious issues arise when the ocean data collection activity at issue serves both scientific and commercial purposes, and when it serves both scientific purposes and the purpose of ensuring the safety of navigation, including weather forecast and disaster risk reduction. The regulation of former category of ocean data collection activities has recently become one of the topics covered by the UN negotiations on the conservation and sustainable use of marine biological diversity of areas beyond national jurisdiction (BBNJ), most recently in the Intergovernmental Conference on Marine Biodiversity of Areas Beyond National Jurisdiction.[50] The relevant discussions will be examined in Section 4.3.3.

As to the latter category of ocean data collection activities, international organizations and networks, such as the World Meteorological Organization (WMO), the International Hydrographic Organization (IHO) and the Global Ocean Observing System (GOOS), share competence over this matter.

WMO is an intergovernmental organization established in 1950.[51] The purposes of this organization include,

a. To facilitate worldwide cooperation in the establishment of networks of stations for the making of meteorological observations or other geophysical observations related to meteorology and to promote the establishment and maintenance of meteorological centers charged with the provision of meteorological services;
b. To promote the establishment and maintenance of systems for the rapid exchange of weather information;
c. To promote standardization of meteorological observations and to ensure the uniform publication of observations and statistics;
d. To further the application of meteorology to aviation, shipping, agriculture, and other human activities; and
e. To encourage research and training in meteorology and to assist in coordinating the international aspects of such research and training.[52]

This organization is well known to researchers interested in the scope of regulation of the UNCLOS marine scientific research regime, because of a letter sent by the Secretary-General of WMO to the Chairman of the Third Committee during UNCLOS III and the reply given by the Chairman. Recently, the

50 For more information on the negotiation process, see the official website of the UN, "INTERGOVERNMENTAL CONFERENCE ON MARINE BIODIVERSITY OF AREAS BEYOND NATIONAL JURISDICTION", available at https://www.un.org/bbnj/.

51 For more information on WMO, see its official website, "about us", available at https://public.wmo.int/en/about-us.

52 Convention of the World Meteorological Organization, 1947, Article 2.

Members of WMO adopted a series of Resolutions on "Marine Observation", in which the relationship between marine observations and marine scientific research has been addressed. The notion of marine observations and the Resolutions will be addressed in Section 4.3.4.

IHO is "an intergovernmental consultative and technical organization that was established in 1921 to support safety of navigation and the protection of the marine environment".[53] IHO is relevant for the current research because of the complicated relationship between marine scientific research and ocean data collection activities that support safe navigation. However, a review of the past events under the framework of IHO indicates that the organization does not provide much information on the relevant subsequent practice on the regulation of marine scientific research or other ocean data collection activities. Therefore, this organization will not be addressed in detail in this chapter.

GOOS is a sustained collaborative system of ocean observations co-sponsored by four organizations: IOC, WMO, United Nations Environment Programme (UNEP), and the International Council of Science.[54] GOOS is established as a coordinative mechanism to integrate the efforts of various global and regional platforms in the field of ocean data collection. An examination of subsequent practice manifest in this system will be provided in Section 4.3.5 of this chapter.

In sum, the following discussion will devote a sub-section to each of the global fora identified above: Section 4.3.2 on IOC/ABE-LOS, Section 4.3.3 on the Intergovernmental Conference on Marine Biodiversity of Areas Beyond National Jurisdiction, Section 4.3.4 on WMO, and Section 4.3.5 on GOOS. The substantive analysis of the subsequent practice manifest in these fora will primarily focus on the statements made by different delegations during the negotiations that took place at these fora. Such an analysis helps discern States' views on issues regarding the legal classification of certain ocean data collection activities. Resolutions adopted and relevant documents issued by these fora will also be examined, especially when the record of the negotiations and meetings is not available. As discussed earlier, to a certain extent, these resolutions and documents represent States' viewpoints on the matters concerned. They may also influence future State practice on said matters.

53 For more information on this organization, see its official website, "About the IHO", available at https://iho.int/en/about-the-iho.

54 For more information on GOOS, see its official website, "GOOS Sponsors", available at http://www.goosocean.org/index.php?option=com_content&view=article&id=8&Itemid=109.

4.3.2 *IOC/ABE-LOS*

This sub-section begins with an overview of the work of the Sub-Group on the Collection of Oceanographic Data and relevant discussions during IOC/ABE-LOS meetings (Section 4.3.2.1), followed by an examination of the outcome of this sub-group, namely the Argo Guidelines (Section 4.3.2.2).

4.3.2.1 The Sub-Group on the Collection of Oceanographic Data

According to IOC Resolution XXII-12, the mandate of the Sub-Group on the Collection of Oceanographic Data is to provide advice on the legal framework within the context of UNCLOS which is applicable to the collection of oceanographic data.[55] The vague wording of this mandate has given rise to extensive discussions during the sub-group's meetings. Controversies that arise include matters concerning: 1) what sort of oceanographic data should be covered by the work of this sub-group, 2) the definition of "collection of oceanographic data" and its relationship with marine scientific research, 3) which tools or platforms that are used for the collection of oceanographic data should be covered, 4) what is the appropriate areal scope to be covered by this sub-group, and 5) whether the sub-group should cover the collection of oceanographic data in general or only those undertaken by or under the auspices of international organizations, or even narrower, only those under the auspices of IOC.[56]

Among the five controversial issues indicated above, the one concerning the definition of oceanographic data collection and its relationship with marine scientific research is the most relevant to the current study. Several delegations argued that the distinction between marine scientific research and the collection of oceanographic data "was in part artificial since these activities were closely interrelated".[57] Some representatives mentioned that the national legislation of their countries considers the collection of oceanographic data to fall under Part XIII of UNCLOS.[58] However, one delegate remarked that "the routine collection of ocean observations is clearly analogous to the collection of marine meteorological data that are distributed openly and for free and for purposes for common good and the protection of natural resources, human life and property", and thus is not considered as marine scientific research

55 "Report of the Twenty-Second Session of the Assembly", Doc. IOC-XXII/3, 2003, Annex II, page 16.

56 For detailed information on the discussions, see for example "Report of the Fourth Session of IOC/ABE-LOS", Doc. IOC/ABE-LOS IV/3, 2004, paras. 60–75; "Report of the Fifth Session of IOC/ABE-LOS", Doc. IOC/ABE-LOS V/3, 2005, at pp. 6–9; "Report of the Sixth Session of IOC/ABE-LOS", Doc. IOC/ABE-LOS VI/3, 2006, at pp. 5–6.

57 "Report of the Sixth Session of IOC/ABE-LOS", Doc. IOC/ABE-LOS VI/3, at p. 5.

58 Ibid., at p. 6.

regulated by Part XIII of UNCLOS.[59] This viewpoint was opposed by the reference to Article 258 of the Convention providing for the same treatment for all scientific research installations and equipment.[60]

With the furtherance of the deliberations on this topic, the distinction between pure and applied marine scientific research was raised.[61] One delegate mentioned that "there is disagreement at the international level with respect to the difference between pure and applied research and in this regard referred [...] to paragraph 92 of [the report of the fifth meeting of the] United Nations Open-Ended Informal Consultative Process on Oceans and the Law of the Sea".[62]

Discussions on the relationship between the collection of oceanographic data and marine scientific research have remained inconclusive.[63] At the sixth session of IOC/ABE-LOS (2006), several delegations advocated "the search of pragmatic solutions".[64] Considering the complexity of the various issues concerning the topic of oceanographic data collection, it was proposed that the most pragmatic way would be to "divide the project in various phases limited to specific methods of data collection, and limited to projects under the auspices of IOC", and "to start drafting guidelines limited to the deployment of

59 Ibid. This position was raised again at the seventh session of the IOC/ABE-LOS meeting, see "Report of the Seventh Session of IOC/ABE-LOS", Doc. IOC/ABE-LOS VII/3, 2007, at p. 7.

60 "Report of the Sixth Session of IOC/ABE-LOS", Doc. IOC/ABE-LOS VI/3, at p. 6. Article 258 of the Convention states, "[t]he deployment and use of any type of scientific research installations or equipment in any area of the marine environment shall be subject to the same conditions as are prescribed in this Convention for the conduct of marine scientific research in any such area." The implication of this article will be addressed in Chapter 7 of this book.

61 "Report of the Fifth Session of IOC/ABE-LOS", Doc. IOC/ABE-LOS V/3, at pp. 7, 9; "Report of the Sixth Session of IOC/ABE-LOS", Doc. IOC/ABE-LOS VI/3, at p. 5. The distinction between pure and applied marine scientific research has been examined in Chapter 3.2.4.1 of this book.

62 "Report of the Fifth Session of IOC/ABE-LOS", Doc. IOC/ABE-LOS V/3, at p. 7. Paragraph 92 reads: "Several delegations made reservations with regard to paragraphs 260 to 262 of the report of the Secretary-General on oceans and the law of the sea (A/59/62). Among other things, they pointed out that the Convention did not provide a definition of marine scientific research and did not mention bioprospecting. It was also noted that the distinction between pure and applied marine scientific research had never been accepted universally, since there was no perceivable difference in the activity or method". See "Report on the work of the United Nations Open-ended Informal Consultative Process on Oceans and the Law of the Sea at its fifth meeting", UN Doc. A/59/122, 2004, para.92.

63 "Report of the Seventh Session of IOC/ABE-LOS", Doc. IOC/ABE-LOS VII/3, at p. 8.

64 "Report of the Sixth Session of IOC/ABE-LOS", Doc. IOC/ABE-LOS VI/3, at p. 6.

profiling floats in the framework of the Argo project".[65] In the seventh session of IOC/ABE-LOS (2007), it was decided to limit the scope of its discussions on the legal framework that is applicable to the collection of oceanographic data by the following means:[66]

i. the deployment of floats on high seas which may drift into EEZs;
ii. the deployment of floats and surface drifting buoys in EEZs;
iii. the deployment of XBTs by ships of opportunity in EEZs.

At the eighth session of IOC/ABE-LOS (2008), the delegations unanimously agreed to first focus on the work on the legal framework for the collection of oceanographic data by means of Argo floats, leaving the treatment of surface drifters and XBTs until a subsequent stage.[67] Since then, the draft legal framework under discussions was only concerned with the collection of oceanographic data in the context of the Argo project.[68]

However, a narrowing down of the scope of the issue did not solve all the problems. Controversies still existed as regards the relationship between the collection of oceanographic data by Argo floats and marine scientific research.

On the one hand, the United Kingdom considered that "the routine collection of data by Argo floats should not be considered as marine scientific research but rather as an operational activity that should be treated in a similar way to meteorological activities".[69] Likewise, the United States considered that the gathering of oceanographic data under the framework of Argo project was "exactly the sort of activity which [WMO] obtained the decision of [UNCLOS III] in 1982 was not marine scientific research governed by Part XIII of the Convention".[70] The US delegation further stated that its previous practice of

65 Ibid., at p. 5. It was commented at the eighth session of IOC/ABE-LOS meeting that "many of the difficulties in making progress until now could be explained by discussing data collection in general, without having a full, in-depth appreciation of a given technology and its applications, something that constituted a lesson learned in the process". See "Report of the Eighth Session of IOC/ABE-LOS", Doc. IOC/ABE-LOS VIII/3, 2008, at p. 3.

66 "Report of the Seventh Session of IOC/ABE-LOS", Doc. IOC/ABE-LOS VII/3, at p. 7.

67 "Report of the Eighth Session of IOC/ABE-LOS", Doc. IOC/ABE-LOS VIII/3, at p. 3.

68 Ibid. Previously, the document serving as the basis for discussions was named "Draft [Practical] Guidelines of IOC, within the Context of UNCLOS, for the Collection of Oceanographic Data by Specific Means", see Draft [Practical] Guidelines of IOC, within the Context of UNCLOS, for the Collection of Oceanographic Data by Specific Means, IOC/ABE-LOS VII/7.

69 "Report of the Thirty-Ninth Session of the Executive Council of IOC", Doc. IOC/EC-XXXIX/3, 2006, para.262; "Report of the Seventh Session of IOC/ABE-LOS", Doc. IOC/ABE-LOS VII/3, at p. 7.

70 "Report of the Eighth Session of IOC/ABE-LOS", Doc. IOC/ABE-LOS VIII/3, at p. 8. For more information on the letter, see Section 4.3.4.2 of this chapter. The US delegation further addressed the position towards the legal status of other means of collecting

providing notification to Argentina of its Argo floats that may drift into Argentina's EEZ was only a matter of courtesy and cooperation, which was done as an exception and without prejudice to its position.[71] On the other hand, other countries disagreed with this position and considered that the collection of data by Argo floats fell under the category of marine scientific research.[72]

Again, there was no consensus reached in the end concerning the classification of this kind of activities – whether they are marine scientific research or not.[73] The extensive discussions of the sub-group ultimately led to the adoption of Resolution EC-XLI.4 adopting the Guidelines for the Implementation of Resolution XX–6 of the IOC Assembly regarding the deployment of profiling floats in the high seas within the framework of the Argo Programme (hereinafter Argo Guidelines).[74]

In the Resolution adopting the IOC Argo Guidelines, the IOC Executive Council "further requests IOC/ABE-LOS to continue its work on the legal framework within the context of UNCLOS that is applicable to the collection of oceanographic data by other specific means".[75]

The discussions around the second means – the deployment of floats and surface drifting buoys in EEZs – did not lead to the adoption of a specific set of guidelines. This is because IOC/ABE-LOS has agreed that "there is no need for specific guidelines on the deployment of Argo floats in EEZs and that such deployment should be considered within the framework of bilateral cooperation and agreements".[76] According to the report of the meeting, this conclusion was based on State practice on this matter. Several delegations provided specific examples indicating "that the regular requests for research

oceanographic data. According to the delegation, "[t]he information gathered by drifting buoys and XBTs is also used for weather forecasting and ocean state estimation. The use of those instruments is, also, not marine scientific research governed by Part XIII of the Convention. [...] The deployment of Argo profiling floats, drifting buoys and XBTs are traditional exercises of the high seas freedom of navigation. They are not subject to coastal state control".

71 Ibid.

72 "Report of the Seventh Session of IOC/ABE-LOS", Doc. IOC/ABE-LOS VII/3, at pp. 6–7; "Report of the Eighth Session of IOC/ABE-LOS", Doc. IOC/ABE-LOS VIII/3, at pp. 8–9.

73 See "Report of the Eighth Session of IOC/ABE-LOS", Doc. IOC/ABE-LOS VIII/3, at pp. 8–9.

74 "Report of the Forty-first Session of the Executive Council of IOC", Doc. IOC/EC-XLI/3, 2008, para.185.

75 "Guidelines for the Implementation of Resolution XX–6 of the IOC Assembly Regarding the Deployment of Profiling Floats in the High Seas within the Framework of the Argo Programme", Resolution EC-XLI.4, 2008.

76 "Report of the Ninth Session of IOC/ABE-LOS", Doc. IOC/ABE-LOS IX/3 Rev., 2009, at p. 8.

authorization have been applied and no specific problems have arisen".[77] According to these delegations, the deployment of Argo floats in EEZs shall be considered as conducting marine scientific research activities, to which the Part XIII regime applies. Some other delegations shared the view that "the deployment of Argo floats in EEZs is a bilateral matter that has worked and continues to work well and, therefore, does not require any guidelines by ABE-LOS". These delegations nonetheless disagreed with the applicable legal framework for such activities.[78] They argued that,

> the routine collection of ocean observations in near-real-time that are distributed freely and openly, and are used for monitoring and forecasting of ocean state, for weather forecasts and warnings, and for climate prediction, is analogous to the collection of marine meteorological data, and therefore is not marine scientific research regulated by Part XIII of UNCLOS.[79]

A question was raised whether the conclusion arrived at in terms of the deployment of Argo floats in the EEZs, namely that there is no need for specific guidelines, also applies to surface drifting buoys.[80] The Chairman of IOC/ABE-LOS indicated that, in his view, the conclusion also covers surface drifters.[81] Members to IOC/ABE-LOS also shared the view that there is no need to set up a new set of guidelines for the deployment of floating devices, such as Argo floats and surface drifting buoys, in the EEZ of a coastal State.[82] In practice, the relevant legal issues have been addressed by bilateral or multilateral agreements.

In terms of the third issue under the consideration of the sub-group – oceanographic data collection activities that involve the deployment of XBTs by ships of opportunity in the EEZs – IOC/ABE-LOS agreed that "there is no need for specific guidelines" for such a kind of activities notwithstanding the different views that were expressed with respect to the applicable legal framework for such activities.[83]

77 Ibid., at p. 6.

78 Ibid.

79 Ibid., at p .7.

80 Ibid., at p. 9.

81 Ibid.

82 "Report of the Twenty-Fifth Session of the Assembly of IOC", Doc. IOC-XXV/3, 2009, at pp. 17–18.

83 "Report of the Ninth Session of IOC/ABE-LOS", Doc. IOC/ABE-LOS IX/3 Rev., at pp. 8–9.

4.3.2.2 The Argo Guidelines

The discussions under the Sub-Group on the Collection of Oceanographic Data led to the adoption of the Argo Guidelines. The Argo Guidelines is a short and brief legally non-binding document that includes a preamble and seven Guidelines. The Guidelines do not address the legal classification of oceanographic data collection within the framework of the Argo Programme. The most critical paragraph of the Argo Guidelines provides that "an IOC Member State must be informed in advance [...] of the deployment in the high seas of any float within the framework of the Argo Programme that may enter its EEZ".[84] Because Resolution EC-XLI.4 acknowledged that "the Argo Programme shall be fully consistent with UNCLOS",[85] one can conclude that the collection of oceanographic data under the Argo Programme is covered by the relevant provisions of UNCLOS. The Guidelines should be seen as a practical arrangement among the Member States within the meaning of UNCLOS. Still, two different interpretations of the notification requirement under the Argo Guidelines may be entertained.

Firstly, one can argue that the Guidelines' requirement of *informing* the coastal State in advance is different from the requirement under Article 246 of UNCLOS concerning the application of *consent*. In other words, the Argo Guidelines treat the collection of oceanographic data by Argo floats differently from marine scientific research. In this case, the Argo Guidelines can be seen as the outcome of the resolution of conflicts concerning unattributed rights in the EEZ of a coastal State,[86] or as the fulfilment of the due regard obligations under Article 58(3) when the collection of oceanographic data under the Argo programme falls under the rights of a third State according to Article 58(1).[87]

Secondly, the notification requirement under the Argo Guidelines can be seen as favorable conditions created for the conduct of marine scientific research under Article 243 of UNCLOS, or as a result of international cooperation under Article 242 of UNCLOS.[88] In line with this interpretation, the collection of oceanographic data under the Argo programme is viewed as marine scientific research.

84 "Guidelines for the Implementation of Resolution XX–6 of the IOC Assembly Regarding the Deployment of Profiling Floats in the High Seas within the Framework of the Argo Programme", Resolution EC-XLI.4, para.1.

85 Ibid.

86 UNCLOS, Article 59. The implications of Article 59 have been discussed in Chapter 3.3.2.4 of this book.

87 Ibid., Article 58(1), (3). The implications of paragraphs (1) and (3) of Article 58 have been discussed in respectively in Chapters 3.3.2.2 and 3.3.2.3 of this book.

88 Ibid., Articles 242, 243.

Because these two different interpretations are possible, it is interesting to note that two approaches existed during the discussions to justify the position considering the collection of oceanographic data by Argo floats as marine scientific research. Some countries, such as the Russian Federation, "agreed with" the Argo Guidelines, *but* "considered that the collection of data by Argo floats falls under marine scientific research".[89] On the other hand, some other countries, such as Japan and Argentina, took the view that "given its characteristics, the Argo initiative could perfectly well be considered in the framework of Art. 247 of UNCLOS, as an activity of a group of IOC Member States on a subject of marine scientific research under the auspices of IOC", and that "the Argo floats are tools of marine scientific research and that the data collected by them are moreover of benefit to marine meteorology".[90]

It is submitted that the discussions during the IOC/ABE-LOS meetings and the adoption of the Argo Guidelines serve as a basis for the future resolution on issues related to ocean data collection. Most notably, the adoption of the Argo Guidelines and the establishment of bilateral and multilateral agreements on the regulation of oceanographic data collection activities involving the use of floats and surface drifting buoys and the deployment of XBTs by ships of opportunity in EEZs give a positive signal. Potentially States would enter into practical arrangements for the regulation of ocean data collection activities undertaken in the EEZ even in cases where the legal classification of the activities concerned is controversial.

The willingness of States to enter into practical arrangements on the said matter is arguably attributed to the common interests in the activities concerned. To be more specific, the basis of the discussions on the topic of the legal framework applicable to the collection of oceanographic data is provided by Resolution XX-6 of the IOC Assembly. The reason for adopting this resolution was to ensure that the Argo Programme could be carried out effectively as a provider of a public good. This reason is recalled in the Chapeau of the Argo Guidelines, in which IOC Member States confirmed, *inter alia*, that "[t]here is a need to ensure that Member States gain maximum benefit from the data of the Argo project".[91] The maximum benefit can only be achieved through

89 "Report of the Forty-first Session of the Executive Council of IOC", Doc. IOC/EC-XLI/3, para.177.

90 "Report of the Thirty-Ninth Session of the Executive Council of IOC", Doc. IOC/EC-XXXIX/3, para.263; "Report of the Seventh Session of IOC/ABE-LOS", Doc. IOC/ABE-LOS VII/3, at p. 6.

91 "Guidelines for the Implementation of Resolution XX–6 of the IOC Assembly Regarding the Deployment of Profiling Floats in the High Seas within the Framework of the Argo Programme", Resolution EC-XLI.4, Chapeau.

cooperation. It has been proposed during IOC/ABE-LOS meetings that the challenge was "to develop a mutual understanding of the real and potential benefits of collecting and sharing of oceanographic data from within a nation's EEZ", and that "such a mutual understanding already exists within the meteorological community [...] because of obvious benefits to weather forecasting and its impact on safety of life at sea".[92] Arguably, by adopting the Argo Guidelines, this mutual understanding has been realized regarding the deployment of Argo floats on the high seas for the purpose of collecting oceanographic data.

The observation that whether States are willing to establish practical arrangements mainly depends on whether the ocean data collection activities can contribute to common interests is also supported by relevant State practice at the regional level. In different regions, States would enter into cooperative arrangements for different practical concerns. Arguably this is because the common interests pursued vary from one region to another. For instance, in the South China Sea region, it is primarily the hope to establish peace and stability in the region and to build trusts among States for the ultimate resolution of regional conflicts that leads to the cooperative arrangements in marine scientific research and ocean data collection activities in general.[93] Whereas in the area covered by the Convention for the Protection of the Marine Environment of the North-East Atlantic (OSPAR Convention),[94] the driving force behind the adoption of practical arrangements, such as the OSPAR Code of Conduct for Responsible Marine Research in the Deep Seas and High Seas

---

92 "Report of the Fourth Session of IOC/ABE-LOS", Doc. IOC/ABE-LOS IV/3, para.68.

93 In the South China Sea region, the Declaration on the Conduct of Parties in the South China Sea provides a basis for cooperating in marine scientific research in the South China Sea region. The successful operation of the Technical Working Group on Marine Scientific Research created under the Workshop on Managing Potential Conflicts in the South China Sea (hereinafter MPC Workshop) also shows that States bordering the South China Sea consider cooperation in marine scientific research as a means to build mutual trusts and resolve regional conflicts. For more information on the MPC Workshop and its role in shaping State practice on marine scientific research, see, for instance, Liselotte Odgaard, *Maritime Security between China and Southeast Asia: Conflict and Cooperation in the Making of Regional Order* (Routledge, 2017), 183–189; IA Satyawan, "Scientific Cooperation to Respond Climate Change in the South China Sea: The Study of Tides and Sea Level Change" (paper presented at the IOP Conference Series: Earth and Environmental Science, 2018), 4; Yann-Huei Song, "The South China Sea Workshop Process and Taiwan's Participation", *Ocean Development & International Law* 41, no. 3 (2010): 253–254; Edgardo D. Gomez, "Marine Scientific Research in the South China Sea and Environmental Security", *Ocean Development & International Law* 32, no. 2 (2001): 209.

94 Convention for the Protection of the Marine Environment of the North-East Atlantic, 1992.

of the OSPAR Maritime Area (hereinafter OSPAR Code of Conduct),[95] was the desire to reduce the adverse impacts of marine scientific research on the marine environment.[96] Therefore, based on their actual needs and the potential common interests that can be identified, States can enter into different forms of cooperative arrangements for the regulation of different kinds of ocean data collection activities.

The implications of the observations above will be further addressed in Chapter 7 of this book.

4.3.3 *Intergovernmental Conference on Marine Biodiversity of Areas beyond National Jurisdiction*

The scope of marine scientific research under UNCLOS and more specifically its connection with access to marine genetic resources have been the subject of discussions during the UN negotiations on the conservation and sustainable use of marine biological diversity beyond areas of national jurisdiction.

In 2015, UNGA decided in its Resolution 69/292, to develop an international legally binding instrument (hereinafter ILBI or the instrument) under UNCLOS on this topic.[97] To this end, a Preparatory Committee (PrepCom) was established, to make substantive recommendations to the General Assembly on the elements of a draft text of an ILBI, and for the Assembly to decide, whether to convene an intergovernmental conference to elaborate the text of the

95 OSPAR Code of Conduct for Responsible Marine Research in the Deep Seas and High Seas of the OSPAR Maritime Area, 2008, Source: OSPAR 08/24/1, Annex 6.

96 OSPAR Convention was adopted as a response to deal with the tremendous pressure on the marine ecosystem from intense human activity that goes on in and around the North-East Atlantic. The OSPAR Code of Conduct was adopted in 2008 to address the unwanted negative side effects of some scientific activities on biodiversity. For more background information on the adoption of the OSPAR Code of Conduct, see the Annual Report of the OSPAR Commission 2007/08, available at https://www.ospar.org/documents?v=7106, at p. 9.

97 "UNGA Resolution on "Development of an international legally-binding instrument under the United Nations Convention on the Law of the Sea on the conservation and sustainable use of marine biological diversity of areas beyond national jurisdiction" of 19 June 2015", UN Doc. A/RES/69/292, para.1. UNGA made the decision on this matter on the basis of the recommendations of the Ad Hoc Open-ended Informal Working Group to study issues relating to the conservation and sustainable use of marine biological diversity beyond areas of national jurisdiction. For more information on this working group and its work, see the official website of UN/DOALOS, "Ad Hoc Open-ended Informal Working Group to study issues relating to the conservation and sustainable use of marine biological diversity beyond areas of national jurisdiction", available at https://www.un.org/depts/los/biodiversityworkinggroup/biodiversityworkinggroup.htm.

agreement.[98] After four sessions, the PrepCom recommended that the General Assembly convene an intergovernmental conference to consider the recommendations of the PrepCom on the elements and to elaborate the text of an ILBI under UNCLOS.[99] In 2017, the General Assembly decided in its Resolution 72/249 to convene an intergovernmental conference with a view to developing the instrument as soon as possible.[100] The intergovernmental conference will meet for four sessions.[101] The third session of the conference was concluded on 30 August 2019; as of the time of writing, the fourth session which was scheduled for 23 March to 3 April 2020 has been postponed to 7 to 18 March 2022.

Negotiations in the PrepCom sessions as well as in the intergovernmental conference focus on:

> the topics identified in the package agreed in 2011, namely, the conservation and sustainable use of marine biological diversity of areas beyond national jurisdiction, in particular, together and as a whole, marine genetic resources, including questions on the sharing of benefits, measures such as area-based management tools, including marine protected areas, environmental impact assessments and capacity-building and the transfer of marine technology.[102]

---

98 Ibid.

99 "Report of the Preparatory Committee established by General Assembly resolution 69/292: Development of an international legally binding instrument under the United Nations Convention on the Law of the Sea on the conservation and sustainable use of marine biological diversity of areas beyond national jurisdiction", UN Doc. A/AC.287/2017/PC.4/2, 2017, para.38.

100 "UNGA Resolution on "International legally binding instrument under the United Nations Convention on the Law of the Sea on the conservation and sustainable use of marine biological diversity of areas beyond national jurisdiction" of 24 December 2017", UN Doc. A/RES/72/249, para.1.

101 Ibid., para.3.

102 "UNGA Resolution on "Development of an international legally-binding instrument under the United Nations Convention on the Law of the Sea on the conservation and sustainable use of marine biological diversity of areas beyond national jurisdiction" of 19 June 2015", UN Doc. A/RES/69/292, para.2; "UNGA Resolution on "International legally binding instrument under the United Nations Convention on the Law of the Sea on the conservation and sustainable use of marine biological diversity of areas beyond national jurisdiction" of 24 December 2017", UN Doc. A/RES/72/249, para.2. Considering the long history of negotiating on this topic, the following analysis will only focus on the positions of States expressed during the PrepCom sessions and the IGC sessions. This selection can be explained by the fact that it is in the negotiations that took place in the PrepCom sessions and the IGC sessions that delegations started to make substantive statements on their position towards substantive issues. The focus of earlier negotiations and work

During the negotiations, the term "marine scientific research" has been brought up numerous times, especially in the discussions on the topic of marine genetic resources. A pertinent question relates to the legal classification of activities involving access to marine genetic resources, or more specifically, whether or to which extent the said activity is to be considered as marine scientific research.

Several delegations proposed distinguishing between marine scientific research and access to marine genetic resources (or bioprospecting),[103] and some of them argued for "dual regulation" of access for marine scientific research and commercial purposes.[104] However, they did not provide any clear indications on how to make such a distinction.

Some States considered it almost impossible to draw a clear line between marine scientific research and bioprospecting because discussions on this matter would inevitably lead to a debate on the distinction between pure and applied marine scientific research, on which there is no agreement at global

was on issues whether the BBNJ issues should be addressed, and if yes, which aspects or elements should be addressed.

103 The term "bioprospecting" is neither used nor defined in UNCLOS or other international legal instruments, including the Convention on Biological Diversity (CBD). A note prepared by the secretariat of CBD defines bioprospecting as "the exploration of biodiversity for commercially valuable genetic and biochemical resources. It can be defined as the process of gathering information from the biosphere on the molecular composition of genetic resources for the development of new commercial products." See "Progress Report on the Implementation of the Programmes of Work on the Biological Diversity of Inland Water Ecosystems, Marine and Coastal Biological Diversity, and Forest Biological Diversity (DECISIONS IV/4, IV/5, IV/7)", Doc. UNEP/CBD/COP/5/INF/7, 2000, para.6. The relationship between bioprospecting and marine scientific research will be further addressed in Chapter 6 of this study.

104 Proponents of this position include G-77/China, the African Group, Mexico, and Singapore. See Elisa Morgera et al., "BBNJ IGC-1 Highlights: Wednesday, 12 September 2018", *IISD - Earth Negotiations Bulletin,* http://enb.iisd.org/download/pdf/enb25176e.pdf, at p. 2; Elisa Morgera et al., "Summary of the First Session of the Intergovernmental Conference on an International Legally Binding Instrument under the UN Convention on the Law of the Sea on the Conservation and Sustainable Use of Marine Biodiversity of Areas Beyond National Jurisdiction: 4–17 September 2018", *IISD - Earth Negotiations Bulletin,* at p. 4. The importance of the distinction between marine scientific research and bioprospecting is also proposed by PSIDS, which states that: "The importance of the distinction between marine scientific research (MSR) and bioprospecting will influence the regulation of such activities." See "PSIDS Submission to the Second Meeting of the Preparatory Committee for the Development of an international legally binding instrument under the United Nations Convention on the Law of the Sea on the conservation and sustainable use of marine biological diversity of areas beyond national jurisdiction (BBNJ PrepCom) (August 2016)", http://www.un.org/depts/los/biodiversity/prepcom_files/streamlined/PSIDS_Submission_aug_2016.pdf.

level.[105] These States cautioned against creating a separate regime for pure and applied marine scientific research or going into detail on the differences between the two.[106]

Other States considered that the free access to *in situ* marine genetic resources is in line with the marine scientific research regime as embodied in UNCLOS.[107] This approach suggests that *in situ* access to marine genetic resources is to be considered as marine scientific research, to which Part XIII of UNCLOS applies.

Most recently, before the commencement of the fourth session of the Intergovernmental Conference, the President of the Conference prepared a revised draft text of an ILBI "to enable delegations to take stock and to facilitate further progress in the negotiations at the fourth session of the intergovernmental conference".[108] Delegations were invited to submit textual proposals for consideration.[109] These proposals have been included in a document titled "Article-by-article compilation of textual proposals for consideration at the

105 "Report on the work of the United Nations Open-ended Informal Consultative Process on Oceans and the Law of the Sea at its fifth meeting", UN Doc. A/59/122, para.92.

106 See for example the statement of Mexico in the second session of the PrepCom, Elisa Morgera et al., "Summary of the Second Session of the Preparatory Committee on Marine Biodiversity beyond Areas of National Jurisdiction: 26 August – 9 September 2016", at p. 3. See also Japan's statement at the third session of the PrepCom, according to which there were numerous unsuccessful attempts to define marine scientific research, Elisa Morgera et al., "Summary of the Third Session of the Preparatory Committee on Marine Biodiversity beyond Areas of National Jurisdiction: 27 March – 7 April 2017", at p. 3.

107 For more information, see the position of the EU in the first session of the IGC, Elisa Morgera et al., "Summary of the First Session of the Intergovernmental Conference on an International Legally Binding Instrument under the UN Convention on the Law of the Sea on the Conservation and Sustainable Use of Marine Biodiversity of Areas Beyond National Jurisdiction: 4–17 September 2018", at p. 4. At the fourth session of the PrepCom, in the deliberations on the issue of access to MGR s, the EU explicitly welcomed reference to UNCLOS Articles 256 (marine scientific research in the Area) and 257 (marine scientific research in the water column beyond the EEZ), and Articles 238–244 (general provisions and international cooperation concerning marine scientific research). This position is shared by CARICOM, suggesting the need to build on UNCLOS provisions on marine scientific research and technology transfer, and China, arguing for free *in situ* access to MGRs as part of marine scientific research. See Elisa Morgera et al., "Summary of the Fourth Session of the Preparatory Committee on Marine Biodiversity beyond Areas of National Jurisdiction: 10–21 July 2017", at pp. 9–10.

108 "Revised draft text of an agreement under the United Nations Convention on the Law of the Sea on the conservation and sustainable use of marine biological diversity of areas beyond national jurisdiction - Note by the President", Doc. A/CONF.232/2020/3, 2019.

109 Ibid., Introduction, para.10.

fourth session dated 15 April 2020".[110] As can be seen from the relevant proposals, opinions on the regulation of *in situ* access to marine genetic resources still vary. Overall, no explicit reference was made to marine scientific research in the proposals concerning *in situ* access to marine genetic resources.

In conclusion, States have expressed divergent positions on the legal classification of access to marine genetic resources. Since the negotiations on BBNJ issues are still on-going, it remains to be seen whether States are willing to make a compromise and to address issues such as the regulation of activities involving access to marine genetic resources and benefit-sharing obligations in the ILBI, despite their differing views. This being said, an examination of the applicability of the UNCLOS marine scientific research regime to activities involving access to marine genetic resources in areas beyond national jurisdiction will be included in Chapter 6 of this book as a case study.

4.3.4 *WMO*

WMO is another international organization that plays an active role in promoting ocean science, especially in the field of a specific kind of ocean data collection activities, called "marine observation". The term "marine observation" has not been defined by WMO. The ordinary meaning of the term "observation" is "the action or process of closely observing or monitoring something or someone".[111] Therefore, marine observation presumably refers to the observation of the state of the marine environment. Because WMO "is the UN system's authoritative voice on the state and behaviour of the Earth's atmosphere, its interaction with the land and oceans, the weather and climate it produces and the resulting distribution of water resources",[112] the objective of marine observation in the context of WMO programs is to observe the state and behavior of the oceans concerning the weather and climate. This assumption is consistent with the purpose of WMO as provided for in Article 2 of the Convention of the World Meteorological Organization:

110 "Textual proposals submitted by delegations by 20 February 2020, for consideration at the fourth session of the Intergovernmental conference on an international legally binding instrument under the United Nations Convention on the Law of the Sea on the conservation and sustainable use of marine biological diversity of areas beyond national jurisdiction (the Conference), in response to the invitation by the President of the Conference in her Note of 18 November 2019 (A/CONF.232/2020/3)", 2020.

111 "Observation", Oxford Dictionary of English (Oxford Reference online version, 3rd edition, Oxford University Press, 2015).

112 For more information, see the official website of WMO, "who we are", available at https://public.wmo.int/en/about-us/who-we-are.

> The purposes of the Organization shall be: (a) [t]o facilitate worldwide cooperation in the establishment of networks of stations for the making of meteorological observations or other geophysical observations related to meteorology [...].[113]

In short, marine observation refers to ocean data collection activities that serve meteorological purposes.

4.3.4.1 WMO Resolutions on Marine Observations

In the Eighteenth Session of the World Meteorological Congress (2019), members of WMO adopted a series of resolutions on "Marine Observation". Of particular interest is Resolution 45 (Cg-18) entitled "Ensuring Adequate Marine Meteorological and Oceanographic Observations and Data Coverage for the Safety of Navigation and the Protection of Life and Property in Coastal and Offshore Areas".[114] This Resolution recognizes, *inter alia*, that

> there is no regulation in place for the collection of marine meteorological and oceanographic measurements within EEZs in support of operational applications of WMO, while the [Argo Guidelines] are operated effectively and fully consistently with UNCLOS.[115]

According to this paragraph, especially the statement that "there is no regulation in place for the collection of marine meteorological and oceanographic measurements [...]", the Resolution considers the activities concerned distinct from marine scientific research. A pertinent question that arises relates to the scope of the activities covered by this Resolution. To be more specific, what can be considered as "the collection of marine meteorological and oceanographic measurements within EEZs in support of operational applications of WMO"? Two qualifications are noted: 1) the collection of marine meteorological and oceanographic measures, and 2) in support of operational applications of WMO.

As to the first element, the Annex to Resolution 45 (Cg-18) includes a list of "marine meteorological and oceanographic variables", the observations of which "are used operationally by WMO applications and are critical for those applications to allow WMO to deliver the services in support of the safety of

113 Convention of the World Meteorological Organization, Article 2.

114 "Abridged Final Report of the Eighteenth session of World Meteorological Congress", Doc. WMO - No.1236, 2019, at pp. 146–150.

115 Ibid., at p. 148.

navigation and the protection of life and property in coastal and offshore areas".[116] According to the overall logic of the Resolution, it transpires that this Resolution only applies to the collection of data concerning the variables that are included in the list. These variables include sea level pressure, surface wind speed and direction, surface air temperature, surface relative humidity, precipitation at the surface, sea surface temperature, sea surface salinity, sea surface currents, directional and non-directional wave observations, visibility, sea-ice, ice accretion, sub-surface temperature and salinity, sea level, atmospheric composition, atmospheric temperature, humidity and wind profiles, all other ocean surface and atmospheric observations that are needed to derive fluxes between the ocean and the atmosphere.[117]

These variables are mainly physical variables concerning conditions of the surface water of the oceans. Compared to biogeochemical variables and biological variables, physical variables have less bearing on natural resources. They, therefore, are less likely to be "of direct significance for the exploration and exploitation of natural resources".[118] Also, confined by the limited number of variables covered by this Resolution, data collected can only serve limited purposes. Besides, the collection of data concerning surface variables is less intrusive than the collection of deep-sea data. Therefore, the collection of data concerning the variables contained in the list is less sensitive from the perspective of coastal States.

Regarding the second element – "in support of operational applications of WMO" – one needs to figure out which WMO programs support the operational application of the organization. In this regard, it is noted that the Resolution makes a specific reference to "the operation of the VOS Scheme and surface observing platforms". The Resolution also reaffirms "the critical importance of the VOS Scheme and operational surface observing platform, for ensuring the provision on a routine basis of adequate marine meteorological and oceanographic observations and data coverage".[119] This statement establishes the close link between the collection of marine meteorological and oceanographic measurements "in support of operational applications of WMO" and the VOS Scheme and operational surface observing platforms.

According to the Resolution, the phrase "surface observing platforms" refers to "operational surface marine meteorological observing platforms

116 Ibid., at p. 150.

117 Ibid.

118 UNCLOS, Article 246(5)(a).

119 "Abridged Final Report of the Eighteenth session of World Meteorological Congress", Doc. WMO - No.1236, at p. 148.

(e.g. moored and drifting buoys, and potentially unmanned surface vehicles)" that are used by the Marine Meteorology and Oceanography Programme and Tropical Cyclone Programme under WMO.[120] The VOS Scheme is a system for ship-based measurement of meteorological data.[121] The role ships play in ocean observation is described with a focus on measurements made within 100 meters of the ocean surface.[122] As such, it seems that the tools and equipment supporting the operational applications of WMO are deployed onboard a vessel or on the surface of the seawater. Thus, they mainly collect data on or near the surface of the oceans. In this regard, compared with other research tools or platforms, such as underwater vehicles, "the operation of the VOS Scheme and surface observing platforms" is less intrusive.

4.3.4.2 Letter of the Chairman of the Third Committee during UNCLOS III to the Secretary-General of WMO on 25 August 1980

Resolution 45 (Cg-18) addresses the issue of the legal framework applicable to marine observations, undertaken in the EEZ of a coastal State, which contribute to the realization of the objectives of WMO. This issue has already been touched upon at UNCLOS III.

At the resumed eighth session of UNCLOS III, WMO raised concerns that the marine scientific research provisions to be included in the new convention might restrict the routine ocean data gathering for weather forecasts.[123] In the resumed ninth session of UNCLOS III, the Chairman of the Third Committee "informed the Committee that he intended to send a letter to the Secretary-General of the World Meteorological Organization".[124] He stated that, in his opinion,

---

120 Ibid., at p. 147.

121 The VOS scheme is an international scheme "first developed almost 150 years ago, by which ships plying the various oceans and seas of the world are recruited for taking and transmitting meteorological observations. VOS ships make a highly important contribution to the Global Observing System (GOS) of the World Weather Watch (WWW), and increasingly to global climate studies". See the official website of WMO, "The Voluntary Observing Ship (VOS) Scheme", available at https://www.wmo.int/pages/prog/amp/mmop/JCOMM/OPA/SOT/vos.html.

122 Shawn R. Smith et al., "Ship-Based Contributions to Global Ocean, Weather, and Climate Observing Systems", *Frontiers in Marine Science* 6, no. 434 (2019).

123 See "Resolution 16 (Cg-VIII) adopted by the World Meteorological Organization at its eighth congress at Geneva in April/May 1979", UN Doc. A/CONF.62/80, in the Official Records of the Third United Nations Conference on the Law of the Sea, Volume XII, 56.

124 "Summary Record of the 46th meeting of the Third Committee: Extract from the Official Records of the Third United Nations Conference on the Law of the Sea, Volume XIV (Summary Records, Plenary, General Committee, First and Third Committees, as well

> the provisions on marine scientific research would not create any difficulties and obstacles hindering adequate meteorological coverage from ocean areas, including areas within the exclusive economic zone, carried out both within the framework of existing international programmes and by all vessels, since such activities had already been recognized as routine observations and data collecting which were not covered by Part XIII of the negotiating text. Furthermore, they were in the common interest of all countries and had undoubted universal significance.[125]

This letter and its content invite different interpretations. The divergences are mainly concerned with two aspects. The first one relates to the legal status of this letter – whether it is only a personal statement of the Chairman of the Third Committee of UNCLOS III, or whether it can be considered as evidence of agreement among the drafters of the Convention. The second aspect concerns the scope of activities that are covered by this letter and thus are excluded from the regulatory scope of the UNCLOS Part XIII regime. Some consider that, according to this letter, marine meteorological observations and other similar activities under the notion of "routine observations and data collecting" shall be excluded from the regulatory scope of the UNCLOS Part XIII regime.[126] In contrast, others consider that this letter cannot be used as evidence to exclude "routine observations and data collecting" from the scope of marine scientific research in general.[127]

In fact, in his report to the Plenary of the Conference, the Chairman of the Third Committee introduced the background of WMO concerns. He stated that:

> The World Meteorological Organization *had specifically in mind activities* carried out under its Voluntary Observing Ships' Scheme which is an important element of the World Weather Watch and *activities* carried out under the projects and programmes of organizations such as the Marine Meteorological Services, the Tropical Cyclone Project and the Integrated Global Ocean Station System.[128]

---

as Documents of the Conference, Resumed Ninth Session)", Doc. A/CONF.62/C.3/SR.46, 1980, para.5.

125 Ibid.

126 See, for instance, "Report of the Sixth Session of IOC/ABE-LOS", Doc. IOC/ABE-LOS VI/3, at p. 6.

127 Katharina Bork et al., "The Legal Regulation of Floats and Gliders - In Quest of a New Regime?", 306.

128 Emphasis added. "Report of the Chairman of the Third Committee: Extract from the Official Records of the Third United Nations Conference on the Law of the Sea, Volume XIV

This statement indicates that the Chairman's viewpoint was only concerned with a limited number of activities in the framework of WMO. Resolution 45 (Cg-18) also buttresses this observation. In its chapeau, the Resolution recalls, *inter alia*, the provisions of Part XIII on marine scientific research of UNCLOS, the report of UNCLOS III including the content of the letter sent by the Chairman of the Third Committee to the Secretary-General of WMO on 25 August 1980, and that "the present Marine Meteorology and Oceanography Programme and Tropical Cyclone Programme, which use both vessels, under the Voluntary Observing Ship (VOS) Scheme, and [...] surface observing platforms, and strive to provide adequate meteorological coverage from the ocean areas, including areas within the exclusive economic zones, falling therefore under the content and the spirit of the letter [...]".[129] These statements indicate that the letter potentially only addresses the legal issues surrounding a limited number of activities under WMO.

4.3.4.3 WMO Resolution 45 (Cg-18) and its Implications for the Interpretation of the Term "Marine Scientific Research" and for Shaping Subsequent Practice

Because WMO Resolution 45 (Cg-18) explicitly excludes relevant WMO marine observations from the scope of marine scientific research under UNCLOS, one may query its implications for interpreting the term "marine scientific research", and for shaping subsequent practice in this regard.

According to the Convention of the World Meteorological Organization, the World Meteorological Congress is the general assembly of delegates representing Members of WMO.[130] In a vote in the Congress, each Member has one vote and decisions shall be by a two-thirds majority of the votes cast for and against except certain circumstances.[131] This means that more than two-thirds of Members of WMO have voted in favor of the draft document of WMO Resolution 45 (Cg-18); otherwise, it would not have been adopted.

It might be controversial whether the Resolution can be considered as a subsequent agreement between the parties to UNCLOS regarding the interpretation of the term "marine scientific research" in the meaning of Article 31(3)(a) of VCLT. Several factors need to be noted. First, the Resolution was adopted

(Summary Records, Plenary, General Committee, First and Third Committees, as well as Documents of the Conference, Resumed Ninth Session)", Doc. A/CONF.62/L.61, 1980, at p. 134.

129 "Abridged Final Report of the Eighteenth session of World Meteorological Congress", Doc. WMO - No.1236, at pp. 146–147.

130 Convention of the World Meteorological Organization, Article 7(a).

131 Ibid., Article 11.

by WMO, rather than a platform that is generally acknowledged to have the competence to adopt resolutions that involve the interpretation of UNCLOS.[132] The legitimacy and credibility of this Resolution may be compromised. Second, the information on the number of States voting for the Resolution is unavailable.[133] It is unclear if the number meets the quantitative requirement, if any, contained in the element of "[the] subsequent agreement between the parties" under Article 31(3)(a) of VCLT.

This being said, considering the broad membership of WMO,[134] the number of States that support the statement made in the Resolution is significant. This indicates that the Resolution will play a crucial role in influencing State practice on this matter. The implications of this resolution for the present research will be further addressed in Chapter 7 on the case study of operational oceanographic activities.

4.3.5 *GOOS*

GOOS is "a sustained collaborative system of ocean observations, encompassing *in situ* networks, satellite systems, governments, UN agencies and individual scientists".[135] The system is governed by three different bodies: the GOOS Steering Committee that provides oversight, the GOOS Expert Panels (respectively on Physics and Climate, Biogeochemistry, and Biology and Ecosystem) that guides system requirements, and Observation Coordination Groups that implement global unified network execution, which is the Observations Programme Area of the WMO-IOC Joint Commission for Oceanography and Marine Meteorology (JCOMM).[136] The GOOS Steering Committee was established in 2011 by IOC under its Resolution XXVI-8, to replace the Intergovernmental

132 A similar concern was raised during the IOC/ABE-LOS meetings about the competence of IOC and IOC/ABE-LOS to interpret UNCLOS provisions on the ground that interpreting the Convention is within the scope of SPLOS and not that of IOC. See "Report of the Fourth Session of IOC/ABE-LOS", Doc. IOC/ABE-LOS IV/3, at p. 9; "Report of the Sixth Session of IOC/ABE-LOS", Doc. IOC/ABE-LOS VI/3, at p. 6.

133 WMO has only published Abridged Final Report of the Eighteenth Session of World Meteorological Congress, which does not include information on the actual voting of the Resolution.

134 As of the time of the 18th session of World Meteorological Congress, WMO has 193 Members. See "Abridged Final Report of the Eighteenth session of World Meteorological Congress", Doc. WMO - No.1236, at p. 3.

135 For more information on the GOOS, see its official website, "The Global Ocean Observing System", available at http://www.goosocean.org/.

136 The official website of the GOOS, "Who we are", available at https://www.goosocean.org/index.php?option=com_content&view=article&id=119&Itemid=120.

IOC-WMO-UNEP Committee for GOOS (I-GOOS)[137] to simplify the governance of GOOS.[138] The Steering Committee is comprised of five Members representing the five IOC regions, and ten Scientific and Technical Experts.[139] The Steering Committee fulfils its mandate to provide oversight for GOOS "under the guidance and governance of the [IOC] Governing Bodies, and with the active participation and support of Member States".[140] In this regard, the activities undertaken by GOOS and its components manifest to a certain extent the subsequent practice of the Member States of IOC.

GOOS was created by IOC in 1991 as a response to the increasing needs of many nations for gathering "the information required to improve forecasts of climate change, the management of marine resources, mitigation of the effects of natural disasters, and the use and protection of the coastal zone and coastal ocean".[141] There was also a strong recognition that "a better understanding of ocean climate and ecosystems, as well as human impacts and vulnerabilities, requires the coordination of a continuous and long-term system of ocean observations".[142] What is also needed is an operational system that facilitates data management and exchange to fulfil the data and information requirements of a broad spectrum of user groups serving various purposes.[143] Against this background, GOOS was established to coordinate observations around the global oceans and to distribute freely and openly the data gathered in real-time to any potential user, through the Observations Program Area of JCOMM.[144]

In 2009, the need for international integration and coordination of interdisciplinary ocean observation was further emphasized in the OceanObs'09 Conference.[145] Based on the "impressive agreement" among 600 participants

---

137 For more information about I-GOOS, see its legacy webpage, "I-GOOS (dissolved 2011)", available at https://www.jcomm.info/index.php?option=com_oe&task=viewGroupRecord&groupID=240.

138 IOC, "Strengthening and Streamlining GOOS", IOC Resolution XXVI–8, 2011.

139 Ibid.

140 Ibid.

141 For more information, see the official website of GOOS, "Overview: History of GOOS", available at http://www.goosocean.org/index.php?option=com_content&view=article&id=10&Itemid=110.

142 For more information, see the official website of GOOS, "why a GOOS?", available at http://www.goosocean.org/index.php?option=com_content&view=article&id=118&Itemid=109.

143 Worth D. Nowlin Jr and Thomas C Malone, "Research and GOOS", *Marine Technology Society Journal* 37, no. 3 (2003): 42.

144 The networked observations are coordinated and implemented by JCOMM. For more information on the JCOMM, see its introduction on the official website, "About JCOMM", available at https://www.jcomm.info/index.php?option=com_content&view=article&id=150&Itemid=97.

145 For more information on this Conference, see http://www.oceanobs09.net/.

from 36 countries to work collectively, a Framework of Ocean Observing was outlined "to guide the ocean observation community as a whole to establish an integrated and sustained global observing system".[146] Since then, GOOS conforms to the approach designed in the Framework of Ocean Observing.

The Framework provides a structure that is centered on Essential Ocean Variables (EOVs),[147] rather than on specific observing systems, platforms, programs, or regions. The contents of the Framework can be divided into three parts: 1) what measurements should be selected as EOVs; 2) how to measure EOVs; 3) how to manage or make available their data products.[148] Data and information on EOVs are gathered by various elements of the ocean observing networks coordinated by JCOMM. All the data and information products are required to "support both research and decision-making in diverse areas such as climate studies and adaptation, disaster warning and mitigation, commerce, and ecosystem-based management".[149] This design helps to avoid duplications of efforts across observing platforms and networks and maximizing the utility of collected data.[150]

This collaborative system dramatically enhances the integration of efforts in the collection of oceanographic data, or EOVs to be more accurate. However, it also further complicates the relationship between marine scientific research and other ocean data collection activities. A single set of data, which are defined by the list of GOOS EOVs, can be collected by different tools or platforms, be it floats, gliders or remote sensing technologies, used by different users for different purposes.[151] As concluded in Chapter 3 of this book, the difference between marine scientific research and other ocean data collection

146 The Task Team for an Integrated Framework for Sustained Ocean Observing, "A Framework for Ocean Observing", Doc. IOC/INF-1284, 2012, at p. 2.

147 For a detailed introduction to EOVs and a list of GOOS EOVs, see http://www.goosocean.org/index.php?option=com_content&view=article&id=14&Itemid=114.

148 The Task Team for an Integrated Framework for Sustained Ocean Observing, "A Framework for Ocean Observing", Doc. IOC/INF-1284, at p. 2.

149 Ibid., at p. 13.

150 Argo Project is one of the components to GOOS through the collaboration under the observations Programme Area of the JCOMM. Other examples include, OceanSITES, the International OceanGliders Program, the Global Ocean Ship-based Hydrographic Investigation Program (GO-SHIP), the Global Sea Level Observing System (GLOSS), and Data Buoy Cooperation Panel (DBCP). For more information on the platforms involved, see the official website of the JCOMM, "Observations Programme Area", available at https://www.jcomm.info/index.php?option=com_content&view=article&id=338&Itemid=38.

151 Potential uses of data on EOVs are provided at the official website of the GOOS, "Strategic Mapping", available at http://www.goosocean.org/index.php?option=com_content&view=article&id=120&Itemid=277.

activities mainly concerns the purposes or objectives of the activity. However, through the integration of efforts in collecting ocean data as noted above, it is hard to say which factor(s) should be decisive when determining the legal classification of the activities involved in GOOS: the type of data that are collected, the tools or platforms that are used for ocean data collection, the user of the collected data, or the subsequent use of the data. The integration of efforts in the collection of ocean data and its implications for the regulation of the activities concerned will be further elaborated upon in Chapters 5 and 7 of this book.

4.4 Concluding Remarks

The investigation into the national legislation and policies on marine scientific research and subsequent practice manifest in global fora points in the same direction – in some cases, States take different views as to what constitutes marine scientific research under UNCLOS. This conclusion is primarily based on the summary of statements by delegations in the IOC/ABE-LOS discussions, and the BBNJ negotiations. However, the adoption of WMO Resolution 45 (Cg-18) indicates that a significant number of States (at least 126 Members, approximately two-thirds of the number of WMO Members as of the time of voting) agree that the collection of data concerning the variables identified in the list annexed to the Resolution, under the VOS Scheme and surface observing platforms, do not constitute marine scientific research, and thus are excluded from the scope of the UNCLOS Part XIII regime. The Resolution also helps clarify the uncertainties arising from the letter sent by the Chairman of the Third Committee at UNCLOS III to the Secretary-General of WMO concerning the applicability of the UNCLOS marine scientific research regime to certain kinds of ocean data collection activities.

However, despite the absence of agreement on the definition of the term "marine scientific research", it appears that the operation of the UNCLOS marine scientific research regime is generally in good shape. States are willing to enter into practical arrangements with each other even if they have different positions on the legal classification of the activities concerned so as to solve practical problems in ocean data collection. Examples of such practical arrangements include the Argo Guidelines and bilateral or multilateral cooperative arrangements on the regulation of oceanographic data collection activities involving the use of floats and surface drifting buoys and the deployment of XBTs by ships of opportunity in EEZs. This could be attributed to the flexibility of the Convention, especially the provisions providing due regard obligations,[152] the basis for the resolution of conflicts concerning unattributed rights in the EEZ of a coastal States,[153] and the obligation of promoting international cooperation and creating favorable conditions for marine scientific research.[154]

Relevant practice indicates that whether States are willing to establish practical arrangements depends on two major factors. The first factor is whether the States concerned share common interests in marine scientific research, or more broadly in ocean data collection. Practice in the South China Sea region and the Convention area of OSPAR indicates that the common interests might be different from one region to another. The second factor concerns the objects and purposes of the ocean data collection activities concerned and the means and methods deployed. States are more likely to reach cooperative agreements in less sensitive fields of research. As indicated by the discussions under the IOC/ABE-LOS sub-group on the collection of oceanographic data, States' willingness to cooperate also depends on the means that are used for ocean data collection, and the type of data that are to be collected.

Cooperation in marine scientific research provides several implications for the current research. Firstly, both multilateral and bilateral cooperative arrangements can create practical approaches that circumvent some of the bureaucratic obligations of the researching State concerning the undertaking of a research project under foreign jurisdiction. Besides, as shown by the OSPAR Code of Conduct, cooperation and collaboration play a vital role in reducing the adverse impact of ocean data collection activities on the marine environment. Implications of these findings will be further addressed in the subsequent chapters of this study, especially Chapters 6 and 7.

Secondly, through cooperation and the integration of efforts in ocean data collection, the line between marine scientific research and other ocean data collection activities is becoming increasingly blurred. Through cooperative platforms, such as GOOS, the same set of data could be collected by different tools or platforms, obtained freely by different users, and utilized for different purposes. It is unclear which factor(s) mentioned above would be determinant in the legal classification of the relevant activities. This being said, it is also noted that this increasingly blurred line does not result in any significant conflict between or among States as one might expect. Partly this is because many of the related activities are conducted in the form of cooperation. It is common in practice that this kind of cooperation covers not only

152 UNCLOS, Articles 56(2), 58(3).
153 Ibid., Article 59.
154 Ibid., Articles 242, 243.

marine scientific research but also other activities, including the conservation and management of marine living resources, exploration activities, and the protection and preservation of the marine environment. The integration of efforts in ocean data collection and its implications for the regulation of the activities concerned will be further elaborated upon in Chapters 5 and 7 of this book.

Lastly, it is worth emphasizing that the Argo Guidelines and WMO Resolution 45 (Cg-18) set out different legal frameworks for the regulation of ocean data collection activities covered by the instruments. Neither of the instruments addresses the legal classification of the activities concerned explicitly.[155] The reasons for the different treatment of the activities concerned and its implication for the legal classification of certain ocean data collection activities will be addressed in Chapter 7 of this book.

Having examined the subsequent State practice on ocean data collection activities, the following chapter will look at rules contained in other international conventions on ocean data collection. It will try to discern the legal implications of such conventions for the legal classification of ocean data collection activities and the understanding of the scope of marine scientific research under UNCLOS.

155 Although WMO Resolution 45 (Cg-18) excludes certain WMO marine observations from the scope of marine scientific research under UNCLOS, it does not define the legal classification of these activities when undertaken in the EEZ of a coastal State – whether it falls under Article 58(1) concerning the rights of other States or Article 59 concerning unattributed rights.

CHAPTER 5

Regulation of Ocean Data Collection Activities under Other International Conventions

5.1 Introduction

As discussed in previous chapters, to understand the scope of marine scientific research and its relationship with other ocean data collection activities, it is necessary to look beyond the text of UNCLOS and examine relevant provisions included in other international conventions. Chapter 2 concludes that the interpretation of pertinent UNCLOS provisions cannot be isolated from subsequent developments, including legal developments that occurred after the adoption of UNCLOS. In this respect, this chapter aims to examine relevant international conventions other than UNCLOS. Relevant customary rules of international law and soft law instruments will not be discussed in this chapter. The reasons for not discussing relevant customary rules of international law include that the identification of customary rules of international law is a highly controversial issue,[1] and it remains largely unclear what customary rules may be applicable for marine scientific research.[2] Besides, many, if not all, customary rules of international law on marine scientific research are already included in UNCLOS, which has been discussed in Chapter 3 of this book. As to soft law instruments, they have been addressed as subsequent practice in Chapter 4.

Examination of rules contained in other international conventions mainly serves two purposes. Firstly, other international conventions serve as an essential means for interpreting the term "marine scientific research". Other international conventions play a role in interpreting the term "marine scientific research" in the context of UNCLOS through 1) contributing to understanding the "ordinary meaning" of the term,[3] 2) being "taken into account" in

1 See, for instance, Tullio Treves, "The Development of the Law of the Sea since the Adoption of the UN Convention on the Law of the Sea: Achievements and Challenges for the Future", 41–43.

2 See, for instance, Tullio Treves, "Marine Scientific Research", para.16.

3 VCLT, Article 31(1). This function of other conventions has illustratively been described as an "elaborate law dictionary", Campbell McLachlan, "The Principle of Systemic Integration and Article 31(3)(c) of the Vienna Convention", 315. See also Martti Koskenniemi, "Fragmentation of International Law: Difficulties Arising from the Diversification and Expansion of

 DOI:10.1163/9789004508590_006

the process of interpretation as "any relevant rules of international law applicable in the relations between the parties",[4] and 3) serving as a supplementary means of treaty interpretation under Article 32 of VCLT.[5]

Secondly, an examination of relevant provisions of other international conventions provides a picture of how ocean data collection activities are regulated, when the legal classification of the activities concerned is unclear or undefined. It might be the case that the ocean data collection activities in the context of other conventions do not fall within the category of marine scientific research under UNCLOS.[6] In this case, the value of relevant provisions of other international conventions for interpreting the term "marine scientific research" under UNCLOS might be limited. Therefore, it is necessary to look

---

International Law (Report of the Study Group of the International Law Commission)", UN Doc. A/CN.4/L.682, paras.445, 447, 450.

4 VCLT, Article 31(3)(c). It remains unclear what "rules of international law" to be taken into account under this provision. For example, as Sands comments, "what [Article 31(3)(c)] actually means in practice is difficult to know since it appears to have been expressly relied upon only very occasionally in judicial practice. It also seems to have attracted little academic comment. There appears to be a general reluctance to refer to Article 31(3)(c)". Philippe Sands, "Sustainable Development: Treaty, Custom and the Cross-Fertilization of International Law", in *International Law and Sustainable Development: Past Achievements and Future Challenges*, edited by Alan Boyle and David Freestone (Oxford University Press, 1999), 49–50. For a further discussion on the exact scope of various elements under Article 31(3)(c), see Panos Merkouris, *Article 31(3)(c) VCLT and the Principle of Systemic Integration: Normative Shadows in Plato's Cave*, 18–24; Campbell McLachlan, "The Principle of Systemic Integration and Article 31(3)(c) of the Vienna Convention", 310–319; Duncan French, "Treaty Interpretation and the Incorporation of Extraneous Legal Rules", 304–307; Ulf Linderfalk, "Who Are 'The Parties'? Article 31, Paragraph 3(c) of the 1969 Vienna Convention and the 'Principle of Systemic Integration' Revisited", *Netherlands International Law Review* 55, no. 3 (2008). A discussion about the scope of this provision in the context of interpreting UNCLOS can be found in James Harrison, "Judicial Law-Making and the Developing Order of the Oceans".

5 VCLT, Article 32. It remains an open question that apart from "preparatory work of the treaty and the circumstances of its conclusion" what to be considered as "supplementary means of interpretation" under this provision. As discussed in Chapter 4, the ILC study group divides subsequent practice into two kinds: 1) subsequent practice that meets the criteria of Article 31(3)(b), and 2) subsequent practice under Article 32 as a means of supplementary means of interpretation. In the same token, there appears to be no immediate reason to reject the assumption that rules contained in other international conventions that do not fit under the criteria of Article 31(3)(c) would play a role in treaty interpretation under Article 32 as a supplementary means of interpretation.

6 As can be noted below, the term "marine scientific research" has rarely been used in any international conventions apart from UNCLOS. Some conventions use the term "scientific research". However, the same term may have different meanings in different contexts, fulfilling different objects and purposes. See ITLOS, *The MOX Plant Case* (*Ireland v. United Kingdom*), *Provisional Measures*, Order of 3 December 2001, paras.50–51.

beyond the terms used under the instruments and focus on the rights and obligations in relation to such activities, to see how they are regulated under instruments that have received wide-ranging support. Besides, as concluded in Chapter 3, UNCLOS sets up the obligations for States concerned to engage in consultation with each other and properly balance the interests that may be involved. In this regard, other international conventions may be relevant in shedding light on the interpretation and implementation of more general legal terms under UNCLOS, such as the due regard obligation. Inspirations can be obtained from these instruments on how to balance the interests involved and what elements could be considered in the consultation.

This chapter only addresses global international conventions that have been widely ratified by States. Conventions with a higher number of parties will, in principle, have more weight both in assisting in interpreting the term "marine scientific research" and in finding out the appropriate regulation of a specific type of ocean data collection activity if the legal classification of the activity concerned remains unclear or controversial.[7]

Based on a review of UNGA resolutions on oceans and the law of the sea,[8] reports of the UN Secretary-General on oceans and the law of the sea,[9] and existing literature on the legal regulation of marine scientific research and other relevant ocean data collection activities,[10] global international conventions

---

7 See Alan Boyle, "Further Development of the Law of the Sea Convention: Mechanisms for Change", 569, 571.

8 For a comprehensive list of UNGA resolutions on Oceans and the Law of the Sea, see the official website of DOALOS, "Oceans and the Law of the Sea in the General Assembly of the United Nations – General Assembly resolutions and decisions", available at http://www.un.org/Depts/los/general_assembly/general_assembly_resolutions.htm.

9 For a comprehensive list of Reports of the Secretary-General on oceans and the law of the sea, see the official website of DOALOS, "Oceans and the Law of the Sea in the General Assembly of the United Nations – Reports of the Secretary-General", available at https://www.un.org/Depts/los/general_assembly/general_assembly_reports.htm.

10 To name but a few, Tullio Treves, "Marine Scientific Research"; Tim Stephens and Donald Rothwell, "Marine Scientific Research"; Florian H.Th. Wegelein, *Marine Scientific Research: The Operation and Status of Research Vessels and Other Platforms in International Law*; Montserrat Gorina-Ysern, *An International Regime for Marine Scientific Research*; Aldo Chircop, "Advances in Ocean Knowledge and Skill: Implications for the MSR Regime"; Harriet Harden-Davies, "The Regulation of Marine Scientific Research: Addressing Challenges, Advancing Knowledge"; Lyle Glowka, "The Deepest of Ironies: Genetic Resources, Marine Scientific Research, and the Area"; Alexander Proelss, "International Legal Challenges Concerning Marine Scientific Research in the Era of Climate Change" (paper presented at the Securing the Ocean for the Next Generation: Papers from the Law of the Sea Institute, UC Berkeley–Korea Institute of Ocean Science and Technology Conference, Seoul, Korea, 2012); Montserrat Gorina-Ysern, "Marine Scientific Research:

that might be of relevance for the current study mainly include the Convention on Biological Diversity (CBD) and its Nagoya Protocol, the United Nations Framework Convention on Climate Change (UNFCCC), the Convention on the Prevention of Marine Pollution by Dumping of Wastes and Other Matter (London Convention) and its London Protocol, and the International Convention on the Regulation of Whaling (ICRW). One commonality shared by the ocean data collection activities covered by these conventions and marine scientific research is that they all involve observations or sampling in the marine environment. The relationship between these activities and marine scientific research will be discussed below. Sections 5.2 to 5.5 of this chapter consecutively examine the relevant provisions contained in CBD and its Nagoya Protocol, UNFCCC, the London Convention and its London Protocol, and ICRW, followed by some concluding remarks in Section 5.6.

5.2 Convention on Biological Diversity and Its Nagoya Protocol

CBD[11] is the first international treaty to take a holistic, ecosystem-based approach to the conservation and sustainable use of biological diversity.[12] According to Article 4 of CBD, it applies to all activities that involve access to and utilization of genetic resources, including marine genetic resources.[13] UNCLOS makes no explicit reference to (marine) genetic resources. CBD defines this term as any material of plant, animal, microbial or other origin

Overview of Major Issues, Programmes and Their Objectives", in *Routledge Handbook of Ocean Resources and Management*, edited by Hance D Smith, Juan Luis Suárez de Vivero, and Tundi S Agardy (Routledge, 2015).

11 CBD. The Convention on Biological Diversity was opened for signature on 5 June 1992 at the United Nations Conference on Environment and Development (the Rio "Earth Summit") and entered into force on 29 December 1993. As of June 2020, it has 196 Parties, 168 Signatures. For more information, see the official website of CBD, "List of Parties", available at https://www.cbd.int/information/parties.shtml.

12 "Study of the Relationship between the Convention on Biological Diversity and the United Nations Convention on the Law of the Sea with Regard to the Conservation and Sustainable Use of Genetic Resources on the Deep Seabed (Decision II/10 of the Conference of the Parties to the Convention on Biological Diversity)", UN Doc. UNEP/CBD/SBSTTA/8/INF/3/Rev.1, 2003, para.68.

13 Article 4 of CBD stipulates that the provisions of CBD apply to "(a) in the case of components of biological diversity, in areas within the limits of its national jurisdiction; and (b) in the case of processes and activities, regardless of where their effects occur, carried out under its jurisdiction or control, within the area of its national jurisdiction or beyond the limits of national jurisdiction". CBD, Article 4.

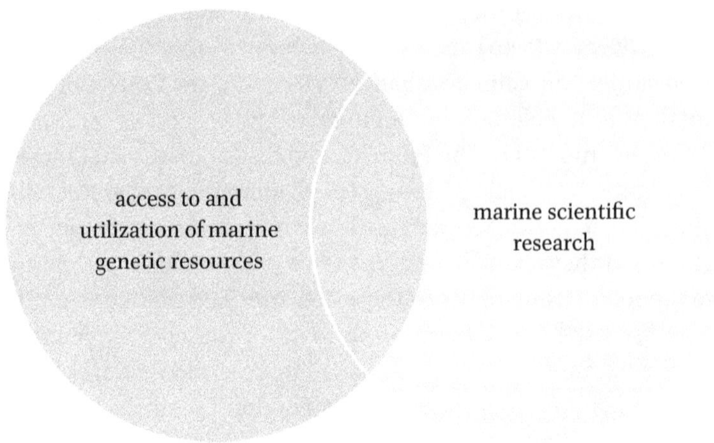

FIGURE 1 The relationship between marine scientific research and the activities regulated under CBD

containing functional units of heredity that is of actual or potential value.[14] The link between CBD and ocean data collection activities (including marine scientific research) can be explained by the fact that some ocean data collection projects take samples of living resources in the marine environment and make use (scientifically or commercially) of the genetic material of such resources.

In 2010, the Nagoya Protocol was adopted.[15] The Protocol further elaborates the rights and obligations enshrined in CBD regarding access to and benefit sharing of genetic resources.

The term "marine scientific research" occurs neither in CBD nor the protocols adopted under its framework. The relationship between marine scientific research and the activities regulated under CBD and its Nagoya Protocol is shown in Figure 1. The two kinds of activities overlap with each other to a certain degree. However, not all marine scientific research projects involve access to marine genetic resources. On the other hand, not all activities concerning marine genetic resources qualify as marine scientific research.[16] To the extent

14 Ibid., Article 2.

15 Nagoya Protocol. The Protocol entered into force on 12 October 2014. As of June 2020, it has 124 Parties, 92 Signatures. For more information, see the official website of the Nagoya Protocol, "Parties to the Nagoya Protocol", available at https://www.cbd.int/abs/nagoya-protocol/signatories/default.shtml.

16 It may constitute exploration of natural resources. A further discussion on the relationship between marine scientific research and exploration is included in Chapter 3.3.2.1 of this book. The legal classification of access to marine genetic resources will be further addressed in Chapter 6.3 of this book.

that the two regimes overlap, relevant provisions of CBD and its protocols may shed light on the interpretation and implementation of the UNCLOS marine scientific research regime.

The most relevant provisions of CBD about marine scientific research or ocean data collection in general are contained in Article 15, which addresses access to genetic resources. This article sets out several requirements for access to genetic resources from the provider Contracting Parties.[17] As a general principle, the authority to determine access rests with the Contracting Party providing genetic resources.[18] Following this principle, it is stipulated that unless otherwise determined by the provider State, access to genetic resources shall be subject to prior informed consent of the provider State,[19] and when granted, shall be based on mutually agreed terms.[20] The State which provides genetic resources shall facilitate access "for environmentally sound uses" by other States, and not "impose restrictions that run counter to the objectives of this Convention".[21] Sections 5.2.1 and 5.2.2 will look into these requirements consecutively.

Apart from the provisions on the regulation of access to marine genetic resources, CBD and the Nagoya Protocol also address issues concerning the utilization of marine genetic resources. Genetic resources are gathered from the (marine) environment for purposes of utilization. As concluded in Chapter 3 of this book, the function or purpose of the activities concerned plays an essential role in the legal classification. For a better understanding of potential uses of marine genetic resources, the following section will also examine the provisions on the utilization of genetic resources (Section 5.2.3).

---

17 Under CBD, the Contracting Party providing genetic resources can be 1) the country of origin of such resources or 2) the Party that has acquired the genetic resources in accordance with this Convention. See CBD, Article 15(3). Since the UNCLOS marine scientific research regime is only concerned with *in situ* access to genetic resources, in order to have comparable sets of requirements, the term "provider Contracting Party" in the following analysis only refers to the country of origin that provides genetic resources to the potential users.

18 Ibid., Article 15(1).

19 Ibid., Article 15(5).

20 Ibid., Article 15(4).

21 Ibid., Article 15(2). As stated in its Article 1, CBD has three fundamental objectives: a) the conservation of biological diversity, b) the sustainable use of its components, and c) the fair and equitable sharing of the benefits arising out of the utilization of genetic resources, including by appropriate access to genetic resources and by appropriate transfer of relevant technologies, taking into account all rights over those resources and to technologies, and by appropriate funding. Ibid., Article 1.

5.2.1 *The Prior Informed Consent Requirement*

The first requirement under CBD that warrants a closer examination is the one concerning prior informed consent.

Both the UNCLOS marine scientific research regime and CBD acknowledge the right of other States to access to marine genetic resources that serves scientific purposes.[22] As to the rights and duties of the coastal State, UNCLOS stipulates that in the exercise of its sovereignty, the coastal State has the exclusive right to regulate, authorize and conduct marine scientific research in its territorial sea.[23] All foreign marine scientific research therein "shall be conducted only with the express consent of under the conditions set forth by the coastal State".[24] In its EEZ or on its continental shelf, the coastal State also has jurisdiction over marine scientific research.[25] Foreign marine scientific research shall be conducted with the consent of the coastal State.[26] In normal circumstances, pursuant to Article 246(3), the coastal State is obliged to grant its consent for marine scientific research projects "to be carried out in accordance with this Convention exclusively for peaceful purposes and in order to increase scientific knowledge of the marine environment for the benefit of all mankind" unless the projects fall under the circumstances under Article 246(5).[27]

However, unlike the provisions set out in Article 246 of UNCLOS, under CBD, the provider Contracting Party is not obliged to grant its consent to the access to genetic resources, either in its territorial sea or in its EEZ or on its continental shelf. This can be explained by the overarching principle of CBD concerning access to genetic resources, *i.e.*, the provider Contracting Party enjoys the sovereign rights over such resources.[28] Access to resources that are under the sovereign rights of the provider State naturally requires its prior consent. It appears unreasonable to render it obligatory for the provider Contracting Party to grant the consent if there is no particular reason to do so. Given that conservation of biological diversity is among its three objectives, CBD provides that if access to genetic resources is "for environmentally sound uses", the

22 UNCLOS, Article 238.

23 Ibid., Article 245.

24 Ibid.

25 Ibid., Articles 56(1)(b), 246(1).

26 Ibid., Article 246(2).

27 Ibid., Article 246(3), (5). The implications of this provision have been addressed in Chapter 3.2.4 of this book.

28 See, for example, CBD, Articles 3, 15(1).

Contracting Party shall facilitate such access.[29] Apart from the conventional obligation to facilitate access "for environmentally sound uses", Article 8(a) of the Nagoya Protocol requires each Party to "create conditions to promote and encourage research which contributes to the conservation and sustainable use of biological diversity".[30]

The fact that the provider Contracting Party is not obliged to grant its consent under CBD can be compared with Article 246(5) of UNCLOS. This provision lists scenarios in which the coastal State may withhold its consent to a foreign marine scientific research project to be conducted in its EEZ or on its continental shelf in its discretion.[31] One such scenario is when the project "is of direct significance for the exploration and exploitation of natural resources".[32] As discussed in Chapter 3.2.4.3 of this book, the scope of marine scientific research covered by this phrase is controversial, especially considering the qualifier "direct". It is hard to say if all marine scientific research activities involving access to marine genetic resources would be considered "of direct significance for the exploration and exploitation of natural resources". According to the logic of UNCLOS, the coastal State has the right to determine whether a research project is of such nature based on the information submitted by the researching State under Article 249(1).[33] In this sense, if the coastal State considers that a research project involving marine genetic resources "is of direct significance for the exploration and exploitation of natural resources" or falls under other scenarios under Article 246(5), the application of relevant CBD provisions and Article 246 of UNCLOS would provide similar outcomes.

Under Article 246(5) of UNCLOS, situations in which the coastal State may withhold its consent to foreign marine scientific research projects are included for the protection of the rights and jurisdiction of the coastal State in its EEZ

29 Ibid., Article 15(2), (5). It has been submitted that in the context of CBD, the overarching principle to protect the provider Contracting Party's sovereign rights over genetic resources is undermined to a certain degree by the purpose of promoting the objective of CBD to conserve and sustainably utilize biological diversity. See Ad Hoc Open-Ended Working Group on Access and Benefit-Sharing, "Report of A Workshop on Access and Benefit-Sharing in Non-Commercial Biodiversity Research", UNEP/CBD/WG-ABS/7/INF/6, 2009, at p. 3. See also Elisa Morgera, Elsa Tsioumani, and Matthias Buck, *Unraveling the Nagoya Protocol: A Commentary on the Nagoya Protocol on Access and Benefit-Sharing to the Convention on Biological Diversity* (Martinus Nijhoff Publishers, 2014), 181.

30 Nagoya Protocol, Article 8(a).

31 UNCLOS, Article 246(5).

32 Ibid., Article 246(5)(a).

33 For a further discussion on this matter, see Chapter 3.2.4.3 of this book.

or on its continental shelf.[34] Looking at the underlying logic of the UNCLOS marine scientific research regime, it is submitted that the obligation for the coastal State to grant consent to foreign marine scientific research projects undertaken in its EEZ or on its continental shelf under Article 246(3) is a manifestation of the consensus of the parties to UNCLOS to promote marine scientific research in general. However, when such projects are undertaken in the territorial sea of the coastal State, or when they fall within the circumstances under Article 246(5), the need to protect the coastal State's sovereignty in its territorial sea and its interests over natural resources, environmental protection, and the construction and use of artificial islands, installations and structures in its EEZ or on its continental shelf should prevail.

From the above comparison, one can see that both CBD (and its Nagoya Protocol) and the UNCLOS marine scientific research regime reflect a delicate balance between the respective interests of the coastal State (in the context of CBD, the provider Contracting Party)[35] and other States. Notably, the two

---

34 This observation is based on the drafting history of Article 246(5). This provision originates from a draft text prepared by the Informal Group of Juridical Experts. This draft text was an expanded version of an article contained in Part III of ISNT reading as:
Marine scientific research beyond the territorial sea, in the economic zone and on the continental shelf, shall be conducted by States as well as by appropriate international organizations in such a manner that the rights of the coastal State, as provided for in this Convention, are respected.
The text proposed by the Group revised this article as:
1. The consent of the coastal State shall be obtained in respect of any scientific research in its economic zone or continental shelf bearing upon the exploration and exploitation of the living or non-living resources.
2. The consent of the coastal State shall in any event be obtained in respect of drilling, or of the use of explosives or means with similar effects on the living organisms of the marine environment or on the sea-bed or subsoil.
3. The consent of the coastal State shall also be obtained in respect of scientific research in its economic zone or continental shelf which would unduly interfere with activities over which the coastal State has jurisdiction as provided for in this Convention.
The connection between these two draft texts indicates that the situations listed under the proposal mooted by the Group were meant to give effect to the idea that marine scientific research in the EEZ or on the continental shelf of a coastal State "shall be conducted [...] in such a manner that the rights of the coastal State, as provided for in this Convention, are respected". For more information on the drafting history of this provision, see Myron H. Nordquist et al., eds., *United Nations Convention on the Law of the Sea, 1982: A Commentary* (*Vol. IV*), 501–505.

35 In order to make the text more concise, in this section, when comparing CBD and the UNCLOS marine scientific research regime, the coastal State also refers to the provider Contracting Party in the context of CBD.

regimes have some similar traits that are relevant to the current research.[36] For pertinent activities conducted in the territorial sea of a coastal State, or for activities conducted in the EEZ or on the continental shelf of the coastal State that fall under Article 246(5) of UNCLOS, both the UNCLOS marine scientific research regime and CBD emphasize the sovereignty or jurisdiction of the coastal State and give the coastal State discretional power to determine whether or not to grant its consent. This similarity indicates an agreement shared among the drafters of UNCLOS and those of CBD to give the coastal State more extensive decision-making power in some instances, in order to protect the coastal State's sovereignty in its territorial sea and its sovereign rights and jurisdiction over the natural resources, environmental protection, and the construction and use of artificial islands, installations and structures in its EEZ or on its continental shelf.

5.2.2 *Requirement of Reaching Mutually Agreed Terms*

The requirement of reaching mutually agreed terms under CBD is comparable to Article 249 of UNCLOS concerning the duties of the researching State which undertakes a marine scientific research project in the EEZ or on the continental shelf of a coastal State.[37] Compared to the mutually agreed terms

36 For an interesting and in-depth comparison of the UNCLOS marine scientific research regime and the Nagoya Protocol, see Charlotte Salpin, "The Law of the Sea: A before and an after Nagoya", 156–183.

37 UNCLOS, Article 249(1). Article 249(1) of UNCLOS provides that
States and competent international organizations when undertaking marine scientific research in the exclusive economic zone or on the continental shelf of a coastal State shall comply with the following conditions:
(a) ensure the right of the coastal State, if it so desires, to participate or be represented in the marine scientific research project, especially on board research vessels and other craft or scientific research installations, when practicable, without payment of any remuneration to the scientists of the coastal State and without obligation to contribute towards the costs of the project;
(b) provide the coastal State, at its request, with preliminary reports, as soon as practicable, and with the final results and conclusions after the completion of the research;
(c) undertake to provide access for the coastal State, at its request, to all data and samples derived from the marine scientific research project and likewise to furnish it with data which may be copied and samples which may be divided without detriment to their scientific value;
(d) if requested, provide the coastal State with an assessment of such data, samples and research results or provide assistance in their assessment or interpretation;
(e) ensure, subject to paragraph 2, that the research results are made internationally available through appropriate national or international channels, as soon as practicable;
(f) inform the coastal State immediately of any major change in the research programme;

requirement under CBD, the conditions with which the researching State is obliged to comply under UNCLOS are more formal or fixed, since basically they are limited to the seven conditions listed in Article 249(1).[38] The requirement of conditioning access to genetic resources on attaining mutually agreed terms under CBD suggests an expectation of negotiations between the provider and potential user of genetic resources, given that an access agreement can only be reached after successful negotiations.[39] The terms agreed upon as a result of negotiations are likely to be more flexible than the conditions listed in Article 249(1) of UNCLOS. In this regard, CBD gives more discretion to the provider State (who enjoys sovereign rights over the genetic resources).

This being said, under UNCLOS, for marine scientific research projects that fall under Article 246(5), conditions established by the laws and regulations of the coastal State "for the exercise of its discretion to grant or withhold consent" prevail over the conditions outlined in Article 249(1).[40] The coastal State is entitled to prescribe additional obligations as compared to those listed in Article 249(1) in its laws and regulations for foreign marine scientific research projects falling within the scope of Article 246(5). Besides, for marine scientific research undertaken in the territorial sea of the coastal State, it can only be conducted "under the conditions set forth by the coastal State",[41] and such conditions are not limited to those specified in Article 249(1) of UNCLOS.

Therefore, similar to the conclusions drawn above for the comparison of prior informed consent between CBD and the UNCLOS marine scientific research regime, when an activity falls under the circumstances of Article 246(5), or when it is conducted in the territorial sea of a coastal State, both the UNCLOS marine scientific research regime and CBD give the coastal State more flexibility in setting the conditions to be complied with by the researching State.

5.2.3 *Utilization of Genetic Resources*

After genetic resources have been gathered, in most cases they will be sent to laboratories for subsequent utilization. CBD does not contain a specific provision on the utilization of genetic resources. A relevant provision is Article 15(7), which deals with the obligation of each Contracting Party to adopt

---

(g) unless otherwise agreed, remove the scientific research installations or equipment once the research is completed.

38 See for instance, Alfred H. A. Soons, *Marine Scientific Research and the Law of the Sea*, 188.

39 Lyle Glowka, Francoise Burhenne-Guilmin, and Hugh Synge, *A Guide to the Convention on Biological Diversity* (IUCN, 1994), 80.

40 UNCLOS, Article 249(2).

41 Ibid., Article 245.

appropriate measures "with the aim of sharing in a fair and equitable way *the results of research and development* and *the benefits arising from the commercial and other utilization* of genetic resources with the Contracting Party providing such resources" upon mutually agreed terms.[42] The separation of "the results of research and development" and "the benefits arising from the commercial and other utilization" of genetic resources indicates that access to genetic resources can serve different uses, with scientific research being one of them.

The different uses of genetic resources have been dealt with in more detail by the Nagoya Protocol, which defines, for the purposes of the Protocol, "utilization of genetic resources" as "to conduct research and development on the genetic and/or biochemical composition of genetic resources".[43] One author has commented that this definition contains two elements – one on the intent underlying the utilization of genetic resources ("research and development"), and the other on the material on which the conduct focuses ("the genetic and/ or biochemical composition of genetic resources").[44] Of relevance for the current discussions is the first element – the intent of the utilization of genetic resources being "research and development". Unlike Article 15(7) of CBD, which considers "research and development" as one potential use of genetic resources,[45] the Nagoya Protocol adopts a relatively narrow definition of the phrase "utilization of genetic resources". Not all activities involving genetic resources are covered by the phrase "utilization of genetic resources" under the Nagoya Protocol. Article 5(1) of the Nagoya Protocol provides that, "benefits arising from the *utilization of genetic resources* as well as *subsequent applications and commercialization* shall be shared in a fair and equitable way".[46] Under the logic of this provision, "subsequent applications and commercialization" of genetic resources fall beyond the scope of "utilization of genetic resources". So, what is covered by the term "utilization of genetic resources", or more specifically the term "research and development"?

The term "research and development" is not defined in the Nagoya Protocol or CBD. The ordinary meaning of the term "research" is "the systematic investigation into and study of materials and sources in order to establish facts

42 Emphasis added. CBD, Article 15(7).

43 Nagoya Protocol, Article 2(c).

44 Elisa Morgera, Elsa Tsioumani, and Matthias Buck, *Unraveling the Nagoya Protocol: A Commentary on the Nagoya Protocol on Access and Benefit-Sharing to the Convention on Biological Diversity*, 63.

45 Other types of utilization have been termed as "commercial and other utilization". See CBD, Article 15(7).

46 Emphasis added. Nagoya Protocol, Article 5(1).

and reach new conclusions".[47] When it is used with "development", it refers to "two intimately related processes by which new products and new forms of old products are brought into being through technological innovation".[48]

Another pertinent provision is Article 8(a) of the Nagoya Protocol, which requires each Party, when developing and implementing its access and benefit-sharing legislation or regulatory requirements, to:

> [c]reate conditions to promote and encourage research which contributes to the conservation and sustainable use of biological diversity, [...] including through simplified measures on *access for non-commercial research purposes*, taking into account the need to address a change of intent for such research.[49]

Unlike the provisions mentioned above, which make a distinction between *access* for commercial purposes and non-commercial purposes, this provision refers explicitly to "non-commercial research purposes". It thus suggests a distinction between *research* for commercial purposes and non-commercial purposes. This distinction is consistent with the notion of "marine scientific research" under UNCLOS, since UNCLOS does not exclude activities which serve commercial purposes from the scope of marine scientific research.[50] As discussed in Chapter 3 of this research, Article 246 of UNCLOS suggests that marine scientific research projects can be "of direct significance for the exploration and exploitation of natural resources", which arguably implies serving commercial purposes.

Article 8(a) of the Nagoya Protocol also recognizes the need to address a change of intent for such research. One author has submitted that almost all activities involving *in situ* access to genetic resources are conducted by researchers, and often researchers with no commercial intent at the time of

---

47 "Research", Oxford Dictionary of English (Oxford Reference online version, 3rd edition, Oxford University Press, 2015).

48 "Research and Development", Encyclopædia Britannica Online, available at www.britannica.com/EBchecked/topic/499010/research-and-development. See also Elisa Morgera, Elsa Tsioumani, and Matthias Buck, *Unraveling the Nagoya Protocol: A Commentary on the Nagoya Protocol on Access and Benefit-Sharing to the Convention on Biological Diversity*, 63; Maria Julia Oliva, "The Implications of the Nagoya Protocol for the Ethical Sourcing of Biodiversity", in *The 2010 Nagoya Protocol on Access and Benefit-sharing in Perspective*, edited by Elisa Morgera, Matthias Buck, and Elsa Tsioumani (Brill Nijhoff, 2013), 378.

49 Emphasis added. Nagoya Protocol, Article 8(a).

50 The condition is, however, that commercial gain is not the sole purpose of the activity concerned. For more discussion on this matter, see Chapters 3.2 and 3.3 of this book.

access.[51] A change of intent may occur either in the event that researchers themselves discover the potential for commercial development or because individuals outside the research team use the published results and information obtained from that research as a starting point for commercial development.[52] As observed by some scholars, this provision aims at relieving or reducing the unnecessary or unintentional burden placed upon scientific research, particularly if it does not have a commercial intent.[53] However, the implementation of this provision remains a challenging task, especially considering the difficulties in drawing the line between commercial and non-commercial research, and in the identification of the change of intent.[54]

In this regard, it is pertinent to refer to Article 17 of the Nagoya Protocol concerning "monitoring the utilization of genetic resources". As a measure to monitor and enhance transparency about the utilization of genetic resources, this article requires each Party to design one or more checkpoints.[55] It further stipulates that the checkpoints established should "be relevant to the utilization of genetic resources, or to the collection of relevant information at, *inter alia*, any stage of research, development, innovation, pre-commercialization or commercialization."[56] This provision suggests that commercialization of genetic resources is only at the final stage of their utilization, following previous steps including research and development. Implications of this finding will be further addressed in Chapter 6 of this book on the legal regulation of access to marine genetic resources.

---

51 Matthias Buck and Clare Hamilton, "The Nagoya Protocol on Access to Genetic Resources and the Fair and Equitable Sharing of Benefits Arising from Their Utilization to the Convention on Biological Diversity", *Review of European Community & International Environmental Law* 20, no. 1 (2011): 59.

52 See Ad Hoc Open-Ended Working Group on Access and Benefit-Sharing, "Report of A Workshop on Access and Benefit-Sharing in Non-Commercial Biodiversity Research", UNEP/CBD/WG-ABS/7/INF/6, at p. 9.

53 Elisa Morgera, Elsa Tsioumani, and Matthias Buck, *Unraveling the Nagoya Protocol: A Commentary on the Nagoya Protocol on Access and Benefit-Sharing to the Convention on Biological Diversity*, 179. See also Matthias Buck and Clare Hamilton, "The Nagoya Protocol on Access to Genetic Resources and the Fair and Equitable Sharing of Benefits Arising from Their Utilization to the Convention on Biological Diversity", 59.

54 See Tom Dedeurwaerdere et al., "Governing Global Scientific Research Commons under the Nagoya Protocol", in *The 2010 Nagoya Protocol on Access and Benefit-Sharing in Perspective*, edited by Elisa Morgera, Matthias Buck, and Elsa Tsioumani (Brill Nijhoff, 2013), 413.

55 Nagoya Protocol, Article 17(1)(a).

56 Ibid., Article 17(1)(a)(IV).

5.2.4 *Interim Conclusions*

In sum, the regulatory scope of CBD and its Nagoya Protocol overlaps to a certain degree with that of the UNCLOS marine scientific research regime. A comparison of the relevant provisions indicates that in certain scenarios, the two sets of regimes create similar rights and obligations for the States concerned. When an activity that involves access to marine genetic resources and that qualifies as marine scientific research is conducted in the territorial sea of the coastal State, or when this activity is conducted in the EEZ or on the continental shelf of the coastal State and falls under Article 246(5) of UNCLOS, both CBD and its Nagoya Protocol and the UNCLOS marine scientific research regime accord the coastal State with discretional power to determine whether or not to grant its consent, and in setting out the conditions to be complied with by the researching State. This finding indicates that when the sovereignty or jurisdiction of the coastal State is affected by the activities concerned, the two regimes tend to lean towards the coastal State. When access to genetic resources is sought for research without commercial intent, both regimes encourage the coastal State to create simplified or less stringent requirements for the researching State and thus seem to lean towards the side of the researching State.

Apart from this, provisions concerning the utilization of genetic resources contained in CBD and its Nagoya Protocol indicate that genetic resources can be used for multiple purposes, including scientific and commercial. Article 8(a) of the Nagoya Protocol further indicates that research on genetic resources can also serve commercial and non-commercial purposes, and also acknowledges the need to address a change of intent. This implication will be discussed in Chapter 6 of this study concerning the international legal regulation of activities involving access to marine genetic resources.

5.3 United Nations Framework Convention on Climate Change

Given the close link between different elements of the ecosystem of the Earth, marine science addresses not only the objects and natural processes occurring in the oceans but also the interface between the oceans and the atmosphere. One of the most prominent topics in the recent decade in this regard is concerned with the relationship between climate change and the oceans. With respect to this connection, UNFCCC becomes relevant.[57]

57 UNFCCC. As of December 2019, there are 197 Parties to the Framework Convention. For more information, see the official website of UNFCCC, "Status of Ratification of the Convention", available at https://unfccc.int/process-and-meetings/the-convention/status-of-ratification/status-of-ratification-of-the-convention.

The relationship between climate change and the oceans, and the relevant legal issues have been discussed by many legal scholars.[58] Most of the discussions focus on the impact of climate change on the oceans, and the legal implications or challenges brought about by such impact. It is noted that the oceans not only bear some of the major effects of climate change; they are also the location of ocean-based activities that aim to adapt to and mitigate the effects of climate change.[59] Such ocean-based activities include reducing emissions from shipping[60] and undertaking climate-related geoengineering activities in the marine environment.[61] Various technologies have been deployed in the oceans for purposes of geoengineering.[62] The most advanced one is called ocean fertilization, which involves the direct or indirect deposition of iron or other nutrients to the open ocean.[63] The legal implications of this technology will be addressed in Section 5.4 of this chapter.

Apart from the issues mentioned above, the oceans also help the adaptation to or mitigation of the effects of climate change by serving as the object of observation and research for a better understanding of the climate system – scientific knowledge on the climate supports climate services and decision-making combating climate change.[64] The understanding of the climate and the oceans are two interdependent processes. On the one hand, as submitted in a number of UN Resolutions on Oceans and the Law of the Sea, nowadays marine science deals with not only research into the marine environment

58 To name but a few, Rosemary Rayfuse, "Climate Change and the Law of the Sea", in *International Law in the Era of Climate Change*, edited by Rosemary Rayfuse and Shirley V. Scott (Edward Elgar Publishing, 2012); Tim Stephens, "Warming Waters and Souring Seas: Climate Change and Ocean Acidification", in *The Oxford Handbook of the Law of the Sea*, edited by Donald Rothwell, et al. (2015); Alan Boyle, "Law of the Sea Perspectives on Climate Change", in *The 1982 Law of the Sea Convention at 30*, edited by David Freestone (Brill Nijhoff, 2013); Philomene Verlaan, "Geo-engineering, the Law of the Sea, and Climate Change", *Carbon & Climate Law Review* 3, no. 4 (2009); Randall S. Abate, ed. *Climate Change Impacts on Ocean and Coastal Law: US and International Perspectives* (Oxford University Press, 2014); Sarra Sefrioui, "Adapting to Sea Level Rise: A Law of the Sea Perspective", in *The Future of the Law of the Sea*, edited by Gemma Andreone (Springer, 2017).

59 Rosemary Rayfuse, "Climate Change and the Law of the Sea", 147.

60 Ibid., 165–166.

61 Alexander Proelss, "International Legal Challenges Concerning Marine Scientific Research in the Era of Climate Change", 3.

62 Ibid.; Philomene Verlaan, "Geo-engineering, the Law of the Sea, and Climate Change", 447.

63 Doug Wallace et al., "Ocean Fertilization: A Scientific Summary for Policy Makers", Doc. IOC/BRO/2010/2, Paris, 2010, http://eprints.uni-kiel.de/11908/1/2010_OceanFertilization_SOLAS.pdf.

64 It is noted that the Paris Agreement emphasized the strengthening of "scientific knowledge on climate, including research, systematic observation of the climate system and early warning systems" as a means of adaptation. See Paris Agreement, 2015, Article 7(a).

itself but also the interface between the oceans and the atmosphere.[65] On the other hand, since the oceans are an indispensable part of the global ecosystem, an in-depth understanding of climatic processes cannot be achieved without sufficient knowledge about the interaction between the climate and the marine environment.

The importance of such research is affirmed not only by the UNCLOS marine scientific research regime[66] but also by UNFCCC. In this regard, the UNCLOS marine scientific research regime and UNFCCC may overlap since both regimes apply to activities involving the collection of data in the marine environment contributing to climate-related research. The following section starts with an introduction to UNFCCC provisions relevant to such research (Section 5.3.1), followed by an analysis of these provisions and their implementation in practice (Section 5.3.2). Interim concluding remarks are included in Section 5.3.3.

5.3.1 *Relevant Provisions of UNFCCC*

The ultimate objective of UNFCCC is the achievement of "stabilization of greenhouse gas concentrations in the atmosphere at a level that would prevent dangerous anthropogenic interference with the climate system".[67] To fulfil this objective, UNFCCC obliges its parties to make various kinds of commitments.[68] One such commitment is listed in Article 4(g) of UNFCCC, which requires all parties to

> [p]romote and cooperate in scientific, technological, technical, social-economic and other research, systematic observation and the development of data archives related to the climate system and intended

65 Under the agenda item of "marine science", a paragraph appears in most of the UNGA resolutions on Oceans and the Law of the Sea, which "stresses the importance of increasing the scientific understanding of the oceans-atmosphere interface". See, for instance, "UNGA Resolution on oceans and the law of the sea of 4 January 2018", UN Doc. A/RES/72/73, para.288. For a comprehensive list of UNGA resolutions on Oceans and the Law of the Sea, see the official website of DOALOS, "Oceans and the Law of the Sea in the General Assembly of the United Nations – General Assembly resolutions and decisions", available at http://www.un.org/Depts/los/general_assembly/general_assembly_resolutions.htm.

66 The obligation of all States and competent international organizations to promote and facilitate the development and conduct of marine scientific research in general is set forth by Article 239 of UNCLOS. Arguably, Articles 242 and 243, which address issues on the promotion of international cooperation and the creation of favorable conditions, also emphasize the importance of the research into the interface between the marine environment and the atmosphere. For a further discussion on this matter, see Chapter 7 of this book.

67 UNFCCC, Article 2.

68 Ibid., Article 4.

> to further the understanding and to reduce or eliminate the remaining uncertainties regarding the causes, effects, magnitude and timing of climate change and the economic and social consequences of various response strategies.[69]

According to this provision, elements including 1) scientific, technological, technical, social-economic and other research, 2) systematic observation and 3) the development of data archives, may contribute to the furtherance of the understanding and the reduction or elimination of the remaining uncertainties about climate change.[70] Of relevance for the current discussion are the elements of research and systematic observations. UNFCCC does not provide any definitions for these elements. The contents of the commitment to promote and cooperate in research and systematic observation are elaborated in Article 5 of UNFCCC. This article requires its Parties to:

a. [s]upport and further develop, as appropriate, international and intergovernmental programmes and networks or organizations aimed at defining, conducting, assessing and financing *research, data collection and systematic observation*, taking into account the need to minimize duplication of effort;
b. [s]upport international and intergovernmental efforts to strengthen *systematic observation and national scientific and technical research* capacities and capabilities, particularly in developing countries, and to promote access to, and the exchange of, data and analyses thereof obtained from areas beyond national jurisdiction; [...][71]

Here, the terms "research" and "systematic observation" are again used in parallel. In order to understand the relationship between the two elements, it is helpful to consider their ordinary meanings. "Observation" refers to "the action or process of closely observing or monitoring something or someone", while "research" refers to "the systematic investigation into and study of materials

69 Ibid., Article 4(1)(g).

70 This logic has been made more prominent in the Kyoto Protocol to the United Nations Framework Convention on Climate Change. Article 10(d) of the Kyoto Protocol concerns the obligation of the Parties to the Protocol to "[c]ooperate in *scientific and technical research* and promote the maintenance and the development of *systematic observation systems* and development of *data archives* to reduce uncertainties related to the climate system, the adverse impacts of climate change and the economic and social consequences of various response strategies [...]". Emphasis added. Kyoto Protocol to the United Nations Framework Convention on Climate Change, 1997, Article 10(d).

71 Emphasis added. UNFCCC, Article 5.

and sources in order to establish facts and reach new conclusions".[72] According to these definitions, both observation and research involve the investigation of something or someone. A relevant distinction between the two is that observation is not focused on drawing conclusions as research is. The following sub-section will look at the actual implementation of the provisions referred to above to test the validity of the argument made on the relationship between "research" and "observation" and to further discern the respective scope of the two elements.

5.3.2 *"Research" and "Systematic Observation" under* UNFCCC

Information on the implementation of research and systematic observation can be found on the official website of UNFCCC.[73] In practice, provisions on "research" under UNFCCC are implemented through cooperation with the World Climate Research Programme (WCRP),[74] the Integrated Assessment Modelling Consortium (IAMC),[75] IOC and other partners and relevant organizations active in climate change-related research.[76] The Intergovernmental Panel on Climate Change (IPCC) also plays a role in climate research.[77] From

72 See "Observation" and "Research", Oxford Dictionary of English (Oxford Reference online version, 3rd edition, Oxford University Press, 2015).

73 Information concerning implementation of research can be found at https://unfccc.int/topics/science/resources/research-background; information concerning the implementation of systematic observation is available at https://unfccc.int/topics/science/workstreams/systematic-observation/overview.

74 "The World Climate Research Programme (WCRP) leads the way in addressing frontier scientific questions related to the coupled climate system—questions that are too large and too complex to be tackled by a single nation, agency or scientific discipline. Through international science coordination and partnerships, WCRP contributes to advancing our understanding of the multi-scale dynamic interactions between natural and social systems that affect climate". For more information, see the official website of WCRP, "About us", available at https://www.wcrp-climate.org/about-wcrp/wcrp-overview.

75 "The Integrated Assessment Consortium (IAMC) is an organization of scientific research organizations. IAMC was created in 2007 in response to a call from the Intergovernmental Panel on Climate Change (IPCC) for a research organization to lead the integrated assessment modeling community in the development of new scenarios that could be employed by climate modelers in the development of prospective ensemble numerical experiments for both the near term and long term". For more information, see the official website of IAMC, "About the Integrated Assessment Modelling Consortium", available at http://www.globalchange.umd.edu/iamc/about/.

76 For more information, see the official website of UNFCCC, "Overview", available at https://unfccc.int/topics/science/resources/research-background.

77 Although it does not carry out its own research, it assesses the information from worldwide climate research in peer-reviewed literature, journals, books and other sources, and has an important function in identifying priority needs for future research activities. Ibid.

the information provided on the websites of these organizations, it appears that under UNFCCC, the term "research" mainly refers to modelling and experiments related to the climate, that are mostly undertaken in laboratories. Notably, this is a relatively narrow definition of the term "research" and is different from the scope of research under UNCLOS, which involves the process of collecting data or samples.[78]

Under UNFCCC, the process of the *in situ* collection of data that are used for climate-related purposes is covered by the term "observation".[79] "Systematic observation", as used in Article 4 of UNFCCC, according to its ordinary meaning, refers to an observational activity that is "undertaken or acting according to a fixed plan or system".[80] Therefore, the relationship between "research" and "systematic observation" under UNFCCC can be phrased as follows: although not all climate data and products resulting from observation contribute to climate research,[81] observation is an essential part or a prerequisite of research. All forms of climate research, including modelling, or experiments, are based on data acquired through observation. Here, an important point to note is that while as suggested by the ordinary meaning of the terms "observation" and "research", observation is not focused on drawing conclusions as research is,[82] in the context of UNFCCC, practice shows that data collected through observations are used for research, *i.e.*, to draw conclusions.

---

78 See Chapter 3 of this book.

79 For more information, see the official website of UNFCCC, "Overview", available at https://unfccc.int/topics/science/workstreams/systematic-observation/overview. See also the Framework for Ocean Observing and the GCOS Implementation Plan. According to the two instruments, the actual observations, are activities that collect the data (on ECVs and EOVs) needed to address specific scientific problems or societal issues. The Task Team for an Integrated Framework for Sustained Ocean Observing, "A Framework for Ocean Observing", Doc. IOC/INF-1284, at p. 7. The GCOS Implementation Plan "describes the proposed implementation of the global observing system for climate [...], sets out the framework for the science community to provide the data and information to implement the global climate observing system, advance scientific research knowledge and support climate services and the development of climate indicators". The latest version of GCOS Implementation Plan is adopted in 2016, "The Global Observing System for Climate: Implementation Needs", Publication No. GCOS 200 (GOOS-214), 2016.

80 "Systematic", Oxford Dictionary of English (Oxford Reference online version, 3rd edition, Oxford University Press, 2015).

81 As mentioned in the latest version of GCOS Implementation Plan, observation can contribute to monitoring, for example, by supporting the estimation of national emissions and removals of greenhouse gas used by Parties to UNFCCC. See "The Global Observing System for Climate: Implementation Needs", Publication No. GCOS 200 (GOOS-214), at pp. XI, XVI.

82 See Section 5.3.1 of the current chapter.

The meaning of the term "observation" can also be seen from the practice of the organizations and programs that carry out observations. In practice, the implementation of observation under UNFCCC is supported through WMO, the Global Climate Observing System (GCOS), Joint Working Group on Climate (WG Climate) of the Committee on Earth Observation Satellites (CEOS) and Coordination Group for Meteorological Satellites (CGMS), and other partners and relevant organizations.[83] The CEOS/CGMS WG Climate contributes to observational activities under UNFCCC by providing relevant data collected from satellites and thus is irrelevant for the current discussions.

WMO is involved in the actual observation through the WMO Integrated Global Observing System (WIGOS), which coordinates existing observing systems that monitor the Earth's atmosphere, land and oceans.[84] WMO is one of the co-sponsors of GCOS,[85] and a subset of WIGOS is used by GCOS for climate observations.[86] GCOS was established in 1992 with the mandate to "regularly assess the status of global climate observations and produce guidance for its improvement".[87] Since 1997, GCOS has been recognized by the COP of UNFCCC as the program that leads to the improvement of systematic observations to meet the needs of UNFCCC.[88] Considering the vital role that GCOS plays in contributing to systematic observations in the context of UNFCCC, it is necessary to have a closer look at the operation of this system.

83 For more information, see the official website of UNFCCC, "Overview", available at https://unfccc.int/topics/science/workstreams/systematic-observation/overview.

84 Ibid. "WIGOS provides an over-arching framework for the coordination and optimized evolution of existing observing systems, which will continue to be owned and operated by a diverse array of organizations and programmes. It supports better use of existing and emerging observational capabilities. Although aimed primarily at improving the WMO observing systems, it also interfaces with co-sponsored and non-WMO observing systems, thereby engaging the essential regional and national actors for the successful integration of these systems." For more information, see the official website of the WMO, "WMO Integrated Global Observing System (WIGOS)", available at https://public.wmo.int/en/about-us/vision-and-mission/wmo-integrated-global-observing-system.

85 Other sponsors are IOC, UNEP and International Council for Science (ISC). For more information, see the official website of GCOS, "The GCOS Story", available at https://gcos.wmo.int/en/about/gcos-story.

86 For more information, see the official website of UNFCCC, "Overview", available at https://unfccc.int/topics/science/workstreams/systematic-observation/overview.

87 For more information, see the official website of GCOS, "About GCOS", available at https://gcos.wmo.int/en/about.

88 See for example, Decision 8/CP.3, Decision 14/CP.4 of the COP to UNFCCC. All decisions and conclusions on research and systematic observation can be found at https://unfccc.int/topics/science/resources/decisions-and-conclusions-on-systematic-observation.

The working method of GCOS is very similar to that of GOOS. As introduced in Chapter 4.3.5 of this book, the operation of GOOS is centered around various Essential Ocean Variables (EOVs). Likewise, GCOS organizes its efforts around Essential Climate Variables (ECVs), which are required to observe Earth's changing climate systematically.[89] Currently, GCOS specifies 54 ECVs in three broad aspects: atmospheric, oceanic and terrestrial.[90] Among them, oceanic ECVs, literally, refer to variables about the oceans that contribute to understanding the climate system. Comparing the lists of ECVs and EOVs, one can note that oceanic ECVs correspond to a large extent with EOVs.[91] Observations, that is, activities that collect data on oceanic ECVs under GCOS and on EOVs under GOOS, are coordinated by the same coordination group – the Observations Programme Area of the WMO-IOC Joint Committee for Oceanography and Marine Meteorology (JCOMM).[92]

JCOMM incorporates research and observing efforts of various platforms that adopt different tools. These tools and platforms include, among others, ship-based meteorological measurements – SOT/VOS, ship-based oceanographic measurements – SOT/SOOP, ship-based areological measurements – SOT/ASAP, sea level gauges – GLOSS, drifting buoys – DBCP, moored buoys – DBCP, interdisciplinary moorings – OceanSITES, profiling floats – Argo, and repeated transects – GO-SHIP.[93]

Through JCOMM, data to be collected through observations are predetermined based on user requirements.[94] To meet diverse needs, data

89 See the official website of the GCOS, "Global Climate Observing System (GCOS)", available at https://gcos.wmo.int/en/home. Apart from specifying ECVs, GCOS also undertakes regular periodic reviews to monitor how these ECVs are observed in practice and prepares implementation plans to ensure continuity of the observational record while improving it where needed. See "The Global Observing System for Climate: Implementation Needs", Publication No. GCOS 200 (GOOS-214), at p. 9.

90 For more information, see the official website of GCOS, "About Essential Climate Variables", available at https://gcos.wmo.int/en/essential-climate-variables/about.

91 Information on EOVs is available at "Essential Ocean Variables", http://www.goosocean.org/index.php?option=com_content&view=article&id=14&Itemid=114.

92 See the official website of GCOS, "Ocean in situ", available at https://gcos.wmo.int/en/networks/ocean. For more detailed discussions on the JCOMM's role in the operation of GOOS, see Chapter 4.3.5 of this study.

93 Emerging elements include OceanGliders, HF radars, Surface based measurements CO2 – SOCONET, animal borne sensors etc. For more information, see the official website of JCOMM, "Observations Programme Area", available at https://www.jcomm.info/index.php?option=com_content&view=article&id=338&Itemid=38. The implications of these tools will be addressed in Chapter 7 of this book.

94 For more information, see The Task Team for an Integrated Framework for Sustained Ocean Observing, "A Framework for Ocean Observing", Doc. IOC/INF-1284; "The Global

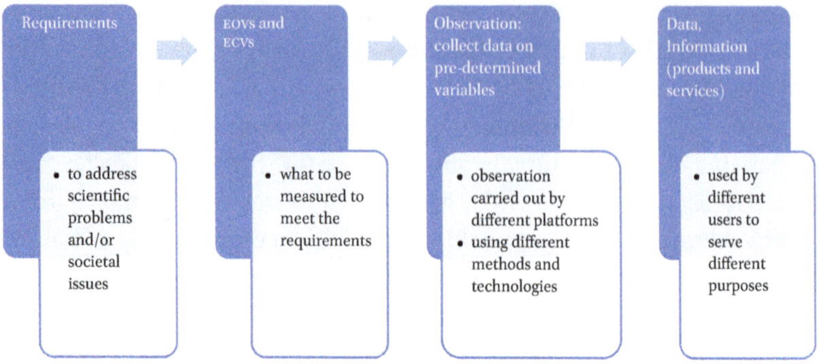

FIGURE 2 Working method of GOOS and GCOS

collected via observations are managed and interpreted to become data products that can be used to provide services and to inform the solutions to scientific problems or decisions on societal issues.[95] As such, a single set of data (on oceanic ECVs or EOVs), which are collected by different platforms coordinated by JCOMM, using different methods or technologies, can be used by different users, for different purposes (see Figure 2).

Practice shows that data collected on oceanic ECVs has been used for various purposes, including monitoring the climate system, detecting climate change, and research to improve understanding, modelling and prediction of the climate system.[96] In this context, ocean data collection activities undertaken by the observing platforms under the coordination of JCOMM are considered as "observations" (rather than "research") under UNFCCC. These are merely the uses that serve climate-related purposes. It is also acknowledged that observations are not only relevant to UNFCCC, but also a broader community.[97] Data collected through observations can also be used to contribute to a better scientific understanding of the marine environment itself, though perhaps in a different form of a data product. In this regard, the collection of the same set

Observing System for Climate: Implementation Needs", Publication No. GCOS 200 (GOOS-214).

95 Sometimes, the raw data acquired through observation cannot be directly used by potential users. In order to meet the requirements of the potential users, the raw data needs to be recovered, compiled and analyzed properly, which is called data management. "The Global Observing System for Climate: Implementation Needs", Publication No. GCOS 200 (GOOS-214), at p. XVI; The Task Team for an Integrated Framework for Sustained Ocean Observing, "A Framework for Ocean Observing", Doc. IOC/INF-1284, at p. 7.

96 "The Global Observing System for Climate: Implementation Needs", Publication No. GCOS 200 (GOOS-214), at p. 110.

97 Ibid., at p. 10.

of oceanic data can be considered both as "marine scientific research" under UNCLOS and as "observation" under UNFCCC. In this regard, Contracting Parties' obligations to promote and cooperate in climate-related "observation" and "research" under Article 4 of UNFCCC can be used as an incentive to facilitate the establishment of practical arrangements for certain ocean data collection activities under UNCLOS.

Besides, it is noted that the legal classification of ocean data collection activities undertaken under certain systems that are coordinated by JCOMM, and the appropriate legal frameworks to be applied to these activities, have been addressed by some international organizations. The IOC Argo Guidelines and WMO Resolution 45 (Cg-18) are the outcomes of these discussions. These documents have been analyzed in Chapter 4 of this study. The implications of these documents for the current research, especially for identifying the appropriate legal framework for certain ocean data collection activities when the legal classification of the activities concerned is unclear or controversial, will be addressed in Chapter 7 of this book.

5.3.3 *Interim Conclusions*

In sum, relevant practice of UNFCCC on "research" does not shed much light on understanding the meaning of the term "marine scientific research" under UNCLOS, because UNFCCC adopts a relatively narrow definition for the term "research". However, practice on "observation" under UNFCCC indicates that potentially an ocean data collection activity may qualify as "marine scientific research" under UNCLOS, and at the same time as "observation" under UNFCCC, when the collected ocean data are used for both climate-related purposes and scientific purposes. In this regard, Contracting Parties' commitments to promote and cooperate in observation under Article 4 of UNFCCC can be interpreted as a catalyst for the States concerned to enter into cooperative arrangements for certain ocean data collection activities when the legal classification of the activities in question – whether they are marine scientific research – remains controversial. The operationalization of this article will be discussed in Chapter 7 of this research.

Pertinent practice on observation under GCOS also shows that in practice, the same set of data can contribute to multiple purposes. Besides, data may be collected by different platforms using different tools or technologies. These facts add to the complexity of discerning the legal classification of a specific activity. It seems that none of the elements (purposes of the activity, tools or technologies adopted in the undertaking of the activity, platforms that collect data) can act in itself as a practical criterion for purposes of legal classification. The implications of this conclusion will be further elaborated in Chapter 7 of this research.

5.4 London Convention and the London Protocol

Another relevant international convention for the current discussions is the London Convention – one of the first international conventions for the protection of the marine environment from human activities.[98] It contributes to the prevention and control of marine pollution by prohibiting the dumping of certain hazardous materials.[99] In 1996, Parties to the London Convention adopted the London Protocol.[100] The London Protocol presents a significant change of approach to regulating the dumping of wastes and other matter as compared to the London Convention. Instead of stating which kinds of material cannot be dumped at sea, the London Protocol prohibits all dumping, except for the possibly acceptable wastes contained in its Annex 1.[101]

Under the London Convention and its London Protocol, one of the most prominent issues related to marine scientific research is marine geoengineering. According to the 2013 Amendment to the London Protocol, the term "marine geoengineering" refers to:

> a deliberation intervention in the marine environment to manipulate natural processes, including to counteract anthropogenic climate change and/or its impacts, and that has the potential to result in deleterious effects, especially where those effaces may be widespread, long-lasting or severe.[102]

According to this definition, activities which fall within the scope of marine geoengineering can hardly be considered as marine scientific research – they do not even seem to involve the collection of ocean data. However, as pointed

98 London Convention. The Convention was adopted in 1972 and entered into force in 1975. As of June 2020, 87 States are Parties to this Convention. See the official website of the International Maritime Organization, "Convention on the Prevention of Marine Pollution by Dumping of Wastes and Other Matter", available at http://www.imo.org/en/OurWork/Environment/LCLP/Pages/default.aspx.

99 Ibid., Article IV.

100 London Protocol. The Protocol entered into force on 24 March 2006 and there are (as of June 2020) 53 Parties to the Protocol. For more information, see the official website of the International Maritime Organization, "Convention on the Prevention of Marine Pollution by Dumping of Wastes and Other Matter", available at http://www.imo.org/en/OurWork/Environment/LCLP/Pages/default.aspx.

101 Ibid., Article 4(1).

102 "Resolution LP.4(8) on the Amendment to the London Protocol to Regulate the Placement of Matter for Ocean Fertilization and Other Marine Geoengineering Engineering Activities", 2013.

out by some scholars, many marine geoengineering techniques are still at the test and modelling stage.[103] Much research needs to be done to assess the feasibility and effects of such techniques. Arguably, when such research is conducted in the marine environment, the activity at issue may qualify as marine scientific research because it aims at increasing the knowledge about the marine environment and its reaction to marine geoengineering activities.[104] In this connection, a series of resolutions adopted by the Parties to the London Convention and the London Protocol concerning marine geoengineering merit a detailed examination.

5.4.1 *Marine Geo-Engineering, "Legitimate Scientific Research" and "Specific Marine Scientific Research"*

At first, Parties to the London Convention and the London Protocol only addressed issues raised by one specific kind of marine geoengineering technique, that is ocean fertilization. Later, in 2013, by adopting Resolution LP.4(8) on the Amendment to the London Protocol to Regulate the Placement of Matter for Ocean Fertilization and Other Marine Geoengineering Activities, the Contracting Parties amended the London Protocol to include marine geoengineering activities in general. [105]

The issue of ocean fertilization was first brought to the attention of the Scientific Group of the London Convention in 1999.[106] At that time, it did not result in any fundamental decision, but a conclusion that the Scientific Group "should continue to keep a watching brief on the relevant research that is being done in this field".[107] In June 2007, based on the consideration of several documents concerning large-scale ocean iron fertilization, the Scientific Groups to the London Convention and the London Protocol released a "Statement

103 Du Haomiao, *An International Legal Framework for Geoengineering: Managing the Risks of an Emerging Technology* (Routledge, 2017), 9; Alexander Proelss, "International Legal Challenges Concerning Marine Scientific Research in the Era of Climate Change", 4–5.

104 However, when the techniques are adopted specifically with a view to "counteract anthropogenic climate change and/or its impacts", the activity concerned can no longer be regarded as marine scientific research.

105 "Resolution LP.4(8) on the Amendment to the London Protocol to Regulate the Placement of Matter for Ocean Fertilization and Other Marine Geoengineering Engineering Activities".

106 For more information, see the official website of the International Maritime Organization, "Ocean Fertilization under the LC/LP", available at http://www.imo.org/en/OurWork/Environment/LCLP/EmergingIssues/geoengineering/OceanFertilizationDocumentRepository/OceanFertilization/Pages/default.aspx.

107 Ibid.

of Concern regarding iron fertilization of the oceans to sequester CO_2".[108] In November of the same year, at the joint meeting of the Contracting Parties to the London Convention and London Protocol, the Parties endorsed the "Statement of Concern" produced by the Scientific Groups.[109] They agreed that the scope of work of the London Convention and London Protocol included ocean fertilization and that these agreements were competent to address this issue in view of their general objective to protect and preserve the marine environment from all sources.[110]

It is worth noting that in 2007, the Scientific Groups' concern was expressed regarding *large-scale* ocean fertilization only. This can be seen from the submissions included in the Statement of Concern, such as "[t]he Scientific Groups [...] took the view that knowledge about the effectiveness and potential environmental impacts of ocean iron fertilization currently was insufficient to justify *large-scale operations*," and "[t]he Scientific Groups noted with concern the potential for *large-scale ocean iron fertilization* to have negative impacts on the marine environment and human health".[111] However, in 2008, when assessing the legitimacy of ocean fertilization activities under the London Convention and the London Protocol – whether such activities run contrary to the aims of these documents[112] – the Scientific Groups and the Working Group on Ocean Fertilization established by the Scientific Groups started to consider whether the concept of scale (spatial and temporal) is a sufficient determinant

108 "Statement of Concern regarding iron fertilization of the oceans to sequester CO2", LC-LP.1/Circ.14, 2007.

109 For more information, see the official website of the International Maritime Organization, "Ocean Fertilization under the LC/LP", available at http://www.imo.org/en/OurWork/Environment/LCLP/EmergingIssues/geoengineering/OceanFertilizationDocumentRepository/OceanFertilization/Pages/default.aspx. See also "Report of the Twenty-Ninth Consultative Meeting and the Second Meeting of Contracting Parties", Doc. LC 29/17, 2007.

110 See the official website of the International Maritime Organization, "Ocean Fertilization under the LC/LP", available at http://www.imo.org/en/OurWork/Environment/LCLP/EmergingIssues/geoengineering/OceanFertilizationDocumentRepository/OceanFertilization/Pages/default.aspx.

111 Emphasis added. "Statement of Concern regarding iron fertilization of the oceans to sequester CO2", LC-LP.1/Circ.14.

112 In the case of ocean fertilization, it constitutes "dumping" under the London Convention and London Protocol unless the activity concerned "is not contrary to the aims of" the Convention and the Protocol. See London Convention, Article III(1)(a), (b); London Protocol, Article 1(4)(1), (2).

in the assessment process and whether ocean fertilization that *serves the purpose of scientific research* can be permitted.[113]

In 2008, the non-legally binding Resolution LC-LP.1 (2008) on the Regulation of Ocean Fertilization was adopted, which provided that ocean fertilization activities, other than "legitimate scientific research", should not be allowed.[114] For purposes of Resolution LC-LP.1, "legitimate scientific research" is defined as those proposals that have been assessed and found acceptable under the assessment framework to be developed by the Scientific Groups.[115] Another element of "legitimate scientific research" provided in this Resolution is that "such research should be regarded as placement of matter for a purpose other than the mere disposal thereof under Article III.1(b)(II) of the London Convention and Article 1.4.2.2 of the London Protocol".[116] This element seemingly implies that such research needs to serve scientific purposes.

In 2010, Parties to the London Convention and the London Protocol adopted the non-legally binding Resolution LC-LP.2 (2010) on the Assessment Framework for Scientific Research Involving Ocean Fertilization (hereinafter 2010 Assessment Framework). This document "provides a tool for assessing proposed activities on a case-by-case basis to determine if the proposed activity constitutes legitimate scientific research that is not contrary to the aims of the London Convention or Protocol".[117]

According to the 2010 Assessment Framework, all proposed activities need to go through an initial assessment, determining whether a proposed activity falls within the definition of ocean fertilization and has proper scientific attributes.[118] Activities that have "proper scientific attributes" should meet the following criteria:

1. the proposed activity *should be designed to answer questions* that will *add to the body of scientific knowledge*. Proposals should state their rationale, research goals, scientific hypotheses and methods, scale, timings and locations with clear justification for why the expected outcomes cannot reasonably be achieved by other methods;

113 See, for instance, "Report of the Thirty-First Meeting of the Scientific Group of the London Convention and the Second Meeting of the Scientific Group of the London Protocol", LC/SG 31/16, 2008, at pp. 6–12; "Report of the Working Group on Ocean Fertilization", LC/SG 31/WP.3/Rev.1, 2008.

114 "Resolution LC-LP.1 (2008) on the Regulation of Ocean Fertilization", para.8.

115 Ibid., para.7.

116 Ibid., para.3.

117 "Resolution LC-LP.2 (2010) on the Assessment Framework for Scientific Research Involving Ocean Fertilization".

118 Ibid., para.1.3(1).

2. *economic interests should not influence* the design, conduct and/or outcomes of the proposed activity. There should not be any financial and/or economic gain *arising directly from the experiment or its outcomes* [...];
3. the proposed activity should be *subject to scientific peer review* at appropriate stages in the assessment process. The outcome of the scientific peer review should be taken into consideration by the Contracting Parties. The peer review methodology should be stated and the outcomes of the peer review of successful proposals should be *made publicly available* together with the *details of the project* [...]; and
4. the proponents of the proposed activity should *make a commitment to publish the results in peer reviewed scientific publications* and include a plan in the proposal to *make the data and outcomes publicly available* in a specified time-frame.[119]

After the initial assessment, the proposal under review is subject to environmental assessment, taking into consideration its problem formulation, site selection and description, exposure assessment, effects assessment, risk characterization and risk management.[120] Based on the result of environmental assessment, a decision will be made that determines whether the proposed activity constitutes "legitimate scientific research".[121]

As such, the regulation of ocean fertilization activities under the London Convention and the London Protocol can be summarized in Figure 3, in which only the green category is permitted under these documents.

The 2010 Assessment Framework was further developed by the 2013 Resolution LP.4(8) on the Amendment to the London Protocol to Regulate the Placement of Matter for Ocean Fertilization and Other Marine Geoengineering Activities, which introduces two new Annexes (Annex 4 and 5) and associated amendments to the London Protocol.[122] However, at the time of writing, the amendments are not yet in force.

Annex 4 (Marine Geoengineering Activities) of the Amendment requires that "[a]n ocean fertilization activity may only be considered for a permit if it is assessed as constituting legitimate scientific research taking into account any specific placement assessment framework".[123] Annex 5 (Assessment Framework for Matter that May Be Considered for Placement under Annex 4)

119 Emphasis added. Ibid., para.2.2.

120 Ibid., para.1.3(2).

121 Ibid., para.1.3(3).

122 "Resolution LP.4(8) on the Amendment to the London Protocol to Regulate the Placement of Matter for Ocean Fertilization and Other Marine Geoengineering Engineering Activities".

123 Ibid., Annex 4.

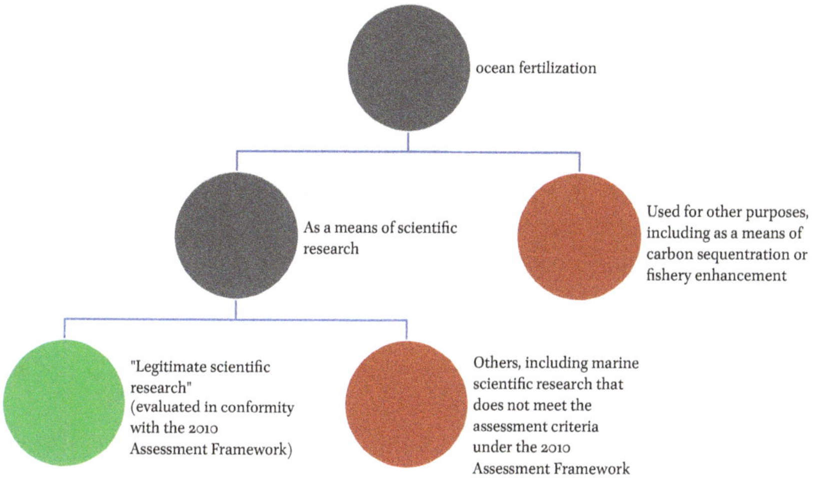

FIGURE 3 Regulation of ocean fertilization under the London Convention and its London Protocol

establishes a legally binding assessment framework for relevant activities.[124] It is worth noting that the term used in Annex 5 is no longer "legitimate scientific research", which is used in 2010 the Assessment Framework and Annex 4 of the Amendment, but "specific marine scientific research".[125] Considering the continuity and internal coherence between Annexes 4 and 5, it is assumed that here "specific marine scientific research" under Annex 5 is an alternative term for "legitimate scientific research" under Annex 4.[126]

Paragraph 7 of Annex 5 acknowledges that "specific marine scientific research" may be required for potential marine geoengineering techniques, in order to, *inter alia*:

> better understand the natural processes which will be affected; understand their potential impacts on the marine environment; understand their potential efficacy for geoengineering purposes; be able to effectively apply the assessment framework(s) to proposals for marine geoengineering.[127]

124 Ibid., Annex 5.

125 Ibid., Annex 5, paras.7–8.

126 The title of Annex 5 is "Assessment Framework for Matter that May Be Considered for Placement under Annex 4", while Paragraph 1(3) of Annex 4 reads "An ocean fertilization activity may only be considered for a permit if it is assessed as constituting legitimate scientific research taking into account any specific placement assessment framework".

127 "Resolution LP.4(8) on the Amendment to the London Protocol to Regulate the Placement of Matter for Ocean Fertilization and Other Marine Geoengineering Engineering Activities", Annex 5, para.7.

In the case of such a "specific marine scientific research" activity, the considerations used for the assessment include:

- the proposed activity is designed to answer questions that will add to scientific knowledge. Proposals should state their rationale, research goals, scientific hypotheses and methods, scale, timings, duration and locations with clear justification for why the expected outcomes cannot reasonably be achieved by other methods.
- the research methodology to be applied should be appropriate and based on best available scientific knowledge and technology. The methodology should be described in sufficient detail to allow a peer review.
- the proposed activity is subject to scientific peer review at appropriate stages in the assessment process.
- economic interests do not influence the design, conduct and/or outcomes of the proposed activity. There should not be any financial and/or economic gain arising directly from the experiment or its outcomes. This does not preclude payment for services rendered in support of the experiment or future financial impacts of patented technology.
- the proponents of the proposed activity make a commitment to publish the results in peer reviewed scientific publications and include a plan in the proposal to make the data and outcomes publicly available in an appropriate and specified time frame.
- the proposed activity has the financial resources available before the work commences to fulfil the program of work.[128]

Compared to the criteria contained in the 2010 Assessment Framework, the considerations listed under the 2013 Resolution LP.4(8) introduced two new elements, which are the requirements for research methodology and the availability of financial resources before the work commences. The latter element – the availability of financial resources – can hardly be considered a criterion for assessing the existence of "proper scientific attributes". Most likely, this element was included to ensure that the proposed activity is not abandoned halfway through due to the lack of financial resources, which could pose harm to the marine environment.

For the remaining considerations, it has been submitted that these criteria "are suitable for developing a general [not limited to ocean fertilization] definition of (marine) (scientific) research under [UNCLOS]".[129] In the 2010

128 Ibid., Annex 5, para.8.

129 Philomène Verlaan, "Marine Scientific Research: Its Potential Contribution to Achieving Responsible High Seas Governance", *The International Journal of Marine and Coastal Law* 27, no. 4 (2012): 808. See also Philomène A Verlaan, "Current Legal Developments: London

Assessment Framework, the criteria are used to assess if an ocean fertilization activity has "proper scientific attributes".[130] Similarly, as concluded in Chapter 3 of this book, as a minimum standard of being "marine scientific research" under UNCLOS, the activity at issue must have some scientific attributes. A pertinent question that arises is whether the criteria for assessing the existence of "proper scientific attributes" for "legitimate scientific research" or "specific marine scientific research" provided by Assessment Frameworks can be used to determine the existence of scientific attributes for marine scientific research under UNCLOS. The following sub-section aims to address this issue.

5.4.2 *Implications for Understanding the Meaning of the Term "Marine Scientific Research"*

When looking at the criteria listed under the Assessment Frameworks, one can see that the scope of "legitimate scientific research" or "specific marine scientific research" under the Assessment Frameworks seems to be narrower than the scope of "marine scientific research" under UNCLOS. For instance, one criterion contained in the Assessment Frameworks requires "[t]here should not be any financial and/or economic gain arising directly from the experiment or its outcomes".[131] However, under UNCLOS, marine scientific research projects can be "of direct significance for the exploration and exploitation of natural resources",[132] which arguably include research projects that directly lead to financial and economic gain.[133] Besides, UNCLOS does not contain any indication that the design, conduct and outcomes of a marine scientific research project shall not be influenced by economic interests,[134] which is among the

Convention and London Protocol", *The International Journal of Marine and Coastal Law* 26, no. 1 (2011): 193.

130 "Resolution LC-LP.2 (2010) on the Assessment Framework for Scientific Research Involving Ocean Fertilization".

131 Ibid., para.2.2; "Resolution LP.4(8) on the Amendment to the London Protocol to Regulate the Placement of Matter for Ocean Fertilization and Other Marine Geoengineering Engineering Activities", Annex 5, para.8.

132 UNCLOS, Article 246(5)(a).

133 This being said, considering the distinction between exploration and exploitation on the one hand, and marine scientific research on the other, commercial gain cannot be the primary purpose of undertaking marine scientific research activities. For more discussion on this matter, see Chapter 3.2.4.3 of this book.

134 This being said, the distinction between marine scientific research on the one hand and exploration and exploration on the other suggests that the design of a marine scientific research project cannot *only* be influenced by economic interests. A further discussion on the distinction between the said activities is included in Chapter 3.3.2.1.

criteria under the Assessment Frameworks.[135] The Assessment Frameworks also provide stricter requirements than the relevant UNCLOS provisions for research methodology, peer review, open publication of research results, data and outcomes.[136]

In this regard, it is submitted that by inserting the qualifiers "legitimate" and "specific", the Assessment Frameworks are not meant to define the term "(marine) scientific research" in general. Instead, they are intended to set out the considerations to be taken into account when assessing whether the research proposals can be permitted under the London Convention and the London Protocol, or in other words, whether they are not "contrary to the aims of the Convention/Protocol".[137] To understand this point, it is pertinent to recall the reason for introducing the concepts of "legitimate scientific research" and "specific marine scientific research" in the first place. The concept of "legitimate scientific research" was for the first time introduced formally by Resolution LC-LP.1 (2008) on the Regulation of Ocean Fertilization, which prohibited ocean fertilization activities, with the only exemption – "legitimate scientific research".[138] In other paragraphs of the same Resolution, it has been provided that

> in order to provide for legitimate scientific research, such research should be regarded as placement of matter for a purpose other than the mere disposal thereof under Article III.1(b)(II) of the London Convention and Article 1.4.2.2 of the London Protocol", and "the [...] assessment framework should include, inter alia, tools for determining whether the proposed activity is contrary to the aims of the Convention and Protocol.[139]

With respect to these statements, it is necessary to recall a pertinent provision contained both in the London Convention and the London Protocol, which states that:

135 "Resolution LC-LP.2 (2010) on the Assessment Framework for Scientific Research Involving Ocean Fertilization", para.2.2; "Resolution LP.4(8) on the Amendment to the London Protocol to Regulate the Placement of Matter for Ocean Fertilization and Other Marine Geoengineering Engineering Activities", Annex 5, para.8.

136 For a further discussion on the UNCLOS requirements on research methods, open publication, see Chapter 3.2 of this study.

137 Ocean fertilization constitutes "dumping" and thus is prohibited under the London Convention and London Protocol, unless the activity concerned "is not contrary to the aims of" the Convention and the Protocol. See London Convention, Article III(1)(a), (b); London Protocol, Article 1(4)(1), (2).

138 "Resolution LC-LP.1 (2008) on the Regulation of Ocean Fertilization", para.8.

139 Ibid., paras.3 and 5.

> 'Dumping' does not include: […] placement of matter for a purpose other than the mere disposal thereof, provided that such placement is not contrary to the aims of this [Convention/Protocol] […].[140]

Given the connection between the statements and the provision quoted above, it can be argued that the Assessment Frameworks are established to evaluate whether a research project that involves ocean fertilization can be considered as "placement of matter for a purpose other than the mere disposal thereof, provided that such placement is not contrary to the aims of" the London Convention and the London Protocol, and thus is legitimate under the two instruments.

It is also noted that when the issue of ocean fertilization was brought to their attention, the Contracting Parties to the London Convention and the London Protocol agreed, based on the Statement of Concern prepared by the Scientific Groups, that the scope of work of the two instruments included ocean fertilization and that they would further study the issue from the scientific and legal perspectives with a view to its regulation.[141] To further study "the issue from the scientific and legal perspectives", a Legal Intersessional Correspondence Group (LICG) on Ocean Fertilization was established. It was instructed to work with the Scientific Groups to respond to questions such as whether, and how, the legal framework of the London Convention and Protocol applies to key scenarios on ocean fertilization, and what would be "contrary to the aims of the Convention/Protocol".[142] As an outcome of the meetings of the LICG on Ocean Fertilization and of the Scientific Groups, it was concluded, among other things, that "the importance of continuing fundamental research was […] noted […] and […] it has been suggested that criteria be established for assessment of research projects"[143] and that "provision should be made for legitimate scientific research".[144] Following these recommendations, the Contracting Parties to the London Convention and the London Protocol adopted the Assessment Frameworks.

In sum, the criteria contained in the Assessment Frameworks were introduced to ensure that the objectives of the London Convention and the London Protocol would not be jeopardized, rather than giving a general definition of

140 London Convention, Article III(1)(a), (b); London Protocol, Article 1(4)(1), (2).

141 "Report of the Twenty-Ninth Consultative Meeting and the Second Meeting of Contracting Parties", Doc. LC 29/17, para.4.23.

142 Ibid., para.4.28.

143 See, for instance, "Ocean Fertilization: Report of the Legal and Intersessional Correspondence Group", LC 30/4, 2008, para.32.

144 "Ocean Fertilization: Report of the Working Group on Ocean Fertilization", LC 30/WP.6, 2008, para.4.2.

the term "(marine) (scientific) research". Given such a purpose, the criteria are formulated in a specific context, that is to only allow scientific research proposals that directly contribute to filling the knowledge gap[145] since otherwise, the operation might be "contrary to the aims of the Convention/Protocol". This is perhaps the reason for including in the 2013 Assessment Framework the consideration concerning the availability of financial resources before the commencement of the project, which is not pertinent to assess the scientific attributes of a research project, but closely related to the likelihood of the project achieving its purpose of gaining scientific knowledge.

Therefore, it is submitted that the criteria contained in the Assessment Frameworks cannot be directly used to define the term "marine scientific research" in general. This being said, the criteria contained in the Assessment Frameworks can serve as a reasonable basis for determining the existence of scientific attributes of an ocean data collection activity. The significance of determining the existence of such attributes will be addressed in Chapter 7 of this book.

5.5 International Convention on the Regulation of Whaling

An exception for scientific research has also been included in international conventions related to the conservation of marine resources. Among the various international conventions of this kind,[146] this section will focus on ICRW. This choice is explained by the fact that the criteria for the treaty phrase "for

---

145 For more information on the element of filling knowledge gap, it is pertinent to refer to a paragraph of the Report of the Thirtieth Meeting of the Scientific Group of the London Convention and the First Meeting of the Scientific Group of the London Protocol Stated that:

> According to the Intergovernmental Panel on Climate Change (IPCC), iron fertilization of the oceans may offer a potential strategy for removing carbon dioxide from the atmosphere by stimulating the growth of phytoplankton and thereby sequestering the carbon dioxide in the form of particulate organic carbon. However, the IPCC also stated that ocean iron fertilization remains largely speculative, and many of the environmental side effects have yet to be assessed.

"Report of the Thirtieth Meeting of the Scientific Group of the London Convention and the First Meeting of the Scientific Group of the London Protocol", LC/SG 30/14, 2007, para.2.24.

146 Numerous international conventions deal with the conservation and management of marine resources. To name but a few, the 1995 Agreement for the Implementation of the Provisions of the United Nations Conventions on the Law of the Sea Relating to the Conservation and Management of Straddling Fish Stocks and Highly Migratory Fish Stocks (hereinafter Fish Stock Agreement), the Convention on the Conservation of Antarctic

purposes of scientific research" under ICRW, that is highly relevant for the current study, has been addressed by the ICJ in the *Whaling in the Antarctic* case.[147] In contrast, other conventions related to the conservation of marine resources only mention "scientific research" as a means that supports conservation and management without shedding any light on understanding the meaning of the term "scientific research".[148]

This section begins with an introduction to ICRW provisions that are relevant for the current discussion (Section 5.5.1), followed by an analysis of the *Whaling in the Antarctic* case and its implications for understanding the meaning of the term "marine scientific research" under UNCLOS (Section 5.5.2).

5.5.1 *Relevant Provisions of ICRW*

ICRW was adopted in 1946 to "provide for the proper conservation of whale stocks and thus make possible the orderly development of the whaling industry".[149] It is the founding document of the International Whaling Commission (IWC).[150] Specific regulations on whaling are contained in an attached Schedule, which is an integral part of ICRW.[151] IWC is responsible for amending the Schedule. In 1982, members of IWC voted by the necessary three-quarters majority to implement a moratorium on commercial whaling, which stated that catch limits for all commercial whaling would be set to zero.[152] An exception to the moratorium is provided by Article VIII(1) of ICRW, which states that,

> [n]otwithstanding anything contained in this Convention any Contracting Government may grant to any of its nationals a special permit authorizing that national to kill, take and treat whales *for purposes of scientific research* subject to such restrictions as to number and subject to such other conditions as the Contracting Government thinks fit, and the

Marine Living Resources, Convention for the Protection of the Natural Resources and Environment of the South Pacific Region.

147 ICJ, *Whaling in the Antarctic* (*Australia v. Japan: New Zealand intervening*).

148 See, for example, the Fish Stock Agreement, which in its general principles calls for the promotion of scientific research and the development of appropriate technologies in support of fisheries conservation and management. In implementing the precautionary approach, the Fish Stock Agreement requires States to obtain and share the best scientific information available.

149 ICRW, 7th Preambular paragraph.

150 Information on the Contracting Governments to IWC is available at the official website of IWC, "Membership and Contracting Governments", available at https://iwc.int/members.

151 ICRW, Article I(1).

152 For more information, see the official website of IWC, "Commercial Whaling", available at https://iwc.int/commercial.

killing, taking, and treating of whales in accordance with the provisions of this Article shall be exempt from the operation of this Convention.[153]

ICRW contains no definition of the term "scientific research". Most provisions of ICRW are of an administrative nature, dealing with matters such as the mandate of IWC,[154] amendments to the Schedule and their function,[155] which do not shed further light on ascertaining the meaning of the phrase "for purposes of scientific research". Given the uncertainty surrounding the meaning of the term "scientific research", the interpretation and application of Article VIII have given rise to controversies in practice. The ICJ *Whaling in the Antarctic* case initiated by Australia against Japan with New Zealand intervening marked the culmination of such controversies.

5.5.2 *The ICJ Whaling in the Antarctic Case and Implications for Understanding the Meaning of the Term "Marine Scientific Research"*

The dispute mainly focused on the research program "JARPA II" carried out by a Japanese research institute, which involved the killing of whales (hereinafter the program). The central question was whether the program fell under Article VIII(1) of ICRW and qualified as a scientific exception to the prohibition of commercial whaling. To fulfil the requirement of Article VIII(1), the program needs to be undertaken "for purposes of scientific research".

Based on the views of a scientific expert, Australia argued that "scientific research" in the context of ICRW had four "essential characteristics", namely:

1. defined and achievable objectives (questions or hypotheses) that aim to contribute to knowledge important to the conservation and management of stocks;
2. "appropriate methods", including the use of lethal methods only where the objectives of the research cannot be achieved by any other means;
3. peer review;
4. and the avoidance of adverse effects on stock.[156]

In its Judgment, the Court responded to each of these four characteristics. As to the first characteristic, the Court observed: "the experts called by both Parties agreed that scientific research should proceed on the basis of particular

---

153 Emphasis added. ICRW, Article VIII(1).
154 Ibid., Articles III, IV.
155 Ibid., Article V.
156 ICJ, *Whaling in the Antarctic* (*Australia v. Japan: New Zealand intervening*), Judgment, para.74.

questions, which could take the form of a hypothesis, although they disagreed about the level of specificity required of such a hypothesis".[157] Although this is a controversial issue, both in the context of the *Whaling in the Antarctic* case and for discerning the scope of marine scientific research under UNCLOS,[158] the Court did not give its opinion on this matter.

About the second characteristic, the Court considered that the relevant resolutions and Guidelines on which Australia and New Zealand rely "do not establish a requirement that lethal methods be used only when other methods are not available".[159] This observation seems to be relevant for interpreting the phrase "appropriate scientific methods and means" under Article 240(b) of UNCLOS. Insofar as it is "compatible with" UNCLOS and relates to marine living resources, the nature of (marine) scientific research does not exclude the use of lethal methods.

Regarding the characteristic of peer review, the Court explicitly stated that it was not convinced that an activity could only qualify as scientific research if the proposals and results are subject to peer view, although this was "common practice in the scientific community".[160] The characteristic of peer review is relevant for understanding the obligations of States under Articles 244[161] and 249(1)(e)[162] of UNCLOS concerning the publication and dissemination of knowledge and information. The Court's finding that scientific research does

157 Ibid., para.77.

158 The requirement under Article 240(b) of UNCLOS that marine scientific research to be conducted with "appropriate scientific methods and means" raised the question whether this provision indicates that in order to qualify as marine scientific research under UNCLOS, the activity at issue must be carried out for the purpose of verifying or falsifying a hypothesis. See Chapter 3.2.2 of this book.

159 ICJ, *Whaling in the Antarctic* (*Australia v. Japan: New Zealand intervening*), Judgment, para.83.

160 Ibid., para.84.

161 Article 244 of UNCLOS stipulates that:
1. States and competent international organizations shall, in accordance with this Convention, make available by publication and dissemination through appropriate channels information on proposed major programmes and their objectives as well as knowledge resulting from marine scientific research.
2. For this purpose, States, both individually and in cooperation with other States and with competent international organizations, shall actively promote the flow of scientific data and information and the transfer of knowledge resulting from marine scientific research, especially to developing States, as well as the strengthening of the autonomous marine scientific research capabilities of developing States through, inter alia, programmes to provide adequate education and training of their technical and scientific personnel.

162 Article 249(1)(e) requires the researching States to "ensure [...] that the research results are made internationally available through appropriate national or international channels, as soon as practicable".

not have to undergo peer review indicates that this is not a generally accepted criterion for (marine) scientific research.

In terms of the fourth characteristic, the Court noticed that there seems to be an agreement among the parties that scientific research must avoid an adverse impact on whale stocks, without expressing its own opinion on this matter.[163] However, it is the current author's view that the avoidance of adverse impact on whaling stocks should be considered as a principle for the conduct of scientific research, rather than a criterion for the legal classification of a specific activity.[164]

After going through all the characteristics advanced by Australia, the Court concluded that it was not persuaded that "scientific research" activities under Article VIII of ICRW must meet the four characteristics advanced by Australia.[165] It was the opinion of the Court that these characteristics reflected activities which can be called "well-conceived scientific research", rather than "serving as an interpretation of the term as used in the Convention".[166] However, the Court did not provide any alternative criteria for or definition of the term "scientific research" as it did not consider it necessary to do so.[167]

Instead of defining the term "scientific research", the Court turned to look at the elements comprising the phrase "for purposes of scientific research" to adjudge whether Japan's whaling program JARPA II was consistent with Article VIII of ICRW.[168] In the view of the Court, the two elements of the phrase "for purposes of scientific research" – "scientific research" and "for purposes of" – are cumulative. As a result, even if a whaling program involves "scientific research", the killing, taking or treating of whales under such a program does not fall within Article VIII unless it is "for purposes of" scientific research.[169]

---

163 ICJ, *Whaling in the Antarctic* (*Australia v. Japan: New Zealand intervening*), Judgment, para.85.

164 For example, according to Article 240(d) of UNCLOS, "marine scientific research shall be conducted in compliance with all relevant regulations adopted in conformity with this Convention including those for the protection and preservation of the marine environment". UNCLOS, Article 240(d). This provision can arguably include the requirement that the conduct of scientific research must avoid adverse impacts on marine resources.

165 ICJ, *Whaling in the Antarctic* (*Australia v. Japan: New Zealand intervening*), Judgment, para.86.

166 Ibid.

167 Ibid. For more discussion on this approach, see, for instance, Anastasia Telesetsky, Donald K. Anton, and Timo Koivurova, "ICJ's Decision in Australia v. Japan: Giving up the Spear or Refining the Scientific Design?", *Ocean Development & International Law* 45, no. 4 (2014): 332–333; Anthony Press, "Science in the Court! The Role of Science in 'Whaling in the Antarctic'", in *Whaling in the Antarctic: the ICJ Judgment and its Implications*, edited by Malgosia Fitzmaurice and Dai Tamada (Brill Nijhoff, 2016), 383–384.

168 ICJ, *Whaling in the Antarctic* (*Australia v. Japan: New Zealand intervening*), Judgment, paras.70–97 and 223–227.

169 Ibid., para.71.

The Court further stated that the decisive element to determine whether a program is "for purposes of" scientific research is whether the research objectives alone would be sufficient to justify the design and implementation of the program.[170] After the assessment, the Court concluded that activities involved in this case could broadly be characterized as "scientific research",[171] but overall the special permits granted by Japan for the killing, taking and treating of whales are not "for purposes of" scientific research under Article VIII, paragraph 1, of ICRW.[172] The Court drew this conclusion based on the reasonableness of the design and implication of the project in relation to its stated objectives, and more specifically Japan's decisions regarding the use of lethal methods and the scale of the use of lethal sampling in the program.[173] It further noted that in the implementation of the program, "funding considerations, rather than strictly scientific criteria, played a role in the program's design".[174] Besides, the Court considered other aspects of the program also "cast doubt on its characterization as a program for purposes of scientific research". These aspects include the open-ended time frame of the program, the limited scientific output to date, and the absence of significant cooperation between the program and other related research projects.[175]

A point worths mentioning is that the Court concluded that the JARPA II activities "can broadly be characterized as 'scientific research'" primarily based on the research objectives of the program presented by Japan and the fact that these objectives fall within the research categories identified by the Scientific Committee in Annexes Y and P, which are adopted to review the special permit granted by the government of States Parties to ICRW under Article VIII of the Convention.[176] The Court did not investigate in detail the *implementation* of the program for purposes of classification – whether it is scientific research or not.[177] It has been submitted that "while the Court seems to have implicitly [...]

170 Ibid., para.97.
171 Ibid., para.127.
172 Ibid., para.227.
173 Ibid., paras.224–226.
174 Ibid., para.225.
175 Ibid., para.226.
176 Ibid., para.127.
177 The Court did, however, looked at the implementation of the program, in particular the fact that the actual take of whales in JARPA II fell short of the sample sizes established in the Research Plan, and the failure of Japan to modify the research program envisaged in the JARPA II Research Plan accordingly, to draw the conclusion that the target sample size for minke whales was set for non-scientific reasons, which was regarded as an important element of program "for purposes of scientific research". See Anthony Press, "Science in the Court! The Role of Science in 'Whaling in the Antarctic'", 376–379.

characterized JARPA II as scientific research, the identification of JARPA II as scientific research does not seem an obvious result".[178]

In terms of the implications of the Judgment on this case for the current analysis, although the decision of the ICJ only has binding force between the parties to the dispute and in respect of this particular case, it has been acknowledged by a Resolution adopted by IWC after the release of the Judgment that such a decision "is a highly authoritative guide on how Article VIII [of ICRW] should be interpreted and applied".[179] In the same Resolution, IWC instructed its Scientific Committee, in its review of new and existing special permit research programs, to provide advice to the Commission concerning the elements mentioned by the ICJ in the Judgment of the *Whaling in the Antarctic* case.[180] By the same token, the reasoning of the ICJ would provide some guidance to interpreting relevant provisions under UNCLOS.[181] It is the viewpoint of the Court that the design and implementation, in relation to the stated objectives, of the program are elements for identifying whether the program is "*for purposes of*" scientific research.[182] Since UNCLOS does not use the term "for purposes of" in its marine scientific research regime, the Court's approach in interpreting the phrase "for purposes of scientific research" cannot be directly used in understanding the meaning of the term "marine scientific research" under UNCLOS. This being said, the Court's interpretation of the term "for purposes of" and its role in the accumulative phrase "for purposes of scientific research" can inform, *inter alia*, the identification of the purpose(s) of an ocean data collection activity.

5.6 Conclusions

As stated in the introductory section of this chapter, the examination of international conventions other than UNCLOS mainly serves two purposes in the context of this study – to assist the interpretation of the term "marine scientific research" under UNCLOS and to provide an overview of the international regulation of ocean data collection activities when the legal classification of the activities concerned is not clearly addressed.

178 Anastasia Telesetsky, Donald K. Anton, and Timo Koivurova, "ICJ's Decision in Australia v. Japan: Giving up the Spear or Refining the Scientific Design?", 332.

179 See "Resolution on Whaling under Special Permit", Doc. Resolution 2014–5, 2014, para.1.

180 Ibid.

181 See Tim Stephens and Donald Rothwell, "Marine Scientific Research", 562, 581.

182 ICJ, *Whaling in the Antarctic (Australia v. Japan: New Zealand intervening)*, Judgment, para.97.

In terms of the first purpose, several implications can be drawn from the analysis of international conventions other than UNCLOS. Relevant provisions of CBD and its Nagoya Protocol suggest that *access* to (marine) genetic resources may serve both commercial and non-commercial purposes. Similarly, *research* on (marine) genetic resources can also be classified into two kinds – commercial and non-commercial. This finding reinforces the interpretation of Article 246(5) of UNCLOS made in Chapter 3, that when the undertaking of an ocean data collection activity includes commercial ends, the activity at issue may still qualify as marine scientific research. Besides, Article 8(a) of the Nagoya Protocol acknowledges the need to address a change of intent for research on genetic resources. Implications of these provisions will be further elaborated upon in Chapter 6 of this study concerning the legal regulation of ocean data collection activities that involve access to marine genetic resources.

In UNFCCC, a provision sets up the obligations for the Contracting Parties to promote and cooperate in "research" and "systematic observation". While UNFCCC does not define these terms, pertinent practice on this provision indicates that the term "research" under UNFCCC only refers to modelling and experimental work that is mostly undertaken in laboratories. Activities that involve the *in situ* collection of data required for such research are covered by the term "observation". As such, it is the practice of observations that is relevant to the current discussion. Because in practice data collected through observation under UNFCCC are not limited to climate-related uses, potentially the same ocean data collection activity may be considered as "observation" in the context of UNFCCC, and as "marine scientific research" in the context of UNCLOS. In this regard, it is argued that Contracting Parties' commitments to promote and cooperate in observation under UNFCCC can be used as an incentive for the States concerned to enter into cooperative arrangements for certain ocean data collection activities when the legal classification of the activities at issue – whether they are marine scientific research – remains controversial. The operationalization of this article will be discussed in Chapter 7 of this book.

As to the London Convention and its London Protocol, subsequent developments of these instruments prohibit marine geoengineering with the only exception of the programs that qualify as "legitimate scientific research" or "specific marine scientific research". The relevant Assessment Frameworks suggest that "legitimate scientific research" and "specific marine scientific research" must have "proper scientific attributes" and set out the criteria for determining the existence of such attributes. It is submitted that these criteria serve as a good basis for determining whether an ocean data collection activity is undertaken for scientific purposes, although they are not intended by the drafters to be directly used to define the term "marine scientific research" in general. To be more specific, it has been concluded that the criteria contained in the Assessment Frameworks were introduced to ensure that the objectives of the London Convention and the London Protocol would not be jeopardized, rather than giving a general definition of the term "(marine) (scientific) research".

Under ICRW, the prohibition of commercial whaling is subject to an exception provided in its Article VIII(1) – when a whaling program is undertaken "for purposes of scientific research". While this phrase is not defined in ICRW, its content has been addressed in detail by the *Whaling in the Antarctic* case. During the proceedings of this case, Australia advanced four "essential characteristics" of "scientific research" in the context of ICRW. In its Judgment, among the four characteristics proposed by Australia, the Court expressly stated that peer review is not one of the criteria for scientific research and that although the use of lethal methods is discouraged, scientific research may still involve the use of such methods. Concerning the criteria on the existence of a hypothesis, the parties concerned agreed that scientific research should proceed based on a certain question, which could take the form of a hypothesis. This reinforces the current author's interpretation of the requirement of "scientific methods" under Article 240(b) of UNCLOS.[183] However, the Parties disagreed about the level of specificity required of such a hypothesis. Therefore, notably, it remained a controversial issue.

In general, the Court chose not to define the term "scientific research", but rather to look at the phrase "for purposes of scientific research" as two cumulative elements – "for purposes of" and "scientific research". Based on information on the implementation of the design of the program, the Court considered that the program was not "for purposes of" scientific research under Article VIII(1) ICRW. Although UNCLOS does not employ the same phrase as ICRW, the ICJ's reasoning in interpreting the phrase "for purposes of scientific research" – whether the research objectives alone would be sufficient to justify the design and implementation of the program – can inform, *inter alia*, the identification of the purpose(s) of an ocean data collection activity. According to the Court, elements for the identification include the decisions regarding the use of the lethal methods (including whether the decisions were made for scientific concerns or commercial reasons), the scale of the use of lethal methods in the program, time frame of the program, the scientific output of the program, and cooperation with other research institutions.

183 See Chapter 3.2.2 of this book.

Concerning the second purpose of looking at other international conventions, provisions of CBD and its Nagoya Protocol concerning the requirements of prior informed consent, mutually agreed terms, and the special considerations to be given to access for non-commercial research purposes, suggest that, similar to the UNCLOS marine scientific research regime, when the sovereignty or jurisdiction of the coastal State is affected by the activities concerned, the CBD regime tends to lean towards the coastal State; whereas when access to (marine) genetic resources is sought without commercial intent, both regimes encourage that the coastal State should create simplified or less stringent requirements for the researching State, and thus seem to lean towards the researching State. This observation will be addressed in Chapters 6 and 7 of this study concerning the legal regulation of two new types of ocean data collection activities, namely access to marine genetic resources and operational oceanography.

Under UNFCCC, pertinent practice on observation (under GCOS) shows that the same set of data (on oceanic ECVs or EOVs), which are collected by different platforms coordinated by the JCOMM, using different methods or technologies, can be used by different users, for different purposes. This kind of practice adds to the complexity of discerning the legal classification of a specific activity. It seems that none of the elements (purposes of the activity, tools or technologies adopted in the undertaking of the activity, platforms that collect data) can act in itself as a practical criterion for purposes of legal classification. This matter will be further elaborated upon in Chapter 7 of this research. In addition, some soft law instruments have been adopted by some international organizations concerning the legal regulation of certain observing elements coordinated by JCOMM, such as the Argo Guidelines and WMO Resolution 45 (Cg-18). Implications of these instruments, especially for considering the appropriate legal framework for certain ocean data collection activities when the legal classification of the activities concerned remains unclear or controversial, will also be addressed in Chapter 7 of this study.

In sum, issues of the law of the sea cannot be considered in isolation and UNCLOS is not the sole regime governing the conduct of ocean data collection activities. From different perspectives, international conventions apart from UNCLOS shed light on understanding the scope of marine scientific research and considering the appropriate legal framework(s) for different kinds of ocean data collection activities. Substantive provisions of these conventions also provide inspiration for the interpretation and implementation of legal terms under UNCLOS in a more general manner, such as the due regard obligation. For instance, relevant provisions of CBD and the Nagoya Protocol indicate the objects and purpose of the activity in question play a vital role in the balancing test as required by the fulfillment of due regard obligations: when the sovereignty or jurisdiction of the coastal State is affected by the activity at issue, both the UNCLOS marine scientific research regime and CBD tend to lean towards the side of the coastal State; whereas when the activity is conducted without commercial intent, both regimes encourage that the coastal State create simplified or less stringent requirements for the researching State. It is further argued that, in the balancing test, the obligations of States under other conventions pertaining to ocean data collection may be considered. For instance, the obligation of States to promote and cooperate in systematic observation under Article 4 of UNFCCC can be used as an incentive for the States concerned to enter into cooperative arrangements for certain ocean data collection activities when the legal classification of the activity at issue remains controversial, or when the States concerned prefer to leave the legal classification of the activity undefined. These observations will be helpful for the discussions in Chapters 6 and 7 of this book concerning the international legal regulation of new developments in the field of ocean data collection.

CHAPTER 6

Access to Marine Genetic Resources and Its Regulatory Framework

6.1 Introduction[1]

As mentioned in the introductory chapter of this book, after setting out the legal framework for ocean data collection activities and options for using the flexibility provided by UNCLOS to cope with new developments in the said field (Chapters 3 to 5), the present study will now illustrate the strengths and limits of UNCLOS and its marine scientific research regime in accommodating "modern" ocean data collection activities, through several specific case studies. Based on the conclusions drawn in the previous chapters, the current chapter and Chapter 7 of this study aim to examine some new developments that are taking place in ocean data collection, ascertain their legal implications and discuss the appropriate legal framework(s) applicable to them. This chapter focuses on access to marine genetic resources and Chapter 7 focuses on operational oceanography. It is the viewpoint of the author that these two kinds of ocean data collection activities raise the most controversial problems concerning the appropriate legal frameworks applicable to them.[2] This assumption is considered to be confirmed by the relevant discussion in various fora as referred to in Chapter 4 of this research.

Access to marine genetic resources is relevant for the present research to the extent that the sampling of such resources can be viewed as a form of ocean data collection. It is noted that access to marine genetic resources

1 An earlier version of this chapter has been published in the journal Ocean Development & International Law, Issue 1, 2020. Chuxiao Yu, "Implications of the UNCLOS Marine Scientific Research Regime for the Current Negotiations on Access and Benefit Sharing of Marine Genetic Resources in Areas Beyond National Jurisdiction", *Ocean Development & International Law* 51, no. 1 (2020): 2–18.

2 As pointed out in Chapter 3 of this book, the distinguishing benchmark for different kinds of ocean data collection activities is arguably the function or purpose of the activity. The boundaries of the UNCLOS marine scientific research regime and hence the legal classification of ocean data collection activities may give rise to different opinions due to the fact that ocean data collection activities can be conducted for different purposes, serving various ends. Access to marine genetic resources and operational oceanography represent two typical examples of "modern" ocean data collection activities that serve multiple purposes, and thus raise typical legal issues regarding their regulation.

 DOI:10.1163/9789004508590_007

does not directly involve the collection of data. However, it is submitted that access to marine genetic resources is not conducted for the purpose of collecting the samples *per se*.[3] Instead, the resources are sampled for the purpose of extracting valuable data therefrom for subsequent research or analysis. In that light, the current chapter will examine the activities concerning access to marine genetic resources as a form of ocean data collection and consider the appropriate legal framework applicable to such activities under UNCLOS.

Before commencing the substantive discussion, it is necessary to delineate the scope of the discussion in this chapter. This chapter only addresses the regulation of access to marine genetic resources in areas beyond national jurisdiction – on the high seas and in the Area. In areas under national jurisdiction, potentially, activities concerning marine genetic resources may be classified either as marine scientific research or activities involving exploration or exploitation of resources over which the coastal State has sovereign rights.[4] In both cases, UNCLOS requires the activities concerned to be subject to the consent of the coastal State.[5] However, the governing principle for the regulation of access to marine genetic resources in areas beyond national jurisdiction is not clearly addressed by UNCLOS. Divergent opinions exist on this matter.[6]

Currently, this matter is under consideration during the discussions at the UN Intergovernmental Conference on Marine Biodiversity of Areas beyond National Jurisdiction with a view to developing an international legally binding

3 Tullio Scovazzi, "Is the UN Convention on the Law of the Sea the Legal Framework for All Activities in the Sea? The Case of Bioprospecting", in *Law, Technology and Science for Oceans in Globalisation: IUU Fishing, Oil Pollution, Bioprospecting, Outer Continental Shelf*, edited by Davor Vidas (Brill, 2010), 312.

4 Craig H Allen, "Protecting the Oceanic Gardens of Eden: International Law Issues in Deep-Sea Vent Resource Conservation and Management", 646.

5 See, for instance, UNCLOS, Articles 2, 19, 56(1), 77, 245, 246(2).

6 See, for instance, "Report of the Secretary-General on oceans and the law of the sea of 12 March 2007", UN Doc. A/62/66, para.200; "Report on the work of the United Nations Open-ended Informal Consultative Process on Oceans and the Law of the Sea at its eighth meeting", UN Doc. A/62/169, 2007, paras.71–81. Relevant literature includes, Tullio Scovazzi, "Is the UN Convention on the Law of the Sea the Legal Framework for All Activities in the Sea? The Case of Bioprospecting"; Robin M. Warner, "Protecting the Diversity of the Depths: Environmental Regulation of Bioprospecting and Marine Scientific Research beyond National Jurisdiction"; Tullio Scovazzi, "The Concept of Common Heritage of Mankind and the Genetic Resources of the Seabed Beyond the Limits of National Jurisdiction", *Agenda Internacional* 14, no. 25 (2007); Louise Angélique de La Fayette, "A New Regime for the Conservation and Sustainable Use of Marine Biodiversity and Genetic Resources Beyond the Limits of National Jurisdiction", *The International Journal of Marine and Coastal Law* 24, no. 2 (2009); Salvatore Arico and Charlotte Salpin, "Bioprospecting of Genetic Resources in the Deep Seabed: Scientific, Legal and Policy Aspects".

instrument (ILBI) under UNCLOS on the conservation and sustainable use of marine biological diversity of areas beyond national jurisdiction. The process of the UN negotiations on this topic has been introduced in Chapter 4.3.3 of this book. During the discussions at the Intergovernmental Conference and the PrepCom prior to the Conference, issues concerning marine genetic resources, including questions on the sharing of benefits, proved to be among the most controversial issues.

An overview of different options was provided by a non-paper prepared by the Chair of PrepCom.[7] In the most recent Intergovernmental Conference, opinions on this matter still vary.[8] Relevant provisions of the revised draft text and the various viewpoints included in the "Article-by-article compilation of textual proposals for consideration at the fourth session dated 15 April 2020" reflect the differing views on issues surrounding marine genetic resources in areas beyond national jurisdiction, in particular the regulation (if any) of access to such resources and the mechanism for the sharing of benefits arising from their utilization.[9]

As indicated by the UNGA Resolution 72/249, the work and results of the Intergovernmental Conference "should be fully consistent with the provisions of [UNCLOS]".[10] In that light, the consideration of the legal framework applicable to access to marine genetic resources in areas beyond national jurisdiction is required to be based on the rights and obligations set out by UNCLOS. Against

---

7 "Chair's streamlined non-paper on elements of a draft text of an international legally-binding instrument under the United Nations Convention on the Law of the Sea on the conservation and sustainable use of marine biological diversity of areas beyond national jurisdiction", 2017, https://www.un.org/Depts/los/biodiversity/prepcom_files/Chairs_streamlined_non-paper_to_delegations.pdf, paras.53–70.

8 Tallash Kantai et al., "Summary of the Third Session of the Intergovernmental Conference (IGC) on the Conservation and Sustainable Use of Marine Biodiversity of Areas Beyond National Jurisdiction: 19–30 August 2019", *IISD - Earth Negotiations Bulletin*, at pp. 7–8.

9 "Revised draft text of an agreement under the United Nations Convention on the Law of the Sea on the conservation and sustainable use of marine biological diversity of areas beyond national jurisdiction - Note by the President", Doc. A/CONF.232/2020/3, Articles 10–11. See also, "Textual proposals submitted by delegations by 20 February 2020, for consideration at the fourth session of the Intergovernmental conference on an international legally binding instrument under the United Nations Convention on the Law of the Sea on the conservation and sustainable use of marine biological diversity of areas beyond national jurisdiction (the Conference), in response to the invitation by the President of the Conference in her Note of 18 November 2019 (A/CONF.232/2020/3)".

10 "UNGA Resolution on "International legally binding instrument under the United Nations Convention on the Law of the Sea on the conservation and sustainable use of marine biological diversity of areas beyond national jurisdiction" of 24 December 2017", UN Doc. A/RES/72/249, para.6.

this backdrop, this chapter begins with an introduction to the characteristics of activities concerning marine genetic resources (Section 6.2). Section 6.3 discusses the legal classification of access to marine genetic resources under UNCLOS, and thus considers the appropriate legal framework for such activities. Section 6.4 draws the implications of applying the framework as discerned in Section 6.3 for establishing the arrangements for access to marine genetic resources in areas beyond national jurisdiction, and the mechanisms for the sharing of benefits arising from the utilization of such resources. Section 6.5 concludes the chapter and offers some final observations.

6.2 Characteristics of Activities Concerning Marine Genetic Resources

There are mainly two stages of activities related to marine genetic resources – access and utilization.[11] As pointed out in the introductory chapter, the present research will only address legal issues arising from ocean data collection activities that are conducted *in situ* in the marine environment. The utilization of marine genetic resources mostly, if not all, takes place after the resources have been collected from the marine environment. Such activity can hardly be considered as ocean data collection in the context of the present research. Therefore, the legal classification of activities involving the utilization of marine genetic resources will not be addressed in this chapter. This being said, marine genetic resources are collected for the purpose of utilization. An introduction to the features of the utilization of the said resources is considered to shed light on understanding the legal implications of access to marine genetic resources. Therefore, the following analysis will consecutively address the features of activities concerning access to and utilization of marine genetic resources.

6.2.1 *Access to Marine Genetic Resources*

Access to marine genetic resources can take place at different places and in different forms, which mainly include *in situ* access, *ex situ* access and *in silico* access.[12] *In situ* access refers to "access to/collection of samples of marine organisms (containing marine genetic resources) within their natural

11 Arianna Broggiato et al., "Mare Geneticum: Balancing Governance of Marine Genetic Resources in International Waters", *The International Journal of Marine and Coastal Law* 33, no. 1 (2018): 22.

12 Evanson Chege Kamau, "Access-Related Issues", *IUCN Information Papers for the Intersessional Workshop on Marine Genetic Resources,* 2013, 23.

surroundings, such as ecosystems and habitats in the high seas or the Area"; *ex situ* access means "access to [marine genetic resources] outside of their natural habitats, which involves [the] transfer of samples previously collected from [the marine environment] that have been analyzed and kept in biorepositories"; *in silico* access refers to "access to information, data and research results for *in silico* testing and the results therefrom".[13]

In situ access to marine genetic resources is primarily carried out by academic or government institutes to increase mankind's knowledge of the oceans and the natural resources therein.[14] Unlike one-time consumptive use of fish, marine genetic resources may be used perpetually in a number of commercial and non-commercial applications when they have been removed from their *in situ* source.[15] Once collected, samples of marine genetic resources can be preserved *ex situ* for future research and development, and the valuable information on genetic materials can be digitalized and thus be freely or partially freely accessed through databases. The emerging best practices in open science have made information and data related to genetic resources more accessible than ever before, and therefore allow *in silico* access to marine genetic resources.[16]

Whether all these types of access shall be included in the regulatory scope of the new instrument remains a controversial issue.[17] As limited by the research scope, the present study will focus on ocean data collection activities that are conducted *in situ* in the marine environment. Activities carried out on land (in the laboratories) concerning objects that have been collected from the marine

13 Ibid.

14 Kim Juniper, "Technological, Environmental, Social and Economic Aspects", *IUCN Information Papers for the Intersessional Workshop on Marine Genetic Resources*, 2013, 18. See also Matthias Buck and Clare Hamilton, "The Nagoya Protocol on Access to Genetic Resources and the Fair and Equitable Sharing of Benefits Arising from Their Utilization to the Convention on Biological Diversity", 59.

15 Lyle Glowka, "The Deepest of Ironies: Genetic Resources, Marine Scientific Research, and the Area", 169.

16 Lyle Glowka, "Evolving Perspectives on the International Seabed Area's Genetic Resources: Fifteen Years After the 'Deepest of Ironies'", in *Law, Technology and Science for Oceans in Globalisation: IUU Fishing, Oil Pollution, Bioprospecting, Outer Continental Shelf*, edited by Davor Vidas (Brill, 2010), 412.

17 This can be seen from the different options for defining the term "access" for the purposes of the ILBI included in the revised draft text. "Revised draft text of an agreement under the United Nations Convention on the Law of the Sea on the conservation and sustainable use of marine biological diversity of areas beyond national jurisdiction - Note by the President", Doc. A/CONF.232/2020/3, Article 1(1). See also, Tallash Kantai et al., "Summary of the Third Session of the Intergovernmental Conference (IGC) on the Conservation and Sustainable Use of Marine Biodiversity of Areas Beyond National Jurisdiction: 19–30 August 2019", at p. 7.

environment fall outside the scope of this study. Therefore, the remaining analysis of this chapter will only address the legal issues arising from *in situ* access to marine genetic resources.

Because *in situ* access means the actual sampling of marine genetic resources in the environment, the term "sampling" will also be used in the following discussion to refer to *in situ* access to marine genetic resources.

6.2.2 *Utilization of Marine Genetic Resources*

The utilization of marine genetic resources can be conducted for commercial or non-commercial (scientific) purposes. The revised draft text of an ILBI reflects different options for defining the phrase "the utilization of marine genetic resources" under the new instrument. If the new instrument is to include a definition of the said phrase,[18] it may refer to "conduct research and development on the genetic and/or biochemical composition of marine genetic resources".[19] Another option is to include "the exploitation thereof" in the definition as well.[20] It is unclear what the term "exploitation" means in the context of the revised draft text. If it refers, as is the case for the ISA Regulations, to the recovery of natural resources for commercial purposes and the production and marketing of certain products,[21] the utilization of marine genetic resources as a means of exploitation requires a substantial amount of catch in order to be profitable.[22] Sampling activities contributing to such a kind of utilization target not the data to be extracted from the resources, but rather the resources themselves. Thus, the exploitation of marine genetic resources and the sampling activities contributing directly to such an end fall outside the scope of the current discussion and will not be addressed in this chapter.

---

18 Several delegations have proposed to exclude the definition of the phrase from the new instrument in their textual proposals. See "Textual proposals submitted by delegations by 20 February 2020, for consideration at the fourth session of the Intergovernmental conference on an international legally binding instrument under the United Nations Convention on the Law of the Sea on the conservation and sustainable use of marine biological diversity of areas beyond national jurisdiction (the Conference), in response to the invitation by the President of the Conference in her Note of 18 November 2019 (A/CONF.232/2020/3)".

19 "Revised draft text of an agreement under the United Nations Convention on the Law of the Sea on the conservation and sustainable use of marine biological diversity of areas beyond national jurisdiction - Note by the President", Doc. A/CONF.232/2020/3, Article 1(15).

20 Ibid.

21 See Chapter 3.3.2.1.1 of this book.

22 See "Report of the Secretary-General on oceans and the law of the sea of 12 March 2007", UN Doc. A/62/66, para.190.

It is also possible that "exploitation" refers to the commercialization of marine genetic resources. In this case, practice shows that marine genetic resources that are collected *in situ* need to be isolated and cultured before they can be studied. After the study, interesting and unique genetic materials may be passed on to industry for biotechnological applications.[23] At this point, the organism and its genetic material may become potentially economically valuable, and such value can only be realized if there are subsequent financial investments, research, and marketing, which is seldomly achieved in practice.[24] Therefore, the percentage of activities concerning marine genetic resources that eventually lead to commercial applications is minor.[25]

The observation above concerning the different stages of utilizing genetic resources is in line with the relevant provisions of the Nagoya Protocol. Article 17(1)(a) indicates that activities concerning marine genetic resources can be divided into different stages, including "research, development, innovation, pre-commercialization or commercialization".[26] Research on marine genetic resources can be commercial or non-commercial.[27] The intent behind such research may change during the process of utilization.[28] However, it remains a challenging task to draw the line between commercial and non-commercial research and to identify the change of intent.[29]

Besides, it has been observed that the distinction between different development stages of genetic resources is difficult to make in practice, "due to the discontinuous paths from the collection of samples in the field

---

23 Lyle Glowka, "The Deepest of Ironies: Genetic Resources, Marine Scientific Research, and the Area", 169; Graham Shimmield, "Extent and Types of Research, Uses and Applications", *IUCN Information Papers for the Intersessional Workshop on Marine Genetic Resources,* 2013; Kim Juniper, "Technological, Environmental, Social and Economic Aspects", 18; Arianna Broggiato et al., "Mare Geneticum: Balancing Governance of Marine Genetic Resources in International Waters", 17.

24 Lyle Glowka, "The Deepest of Ironies: Genetic Resources, Marine Scientific Research, and the Area", 169; Graham Shimmield, "Extent and Types of Research, Uses and Applications".

25 Arianna Broggiato et al., "Mare Geneticum: Balancing Governance of Marine Genetic Resources in International Waters", 23.

26 Article 17 of the Nagoya Protocol requires the checkpoints established for the purposes of monitoring and enhancing transparency about the utilization of the genetic resources "to be relevant to the utilization of genetic resources, or to the collection of relevant information at, *inter alia*, any stage of research, development, innovation, pre-commercialization or commercialization". Nagoya Protocol, Article 17(1)(a)(IV)(a).

27 Ibid., Article 8(a).

28 Ibid. This matter has been fuller discussed in Chapter 5.2.3 of this study.

29 See Tom Dedeurwaerdere et al., "Governing Global Scientific Research Commons under the Nagoya Protocol", 413.

through to commercialization".[30] One exception is commercialization. The line between commercialization, which is the final stage of the utilization, and other development stages is relatively easier to draw. This is because commercialization typically involves the production and marketing of specific products or the application of intellectual property rights, which will be known to the public.

6.3 Appropriate Legal Framework for the Sampling of Marine Genetic Resources

Bearing in mind the features of activities concerning marine genetic resources, this section considers the appropriate legal framework for *in situ* access to marine genetic resources. To address this matter, it is necessary to discern the legal classification of such activities.

As concluded in Chapter 3, the purpose of an ocean data collection activity is an essential element for discerning the legal classification of the activity in the context of UNCLOS. Sampling of marine genetic resources can be conducted for commercial or scientific purposes or both. In most cases, such activities are carried out by academic or government institutes to increase mankind's knowledge of the ocean and the natural resources therein.[31] Oftentimes, these activities are conducted by researchers with no commercial intent at the time of access.[32] The legal classification of such activities is relatively clear in light of the conclusions drawn in Chapter 3 – they fall squarely within the scope of marine scientific research under UNCLOS.

Marine genetic resources can also be sampled for both scientific and commercial purposes. Genetic resources are also collected as part of scientific research projects, which often involve partnerships between public research institutes and biotechnology companies.[33] It is becoming increasingly common for activities undertaken for scientific purposes, especially those related to biological and geological sampling, to have links to onshore commercial

30 Thomas Greiber, "Meaning and Scope", *IUCN Information Papers for the Intersessional Workshop on Marine Genetic Resources*, 2013, 3.

31 Kim Juniper, "Technological, Environmental, Social and Economic Aspects", 18.

32 Matthias Buck and Clare Hamilton, "The Nagoya Protocol on Access to Genetic Resources and the Fair and Equitable Sharing of Benefits Arising from Their Utilization to the Convention on Biological Diversity", 59.

33 "Report of the Secretary-General on oceans and the law of the sea of 12 March 2007", UN Doc. A/62/66, para.145.

activities.[34] Considering the high costs in terms of financial and human resources of venturing into the marine environment, the consortia of different actors, such as government, academia and industry, have been created to share expertise, risks and expenses in such activities.[35] In this regard, a sampling activity will have to serve multiple ends to satisfy the needs of all the actors involved.

Some scholars term activities involving marine genetic resources described above as "bioprospecting".[36] This term is neither used nor defined in UNCLOS or other international legal instruments, including CBD. A note prepared by the secretariat of CBD defines the term as:

> the exploration of biodiversity for commercially valuable genetic and biochemical resources. It can be defined as the process of gathering information from the biosphere on the molecular composition of genetic resources for the development of new commercial products.[37]

According to this definition, bioprospecting is, in a sense, equivalent to exploration under UNCLOS, which is conducted specifically to make use of the commercial value of genetic resources. As such, this definition indicates a clear distinction between marine scientific research and bioprospecting.

---

34 "Report of the Secretary-General on oceans and the law of the sea of 4 March 2004", UN Doc. A/59/62, para.260.

35 Lyle Glowka, "The Deepest of Ironies: Genetic Resources, Marine Scientific Research, and the Area", 173; Florian H.Th. Wegelein, *Marine Scientific Research: The Operation and Status of Research Vessels and Other Platforms in International Law*, 21.

36 See, for instance, Salvatore Arico and Charlotte Salpin, "Bioprospecting of Genetic Resources in the Deep Seabed: Scientific, Legal and Policy Aspects"; Andree Kirchner, "Bioprospecting, Marine Scientific Research and the Patentability of Genetic Resources", in *Serving the rule of international maritime law: essays in honour of Professor David Joseph Attard*, edited by Norman A. Martínez Gutiérrez (London: Routledge, 2009); Morten Walløe Tvedt and Ane E Jørem, "Bioprospecting in the High Seas: Regulatory Options for Benefit Sharing", *The Journal of World Intellectual Property* 16, no. 3–4 (2013); Ane Jørem and Morten Walløe Tvedt, "Bioprospecting in the High Seas: Existing Rights and Obligations in View of A New Legal Regime for Marine Areas Beyond National Jurisdiction"; Marjo Vierros et al., "An Update on Marine Genetic Resources: Scientific Research, Commercial Uses and a Database on Marine Bioprospecting" (paper presented at the side event of the eighth meeting of United Nations Informal Consultative Process on Oceans and the Law of the Sea, 2007).

37 "Progress Report on the Implementation of the Programmes of Work on the Biological Diversity of Inland Water Ecosystems, Marine and Coastal Biological Diversity, and Forest Biological Diversity (DECISIONS IV/4, IV/5, IV/7)", Doc. UNEP/CBD/COP/5/INF/7, para.6.

On the other hand, the UN Secretary-General's Report on oceans and the law of the sea (2007) stated that the frontier between bioprospecting and scientific investigation is becoming increasingly unclear.[38] The report further pointed out that in recent years, the term "biodiscovery" has been preferred to the term "bioprospecting" to put greater emphasis on the investigative aspect of the activities concerned and less on the idea of future exploitation.[39] Besides, unlike the note prepared by the secretariat of CBD, the report equates "bioprospecting" to "research and development" – a notion under the Nagoya Protocol.[40] As discussed in Chapter 5.2.3 of this book, the notion of "research and development" under the Nagoya Protocol also includes research on genetic resources without commercial intent. As such, it seems that the introduction of new concepts, including "bioprospecting", does not contribute to understanding the legal classification of activities concerning marine genetic resources, and may cause terminological chaos. Therefore, this section will not use these newly introduced terms but instead rely on the terms included in CBD and the Nagoya Protocol to help discern the legal classification of access to marine genetic resources under UNCLOS.[41] It is noted that the revised draft text of an ILBI does not use the term "bioprospecting" either. Options to refer

38 "Report of the Secretary-General on oceans and the law of the sea of 12 March 2007", UN Doc. A/62/66, para.145. The report stated that, "types of activities related to [marine genetic resources] generally include scientific investigation of the oceans and their biological processes; research and development or 'bioprospecting'; and exploitation".

39 Ibid., para.150.

40 Ibid., paras.145, 150.

41 The necessity to rely on the terms used in CBD and the Nagoya Protocol for legal classification can be explained by the fact that UNCLOS provisions concerning prospecting and exploration are mostly drafted with mineral resources and fisheries in mind. In contrast, CBD and the Nagoya Protocol are adopted with a specific view to the regulation of activities concerning genetic resources, including marine genetic resources. Therefore, a comparison of the terms under these instruments may shed some further light on the legal classification of activities concerning marine genetic resources. Because the new instrument is to be adopted under the framework of UNCLOS, this section will discern the legal classification of activities concerning marine genetic resources in the context of UNCLOS, with the implications of the connection between the different terms under CBD and the Nagoya Protocol. It has been submitted that "in many cases the CBD supplements the [UNCLOS] regime governing access to living and genetic resources of the sea. Thus the two conventions must be read together when examining [marine scientific research] questions arising within that are party to both". See Craig H. Allen, "Protecting the Oceanic Gardens of Eden: International Law Issues in Deep-Sea Vent Resource Conservation and Management", 639.

to the sampling of marine genetic resources include "collection of" and "access to" marine genetic resources.[42]

With respect to "access to" marine genetic resources for both scientific and commercial purposes, opinions on the legal classification of the activities concerned vary.[43] Under UNCLOS, terms that can be used to denote ocean data collection activities with commercial purposes include "marine scientific research", "prospecting" and "exploration".[44] As discussed in Chapter 3 of this study, the fundamental difference between the three terms is that while the latter two terms – "prospecting" and "exploration"– refer to activities exclusively serving the purpose of commercial gain, activities under the term "marine scientific research" are not undertaken purely for commercial purposes.

Some scholars opine that access to marine genetic resources cannot be considered as marine scientific research under UNCLOS, mainly for the reason that, according to them, marine scientific research is generally understood to have a non-commercial purpose.[45] In contrast, sampling of marine genetic resources may have a commercial intent. However, the viewpoint that marine scientific research shall be conducted without any commercial purpose is debatable.

As concluded in the previous chapters of this book, no UNCLOS provision or subsequent agreement requires marine scientific research to be conducted solely for the purpose of increasing knowledge of the marine environment.[46]

---

42 "Revised draft text of an agreement under the United Nations Convention on the Law of the Sea on the conservation and sustainable use of marine biological diversity of areas beyond national jurisdiction - Note by the President", Doc. A/CONF.232/2020/3, Article 10.

43 The divergent opinions expressed at the UN BBNJ process on this matter have been discussed in Chapter 4.3.3 of this book.

44 As addressed earlier, sampling activities as a means of exploitation within the meaning of UNCLOS are not ocean data collection activities in the context of the present research and thus fall outside the scope of this chapter.

45 Thomas Greiber, "Access and Benefit Sharing in Relation to Marine Genetic Resources from Areas Beyond National Jurisdiction: A Possible Way Forward", *Bonn: IUCN (BfN-Skripten, no. 301)* (2011): 15; Salvatore Arico and Charlotte Salpin, "Bioprospecting of Genetic Resources in the Deep Seabed: Scientific, Legal and Policy Aspects", 33. This view was also shared by the CBD Secretariat, which in its report on "Study of the relationship between the Convention on Biological Diversity and the United Nations Convention on the Law of the Sea with regard to the Conservation and Sustainable Use of Genetic Resources on the Deep Seabed" stated that, "[i]n the absence of a formal definition, marine scientific research could be defined as an activity that involves collection and analysis of information, data or samples aimed at increasing mankind's knowledge of the environment, and is not undertaken with the intent of economic gain". Doc. UNEP/CBD/SBSTTA/8/INF/3/Rev.1, 22 February 2003, para.47.

46 For more information, see the concluding remarks of Chapters 3 and 4 of this book.

Marine scientific research that contributes purely to furthering scientific knowledge of the marine environment is usually termed as pure marine scientific research, as opposed to applied marine scientific research.[47] An investigation of the drafting history of Article 246 of UNCLOS indicates that the distinction between pure and applied marine scientific research is not preserved in UNCLOS, and marine scientific research under the Convention covers both kinds of research projects.[48] Besides, it is argued that by including the phrase "of direct significance for the exploration and exploitation of natural resources", especially the qualifier "direct", in Article 246(5) of UNCLOS, the Convention recognizes that marine scientific research can be carried out with a view to the commercial utilization of the research objects.[49]

In fact, for centuries, marine scientific research has been used to provide insights for the discovery, exploration and exploitation of resources and to provide States with the basis for an advantageous position in marine affairs.[50] This observation is shared by the UN Secretary-General's Report on the oceans and the law of the sea, which commented that:

> [i]n the absence of a formal definition, it has been suggested that marine scientific research under UNCLOS encompasses both the study of the marine environment and its resources with a view to increasing humankind's knowledge (so-called "pure" or "fundamental" research), and research for the subsequent exploitation of resources (so-called "applied" research).[51]

Therefore, *in situ* access to marine genetic resources both for scientific and commercial purposes constitutes marine scientific research under UNCLOS. Such an activity is not to be considered as exploration or prospecting. Exploration refers to research and analytical activities specifically contributing to the subsequent exploitation,[52] while prospecting means the search for deposits

---

47 See Chapter 3.2.4.1.

48 See Chapter 3.2.4.1. See also Craig H. Allen, "Protecting the Oceanic Gardens of Eden: International Law Issues in Deep-Sea Vent Resource Conservation and Management", 643–644.

49 See Chapter 3.2.4.3.

50 Montserrat Gorina-Ysern, "Principles of International Law of the Sea Governing Coastal State Access to Marine Scientific Research Results" (University of New South Wales, 1995), 66–67.

51 "Report of the Secretary-General on oceans and the law of the sea of 12 March 2007", UN Doc. A/62/66, para.203.

52 See Chapter 3.3.2.1.

including the estimation of, among others, the economic values of the resources.[53] Arguably, prospecting preceded the resources exploration phrase, and exploration directly contributes to exploitation.[54] Based on the definitions given by the ISA Regulations, it seems that the difference between prospecting and exploration is that the former means the searching for deposits starting from scratch, while the latter refers to the search based on certain previously gathered data and information or confirmed hypothesis.[55]

In sum, both prospecting and exploration denote activities undertaken directly with a view to commercial gains, although the level of certainty to achieve such commercial gains differs for the two kinds of activities. Therefore, in the context of the current discussion, sampling of marine genetic resources for both scientific and commercial purposes is not to be considered as prospecting or exploration.

One may ask whether access to marine genetic resources (as a form of ocean data collection) can be conducted purely for commercial purposes. Very likely, the answer is negative. As demonstrated earlier, after marine genetic resources are collected, they will be processed in laboratories and enter the stage of research. Initially, most of such research is conducted for purposes of increasing scientific knowledge of the resources. If interesting and unique genetic materials are discovered during the research, and the researcher considers the materials be of commercial value, the materials will be further studied and developed. Some genetic materials may be passed on to biotechnology companies for subsequent applications in cases where the commercial value of the materials has been verified through research and development. It is until this point that the marine genetic resources that are collected may become potentially economically valuable. In light of all these procedures, arguably, it is sporadic that the marine genetic resources are sampled purely for commercial purposes since the commercial value of the resources is not known at the time of sampling.

One may inquire further whether it might be the case that marine genetic resources are (re)sampled after the value of such resources has been verified through previous research and development. Again, very likely, the answer is negative. As mentioned earlier, unlike one-time consumptive uses of fish,

---

53 See Chapter 3.3.4.1.1.

54 Craig H. Allen, "Protecting the Oceanic Gardens of Eden: International Law Issues in Deep-Sea Vent Resource Conservation and Management", 644. See also Michael W. Lodge, "International Seabed Authority's Regulations on Prospecting and Exploration for Polymetallic Nodules in the Area", *Journal of Energy & Natural Resources Law* 20, no. 3 (2002): 282.

55 See Chapter 3.3.4.1.1.

once collected, the samples of marine genetic resources can be cultured and preserved *ex situ* for future use, and the valuable data of such resources can be digitalized and saved on file. There is no need to resample marine genetic resources unless the resources are not sampled for the purpose of extracting data of the resources.

This being said, it is possible that with the development of technology and the accumulation of knowledge and research experiences, the likelihood of identifying commercially valuable information at the time of sampling will increase.[56] In other words, the nature and level of interest in marine genetic resources may change in the future. Potentially, sampling of marine genetic resources will be undertaken with an increasing level of commercial interests. As a result, the sampling activities are more likely to be conducted with commercial purposes.[57] Arguably, in this case, the related activities may be considered as prospecting under UNCLOS.[58] However, research indicates that knowledge about marine genetic resources in areas beyond national jurisdiction, especially in the deep sea, is generally lacking.[59] The level of certainty that the sampling of marine genetic resources in areas beyond national jurisdiction contributes to commercial gains is scarce at the moment.[60] Considering the knowledge gap and the various and difficult stages before the commercialization of such resources, the above observation that the sampling of marine

56 For more information on the evolving capacity to venture into the marine environment and extract valuable materials from marine genetic resources in areas beyond national jurisdiction and the increasing prospects for research for commercial purposes, see Graham Shimmield, "Extent and Types of Research, Uses and Applications"; Marjo Vierros et al., "An Update on Marine Genetic Resources: Scientific Research, Commercial Uses and a Database on Marine Bioprospecting"; Lyle Glowka, "Evolving Perspectives on the International Seabed Area's Genetic Resources: Fifteen Years After the 'Deepest of Ironies'".

57 It is perhaps for this reason that there has been a call for an "examination of the nature and level of interest in marine biological diversity in areas beyond national jurisdiction, and in particular commercial interest in genetic resources from the deep sea". See Marjo Vierros et al., "An Update on Marine Genetic Resources: Scientific Research, Commercial Uses and a Database on Marine Bioprospecting".

58 In view of the current author, such activities do not qualify as exploration under UNCLOS, as the threshold of the level of certainty to achieve commercial gains of exploration can hardly met.

59 See, for instance, Marjo Vierros et al., "An Update on Marine Genetic Resources: Scientific Research, Commercial Uses and a Database on Marine Bioprospecting".

60 For instance, it has been observed that "it has not been possible to identify gene patents from organisms located solely in areas beyond national jurisdiction". Andrew Merrie et al., "An ocean of surprises – Trends in human use, unexpected dynamics and governance challenges in areas beyond national jurisdiction", *Global Environmental Change* 27(2014): 23.

genetic resources can be undertaken purely for commercial purposes and thus be considered as prospecting is merely hypothetical.

Therefore, ocean data collection activities involving access to marine genetic resources in areas beyond national jurisdiction are not conducted purely for commercial purposes at the moment and thus cannot be considered as prospecting or exploration in the context of UNCLOS. As to future activities, potentially the intent of sampling marine genetic resources will change as a result of an increasing level of interest in the commercial value of marine genetic resources. However, as noted earlier, it remains a challenging task to draw the line between commercial and non-commercial research and to identify the change of intent.[61] In the context of UNCLOS, the identification of the change of intent is even more complicated, given that marine scientific research can be "of direct significance for exploration and exploitation of natural resources".[62] In this scenario, it is more reasonable, or more feasible at least, to consider activities concerning access to marine genetic resources in areas beyond national jurisdiction, which are carried out primarily to understand the unique biodiversity therein and the surrounding marine environment, as marine scientific research, to which the UNCLOS marine scientific research regime applies, unless there is sufficient evidence suggesting such activities are to be viewed as prospecting.[63]

The following section will apply pertinent UNCLOS provisions on marine scientific research and prospecting to access to marine genetic resources and examine the implications of such provisions for some controversial issues surrounding marine genetic resources in the BBNJ negotiation process.

6.4 Applying the Relevant UNCLOS Provisions to Activities Involving Marine Genetic Resources

Since the preceding discussion concludes that at the moment sampling of marine genetic resources qualifies as marine scientific research, this section will mainly focus on the implications of the UNCLOS marine scientific research regime on the critical issues concerning marine genetic resources in

61 See Tom Dedeurwaerdere et al., "Governing Global Scientific Research Commons under the Nagoya Protocol", 413. Besides, it has been pointed out that "most of [prospecting activities] may be carried out under the cover of marine scientific research". See Michael W Lodge, "International Seabed Authority's Regulations on Prospecting and Exploration for Polymetallic Nodules in the Area", 283.

62 UNCLOS, Article 246(5)(a).

63 This matter will be further addressed in Section 6.4 of the current chapter.

the ongoing negotiations.[64] The application of relevant UNCLOS provisions to cases where sampling of marine genetic resources constitutes prospecting will also be addressed.

Issues that are dealt with in this section include whether *in situ* access to marine genetic resources in areas beyond national jurisdiction needs to be regulated and if yes, under what conditions (Section 6.4.1); and whether an obligation of benefit sharing should be included in the new instrument (Section 6.4.2).

6.4.1 *The Application of the Relevant UNCLOS Provisions to* in Situ *Access to Marine Genetic Resources in Areas beyond National Jurisdiction*

An application of the UNCLOS marine scientific research regime to *in situ* access to marine genetic resources in areas beyond national jurisdiction leads to the following implications.

Based on the marine scientific research regime on the high seas and in the Area, *in situ* access to marine genetic resources that is not exclusively for commercial purposes can be carried out freely without the obligations of notification or consent, since no such requirements are contained in the relevant provisions of UNCLOS. This submission is in line with the common ground agreed to by all delegations during the UN BBNJ negotiations that the new instrument shall not hamper the development of marine scientific research. However, this does not mean that under the UNCLOS marine scientific research regime, the sampling of marine genetic resources in areas beyond national jurisdiction is free of obligations.

Firstly, as stipulated by the Convention, all marine scientific research shall be conducted in accordance with the general principles outlined in Article 240. These principles require, *inter alia*, all marine scientific research to be conducted with appropriate scientific methods and means and in compliance with all relevant regulations, including those for the protection and preservation of the marine environment.[65] Implications of the requirement on the use of appropriate scientific methods and means have been addressed in Chapter 3.2.2. Besides, the ICJ's reasoning in the *Whaling in the Antarctic* case on the use of lethal methods and the scale of such use in scientific research provides a reasonable basis for determining whether access to marine genetic

64 An examination of UNCLOS provisions in relation to marine scientific research on the high seas and in the Area is provided in Chapter 3 of this study.

65 UNCLOS, Article 240. For more discussions on the content of the general principles, see Chapter 3.2.2 of this study.

resources is conducted with "appropriate scientific methods and means".[66] Article 240 of UNCLOS also requires *in situ* access to marine genetic resources to be carried out under relevant environmental protection obligations. In this regard, it is relevant to recall that issues concerning marine genetic sources are negotiated with the other three elements that are included in the "package deal", two of which are environmental protection related.[67] Therefore, the importance of protecting the marine environment and conserving the natural resources therein during sampling is significant.

An option to promote the protection of the marine environment and the conservation of natural resources would be to establish standards and criteria to encourage responsible sampling activities. These standards and criteria could be set up during the upcoming negotiations on BBNJ issues. They can also be established by researchers in the form of a code of conduct. Indeed, some nongovernmental initiatives to ensure responsible research by the scientific community have already been adopted. Examples include the "InterRidge Statement of Commitment to Responsible Research Practices at Deep-Sea Hydrothermal Vents"[68] and the "Code of Conduct for Marine scientific research Vessels" proposed by the Marine Board of the European Science Foundation and adopted at the International Research Ship Operators' Meeting (ISOM).[69]

Secondly, according to Article 244(1) of UNCLOS, States and competent international organizations that carry out marine scientific research are under an obligation to publish and disseminate "through appropriate channels information on proposed major programmes and their objectives".[70]

66 See Chapter 5.5.2.

67 Negotiations in the Intergovernmental Conference focus on "the topics identified in the package agreed in 2011, namely, the conservation and sustainable use of marine biological diversity of areas beyond national jurisdiction, in particular, together and as a whole, marine genetic resources, including questions on the sharing of benefits, measures such as area-based management tools, including marine protected areas, environmental impact assessments and capacity-building and the transfer of marine technology". See "UNGA Resolution on "Development of an international legally-binding instrument under the United Nations Convention on the Law of the Sea on the conservation and sustainable use of marine biological diversity of areas beyond national jurisdiction" of 19 June 2015", UN Doc. A/RES/69/292, para.2; "UNGA Resolution on "International legally binding instrument under the United Nations Convention on the Law of the Sea on the conservation and sustainable use of marine biological diversity of areas beyond national jurisdiction" of 24 December 2017", UN Doc. A/RES/72/249, para.2.

68 "InterRidge Statement of Commitment to Responsible Research Practices at Deep-Sea Hydrothermal Vents," available at http://www.interridge.org/IRStatement.

69 "Code of Conduct for Marine scientific research Vessels," 2007, available at https://www.irso.info/wp-content/uploads/International_RV_Code_final.pdf.

70 UNCLOS, Article 244(1).

Soons observes that "major programmes" seem to refer to all marine scientific research programs that involve the conduct of research activities in areas that are not under the jurisdiction of the researching State itself, or which "are of more than purely local interest".[71] As such, all *in situ* access to marine genetic resources in areas beyond national jurisdiction can be regarded as "major programmes" under Article 244(1) of UNCLOS. According to this provision, States or competent international organizations that carry out activities involving *in situ* access to marine genetic resources (not for commodities) would be obliged to publish and disseminate information on the proposed activities and their objectives "through appropriate channels". These channels could be decided during the upcoming negotiations.

Thirdly, according to Article 143 of UNCLOS, the conduct of *in situ* access to marine genetic resources by States Parties in the Area needs to fulfill several procedural obligations. For example, States Parties are to participate in international programs, encourage cooperation in marine scientific research by personnel of different countries and of the ISA, and ensure that sampling programs are developed through the ISA or other international organizations for the benefit of developing States and technologically less developed States.[72] These requirements can be considered as the detailing of "for the benefit of mankind as a whole" obligation,[73] and need to be taken into consideration when negotiating the substantive rules concerning *in situ* access to marine genetic resources in the Area.

For the hypothetical situations in which sampling activities constitute prospecting under UNCLOS in the future, relevant provisions of the Convention may lead to the following observations. When such activities are conducted on the high seas, Article 87 of the Convention applies. Although prospecting is not explicitly referred to in this article, it is commonly understood that the principle of freedom of the high seas encompasses a broader scope of activities than those listed under Article 87(1).[74] Therefore, arguably prospecting can be

---

71 Alfred H. A. Soons, *Marine Scientific Research and the Law of the Sea*, 243; Alexander Proelss, ed. *United Nations Convention on the Law of the Sea: A Commentary*, 1461.

72 UNCLOS, Article 143(3).

73 Article 143(1) requires marine scientific research in the Area to be carried out for the benefit of mankind as a whole. For a more detailed discussion on this obligation, and its connection to the "common heritage of mankind" principle, see Chapter 3.3.4.2 of this study.

74 Douglas Guilfoyle, "The High Seas", in *The Oxford Handbook of the Law of the Sea*, edited by Donald Rothwell, et al. (2015), 206; Alexander Proelss, ed. *United Nations Convention on the Law of the Sea: A Commentary*, 679–682.

undertaken freely on the high seas insofar as it is not incompatible with "conditions laid down by this Convention and by other rules of international law".[75]

The applicable rules for such activities in cases where they are conducted in the Area are more complicated than the situation of those conducted on the high seas. The preliminary question is what regime is applicable – the regime for the high seas or the regime for the Area. If the regime for the high seas applies, the observation made in the above paragraph would apply; and if the regime for the Area applies, the situation becomes different.

It is noted that that the UNCLOS provisions concerning prospecting in the Area are mostly drafted with mineral resources in mind.[76] As mentioned earlier, the term "prospecting" is not defined in UNCLOS. A definition of this term can be found in the series of ISA Regulations on prospecting and exploration fexor different types of mineral resources in the Area. Such a definition is also drafted with mineral resources in mind.[77] However, it is submitted that prospecting of mineral resources and prospecting of marine genetic resources share one essential commonality: both activities are different from marine scientific research and both constitute an important phase preliminary to and distinct from exploration.[78] Besides, both activities only involve the taking of a small quantity of samples.[79] If and to the extent that the provisions under UNCLOS and the ISA Regulations on prospecting[80] can be interpreted or expanded to cover marine genetic resources, an application of these provisions to access to marine genetic resources purely for commercial reasons may entail the following consequences.[81]

75 UNCLOS, Article 87(1).

76 Lyle Glowka, "The Deepest of Ironies: Genetic Resources, Marine Scientific Research, and the Area", 152–154.

77 See, for instance, Regulations on Prospecting and Exploration for Polymetallic Nodules in the Area, Regulation 1(3)(e).

78 Michael W Lodge, "International Seabed Authority's Regulations on Prospecting and Exploration for Polymetallic Nodules in the Area", 282.

79 According to the ISA Regulations, "[a] prospector may [...] recover a reasonable quantity of minerals, being the quantity necessary for testing, and not for commercial use". See, for instance, Regulations on Prospecting and Exploration for Polymetallic Sulphides in the Area, Regulation 2(4).

80 A brief examination of these provisions has been included in Chapter 3.3.4.1 of this book.

81 It should be noted that several prerequisites need to be fulfilled to invite the application of the consequences – 1) the sampling of marine genetic resources is purely for commercial purposes, which is only a hypothetical situation at the moment; 2) the UNCLOS regime for the Area is to be applied; and 3) relevant provisions on prospecting in the Area can be interpreted or expanded to cover marine genetic resources. Therefore, the following "consequences" can be best considered as a proposal *de lege ferenda*.

First, access to marine genetic resources in the Area for prospecting is subject to a notification requirement,[82] and the activity "may commence only after the prospector has been informed by the [ISA] Secretary-General that its notification has been recorded".[83] The notification submitted to the ISA shall contain, among others, "[a] general description of the prospecting programme, including the proposed date of commencement and its approximate duration", and "[a] satisfactory written undertaking" pursuant to Article 2 of Annex III to UNCLOS and Regulation 3(4)(d) of the ISA Regulations. A prospector is obliged to "inform the [ISA] Secretary-General in writing of any change in the information contained in the notification".[84] Second, similar to the case of marine scientific research, the sampling of marine genetic resources for prospecting is subject to a number of requirements concerning the protection of the marine environment.[85] Third, each prospector may only take "a reasonable quantity" of samples of marine genetic resources, "being the quantity necessary for testing and not for commercial use".[86] Arguably, this requirement is also enshrined in the criteria for marine scientific research.

Based on the preceding analysis, it seems that the main difference in terms of the legal implications between access to marine genetic resources for marine scientific research and access for prospecting is concerned with the requirement of notification.

Because sampling of marine genetic resources is hardly conducted for prospecting purposes in the near future, it is suggested that for negotiating the new instrument, the regulation of *in situ* access to marine genetic resources in areas beyond national jurisdiction be based on the UNCLOS marine scientific research regime – access can be conducted without the obligation of prior notification on the condition that information on the proposed activities and their objectives should be published and disseminated "through appropriate channels" to be decided during the upcoming negotiations. To address the concern that in the future, sampling of marine genetic resources may be conducted for prospecting, a competent international organization can be designated to review the development of biotechnology and the knowledge about marine genetic resources in areas beyond national jurisdiction. When the organization considers that the information mentioned above suffices in proving that

82 See, for instance, Regulations on Prospecting and Exploration for Polymetallic Nodules in the Area, Regulation 3.

83 See, for instance, ibid., Regulation 2(1).

84 See, for instance, ibid., Regulation 4(4).

85 See, for instance, ibid., Regulations 2(2), 5.

86 See, for instance, ibid., Regulation 2(4).

sampling activities may be conducted for prospecting, the organization could be charged with the task of drafting guidelines to regulate sampling of marine genetic resources for prospecting. For drafting the guidelines, references can be made to the provisions contained in UNCLOS and the ISA Regulations on prospecting of mineral resources. One focus of such guidelines would be the creation of notification requirement for the sampling of marine genetic resources in the Area.

6.4.2 *Implication of the Relevant UNCLOS Provisions for Benefit-Sharing Arrangement*

The sharing of benefits arising from the utilization of marine genetic resources is another controversial topic surrounding marine genetic resources in areas beyond national jurisdiction. The following section will focus on the relevant UNCLOS provisions on marine scientific research and prospecting to identify the benefit-sharing alternatives provided for by this Convention.

The most controversial issues concerning benefit sharing include whether an obligation of benefit sharing should be included in the new instrument and, if the answer is yes, what kind of benefit-sharing obligations should be included, *i.e.,* monetary and/or nonmonetary. To address these questions, one needs to look at the features of activities concerning the utilization of marine genetic resources, since benefits (both monetary and nonmonetary) can only be generated after utilization. It is only at the final stage (commercialization) that the utilization of marine genetic resources can lead to monetary benefits. Before commercialization, since no commercial gains are generated from the utilization of marine genetic resources, there would naturally be no sharing of monetary benefits. Commercialization, in a sense, can be equivalent to exploitation under UNCLOS, which is distinct from marine scientific research and prospecting. In this respect, UNCLOS provisions on marine scientific research or prospecting do not provide any direction regarding the establishment of monetary benefit-sharing obligations in the new instrument.

Although relevant UNCLOS provisions are not applicable when considering monetary benefit-sharing issues, it is worth noting the following. Since very few sampling activities lead to commercial gains, establishing monetary obligations tied to sampling is likely to reduce the incentive to innovate and is not conducive to the overall development of scientific research and the increase of knowledge about the oceans. Besides, as a result of researchers' unwillingness to share monetary benefits, they might find various ways to avoid such obligations, and in a worse scenario, might leave their activities unregulated and hence cause adverse effects to the marine environment.

The drawbacks just described could be overcome to a certain extent by opting for forms of nonmonetary benefit sharing.[87] It is argued that the obligations set out by relevant UNCLOS provisions provide the legal basis for including nonmonetary benefit-sharing obligations in the new instrument. For activities concerning the marine genetic resources that constitute marine scientific research, the UNCLOS Part XIII regime applies. Relevant provisions in this aspect are contained in Article 244 of UNCLOS, which sets out the obligation for researching States to share with others, especially developing States, information, data and research results of marine scientific research.[88] As is opined by some scholars, public availability and free exchange add to the sum of human scientific knowledge on a particular subject, and therefore, can be presumed to benefit humankind.[89] In other words, the sharing of information, data and research results can be regarded as the fulfillment of nonmonetary benefit sharing obligations.

In this connection, it is suggested that a clearing-house mechanism be established for marine genetic resources in areas beyond national jurisdiction, where information of sampling activities, data of marine genetic resources, and research results would be shared in the international community.[90] This arrangement has several advantages.

First, it could serve as a means to share the benefits arising from the utilization of marine genetic resources in areas beyond national jurisdiction under Article 244 of UNCLOS. It is noted that the sharing of information, data and research results might raise concerns as to the interests in developing patents on the basis of marine genetic resources as a result of successful subsequent applications. This concern surely warrants attention since respecting the rights and interests to intellectual properties is a crucial element to secure investment flows in the biotechnological industry, and in the long run, to prosper the development of economy and science. In this respect, it has been

87 Morten Walløe Tvedt and Ane E. Jørem, "Bioprospecting in the High Seas: Regulatory Options for Benefit Sharing", 154.

88 UNCLOS, Article 244.

89 Alfred H. A. Soons, *Marine Scientific Research and the Law of the Sea*, 242–243; Lyle Glowka, "The Deepest of Ironies: Genetic Resources, Marine Scientific Research, and the Area", 172.

90 Article 11(3)(b) of the revised draft text of the ILBI reflects that the establishment of the clearing-house mechanism is one of the options for non-monetary benefit sharing. See "Revised draft text of an agreement under the United Nations Convention on the Law of the Sea on the conservation and sustainable use of marine biological diversity of areas beyond national jurisdiction - Note by the President", Doc. A/CONF.232/2020/3, Article 11(3)(b).

suggested to establish a mechanism that allows an embargo period for the researching States or organizations to keep the information and data private for a certain period, for instance, to secure confidentiality before the publication of the results of the research or the grant of a patent.[91] But the entitlement to an embargo period is conditional, for example, upon the requirement for researching States or international organizations to pay certain fees to a to-be-established organization under the new instrument, and the length of the period is not indefinite.[92] This suggestion provides a good balance between facilitating marine scientific research on the one hand and safeguarding intellectual property interests on the other.

Second, establishing a clearing-house mechanism would be beneficiary to the conservation of biodiversity and preservation of the marine environment, since the sharing of such information, data and research results can avoid duplicated visits to an area beyond national jurisdiction and repeated collecting of genetic resources. This is significant, especially when considered over a more extended period, as investigative and sampling activities have been identified as one of the causes of environmental degradation and biodiversity loss, especially in the deep sea.

Third, this kind of nonmonetary benefit sharing has the potential to reduce research and technological gaps between different States. Compared with *in situ* access to marine genetic resources, *in silico* access, which is made possible by this form of nonmonetary benefit sharing, is much more affordable and accessible for technologically less developed States. This kind of arrangement is also conducive to the "strengthening of the autonomous marine scientific research capabilities" of developing States[93] and can be linked to another component of the new instrument – capacity building. It can be hoped that, in the future, this arrangement can contribute to a more equitable situation.

Last, the establishment of a clearing-house mechanism, which makes information, data and research results readily available, can foster future marine scientific research and spur innovation, and thus creates a positive circle for marine scientific research concerning marine genetic resources.

For the hypothetical situation where sampling of marine genetic resources amounts to prospecting in the future, the scenario might be different in terms of benefit-sharing obligations. UNCLOS does not contain any provision on the regulation of prospecting activities on the high seas. The general provisions

---

91 Arianna Broggiato et al., "Mare Geneticum: Balancing Governance of Marine Genetic Resources in International Waters", 8.

92 Ibid., 10, 21–22.

93 UNCLOS, Article 244(2).

included in the regime for the high seas do not shed any further light on benefit sharing. Therefore, when sampling of marine genetic resources for prospecting is conducted on the high seas, UNCLOS does not provide any direction as to the establishment of benefit-sharing obligations.

When such activities are conducted in the Area, if the UNCLOS regime for the Area applies, and if and to the extent that the relevant provisions on prospecting of mineral resources under UNCLOS and the ISA Regulations cover marine genetic resources, a provision relevant for the current discussion is contained in Regulation 7 of the ISA Regulations. This provision sets out an obligation for the ISA Secretary-General to "ensure the confidentiality of all data and information contained in the reports" submitted by the prospector to the ISA under Regulation 6, with the exception of data and information "relating to the protection and preservation of the marine environment".[94] Other data and information may only be released by the ISA Secretary-General with the consent of the prospector.[95] As such, the benefit-sharing obligation for sampling marine genetic resources for prospecting in the Area may be different from that for sampling for marine scientific research.

As argued earlier, at the moment, sampling of marine genetic resources is to be considered as marine scientific research. It is suggested that the mechanism for benefit sharing to be included in the new instrument be based on the UNCLOS marine scientific research regime. In the future, when sampling of marine genetic resources may be conducted for purposes of prospecting, the difference for the obligation of benefit sharing as noted above can be considered in formulating the guidelines as mentioned in Section 6.4.1.

6.5 Conclusions

Previous chapters have concluded that the decisive factor for determining the legal classification of an ocean data collection activity is the purpose of conducting the activity. If the activity is conducted purely for commercial purposes, it may be classified as prospecting, exploration or exploitation. Because marine scientific research is different from these activities, it is not to be undertaken solely for the purpose of commercial gain.

As to *in situ* access to marine genetic resources, such activities can be conducted for scientific purposes or both for commercial and scientific purposes.

94 See, for instance, Regulations on Prospecting and Exploration for Polymetallic Nodules in the Area, Regulation 7(1).

95 Ibid., Regulation 7(2).

Practice shows that the actual access to marine genetic resources is mostly conducted by researchers specifically with the view to better understanding the biodiversity of the marine environment. In this case, the related activities fall squarely under the meaning of marine scientific research.

For sampling activities that are undertaken for both scientific and commercial purposes, it is argued that these activities also qualify as marine scientific research under UNCLOS. No provision of UNCLOS or subsequent agreement indicates that marine scientific research is only to be carried out purely for scientific purposes. Besides, by including the phrase "of direct significance for the exploration and exploitation of natural resources", especially the qualifier "direct", in Article 246(5), the Convention recognizes that marine scientific research can be carried out with a view to the commercial utilization of the research objects.

It is argued that considering the features of activities concerning marine genetic resources and the current state of biotechnology and knowledge about marine genetic resources in areas beyond national jurisdiction, *in situ* access to marine genetic resources can hardly be conducted purely for commercial purposes at the moment. Therefore, the related activities cannot be considered as prospecting or exploration under UNCLOS. This being said, potentially with the development of biotechnology and the accumulation of knowledge and research experiences, in the future, the level of interests in the commercial value of marine genetic resources in areas beyond national jurisdiction will increase. As a result, hypothetically, access to such resources may be conducted purely for commercial purposes and thus may amount to prospecting under UNCLOS.

After discerning the legal classification of *in situ* access to marine genetic resources – at the moment the related activities are to be considered marine scientific research under UNCLOS and in the future, hypothetically, some of such activities may amount to prospecting, Section 6.4 looks at the implications of applying the relevant UNCLOS provisions to the related activities for establishing the arrangements for *in situ* access to marine genetic resources in areas beyond national jurisdiction, and the mechanisms for the sharing of benefits arising from the utilization of such resources.

By applying the UNCLOS marine scientific research regime to *in situ* access to marine genetic resources in areas beyond national jurisdiction, the following implications result. All States and competent international organizations enjoy the right to freely access *in situ* marine genetic resources in areas beyond national jurisdiction subject to certain obligations. For instance, *in situ* access to marine genetic resources should be conducted with "appropriate scientific methods and means" and be subject to the obligations of environmental protection. Besides, States or competent international organizations that carry out *in situ* access to marine genetic resources would be obliged to publish and disseminate information on the proposed activities and their objectives "through appropriate channels". It is submitted that these channels could be decided during the upcoming negotiations. Last, *in situ* access to marine genetic resources by States Parties in the Area should follow the procedural obligations set out in Article 143(3) of UNCLOS.

As regards benefit sharing, the UNCLOS marine scientific research regime provides the legal basis for establishing nonmonetary benefit-sharing obligations. It is suggested that a clearing-house mechanism be established as a means of nonmonetary benefit sharing and as an effective way to conserve biodiversity and preserve the marine environment in areas beyond national jurisdiction, to reduce the gaps between developed States and developing States, and to foster research.

However, the application of the UNCLOS marine scientific research regime to activities concerning marine genetic resources is not free of problems. In particular, the requirement of open publication of information, data and research results leads to some concerns as to the interests in developing patents on the basis of marine genetic resources. It has been suggested that this concern could be addressed by allowing an embargo period to keep the information and data private for a certain period.

Because at the moment the sampling of marine genetic resources falls under the scope of marine scientific research, it is suggested that provisions on access and benefit sharing of the new instrument be based on the UNCLOS marine scientific research regime.[96] To address the concern that, hypothetically, the related activities may be conducted for prospecting in the future, an international organization can be designated in the new instrument to review the development of biotechnology and the knowledge about marine genetic resources in areas beyond national jurisdiction. When the organization considers the information mentioned above suffices in proving the sampling activities may be conducted purely for commercial purposes, the organization may draft guidelines to regulate sampling of marine genetic resources for prospecting. For the purpose of the guidelines mentioned above, references

96 As indicated by the UNGA Resolution 72/249, the work and results of the intergovernmental conference "should be fully consistent with the provisions of [UNCLOS]". See "UNGA Resolution on "International legally binding instrument under the United Nations Convention on the Law of the Sea on the conservation and sustainable use of marine biological diversity of areas beyond national jurisdiction" of 24 December 2017", UN Doc. A/RES/72/249, para.6.

can be made to the provisions contained in UNCLOS and the ISA Regulations on prospecting of mineral resources. Although these provisions are drafted specifically with mineral resources in mind, they provide a reasonable basis for formulating guidelines for the regulation of sampling of marine genetic resources for prospecting. When the sampling activities qualify as prospecting and to the extent that the provisions contained in UNCLOS and the ISA Regulations on prospecting can be expanded to include marine genetic resources, the following observations on the arrangement for access and benefit sharing can be made: first, sampling of marine genetic resources for prospecting in the Area is subject to a notification requirement, and such notification is to be sent to the ISA or another international organization to be established in the new instrument; second, there would be no benefit-sharing obligations for the sampling of marine genetic resources for prospecting on the high seas, and when the related activities are conducted in the Area, the obligation of benefit sharing will be lighter than in the case of sampling of marine genetic resources for marine scientific research.

CHAPTER 7

Operational Oceanography and Its Regulatory Framework

7.1 Introduction

This chapter offers the second case study of this book with a view to assessing the strengths and limits of UNCLOS and its marine scientific research regime in accommodating "modern" ocean data collection activities.[1,2] The object of the case study in this chapter is operational oceanography. This chapter aims to ascertain the legal classification of this kind of ocean data collection activities and discuss the options for their regulation under UNCLOS. It begins with an introduction to the concept of "operational oceanography" and the characteristics of this kind of activities (Section 7.2). Section 7.3 discusses the legal classification of operational oceanographic activities. It is argued that the legal classification of activities under the notion of "operational oceanography" may vary and, accordingly, different rules would apply. Section 7.4 examines the implications of applying relevant UNCLOS provisions to different categories of operational oceanographic activities respectively. Based on the observations made in Section 7.4, Section 7.5 proposes future regulatory options for operational oceanography. Concluding remarks are contained in Section 7.6.

Unlike the discussions included in Chapter 6 on access to marine genetic resources in areas beyond national jurisdiction, this chapter will mainly address the legal issues raised by operational oceanography in areas under national jurisdiction, or more specifically in the EEZs, because it is in such areas that the conduct of operational oceanographic activities might lead to controversies or conflicts.

1 Part of analysis included in this chapter has been published in the journal *Marine Policy*. See Chuxiao Yu, "Operational oceanography as a distinct activity from marine scientific research under UNCLOS? – An analysis of WMO Resolution 45 (Cg-18)." *Marine Policy* 143 (2022): 105131.

2 See Chapter 1 of this study.

 | DOI:10.1163/9789004508590_008

7.2 What Is "Operational Oceanography"?

The term "operational oceanography" is not used in UNCLOS or any other international legal documents. Up until now, there is no generally accepted definition of the term.[3] This section introduces the definitions given by international organizations that undertake operational oceanographic activities and scholars who have expertise in this field and identifies some characteristics of this sort of activities (Section 7.2.1). Section 7.2.2 provides an overview of the platforms that are deployed for purposes of operational oceanography, which is considered to provide necessary background information for an in-depth analysis of issues regarding its legal classification and appropriate regulatory framework.

7.2.1 *Definition of the Term "Operational Oceanography" and Features of this Kind of Activities*

Several international organizations provide definitions of the term "operational oceanography". In its report submitted to the first session of IOC/ABE-LOS, the GOOS Project Office defined operational oceanography as:

> the activity of routinely making, disseminating, and interpreting measurements of the seas and oceans and atmosphere, so as to
>
> i. provide continuous forecasts of the future condition of the sea as far ahead as possible;
> ii. provide a description of the present state of the sea including living resources, with optimal accuracy;
> iii. assemble long term climatic data sets to describe past states, and time series showing trends and changes.[4]

A similar definition has been given by EuroGOOS, according to which, operational oceanography "can be defined as the activity of systematic and long-term routine measurements of the seas and oceans and atmosphere, and their rapid interpretation and dissemination".[5]

This definition has been echoed by some scholars. For example, Roach has defined operational oceanography as "the routine collection of ocean observations in all maritime zones, such as temperature, pressure, current, salinity,

---

3 "Technical Workshop Enhancing Ocean Observations and Research, and the Free Exchange of Data, to Foster Services for the Safety of Life and Property: Final Report", at p. 30. See also "Technical Report on Scoping of Operational Oceanography", Doc. IOC/INF-1291, 2012, at p. 3.

4 "Report by GPO on "the Argo Project" Developments", Doc. IOC/ABE-LOS I/10, pp. 4–5.

5 See the official website of EuroGOOS, "What is operational oceanography?", available at http://eurogoos.eu/about-eurogoos/what-is-operational-oceanography/.

and wind".[6] He further pointed out that operational oceanographic programs "have the same characteristics: sustained, systematic, reliable, and robust mission activities with an institutional commitment to deliver appropriate, public, cost-effective products and services".[7] Bork *et al.*, considered that the activities are operational in the way that the collected data are transmitted in a timely fashion, mostly less than once a week, to one or more data centers that provide access to the data to various users.[8] Soons has submitted that the US used the notion "operational oceanography" to point to "the routine collection of ocean variables transmitted in real time and publicly available, although there remains lack of clarity about the use of data".[9]

Based on the definition given by the GOOS Project Office, EuroGOOS, and those by scholars, one can note that the term has been used to denote a group of activities. The exact meaning of the concept may not be clear, but some features of activities falling under this concept can be identified.

Most notably, one feature of operational oceanography is that its primary **function/objective** is to provide an assessment of the current and past state of the marine environment and to make predictions about its future state.[10] To achieve this objective, a substantive amount of *in situ* data concerning the marine environment is required. To this end, a global network that coordinates ocean data collection activities serving operational purposes – GOOS – has been established.[11] Under the working method outlined in the Framework for Ocean Observing, to make ocean data collection activities more cost-effective, and based on observational needs agreed upon by States, GOOS identifies the essential variables to be measured (EOVs), the approach to measuring them, and how the data and relevant products will be managed and distributed.[12]

6 J. Ashley Roach, "Defining Scientific Research: Marine Data Collection", in *Law, Science & Ocean Management*, edited by Myron Nordquist, et al. (Brill, 2007), 544.

7 Ibid., 550.

8 Katharina Bork et al., "The Legal Regulation of Floats and Gliders - In Quest of a New Regime?", 301.

9 "Technical Workshop Enhancing Ocean Observations and Research, and the Free Exchange of Data, to Foster Services for the Safety of Life and Property: Final Report", at p. 30.

10 See for instance, "Technical Report on Scoping of Operational Oceanography", Doc. IOC/INF-1291; Peter Ryder, "Marine Scientific Research and Operational Oceanography in the Context of the UN Convention on the Law of the Sea", Doc. IOC-WMO-UNEP/I-GOOS-VI/10, 2003, at pp. 10–14; Peter Ryder, "A possible migration from marine scientific research to operational oceanography in the context of the United Nations Convention on the Law of the Sea (UNCLOS)", *Elsevier Oceanography Series* 69(2003): 27–29.

11 For more detailed introduction to the mandate and working method of GOOS, see Chapter 4.3.5 of this study. See also The Task Team for an Integrated Framework for Sustained Ocean Observing, "A Framework for Ocean Observing", Doc. IOC/INF-1284.

12 Ibid., at p. 2.

Originally, operational oceanographic activities mainly contribute to the provision of data and information that support climate science and operational forecast systems.[13] More recently, data that are collected through such activities have been used for more diversified purposes to satisfy the expanding observational needs.[14]

Observational needs can be broadly classified into two kinds – societal and scientific.[15] Societal needs mainly come from observing requirements agreed upon by States through intergovernmental organizations, such as IOC and WMO, in relation to the provision of operational services through ocean hazard early warnings, weather and ocean forecasting,[16] or under various conventions, such as the obligations under UNFCCC to promote and cooperate in research and systematic observation related to the climate system,[17] and the obligations under CBD to identify and monitor components of biological diversity important for its conservation and sustainable use.[18] For scientific needs, operational oceanographic activities coordinated under GOOS are focused primarily on physical ocean variables required to better understand the climate.[19] Outside GOOS, operational oceanographic activities have also been conducted at both national and regional levels, serving a wide range of observational needs, which are not limited to the ones identified by GOOS.[20]

Based on these observational needs, the **data to be collected** will be identified. For operational oceanographic activities coordinated under GOOS, the GOOS Expert Panels articulate requirements in terms of the data to be collected – the Essential Ocean Variables (EOVs).[21] Since its inception, operational oceanography mainly serves climate science and forecasting, and thus most operational oceanographic programs target meteorological and physical data. Along with the expanding observational needs, data that are collected

13 IOC, "The Global Ocean Observing System 2030 Strategy", IOC Brochure 2019-5 (IOC/BRO/2019/5 rev.), Paris, 2019, at p. 2.

14 Ibid.

15 The Task Team for an Integrated Framework for Sustained Ocean Observing, "A Framework for Ocean Observing", Doc. IOC/INF-1284, at p. 18.

16 Peter Ryder, "A possible migration from marine scientific research to operational oceanography in the context of the United Nations Convention on the Law of the Sea (UNCLOS)", 33.

17 UNFCCC, Article 4(1)(g). See also Chapter 5.3.1 of this book.

18 CBD, Article 7.

19 The Task Team for an Integrated Framework for Sustained Ocean Observing, "A Framework for Ocean Observing", Doc. IOC/INF-1284, at p. 18.

20 See Peter Ryder, "Marine Scientific Research and Operational Oceanography in the Context of the UN Convention on the Law of the Sea", Doc. IOC-WMO-UNEP/I-GOOS-VI/10, Annex A - Scenarios of research carried out in territorial seas and EEZs, at pp. 25–34.

21 The Task Team for an Integrated Framework for Sustained Ocean Observing, "A Framework for Ocean Observing", Doc. IOC/INF-1284, at pp. 2, 8.

through operational oceanographic activities have also become more diversified. In this connection, it is worth mentioning that the EOVs identified by GOOS are subject to frequent update, taking into account elements including the relevance of the variables in addressing the overall GOOS themes – climate, operational ocean services, and ocean health.[22]

To meet the observational requirements identified by States, especially those in relation to the provision of operational forecasting services, data concerning the marine environment need to be collected continuously and systematically.[23] This relates to the **manner** in which data are collected. In order to provide data about the present state of the sea and its future state as far in advance as possible, operational oceanographic activities are carried out on a routine and systematic basis, which are concerned with continuous and long-term observations of the marine environment.[24]

On efficiency grounds, ocean data that are used for purposes of operational oceanography are mostly collected by advanced **tools and platforms** using the latest technological developments in measurement and communication.[25] To be more cost-effective, most of the operational oceanographic activities are undertaken by autonomous tools.[26]

To provide assessment and forecasting in a real or near real-time manner, most data that are collected by operational oceanographic activities are distributed timely, freely and openly.[27] This concerns another feature of operational oceanography, which is about **data availability and open publication.** Open access to data collected through operational oceanographic programs contributes to the optimal use of the data, facilitates the collaboration

22 Ibid., at p. 18. See also the official website of GOOS, "Essential Ocean Variables (with link to disciplinary panels)", available at https://www.goosocean.org/index.php?option=com_content&view=article&id=170&Itemid=114.

23 Ibid., at p. 5. See also "Technical Report on Scoping of Operational Oceanography", Doc. IOC/INF-1291, at pp. 1, 3; IOC, "The Global Ocean Observing System 2030 Strategy", IOC Brochure 2019-5 (IOC/BRO/2019/5 rev.), at p. 7.

24 Florian H.Th. Wegelein, *Marine Scientific Research: The Operation and Status of Research Vessels and Other Platforms in International Law*, 20; Peter Ryder, "A possible migration from marine scientific research to operational oceanography in the context of the United Nations Convention on the Law of the Sea (UNCLOS)".

25 "Technical Report on Scoping of Operational Oceanography", Doc. IOC/INF-1291, at p. 3.

26 Peter Ryder, "Marine Scientific Research and Operational Oceanography in the Context of the UN Convention on the Law of the Sea", Doc. IOC-WMO-UNEP/I-GOOS-VI/10, para.5.6. See also IOC, "The Global Ocean Observing System 2030 Strategy", IOC Brochure 2019-5 (IOC/BRO/2019/5 rev.), at p. 12.

27 The Task Team for an Integrated Framework for Sustained Ocean Observing, "A Framework for Ocean Observing", Doc. IOC/INF-1284, at p. 13.

across disparate observing systems, and plays a vital role in raising public awareness of the significance of operational oceanography and in narrowing the gap between developing and developed countries in terms of ocean observations.[28] Through the promotion of open publication, data collected through operational oceanographic activities can be freely accessed by different users for different purposes. Such purposes are no longer limited to the ones concerning the provision of assessment and forecasting services. In this regard, as submitted by Soons, there remains a lack of clarity about the use of data collected by activities falling under the notion of "operational oceanography".[29]

From the preceding analysis, one can note that the features about the data that are collected, the manner in which data are collected, the tools that are deployed to collect data, and the open publication and availability of data, all contribute to the realization of the objective of operational oceanographic activities. These features will be elaborated upon further in the analysis of the legal classification of operational oceanography in Section 7.3. In order to provide the necessary background information for the discussion in the following part of the chapter, the next sub-section will first provide an overview of the tools and platforms that are used in the marine environment for the undertaking of operational oceanographic activities.[30]

---

28 Ibid.

29 "Technical Workshop Enhancing Ocean Observations and Research, and the Free Exchange of Data, to Foster Services for the Safety of Life and Property: Final Report", at p. 30. See also Florian H.Th. Wegelein, *Marine Scientific Research: The Operation and Status of Research Vessels and Other Platforms in International Law*, 226.

30 Operational oceanography can also be conducted in the atmosphere by means of remote sensing technologies. See IOC, "The Global Ocean Observing System 2030 Strategy", IOC Brochure 2019-5 (IOC/BRO/2019/5 rev.), at p. 12. Since it has been generally acknowledged that space activities are covered by a separate international legal regime, this study will only focus on activities that are conducted *in situ* the marine environment. Apart from the platforms that are *in situ* the marine environment and that are placed in space, instruments or equipment can also be installed onshore for the purposes of operational oceanography. An example is the HF (High Frequency) radar system. The HF radar system is located near the water's edge and measures the speed and direction of ocean surface currents in near real-time over a large region of the coastal oceans (from a few kilometers offshore up to about 200 kilometers). For more information on HF radar system, see the official website of the U.S. Integrated Ocean Observing System (IOOS), "About HF Radar", available at https://ioos.noaa.gov/project/hf-radar/. However, since the radar installations are located on the land territory of a coastal State, it is debatable whether the law of the sea would apply in such a circumstance.

7.2.2 *Types of Platforms that Are Used for* In Situ *Operational Oceanography*

There are several ways to distinguish different types of platforms, *i.e.*, manned and unmanned, or fixed and free.[31] In this sub-section, *in situ* platforms that are deployed to undertake operational oceanographic activities are divided into three major categories, namely ship-based measurements,[32] surface observing devices and subsurface profilers.

7.2.2.1 Ship-Based Measurements

Ships play a distinctly different role in operational oceanography as compared to in traditional marine scientific research, as they are usually not specifically designed for research purposes.[33] Ships that are used for operational oceanography are mainly coordinated by the Ship Observations Team (SOT), which is an ocean observation element under the coordination of JCOMM.[34] The work of SOT consists of several enduring data collection programs, including voluntary observing ships (VOS)[35] and ships of opportunity (SOOP)[36] that deploy

---

31 For a comprehensive introduction to current means of research and their implications for coastal States' interest, see Florian H.Th. Wegelein, *Marine Scientific Research: The Operation and Status of Research Vessels and Other Platforms in International Law*, 37–55.

32 It is noted that the term "ships" has not been defined in UNCLOS. Other international conventions seem to give different definitions for this term. For the purpose of the current discussion, the main differences between a ship and a device arguably include that the former is self-propelled and has the capacity to be used as a means of transportation on water of goods, people, or both while the latter is not. For a further discussion on the definition(s) of ships and vessels, see Tobias Hofmann and Alexander Proelss, "The Operation of Gliders Under the International Law of the Sea", *Ocean Development & International Law* (2015): 174–177.

33 Florian H.Th. Wegelein, *Marine Scientific Research: The Operation and Status of Research Vessels and Other Platforms in International Law*, 41.

34 For more information on the mandate and function of JCOMM, see Chapter 4.3.5 of this study. For more information on SOT, see the official website of WMO, "Ship Observations Team (SOT)", available at https://www.wmo.int/pages/prog/amp/mmop/sot.html.

35 The VOS scheme is an international scheme "first developed almost 150 years ago, by which ships plying the various oceans and seas of the world are recruited for taking and transmitting meteorological observations. VOS ships make a highly important contribution to the Global Observing System (GOS) of the World Weather Watch (WWW), and increasingly to global climate studies". See the official website of WMO, "The Voluntary Observing Ship (VOS) Scheme", available at https://www.wmo.int/pages/prog/amp/mmop/JCOMM/OPA/SOT/vos.html.

36 The SOOP Programme "makes use of volunteer merchant ships which routinely transit strategic shipping routes. Ships' officers are trained to deploy Expendable Bathythermographs (XBTS) at predetermined sampling intervals to acquire temperature profiles in the open ocean. Selected data which accurately represent the entire data profile are

Expendable Bathythermographs (XBTs) at predetermined sampling intervals to acquire temperature profiles in the marine environment. According to JCOMM's division of its various networks, VOS mainly target meteorological measurement, while SOOP oceanographic measurement.[37]

Apart from SOT, the Global Ocean Ship-Based Hydrographic Investigations Program (GO-SHIP) is another ship-based system that serves operational oceanographic purposes.[38] Two differences between SOT and GO-SHIP can be identified: first, GO-SHIP involves the use of vessels that are specifically designed for data collection; second, under GO-SHIP, ocean data involved are more diversified than SOT and are collected by vessels that travel along predetermined routes.

Other ship-based systems in the context of the current discussion include weather stations, both automatic and manned.[39] Data collected by these stations are by definition related to weather.

---

transmitted by satellites to shore centers, for insertion and exchange on the GTS, and assimilation into operational ocean models. System performance is monitored continuously, and sampling strategies are adjusted in the light of new scientific understanding, evolving requirements, in particular those of GOOS and GCOS, and new technologies and systems, most notably Argo. The SOOP data are vital in particular to seasonal to interannual climate prediction. The program is managed by the SOOP Implementation Panel (SOOPIP), also a part of the JCOMM Ship Observations Team, and supported by a technical coordinator. The SOOP coordinator maintains a dedicated SOOP website". See the official website of WMO, "Ship of Opportunity Programme", available at https://www.wmo.int/pages/prog/amp/mmop/JCOMM/OPA/SOT/soop.html.

37 See the JCOMM Report Card 2018, available at http://www.jcommops.org/reportcard2018/. See also Peter Ryder, "Marine Scientific Research and Operational Oceanography in the Context of the UN Convention on the Law of the Sea", Doc. IOC-WMO-UNEP/I-GOOS-VI/10, at p. 6.

38 GO-SHIP "brings together scientists with interests in physical oceanography, the carbon cycle, marine biogeochemistry and ecosystems, and other users and collectors of ocean interior data, and coordinates a network of globally sustained hydrographic sections as part of the global ocean/climate observing system including physical oceanography, the carbon cycle, marine biogeochemistry and ecosystems. GO-SHIP provides approximately decadal resolution of the changes in inventories of heat, freshwater, carbon, oxygen, nutrients and transient tracers, covering the ocean basins from coast to coast and full depth (top to bottom), with global measurements of the highest required accuracy to detect these changes. [...] GO-SHIP data are publicly available without restriction". See the official website of GO-SHIP, "About GO-SHIP", available at http://www.go-ship.org/About.html.

39 An introduction of all the observation platforms serving the objectives of WMO is provided on the official website of WMO, "Observations", available at https://public.wmo.int/en/our-mandate/what-we-do/observations.

7.2.2.2 Surface Observing Devices

The term "devices" in the current context refers to all structures, platforms, installations, buoys or other devices, not being a ship, together with their appurtenant equipment deployed at sea for the purpose of collecting, storing or transmitting samples and data relating to the marine environment or the atmosphere or the uses thereof.[40] Several distinctions between surface observing devices and ship-based measurements can be identified. Firstly, as indicated by the definition of "devices", platforms that are discussed under this categorization do not involve the use of ships. The second difference is that most, if not all, of the vessels, are manned, while surface observing devices are generally automatic.

Surface devices that are used for operational oceanographic purposes are mainly coordinated by the Data Buoy Cooperation Panel (DBCP), which constitutes the data buoy component of JCOMM and GOOS.[41] The actual implementation of buoy deployments is coordinated at the regional level through its Action Groups, including the Global Drifter Programme (GDP), the Ocean Sustained Interdisciplinary Timeseries Environment observation System (OceanSITES),[42] the Tropical Moored Buoy Implementation Panel (TIP),

---

40 This definition is borrowed from the definition of ocean data acquisition system (ODAS) in the second revision of the Draft Convention on the Legal Status of Ocean Data Acquisition Systems, Aids and Devices (ODAS). See Draft Convention on the Legal Status of Ocean Data Acquisition Systems, Aids and Devices (ODAS): Second Revision, 1993, Article 1(2).

41 DBCP is an official joint body of WMO and IOC. Its primary objective "is to maintain and coordinate all components of the network of over 1250 drifting buoys and 400 moored buoys, which provides measurements such as sea-surface temperature, surface current velocity, air temperature and wind speed and direction. This data is useful for Weather and Ocean Forecasts and research and additionally can be used to complement or validate remotely-sensed data and operational models. The DBCP also explores and evaluates new technologies and uses those which prove successful to improve operations". See the official website of DBCP, "About the DBCP", available at http://www.jcommops.org/dbcp/overview/about.html.

42 OceanSITES "is a worldwide system of long-term, deepwater reference stations measuring dozens of variables and monitoring the full depth of the ocean, from air-sea interactions down to 5,000 meters. Since 1999, the international OceanSITES science team has shared both data and costs in order to capitalize on the potential of the moorings and ship-based time series. The growing network now consists of about 30 surface and 30 subsurface arrays. Satellite telemetry enables near real-time access to OceanSITES data by scientists and the public. OceanSITES is an integral part of the Global Ocean Observing System. The network complements satellite imagery and other in-situ observation data (like Argo floats) by extending the dimensions of time and depth". See the official website of OceanSITES, "Putting eyes and ears in the deep ocean", available at http://www.oceansites.org/about.html.

and the International Tsunameter Partnership (ITP).[43] Devices deployed under DBCP can be divided into two kinds: drifters and moorings. Drifters are designed to move with the currents. In contrast, moorings are fixed at a given position and measure the change of parameters against a defined location.

Another example of surface observing devices is tide gauges, which are used to monitor the sea level in a given location. A network of 290 tide gauges is coordinated under the Global Sea Level Observing System (GLOSS).[44]

7.2.2.3 Subsurface Profilers

Observing devices can also be used underwater to monitor subsurface conditions. In the case of operational oceanography, such devices mainly include floats, ocean gliders and animal-borne sensors.

A float has been defined as "an autonomous vehicle used for collection of [...] data [...] and floating passively at a pre-programmed pressure level until at predetermined time intervals rising to the ocean surface to broadcast its position and, as the case may be, collected data to a satellite".[45] A typical example of this kind of devices is an Argo float. Argo is a global array of nearly 4,000 free-drifting profiling floats that measure the temperature and salinity of the upper 2000 meters of the ocean.[46] After the launch of the Argo Project, a new generation of autonomous floats that can sample the full ocean volume

---

43 See the official website of WMO, "Data Buoy Co-Operation Panel", available at https://www.wmo.int/pages/prog/amp/mmop/dbcp.html.

44 The number of tide gauges is as of the time of writing. GLOSS is a component of GOOS, which "is establishing a well-designed, high-quality sea level observing network to support a broad research and operational user base". For more information, see the official website of GLOSS, available at https://www.gloss-sealevel.org/.

45 Draft [Practical] Guidelines of IOC, within the Context of UNCLOS, for the Collection of Oceanographic Data by Specific Means, IOC/ABE-LOS VII/7, para.7(II); "Evolving Capabilities of the Argo Global Array of Profiling Floats - Information Document", Doc. IOC/INF-1344, 2017. A similar definition is given by Wegelein, according to whom, floats are designed to be neutrally buoyant in water of a certain density, which usually corresponds to a certain depth. Modern technologies have enabled such devices to be programmed to change depth at a given moment. When the floats come to the surface, they transmit the data collected to a satellite and return again to their allocated depth. See Florian H.Th. Wegelein, *Marine Scientific Research: The Operation and Status of Research Vessels and Other Platforms in International Law*, 45.

46 The Argo Project has already grown to be a major component of the ocean observing system. This project allows, for the first time, continuous monitoring of the temperature, salinity, and velocity of the upper ocean, with all data being relayed and made publicly available within hours after collection. For more information, see the official website of Argo, "Current Status of Argo", available at http://www.argo.ucsd.edu/About_Argo.html.

was introduced, which is called Deep Argo.[47] In addition, IOC Members have approved the global implementation of six new biogeochemical parameters for Argo floats.[48] Argo floats that are capable of measuring the new parameters are called Biogeochemical Argo floats.[49]

Ocean gliders are a relatively new type of data-acquisition floats, which are coordinated globally by the OceanGliders Programme.[50] The main difference between floats and ocean gliders is that the latter are able to navigate designated waypoints while the former can only move horizontally with currents.[51]

Operational oceanography can also be conducted by marine animals, or more accurately by animal-borne sensors. In recent years, the rapid advances in miniaturizing the size of electronic sensors and the techniques to attach sensors to marine animals have introduced a new technology to record the behavior of marine animals as well as their interaction with the marine environment, which is called bio-logging.[52] Marine Mammals Exploring the Oceans Pole to Pole (MEOP) is the principal global system coordinating such activities.[53]

---

47 "Deep Argo float models include the Deep SOLO and Deep APEX capable of reaching 6000 m, and the Deep ARVOR and Deep NINJA designed to sample to 4000 m. Regional Deep Argo arrays in the Southwest Pacific Basin, South Australian Basin, Australian Antarctic Basin, and North Atlantic Ocean are leading the way forward to implement a standing Deep Argo array of 1228 floats." See the official website of Argo, "What Is Deep Argo?", available at http://www.argo.ucsd.edu/Deep_Argo.html.

48 See IOC Executive Council, "Evolving Capabilities of the Argo Global Array of Profiling Floats", Decision IOC/EC-LI/4.8, 2018.

49 For more information on Biogeochemical Argo, see the official website of Argo, "What Is Biogeochemical-Argo?", available at http://www.argo.ucsd.edu/BGC_Argo.html.

50 For more information on OceanGliders, see its official website, "OceanGliders in brief", available at https://www.oceangliders.org/about-us/.

51 See Florian H.Th. Wegelein, *Marine Scientific Research: The Operation and Status of Research Vessels and Other Platforms in International Law*, 45–46; Tim Stephens and Donald Rothwell, "Marine Scientific Research", 575.

52 Trevor McIntyre, "Trends in tagging of marine mammals: a review of marine mammal biologging studies", *African Journal of Marine Science* 36, no. 4 (2014); Lars Boehme et al., "Biologging in the global ocean observing system" (paper presented at the OceanObs 09: Sustained Ocean Observations and Information for Society (Vol. 2), Venice, Italy, 21–25 September 2009, 1, 2010); Rob Harcourt et al., "Animal-borne telemetry: an integral component of the ocean observing toolkit", *Frontiers in Marine Science* 6(2019).

53 The core missions of the MEOP consortium are "(1) the production of a quality-controlled database of oceanographic data obtained with instrumented marine animals, and (2) to maintain the present data portal from where information and data can be accessed easily. MEOP also acts as a natural bridge between the scientific teams that deploy the tags and the scientists who use the data." For more information about the MEOP, see its official

Some of the platforms discussed above and the pertinent legal issues arising therefrom have been discussed in various international fora.[54] Results of such discussions include the IOC Argo Guidelines on the regulation of the deployment of Argo floats in the high seas,[55] and WMO Resolution 45 (Cg-18) concerning the operation of the VOS Scheme and surface observing platforms in support of operational applications of WMO.[56] However, because these instruments only address the legal issues raised by certain types of platforms that are used to collect ocean data, it remains unclear what would be the appropriate legal framework(s) for operational oceanographic activities that are not covered by these instruments. In this context, it is necessary to discern the legal classification of operational oceanographic activities in a general sense. To help address this issue, the impact of the discussion of other fora and the outcomes of the discussion will be taken into account. Because UNCLOS is generally recognized as the fundamental jurisdictional framework for oceans governance and the present research is primarily embedded in the framework of UNCLOS,[57] pertinent provisions of UNCLOS will be consulted in the subsequent section for purposes of legal classification.

7.3 Legal Classification of Operational Oceanography

Different viewpoints have been expressed on the legal classification of operational oceanography – some States consider operational oceanography as marine scientific research which falls under the regulatory scope of Part XIII of UNCLOS, others disagree and hold the view that the related activities can be conducted in areas under the jurisdiction of a coastal State without seeking for its consent.[58] For the latter viewpoint, there are potentially two justifications under UNCLOS: 1) operational oceanography constitutes a type of "other internationally lawful uses of the sea related to" the freedoms of other States in the EEZ of a coastal State,[59] and 2) it falls under the scope of Article 59 of the Convention concerning unattributed rights in the EEZ of a coastal State.[60]

website, "What is MEOP?", available at http://www.meop.net/meop-portal/what-is-meop.html.

54 See Chapter 4 of this study.

55 See Chapter 4.3.2.2 of this study.

56 See Chapter 4.3.4 of this study.

57 See Chapter 1 of this study.

58 An evaluation of the different viewpoints is given in Chapter 4.3.2.1 of this study.

59 UNCLOS, Article 58(1).

60 Ibid., Article 59.

Nevertheless, it is submitted that not all ocean data collection activities falling under the notion of "operational oceanography" necessarily belong to the same legal category. It might be the case that certain operational oceanographic activities should be considered as marine scientific research, some constitute "other internationally lawful uses of the sea related to" the freedoms under Article 58(1) of UNCLOS, and some fall into neither of these categories. The different treatment of ocean data collection activities under the IOC Argo Guidelines and WMO Resolution 45 (Cg-18) buttresses this observation. Arguably, ocean data collection activities covered by these two instruments fall under the notion of "operational oceanography" as they meet all the features identified in Section 7.2.1 of this chapter.[61] Under the IOC Argo Guidelines, although the legal classification of the activities concerned is not addressed, the Guidelines require that when Argo floats that have been deployed in the high seas may enter the EEZ of a coastal State, the coastal State must be informed in advance.[62] In contrast, the WMO Resolution recognizes that "the VOS Scheme and surface observing platforms are not covered by UNCLOS Part XIII on marine scientific research and can consequently be freely operated in the EEZs".[63] An examination of the reason(s) that operational oceanographic activities have been treated differently is considered to help identify the elements that are of significance for discerning the legal classification of operational oceanography in general terms (Section 7.3.1). Section 7.3.2 looks at pertinent UNCLOS provisions to define the role of the features of operational oceanography identified above for the purposes of discerning the legal classification of operational oceanographic activities. Based on the conclusions drawn in the previous sub-sections, Section 7.3.3 discusses the legal classification of operational oceanography under UNCLOS. Interim concluding remarks are contained in Section 7.3.4.

61 See "IOC Assembly Resolution on the Argo Project", IOC/Resolution XX–6, 1999. The Resolution states that the data and data products derived from Argo floats support operational oceanography and marine meteorology. See also "Abridged Final Report of the Eighteenth session of World Meteorological Congress", Doc. WMO - No.1236, at p. 148. According to WMO Resolution 45 (Cg-18), ocean data collection activities covered by this resolution support the operational applications of WMO.

62 "Guidelines for the Implementation of Resolution XX–6 of the IOC Assembly Regarding the Deployment of Profiling Floats in the High Seas within the Framework of the Argo Programme", Resolution EC-XLI.4, Annex to Resolution EC-XLI.4, para.1.

63 "Abridged Final Report of the Eighteenth session of World Meteorological Congress", Doc. WMO - No.1236, at p. 149.

7.3.1 *A Comparison of the IOC Argo Guidelines and WMO Resolution 45 (Cg-18)*

To understand the reason(s) that the IOC Argo Guidelines and WMO Resolution 45 (Cg-18) establish different regulatory frameworks for the activities covered by the two instruments respectively, it is necessary to consider the difference(s) between the two kinds of activities involved. To this end, the following aspects can be identified.

7.3.1.1 The Function and Objective of the Activity

For activities covered by WMO Resolution 45 (Cg-18), the data obtained mainly serve the purpose of ensuring the safety of navigation, and the protection of life and property in coastal and offshore areas.[64] These data also contribute to coping with the consequences of climate change, improving prediction skills in relation to climate change at all time scales, and meeting the needs of WMO-coordinated research programs.[65] This can be related to the mandate of WMO, which is the monitoring and forecasting of the ocean state, natural hazard warnings and weather forecasts, and climate prediction.[66]

As to the Argo project, as stated in the IOC Assembly Resolution XX–6 on the Argo Project, the project was created to contribute to short-term ocean forecasting, and seasonal to inter-annual atmospheric forecast, with consequent benefits for the protection of life and property.[67] After the launch of the project, other observational needs have been acknowledged by States, including to determine ocean biological productivity and to observe and predict the effects of climate change on ocean metabolism, carbon uptake, and marine living resources.[68] These newly emerged observational needs have been met by the introduction of Biogeochemical Argo in recent years.[69]

A comparison of the function of the activities covered by the two instruments indicates that both of them contribute to ocean forecasting and climate prediction, which have indirect benefits of ensuring the safety of navigation and the protection of life and property. However, unlike activities covered

---

64 Ibid., at p. 147.

65 Ibid., at p. 148.

66 For more information, see the mandate of WMO, "What we do", available at https://public.wmo.int/en/our-mandate/what-we-do.

67 "IOC Assembly Resolution on the Argo Project", IOC/Resolution XX–6.

68 "Evolving Capabilities of the Argo Global Array of Profiling Floats - Information Document", Doc. IOC/INF-1344, para.17. See also Biogeochemical-Argo Planning Group, "The Scientific Rationale, Design and Implementation Plan for a Biogeochemical-Argo Float Array", 2016, at p. 6.

69 See IOC Executive Council, "Evolving Capabilities of the Argo Global Array of Profiling Floats", Decision IOC/EC-LI/4.8.

by WMO Resolution 45 (Cg-18), which are conducted under the auspices of WMO alone, and thus have a focus on marine meteorology, the Argo project represents a significant component of the Global Ocean Data Assimilation Experiment (GODAE) initiated in the context of the UN-sponsored programs of GOOS, GCOS and Climate and Ocean: Variability, Predictability and Change (CLIVAR),[70] which have a broader focus than WMO. As a result, along with the expanding user requirements attached to GOOS, GCOS and CLIVAR, the function of activities undertaken under their auspices, including the Argo project, becomes more diversified.

7.3.1.2 Variables Measured

Variables that are measured by operational oceanographic activities are determined by the function of the activities. Because the function of WMO observations has a focus on meteorology, data that are collected by these activities are mostly meteorological ones. As discussed in Chapter 4.3.4.1, WMO Resolution 45 (Cg-18) only applies to the collection of data concerning the variables that are included in the Annex to the Resolution.[71] In contrast, variables measured by Argo floats traditionally include temperature and salinity, and have been expanded to include six biogeochemical variables: pH, oxygen, nitrate, chlorophyll fluorescence, suspended particles and downwelling irradiance.[72] Besides, some pilot Argo have tested passive acoustic listeners, which provide information on wind, rainfall at the surface, marine mammals, and seismic activity.[73]

Notably, variables measured by activities under WMO Resolution 45 (Cg-18) are mainly physical variables related to the conditions of the surface water of the oceans. Compared to biogeochemical variables and biological variables, in most cases, physical variables have less bearing on natural resources, and therefore are less likely to be relevant for the exploration and exploitation of natural resources. Also, confined by the limited number of variables covered by this Resolution, purposes that can be served by using the data product are also limited.

---

70 "IOC Assembly Resolution on the Argo Project", IOC/Resolution XX–6.

71 These variables include, "sea level pressure, surface wind speed and direction, surface air temperature, surface relative humidity, precipitation at the surface, sea surface temperature, sea surface salinity, sea surface currents, directional and non-directional wave observations, visibility, sea-ice, ice accretion, sub-surface temperature and salinity, sea level, atmospheric composition, atmospheric temperature, humidity and wind profiles, all other ocean surface and atmospheric observations that are needed to derive fluxes between the ocean and the atmosphere". "Abridged Final Report of the Eighteenth session of World Meteorological Congress", Doc. WMO - No.1236, at p. 150.

72 IOC Executive Council, "Evolving Capabilities of the Argo Global Array of Profiling Floats", Decision IOC/EC-LI/4.8.

73 "Evolving Capabilities of the Argo Global Array of Profiling Floats - Information Document", Doc. IOC/INF-1344, para.18.

In addition, WMO Resolution 45 (Cg-18) applies to the collection of data by means of vessels under the VOS Scheme and surface observing platforms.[74] As such, activities covered by the resolution are either conducted onboard a vessel or by platforms that only float on the surface of the oceans. In contrast, Argo floats measure data of the upper 2000 meters of the ocean. Recently the introduction of Deep Argo floats has enabled the sampling of the full ocean volume.[75] The collection of data concerning surface variables are, in most cases, less intrusive than the collection of deep-sea data.

Therefore, the collection of data in relation to the variables contained in the list annexed to WMO Resolution 45 (Cg-18) is less sensitive from the perspective of coastal States.

7.3.1.3 Conclusions

The major differences between activities that are covered by WMO Resolution 45 (Cg-18) and the IOC Argo Guidelines relate to the function of and variables obtained by the activities. These differences have led to the adoption of different regulatory frameworks for the activities. However, as can be seen from the discussion on the features of operational oceanographic activities above, data that are collected are primarily determined by the function of the activity. It is submitted that, as concluded in Chapter 3 of this study, for the purpose of legal classification and considering the appropriate legal framework(s), the function of the activity is of particular significance. The type of data that is collected can be seen as a good indication of the function or objective served by the activity.

7.3.2 *The Role of the Features of Operational Oceanography in Legal Classification*

To determine the legal classification of operational oceanography, it is necessary to reiterate the features of this kind of activities. Apart from the function of the activities and the data that are obtained, Section 7.2.1 identifies three other features of operational oceanographic activities: 1) the manner in which

---

74 "Abridged Final Report of the Eighteenth session of World Meteorological Congress", Doc. WMO - No.1236, at p. 148. For more detailed discussions on this matter, see Chapter 4.3.4.1 of this study.

75 "Deep Argo float models include the Deep SOLO and Deep APEX capable of reaching 6000 m, and the Deep ARVOR and Deep NINJA designed to sample to 4000 m. Regional Deep Argo arrays in the Southwest Pacific Basin, South Australian Basin, Australian Antarctic Basin, and North Atlantic Ocean are leading the way forward to implement a standing Deep Argo array of 1228 floats". See the official website of Argo, "What Is Deep Argo?", available at http://www.argo.ucsd.edu/Deep_Argo.html.

the activity is conducted, 2) open publication and data availability, and 3) tools and platforms that are used for the collection of ocean data. This sub-section examines relevant provisions of UNCLOS to determine whether these three elements can be used as criteria for discerning the legal classification of operational oceanography under UNCLOS.

In terms of the manner in which the ocean data collection activity is conducted, operational oceanographic activities are mostly carried out on a routine and systematic basis. Throughout the text of UNCLOS, there is no single provision indicating that this element has the effect of altering its legal classification. No limits have been set by UNCLOS provisions on the frequency or the continuity of conducting an ocean data collection activity.

As to the element of data availability and open publication, all the data collected by operational oceanographic activities are made freely available and can be accessed in real-time or near real-time by different users. Under UNCLOS, the distribution of data and information derived from ocean data collection activities are generally encouraged, with the only exceptions provided for in Articles 249(2) and 302. According to Article 249(2) of UNCLOS, if the project is carried out in the EEZ or on the continental shelf of a coastal State, the publication of research results that are "of direct significance for the exploration and exploitation of natural resources" shall be subject to "the conditions established by the laws and regulations of the coastal State for the exercise of its discretion to grant or withhold consent".[76] This exception only applies to certain marine scientific research projects. As a general provision for marine scientific research, Article 244(2) requires States to "actively promote the flow of scientific data and information and the transfer of knowledge resulting from marine scientific research".[77] As such, the element of data availability and open publication is not a criterion that distinguishes operational oceanography from marine scientific research. Article 302 acknowledges the right of a State not to disclose "information the disclosure of which is contrary to the essential interests of its security".[78] Arguably, open publication of data collected by operational oceanographic activities is not considered to be contrary to "the essential interests of [the] security" of a State. However, as a general provision that applies to all activities regulated by UNCLOS, Article 302 does not shed much light in terms of the legal classification of operational oceanography under the Convention.

76 UNCLOS, Article 249(2).
77 Ibid., Article 244(2). See Chapter 3.2.3 of this study.
78 Ibid., Article 302.

With respect to the tools and platforms that are used, as submitted earlier, on cost-effectiveness grounds, most operational oceanographic activities are undertaken by autonomous devices. Throughout the Convention, no provision indicates that the tools or platforms used in ocean data collection activities may alter the legal classification of the activities concerned. This being said, it is worth noting that Article 258 of the Convention stipulates that,

> [t]he deployment and use of any type of scientific research installations or equipment [...] shall be subject to the same conditions as are prescribed in this Convention for the conduct of marine scientific research.[79]

This provision does not address the legal classification of ocean data collection activities. However, it is relevant for the current discussion in the sense that this provision subjects all "scientific research" activities that involve the deployment and use of installations or equipment to the marine scientific research regime of the Convention.

Although Article 258 is placed under Part XIII of UNCLOS, which specifically addresses the issue of marine scientific research, arguably its scope of application is not limited to marine scientific research projects.[80] As observed by Virginia Commentary, "scientific research and marine scientific research are not the same thing, although the latter comes within the scope of the former".[81] Soons has pointed out that the wording of "scientific research installations or equipment", rather than "marine scientific research installations or equipment", suggests that Article 258 covers installations and equipment not only for marine scientific research but for other scientific research as well.[82] This interpretation is reinforced by the drafting history of Article 258. At the sixth session of UNCLOS III, a proposal concerning the replacement of "scientific research installations and equipment" with "marine scientific research installations and equipment" did not win much support.[83] This matter was brought up by the Drafting Committee again in the resumed ninth session

79 Ibid., Article 258.

80 Alfred H. A. Soons, *Marine Scientific Research and the Law of the Sea*, 230–231; Florian H.Th. Wegelein, *Marine Scientific Research: The Operation and Status of Research Vessels and Other Platforms in International Law*, 137; Alexander Proelss, ed. *United Nations Convention on the Law of the Sea: A Commentary*, 1734.

81 Myron H. Nordquist et al., eds., *United Nations Convention on the Law of the Sea, 1982: A Commentary (Vol. IV)*, 502.

82 Alfred H. A. Soons, *Marine Scientific Research and the Law of the Sea*, 230–231.

83 Myron H. Nordquist et al., eds., *United Nations Convention on the Law of the Sea, 1982: A Commentary (Vol. IV)*, 618–619.

of the Conference, which recommended the insertion of the word "marine" before "scientific research" as an effort to ensure consistent usage of terminology throughout Part XIII.[84] Again, the recommendation was not accepted.[85] As such, for operational oceanographic activities that do not constitute marine scientific research under UNCLOS, the Part XIII regime would still be applicable if they use or deploy "installations" or "equipment" and fall under the notion of "scientific research". Implications of this observation will be further elaborated upon later.[86]

In sum, none of the three elements – the manner in which the activity is conducted, open publication and data availability, and tools and platforms that are used – allows discerning the legal classification of operational oceanography in the context of UNCLOS. However, tools and platforms that are used may influence the regulatory framework applicable to certain operational oceanographic activities.

7.3.3 *Legal Classification of Operational Oceanography in the Context of UNCLOS*

The above analysis leads to the conclusion that two elements – the function of the activity and the data collected by the activity – are decisive for the legal classification of operational oceanographic activities. Focusing on these two elements, this sub-section examines relevant provisions of UNCLOS to discern the legal classification of operational oceanography under the Convention. As pointed out in Section 7.1, this chapter focuses on the legal issues surrounding the conduct of operational oceanographic activities in the EEZs, and hence the following analysis will look at the relevant provisions concerning the EEZ in relation to ocean data collection. In particular, this chapter will discern the relationship between operational oceanography and marine scientific research (Section 7.3.3.1), in what instances operational oceanography is to be considered as "other internationally lawful uses of the sea related to" the freedoms of other States in the EEZ of a coastal State (Section 7.3.3.2), and in what instances it falls under the scope of Article 59 of the Convention concerning unattributed rights in the EEZ of a coastal State (Section 7.3.3.3).

---

84 Ibid., 619.

85 Ibid. The decision was made in an informal setting, of which no record exists. Therefore, the reason for not accepting the recommendation can only be inferred.

86 See Section 7.4.1 of this chapter.

7.3.3.1 Operational Oceanography and Marine Scientific Research

Relevant provisions concerning the nature of and criteria for marine scientific research have been examined in Chapter 3.2 of this study. That examination concludes that to constitute marine scientific research under UNCLOS, an ocean data collection activity should have some scientific attributes.[87] Elements that are crucial for assessing the existence of scientific attributes include: 1) whether the project at issue is undertaken with a scientific hypothesis, and 2) whether information and knowledge resulting from research projects are published and disseminated.[88] With respect to the latter element, as discussed above, the element of open publication and data availability is one of the features of operational oceanographic activities. As such, the crux of the matter is to examine if operational oceanographic activities are carried out with a scientific hypothesis.

The requirement of the existence of a scientific hypothesis is inferred from a provision contained in Article 240 of UNCLOS, which provides that all marine scientific research projects shall be conducted with "appropriate scientific methods [...]".[89] As discussed in Chapter 3.2.2 of this study, the ordinary meaning of the term "scientific method" suggests that under this provision, the undertaking of marine scientific research projects should follow a step-by-step approach to solving problems, that is to "identify and define the problem, accumulate data, formulate a hypothesis, conduct experiments to prove hypothesis, interpret results in an objective manner and repeat".[90]

Regarding operational oceanographic activities, it has been submitted that they mainly aim at providing continuous and long-term observations of the marine environment to provide data about the present state of the sea.[91] In this sense, operational oceanography can be called "descriptive oceanography"[92]

---

87 See Chapter 3.2.5 of this study.

88 Ibid.

89 UNCLOS, Article 240(b).

90 "Scientific method", The Law Dictionary (Featuring Black's Law Dictionary Free Online Legal Dictionary 2nd Ed.), available at https://thelawdictionary.org/scientific-method/.

91 Peter Ryder, "A possible migration from marine scientific research to operational oceanography in the context of the United Nations Convention on the Law of the Sea (UNCLOS)"; Florian H.Th. Wegelein, *Marine Scientific Research: The Operation and Status of Research Vessels and Other Platforms in International Law*, 20; Tobias Hofmann and Alexander Proelss, "The Operation of Gliders Under the International Law of the Sea", 172.

92 Descriptive oceanography aims at describing and explaining how and why the ocean system works through observations. See, for instance, Lynne D. Talley et al., *Descriptive Physical Oceanography: An Introduction (Sixth Edition)* (Academic Press, 2011), 1; André Gougenheim, "Oceanography and Hydrography—Basic Research and Descriptive Oceanography", *The International Hydrographic Review* (1965).

that is conducted without a clear scientific hypothesis.[93] However, as discussed above, along with the expanding observational needs, the function of operational oceanographic activities is no longer limited to the provision of ocean forecasting and climate predictions. Increasing scientific knowledge through verifying or falsifying scientific hypotheses is also one of the objectives pursued by the undertaking of operational oceanographic activities.[94] Arguably, when an operational oceanographic activity is conducted with a scientific hypothesis, it can be considered as marine scientific research. It is noted that UNCLOS does not provide any indication as to the level of specificity of the hypothesis. In the *Whaling in the Antarctic* case, although the criterion for defining a hypothesis was discussed by the experts called by both Parties, the Court observed that the Parties disagreed about the level of specificity required of such a hypothesis.[95] Therefore, the assessment of the existence of a scientific hypothesis remains a controversial issue, which can be resolved by accumulating best practices in this field.

Another factor that adds to the complexity of legal classification is that in practice, a single undertaking of operational oceanography potentially serves not only scientific purposes, but also other ends. Observation needs are fulfilled by the collection and management of different sets of ocean data. Different sensors that measure a variety of variables can be attached to one single tool or platform that is used for operational oceanography.[96] On the one hand, a single set of data may serve multiple purposes, scientific and non-scientific (one expedition, one tool or platform, one set of data collected by one sensor, multiple purposes served). On the other hand, it could also be the case that data collected by some sensors attached to the tool or platform contribute to verifying or falsifying a scientific hypothesis, while others do not (one expedition, one tool or platform, different sensors collecting different sets of data, multiple purposes served). It is debatable whether, in such circumstances, the operational oceanographic activity at issue qualifies as marine scientific research.[97]

93 Alexander Proelss, ed. *United Nations Convention on the Law of the Sea: A Commentary*, 460–461.

94 The Task Team for an Integrated Framework for Sustained Ocean Observing, "A Framework for Ocean Observing", Doc. IOC/INF-1284, at p. 18.

95 ICJ, *Whaling in the Antarctic* (*Australia v. Japan: New Zealand intervening*), Judgment, para.86.

96 For instance, Biogeochemical Argo floats are capable of gathering data concerning eight variables. See "Evolving Capabilities of the Argo Global Array of Profiling Floats - Information Document", Doc. IOC/INF-1344.

97 Florian H.Th. Wegelein, *Marine Scientific Research: The Operation and Status of Research Vessels and Other Platforms in International Law*, 227.

UNCLOS does not provide any clear indication on this matter, although relevant provisions suggest that marine scientific research projects could serve multiple purposes insofar as one of such purposes should be scientific.[98]

In conclusion, when an operational oceanographic activity is undertaken with a scientific hypothesis, it is to be considered as marine scientific research under UNCLOS. Nevertheless, considering the difficulty in assessing the existence of a scientific hypothesis, and the potential controversies concerning whether and to which extent operational oceanographic activities serving both scientific and non-scientific purposes qualify as marine scientific research, in practice, the determination of the legal classification of operational oceanography, especially its relationship with marine scientific research, remains a challenging task.

7.3.3.2 Operational Oceanography and "Other Internationally Lawful Uses of the Sea Related to" the Freedoms under Article 58(1)

According to Article 58(1) of UNCLOS, in the EEZ of a coastal State, all States enjoy

> the freedoms [...] of navigation and overflight and of the laying of submarine cables and pipelines, and other internationally lawful uses of the sea related to these freedoms, such as those associated with the operation of ships, aircraft and submarine cables and pipelines, and compatible with the other provisions of this Convention.[99]

This provision is relevant for the current analysis, because if an operational oceanographic activity constitutes "internationally lawful uses of the sea related to these freedoms", it can be undertaken freely in the EEZ of a coastal State and is not to be considered marine scientific research requiring a prior consent from the coastal State.[100]

As argued in Chapter 3.3.2.2 of this study, three qualifications are included in this provision, including that such uses shall be: 1) "related to" the freedoms explicitly mentioned in Article 58(1), 2) "internationally lawful", and 3)

98 See the conclusions of Chapter 3.

99 UNCLOS, Article 58(1).

100 It is submitted in Chapter 3.3.2.2 of this study that ocean data collection activities are not to be considered as "navigation", "overflight" or "laying of submarine cables and pipelines", notwithstanding the fact they can be undertaken by means of navigation, overflight or laying of submarine cables and pipelines.

"compatible with the other provisions of this Convention". The first qualification is the most pertinent to the current discussion.[101]

For the first qualification, the Convention does not indicate how close the relationship should be. Given the open-ended nature of this qualification, it is impractical to list all such uses. What is commonly understood is that this phrase includes the activities that form a regular, common or even necessary requirement for the exercise of the freedoms of navigation, overflight and the laying of pipelines and cables.[102] In the context of the present discussion, it has been submitted that for a ship collecting ocean data that are required for the safe passage of the ship itself (such as water depth, wind speed and direction), the ocean data collection activity involved is to be considered as "uses associated with the operation of ships", and thus falls under "other internationally lawful uses of the sea related to" navigation.[103] However, in most cases, the function of operational oceanographic activities is not merely to ensure the safe passage of the ship itself. Some operational oceanographic activities are undertaken for ocean forecasting and climate prediction, with indirect benefits of ensuring the safety of navigation, overflight, and of the laying of submarine cables and pipelines. It is the viewpoint of some authors that such activities can be broadly considered as "related to" the mentioned freedoms.[104] However, this interpretation is not without controversy, especially considering the different interpretations of the phrase "related to" the freedoms mentioned in Article 58(1). Therefore, similar to the case for discerning the relationship between operational oceanography and marine scientific research, for operational oceanographic activities that serve multiple purposes, and one of such purposes is to ensure the safety of navigation, their legal classification is more controversial.

Besides, to determine in what instances the related activities constitute "other internationally lawful uses of the sea related to" the freedoms, one needs to examine whether the activities fulfil the other two qualifications under Article 58(1).[105]

101 A detailed discussion on the three qualifications and their implication for the legal classification of ocean data collection activities are included in Chapter 3.3.2.2 of this study.

102 See, for instance, Alexander Proelss, ed. *United Nations Convention on the Law of the Sea: A Commentary*, 452–453; Kaiyan Homi Kaikobad, "Non Consensual Aerial Surveillance in the Airspace over the Exclusive Economic Zone for Military and Defence Purposes", 521.

103 Alfred H. A. Soons, *Marine Scientific Research and the Law of the Sea*, 149.

104 Kaiyan Homi Kaikobad, "Non Consensual Aerial Surveillance in the Airspace over the Exclusive Economic Zone for Military and Defence Purposes", 538. A detailed discussion on this matter is included in Chapter 3.3.2.2 of this book.

105 More discussion on the other two qualifications is contained in Chapter 3.3.2.2 of this book.

7.3.3.3 Operational Oceanography and the Role of Article 59

Article 59 of UNCLOS sets out the basis for resolving conflicts that arise from situations where the Convention does not attribute rights or jurisdiction to the coastal State or other States.[106] One author has submitted that operational oceanography constitutes a typical example of activities that fall under the scope of Article 59.[107] However, as a supplementary provision to Articles 56 and 58, this provision may only come into play when the undertaking of operational oceanographic activity in the EEZ of a coastal State falls neither under the jurisdiction of the coastal State nor under the scope of "other internationally lawful uses of the sea related to" the the freedoms under Article 58(1).[108] As discussed above, among the activities falling under the notion of "operational oceanography", those serving scientific purposes may qualify as marine scientific research, and those "related to" the freedom of navigation, overflight and of the laying of submarine cables and pipelines fall under Article 58(1). These activities naturally do not fall under the scope of Article 59. In cases where the operational oceanographic activity fulfils none of the purposes identified above, Article 59 should be invoked.

7.3.4 *Interim Conclusions*

In sum, the legal classification of operational oceanographic activities cannot be discerned categorically. For purposes of legal classification, the function of the activity is of paramount significance. As will be demonstrated below, data that are collected can be used as a good indication of the function of or objective served by the activity.

When undertaken in the EEZ of a coastal State, an operational oceanographic activity: 1) may qualify as marine scientific research (when it is conducted with a scientific hypothesis), 2) may constitute "other internationally lawful uses of the sea" under Article 58(1) of the Convention (in particular when it is undertaken to ensure the safety of navigation, overflight, or of the

---

106 UNCLOS, Article 59. This article provides that:

> In cases where this Convention does not attribute rights or jurisdiction to the coastal State or to other States within the exclusive economic zone, and a conflict arises between the interests of the coastal State and any other State or States, the conflict should be resolved on the basis of equity and in the light of all the relevant circumstances, taking into account the respective importance of the interests involved to the parties as well as to the international community as a whole.

107 Alexander Proelss, ed. *United Nations Convention on the Law of the Sea: A Commentary*, 460–461.

108 A fuller discussion on the role of Article 59 in addressing the classification and regulation of ocean data collection activities are included in Chapter 3.3.2.4 of this study.

laying of submarine cables and pipelines), 3) may concern an unattributed right falling under Article 59. The subsequent section will look at the result(s) of applying the relevant provisions to these scenarios and examine whether and to what extent the application provides similar outcomes.

Nevertheless, considering the difficulty of determining the existence of a scientific hypothesis in practice (for discerning the relationship between the activity at issue and marine scientific research), and the uncertainties or controversies over the legal status of operational oceanographic activities that serve multiple purposes, determining the legal classification of some operational oceanographic activities under UNCLOS remains a challenging task. The legal implications of these activities will be addressed in Section 7.5 of this chapter.

7.4 Different Scenarios: Application of the Relevant UNCLOS Provisions to Operational Oceanography

In this section, sub-sections 7.4.1 to 7.4.3 respectively look at the implications of applying the UNCLOS Part XIII regime to operational oceanographic activities that qualify as marine scientific research, of applying Article 58 to those constituting "other internationally lawful uses related to" the freedoms under Article 58(1), and of applying Article 59 to those that are concerned with unattributed rights in the EEZ of a coastal State. Interim concluding remarks and some observations pertinent to the discussions in the next section are contained in sub-section 7.4.4.

7.4.1 *The UNCLOS Marine Scientific Research Regime and Operational Oceanography*

As discussed in Section 7.3.2 of the current chapter, the UNCLOS Part XIII regime applies not only to operational oceanographic activities that qualify as marine scientific research, but also to all "scientific research" activities that involve the deployment and use of installations or equipment. A pertinent question that arises is in what instances operational oceanographic activities should be considered as "scientific research". Since the Convention does not define the term "scientific research", one has to resort to its ordinary meaning.[109]

109 It is noted that the term "scientific research" and its meaning have been addressed in the ICJ *Whaling in the Antarctic* case. The Court considered that the criteria advanced by Australia concerning 1) defined and achievable objectives (questions or hypotheses) that aim to contribute to knowledge important to the conservation and management of stocks, 2)

This term commonly refers to "an investigation of a question, problem or phenomenon conducted according to the rules and principles of science".[110] Some operational oceanographic activities are undertaken systematically to measure the state of the marine environment. Arguably, these activities can be broadly considered as scientific research. There are also instances where operational oceanographic activities are not intended to study or explain a phenomenon, or its relationship with other phenomena.[111] It is submitted that such activities do not fall under the scope of "scientific research". Besides, Article 258 only applies to activities involving the use or deployment of installations or equipment, while some operational oceanographic activities are conducted by vessels. Naturally, Article 258 does not apply to such activities either.[112] Therefore, pursuant to Article 258 and in the context of the current discussion, the Part XIII regime may apply to certain operational oceanographic activities even if such activities do not amount to marine scientific research. As such, the following discussion on the implications of applying the UNCLOS Part XIII regime to operational oceanographic activities that constitute marine scientific research also applies to operational oceanographic activities that are not marine scientific research, but rather scientific research activities that involve the use and deployment of installations or equipment.

As briefly mentioned in the Chapter 1.1 of this book, an application of the UNCLOS marine scientific research regime to certain new forms of ocean data collection activities will lead to some challenges in practice. Arguably, some operational oceanographic activities are among those "modern" ocean data collection activities. In this regard, this sub-section begins with an introduction to the challenges of applying the UNCLOS marine scientific research regime to (certain) operational oceanographic activities (Section 7.4.1.1), which is followed by an examination of the relevant provisions that potentially offer

"appropriate methods", 3) peer review, and 4) the avoidance of adverse effects on stock, reflected activities which can be called "well-conceived scientific research", rather than "serving as an interpretation of the term as used in the Convention". However, the Court did not consider it "necessary to devise alternative criteria or to offer a general definition of 'scientific research'". ICJ, *Whaling in the Antarctic* (*Australia v. Japan: New Zealand intervening*), Judgment, paras.73–86. An analysis of this case and its implications for understanding the meaning of the term "scientific research" is included in Chapter 5.5.2 of this study.

110 Alfred H. A. Soons, *Marine Scientific Research and the Law of the Sea*, 124.

111 "Technical Report on Scoping of Operational Oceanography", Doc. IOC/INF-1291, at p. 3.

112 However, it is also noted that given the requirements to provide systematic and long-term observations, operational oceanographic activities undertaken by vessels in most cases require the use of some types of installation or equipment – one will not estimate temperature or wind force solely on the basis of sensory perception.

options to respond to these challenges (Section 7.4.1.2). Section 7.4.1.3 offers some interim concluding remarks.

7.4.1.1 Challenges for Implementation

The most significant implication derived from the application of the UNCLOS marine scientific research regime to operational oceanography, which usually involves the use of autonomous instruments, is the difficulty of fully implementing the prior consent requirements when the research instruments will enter areas within the national jurisdiction of a coastal State.

Under UNCLOS, marine scientific research projects which are proposed to be undertaken in areas under the jurisdiction of a coastal State require the prior consent of that State.[113] For this purpose, when the project is planned to be undertaken in the EEZ or on the continental shelf of a coastal State, the relevant information should be sent to the State at least six months prior to the commencement of the research project.[114] In practical terms, these requirements would be difficult to fulfil if autonomous instruments are deployed for ocean data collection purposes.[115] It is the nature of autonomous instruments that, once deployed in the marine environment, they may be carried by ocean currents and flow passively in the oceans. It is impracticable to predict their route precisely or to influence it. It is therefore unpredictable when and where the instruments might enter the EEZ of a coastal State.[116] As such, it is hardly possible to obtain the coastal State's consent in accordance with the time limit provided for by the Convention.

This problem can be most vividly illustrated by the use of bio-logging technology in the field of operational oceanography.[117] When data-collecting sensors are attached to marine animals, which may migrate into the territorial sea or the EEZ of the coastal State, and the sensors record certain kinds of oceanographic data therein. The highly variable and hardly predictable behavior of marine animals makes it impracticable to accurately forecast the precise

---

113 UNCLOS, Articles 245, 246.

114 Ibid., Article 248.

115 Tim Stephens and Donald Rothwell, "Marine Scientific Research", 575.

116 Katharina Bork et al., "The Legal Regulation of Floats and Gliders - In Quest of a New Regime?", 311.

117 Richard J. McLaughlin, "UNCLOS and the Growing Use of Electronic Tagged Marine Animals as Autonomous Ocean Profilers", 489–501; Richard Apostle, Tsafrir Gazit, and Marcus Haward, "Ocean Tracking and Marine Species Protection in Australia and Canada: Science, Technology, and Knowledge Brokering", *Ocean Development & International Law* 47, no. 4 (2016); James Kraska, Guillermo Ortuño Crespo, and David W. Johnston, "Bio-logging of marine migratory species in the law of the sea", 394–400.

route that individual animals may travel, and there is no efficient and acceptable way to direct (or interfere with) the movement of these animals.[118] In this regard, the implementation of the consent regime as provided for in Part XIII of UNCLOS is problematic. It would be difficult to argue that researchers using such a method have to fully comply with the prior consent requirements when the marine animals enter areas under the jurisdiction or sovereignty of other States.[119]

In fact, the legal implications of using autonomous instruments for the marine scientific research regime have been discussed during the IOC/ABE-LOS meetings.[120] Some scholars have opined that such new methods of ocean data collection "have by-passed" the existing legal regime; thus the use of these methods does not need to fulfil the outdated requirements set out for marine scientific research in the Convention, just like satellite remote sensing did decades earlier.[121] In the view of the current author, this observation seems to fail to understand the reason for excluding satellite remote sensing from the scope of the legal regime for marine scientific research in UNCLOS. Unlike autonomous vehicles, the use of remote sensing technology to conduct ocean data collection activities was discussed in other fora at the same time as UNCLOS III or even earlier, and it was agreed at UNCLOS III that it should be covered by other international rules than the law of the sea.[122] For autonomous instruments, the relevant drafting history indicates that research tools and platforms other than vessels have been envisaged and discussed during UNCLOS III. States intended to include the activities involving the use of these tools and platforms in the scope of the UNCLOS marine scientific research

118 Richard J. McLaughlin, "UNCLOS and the Growing Use of Electronic Tagged Marine Animals as Autonomous Ocean Profilers", 496; James Kraska, Guillermo Ortuño Crespo, and David W. Johnston, "Bio-logging of marine migratory species in the law of the sea", 395–396; Richard J. McLaughlin, "Bio-Logging as Marine Scientific Research Under the Law of the Sea: A Commentary Responding to James Kraska, Guillermo Ortuño Crespo, David W. Johnston, Bio-Logging of Marine Migratory Species in the Law of the Sea, Marine Policy 51 (2015) 394–400", 180.

119 Richard J. McLaughlin, "UNCLOS and the Growing Use of Electronic Tagged Marine Animals as Autonomous Ocean Profilers", 496; James Kraska, Guillermo Ortuño Crespo, and David W Johnston, "Bio-logging of marine migratory species in the law of the sea", 394.

120 For more information on these discussions, see the summary records of the meetings of IOC/ABE-LOS, especially, "Report of the Sixth Session of IOC/ABE-LOS", Doc. IOC/ABE-LOS VI/3, at pp. 5–6; "Report of the Seventh Session of IOC/ABE-LOS", Doc. IOC/ABE-LOS VII/3, at pp. 4–9; "Report of the Eighth Session of IOC/ABE-LOS", Doc. IOC/ABE-LOS VIII/3, at pp. 2–9. See also Chapter 4.3.2.1 of this book.

121 James Kraska, Guillermo Ortuño Crespo, and David W Johnston, "Bio-logging of marine migratory species in the law of the sea", 400.

122 Alfred H. A. Soons, *Marine Scientific Research and the Law of the Sea*, 5.

regime. This is considered to be supported by the drafting history of Article 240(b) of UNCLOS, which sets out a general principle for all marine scientific research. This provision evolved from proposals that made specific reference to research means, which may be used for marine scientific research, such as vessels, aircraft, devices, equipment or installations. A pertinent article contained in ISNT provided that:

> [i]n conducting marine scientific research in accordance with the provisions of this Convention States and competent international organizations shall use appropriate scientific methods and may utilize vessels, aircraft, devices, equipment or installations.[123]

The reference to these specific means was deleted in the subsequent draft texts of the Convention. It is submitted that this deletion reflects the intention of the drafters to leave this provision open to a broad interpretation concerning scientific methods and means.[124]

In this connection, it is noted that the DOALOS Revised Guide on marine scientific research has suggested that in the application of the relevant UNCLOS provisions, "[t]he increasing sophistication of research platforms and other means of collecting data should be taken into account".[125] Here, "the increasing sophistication of research platforms and other means of collecting data" primarily denotes the growing use of autonomous platforms and more advanced equipment and sensors for marine scientific research, which is driven by the increased cost of ship-borne research and the expanding demand for continuous, high-resolution, long-term ocean observations for both research and societal needs.[126] Therefore, new methods of ocean data collection cannot "by-pass" the existing legal regime on marine scientific research.

Another challenge raised by the application of the UNCLOS marine scientific research regime to (some) operational oceanographic activities is that the rigid consent requirements may impede the development of science and sufficient coverage of meteorological observations, which is indispensable for ensuring the safety of life and property at sea.

---

123 Informal single negotiating text, Part III, UN. Doc. A/CONF.62/WP.8/Part III, part II, Article 6.

124 Myron H. Nordquist et al., eds., *United Nations Convention on the Law of the Sea, 1982: A Commentary* (*Vol. IV*), 461; Alexander Proelss, ed. *United Nations Convention on the Law of the Sea: A Commentary*, 1621–1622.

125 UN/DOALOS, "Marine Scientific Research: A Revised Guide to the Implementation of the Relevant Provisions of the United Nations Convention on the Law of the Sea", para.118.

126 Ibid., Introduction, at p. v.

Considering these challenges, a pertinent question that arises is that what these challenges entail? Do they annul the application of the marine scientific research regime to such new uses? In the view of the current author, the answer is negative. Operational oceanography represents an illustrative example that existing legal regimes may fall short in addressing the legal issues raised by new technologies. However, as observed by one scholar:

> when technological innovations occur, they do not eliminate existing treaty obligations, but instead encourage new and innovative legal adjustments and policies to respond to the unforeseen problems.[127]

As has been discussed in Chapter 2 of this book, UNCLOS is a "living instrument" and has the ability to adapt to new developments. In most cases, the provisions of the Convention are drafted in a way to resolve new problems not envisaged at the time of UNCLOS III.[128] Presumably, this observation also holds true, where the marine scientific research regime is concerned. In this connection, the next sub-section will look at pertinent provisions of the Convention and evaluates whether the UNCLOS Part XIII regime is still adequate and allows responding to the above-mentioned challenges.

7.4.1.2 Opportunities for Future Development

As discussed above, the major challenges of applying the UNCLOS marine scientific research regime to operational oceanography include: 1) the difficulty of fully implementing prior consent requirements, and 2) the risk of impeding the development of marine science and timely provision of operational services.[129] It is submitted that these challenges can be mitigated by taking into consideration certain provisions of UNCLOS – as proposed by Jarmache, an approach to respond to the challenges would be to use the flexibility embedded

---

127 Richard J. McLaughlin, "Bio-Logging as Marine Scientific Research Under the Law of the Sea: A Commentary Responding to James Kraska, Guillermo Ortuño Crespo, David W. Johnston, Bio-Logging of Marine Migratory Species in the Law of the Sea, Marine Policy 51 (2015) 394–400", 181.

128 Tullio Treves, "The International Tribunal for the Law of the Sea and the Rule of Law", 69. See also Bernard H. Oxman, "Tools for Change: The Amendment Procedure", 199.

129 Operational services mainly include the provision of ocean hazard early warning, weather and ocean forecasting, and the contribution to the development of a path towards sustainable development. For more information, see the official website of GOOS, "GOOS Themes: Operational Services", available at https://www.goosocean.org/index.php?option=com_content&view=article&id=5&Itemid=105.

in the UNCLOS Part XIII regime.[130] This sub-section looks into some UNCLOS provisions contributing to the flexibility of Part XIII which potentially provide some leeway for the cumbersome obligations for researching States that are undertaking marine scientific research in the form of operational oceanography in waters under the jurisdiction of a coastal State. These provisions are included in Articles 242, 243, and 247. Implications of these provisions will be addressed consecutively in the following analysis.

Before commencing the substantive discussion, it is necessary to point out that none of these provisions overrides the consent requirements contained in Articles 245 and 246 of the Convention. Rather, they set out options for obtaining the consent in a different (and simplified) way as a response to the challenges identified above.

7.4.1.2.1 *Implications of Article 242*

The first article that warrants an examination is Article 242. Paragraph 1 of this article sets out the general obligation for States and competent international organizations to "promote international cooperation in marine scientific research for peaceful purposes."[131] Paragraph 2 of this article and Article 243 are among the provisions that provide more specific measures that give concreteness to such a general obligation.[132] Besides, some international instruments adopted after UNCLOS also emphasize the obligation of States to cooperate in marine scientific research, especially instruments concerning the conservation of marine living resources and the protection of the marine environment.[133] Other relevant fields in which significance has been attached to cooperation in marine science are climate change mitigation and adaptation, and disaster risk reduction.[134]

One of the challenges of applying the Part XIII regime to operational oceanography is that it may impede the collection of data that are indispensable for the safety of life at sea and the protection of life and property in coastal and offshore areas. It is submitted that this concern can be, at least partly,

---

130 "Technical Workshop Enhancing Ocean Observations and Research, and the Free Exchange of Data, to Foster Services for the Safety of Life and Property: Final Report", at p. 30.

131 UNCLOS, Article 242(1).

132 Alexander Proelss, ed. *United Nations Convention on the Law of the Sea: A Commentary*, 1631.

133 Yoshifumi Tanaka, "Obligation to Co-Operate in Marine Scientific Research and the Conservation of Marine Living Resources", 945–951.

134 International legal instruments that are relevant include UNFCCC, the Paris Agreement and the Sendai Framework for Disaster Risk Reduction.

addressed by Article 242(2). As a means to promote international cooperation under Article 242(1), Article 242(2) provides that:

> without prejudice to the rights and duties of States under this Convention, a State, in the application of this Part, shall provide, as appropriate, other States with a reasonable opportunity to obtain from it, or with its cooperation, information necessary to prevent and control damage to the health and safety of persons and to the marine environment.[135]

On the face of it, this paragraph seems to be a detailed obligation for States to share information that is necessary to prevent and control damage to the health and safety of persons and to the marine environment. However, a closer examination of its wording reveals that this paragraph is not concerned with the provision of such information *per se*, but rather the provision with other States of a reasonable opportunity to obtain the mentioned information. As submitted by Soons, this paragraph provides for "a special regime for a particular category of marine scientific research" that applies to the collection, in areas under coastal State jurisdiction, of information/data "necessary to prevent and control damage to health and safety of persons and the environment".[136] It is observed that such information or data include:

> data necessary for studies of great social importance, such as studies for the purpose of predicting earthquakes or tsunamis, or certain dangerous atmospheric conditions (such as hurricanes and the monsoon), or for identifying and controlling cases of serious pollution, in order to be able to prevent or minimize the harmful effects of such natural disasters or man-made conditions.[137]

This reading of the provision is supported by the relevant drafting history. This paragraph evolved from an informal proposal made by the United States at UNCLOS III which reads as:

> The *coastal State* in the application of this Part shall provide other States with reasonable opportunity to obtain from it, or with its cooperation, information necessary to prevent and control damage to the health, safety

135 UNCLOS, Article 244(2).

136 Alfred H. A. Soons, *Marine Scientific Research and the Law of the Sea*, 241.

137 Ibid. See also Myron H. Nordquist et al., eds., *United Nations Convention on the Law of the Sea, 1982: A Commentary* (*Vol. IV*), 471–472.

> and environment of persons not subject to the jurisdiction of the coastal State, *such as research and monitoring data regarding weather, currents, pollution and other general processes and their causes and effects.*[138]

The Virginia commentary observes that no formal or informal explanations had been provided for the omission of the examples included in the proposal, but there is no reason to suppose that such an omission would result in a materially different reading of the provision.[139] In the context of the current discussion, it can be reasonably argued that data that are usually collected by operational oceanographic activities fall under the scope of this provision. Accordingly, the coastal State is under an obligation to provide other States "a reasonable opportunity" to obtain such information from it, or with its cooperation.

Under Article 242(2), there are two ways for other States to acquire such information from the coastal State.[140] First, when such information has been acquired by the coastal State, other States shall be given a reasonable opportunity to obtain the information from it. Second, if a State considers the collection of certain ocean data will lead to the mentioned information, the coastal State shall provide the researching State "a reasonable opportunity" to collect the data with its cooperation. Of particular relevance for the current discussions is the latter one. The researching State may enter into a cooperative agreement with the coastal State for the collection of the data concerned.

"A reasonable opportunity" is an ambiguous, and on the positive side, a flexible phrase. From the perspective of the coastal State, there are multiple means to provide such an opportunity. For instance, it may simplify the clearance

---

138 Emphasis added. See Myron H. Nordquist et al., eds., *United Nations Convention on the Law of the Sea, 1982: A Commentary* (*Vol. IV*), 469. The United States further addressed the rationale of this paragraph in its explanatory notes attached to that proposal, according to which, with regard to Article 242,

> [i]nternational law in principle regulates the manner in which a State may use areas subject to its jurisdiction when such use causes harm outside its jurisdiction. The specific application of this general principle depends on the subject-matter. Article 195, paragraph 2 [article 194 of the Convention], is an application of the principle relevant to pollution. This new article would *apply the same principle to marine scientific research* where, for example, understanding of the monsoon may be critical to the development, and indeed the survival, of millions.

139 Ibid., 471.

140 It is noted that this provision not only applies to coastal States but also researching States that have collected such information. These researching States are also under an obligation to "provide, as appropriate, other States with a reasonable opportunity" to obtain from them such information. See ibid.

procedure for such a project or choose to grant its consent even if it has the discretional power to withhold the consent in accordance with Article 246(5) of the Convention.[141]

Arguably, this provision can be read as providing an opportunity for the researching State to be more actively involved in the process of obtaining the consent from the coastal State, instead of idly waiting for the consent to be given. In other words, it establishes a two-way communication process as opposed to a one-way road of obtaining the consent as manifested in Articles 246(2) and 248 of the Convention. In addition, because Article 242(2) creates an obligation for the coastal State to provide "a reasonable opportunity", in a sense, this provision also provides some leverage for the researching State to persuade the coastal State to grant its consent in the two-way communication.

7.4.1.2.2 *Implications of Article 243*

Article 243 is another provision giving concreteness to the general obligation of international cooperation contained in Article 242(1). Under Article 243, States and competent international organizations are under an obligation to:

> cooperate, through the conclusion of bilateral and multilateral agreements, to create favourable conditions for the conduct of marine scientific research […] and to integrate the efforts of scientists in studying the essence of phenomena and processes occurring in the marine environment and the interrelations between them.[142]

Since most operational oceanographic activities aim at "studying the essence of phenomena and processes occurring in the marine environment and the interrelations between them", they neatly fall under the scope of this provision.

According to this article, the creation of "favourable conditions" is to take place through the conclusion of bilateral or multilateral agreements.[143] The drafting history of Article 243 indicates that, aside from facilitating international cooperation in marine scientific research, this provision was also intended to "balance the interests of any given coastal States with the interests

141 It is noteworthy that since Article 242(2) is "without prejudice to the rights and duties of States under the Convention", the coastal State remains entitled to withhold its consent if such a project falls within the circumstances listed in Article 246(5). UNCLOS, Articles 242(2), 246(5); Alfred H. A. Soons, *Marine Scientific Research and the Law of the Sea*, 241.

142 UNCLOS, Article 243.

143 Ibid.

of other coastal States and the international community".[144] In this regard, it is submitted that like some other provisions of the Part XIII regime, this provision tries to provide a way for the researching state of being more actively involved in the process of obtaining the consent from the coastal State.

As one can note, this provision has been formulated in a rather vague fashion. It has been observed that presumably, the "favourable conditions" referred to in this provision "concern the situation that States have agreed on a basis of reciprocity to apply simplified or less strict procedures for obtaining consent to do research in areas under their jurisdiction".[145] The States concerned enjoy the discretion to choose the specific conditions themselves. The Convention again leaves States and competent international organizations with broad discretion as to the form and contents of such agreements. Thus, it appears compatible with the aim of this provision for States and competent international organizations, when fulfilling their obligations under this provision, to enter into treaties, as well as soft law instruments, such as the decisions adopted by international organizations.[146] Any agreement would be consistent with this provision as long as it aims at creating favorable conditions for the conduct of marine scientific research and the integration of research efforts.[147]

In the context of the current discussion, for operational oceanographic activities that qualify as marine scientific research under UNCLOS, such agreements could be established, as a means to create simplified or less stringent requirements for applying the consent from the coastal State.

7.4.1.2.3 *Implications of Article 247*

Another option for using the flexibility of the UNCLOS marine scientific research regime is provided in Article 247, which stipulates that:

> [a] coastal State which is a member of or has a bilateral agreement with an international organization, and in whose exclusive economic zone or on whose continental shelf that organization wants to carry out a marine scientific research project, directly or under its auspices, shall be deemed to have authorized the project to be carried out in conformity with the agreed specifications if that State approved the detailed project when the

144 Myron H. Nordquist et al., eds., *United Nations Convention on the Law of the Sea, 1982: A Commentary* (*Vol. IV*), 476.

145 Alfred H. A. Soons, *Marine Scientific Research and the Law of the Sea*, 242.

146 Alexander Proelss, ed. *United Nations Convention on the Law of the Sea: A Commentary*, 1639.

147 Ibid.

> decision was made by the organization for the undertaking of the project, or is willing to participate in it, and has not expressed any objection within four months of notification of the project by the organization to the coastal State.[148]

This article constitutes an exception to the normal consent regime as provided in Article 246 of the Convention, which applies to marine scientific research projects undertaken by or under the auspices of international organizations.[149] It intends to simplify the procedure for the application of the consent from the coastal State to the undertaking of marine scientific research projects in its EEZ or on its continental shelf.[150] However, in practice, this provision has never been invoked since the adoption of the Convention. The fundamental reason arguably is the different interpretations of the scope of marine scientific research.

During the IOC/ABE-LOS discussions on the matter of the legal framework applicable to the collection of oceanographic data in the EEZ, it was proposed that Article 247 of UNCLOS could be used to address legal issues related to the deployment of Argo floats in EEZs.[151] This proposal was rejected by some delegations. According to them, the Part XIII regime does not apply to the deployment of Argo floats in EEZs.[152] In connection to the proposal relating to Article 247, a delegation recalled that the basis of all discussions on issues regarding the collection of oceanographic data by specific means was that a reference in whatever form to Article 247 should be avoided since that article is contained

148 UNCLOS, Article 247.

149 The first proposal concerning the draft text of this article was introduced at a relatively late stage of the UNCLOS III negotiations. At the time, States had already reached an agreement on setting up a consent regime for the conduct of all kinds of marine scientific research projects in areas under the jurisdiction of a coastal State. The reason of introducing this provision, in the words of the President of the Conference, was "[t]o meet the concerns of several delegations which felt that research projects undertaken under the auspices of or by an international organization should be facilitated through a special regime". For more information on the drafting history of this provision, see Myron H. Nordquist et al., eds., *United Nations Convention on the Law of the Sea, 1982: A Commentary* (*Vol. IV*), 520–525; Alfred H. A. Soons, "The Background of Article 247 of the UN Convention on the Law of the Sea (UNCLOS)", in *Procedure for the Application of Article 247 of the United Nations Convention on the Law of the Sea by the Intergovernmental Oceanographic Commission of UNESCO*, edited by UNESCO/IOC/LAW OF THE SEA (IOC/LOS) (Paris: 2007).

150 Alexander Proelss, ed. *United Nations Convention on the Law of the Sea: A Commentary*, 1669.

151 "Report of the Ninth Session of IOC/ABE-LOS", Doc. IOC/ABE-LOS IX/3 Rev., at p. 7.

152 Ibid.

in Part XIII, which is entitled "Marine Scientific Research" – a reference to that article would imply that activities undertaken under the Argo project should be considered as marine scientific research.[153]

Another reason for the reluctance to make use of this provision is concerned with the divergent viewpoints as to how this provision should be invoked.[154] Several issues remain uncertain.[155] What can be considered as a "decision" under this provision? How detailed must the decision be? How should the State give its consent or express its willingness to participate in the international organization?

The first two questions relate to the meaning of the term "decision" under this article. Soons has argued that the term "decision" under the current provision in normal circumstances refers to the decision made by the international organization during the final stage of the preparation of the marine scientific research project.[156] More importantly, to guarantee the practical effect of such a decision, it is preferable to expressly specify in the text of the decision that it is approved under the meaning of Article 247.[157] This approach has been endorsed by the IOC Procedure of the Implementation of Article 247 of UNCLOS (hereinafter IOC Procedure).[158] Paragraph 5 of the Procedure provides that,

153 Ibid., at pp. 7–8.

154 As observed by the Virginia Commentary,

> [t]he mere fact that the coastal State is a member of, or has a bilateral agreement with, the international organization concerned does not in itself suffice to create the presumption of its authorization for a given research project. The coastal State is deemed to have authorized a particular project only if it has approved the detailed project when the decision was made by the organization to undertake the project, or when that State is willing to participate in the project, and has not expressed any objection to that detailed project within four months of the notification of the project by the organization to the coastal State.

See Myron H. Nordquist et al., eds., *United Nations Convention on the Law of the Sea, 1982: A Commentary* (*Vol. IV*), 523.

155 Alexander Proelss, ed. *United Nations Convention on the Law of the Sea: A Commentary*, 1670, at note 32.

156 Alfred H. A. Soons, *Marine Scientific Research and the Law of the Sea*, 181.

157 Ibid. Soons also points out the disadvantages of the inclusion of an express reference to Article 247, which are 1) it would prolong discussions in the organization on the decision (and the entire project), and 2) it entails the risk of more politicization and bureaucratization of the organization.

158 Procedure for the Application of Article 247 of UNCLOS by the Intergovernmental Oceanographic Commission of UNESCO, 2005. The full text of the Procedure is available at the official website of IOC/ABE-LOS, "Procedu-re for Implementation", available at http://www.ioc-unesco.org/index.php?option=com_content&view=article&id=309&Itemid=100024.

> [a] decision that the Commission undertake a marine scientific research project under Article 247 of the Convention shall be taken by the Assembly by means of the adoption of a resolution. The draft for such a resolution [...] shall explicitly indicate that its adoption is for the purpose of applying Article 247 of the Convention.[159]

As to the third question, the IOC Procedure only acknowledges a State's approval of the project when it votes in favor of the resolution as referred to in Paragraph 5 of the Procedure.[160]

Notably, this represents a relatively narrow interpretation of Article 247. However, as pointed out earlier, the issues discussed above are open questions that potentially invite different interpretations. Besides, the terminology used in this provision – "international organization", rather than "competent international organization" as other provisions in the same Section – indicates a broader scope of application of this provision.[161] To be more specific, in the words of Soons:

> Article 247 can be used by any global or regional international organization with competence in the field of marine scientific research. It is up to each organization to adopt its own internal procedure for this purpose.[162]

Accordingly, international organizations other than IOC are in a position to adopt more flexible approaches than the IOC Procedure. For instance, it could be provided that the decision under Article 247 can be adopted informally, or without explicit reference to Article 247; that a State's approval of the project can be inferred when it participates actively in the discussions and formulation of a research project undertaken by or under the auspices of an international organization and shows its "positive stance"[163] to the undertaking

159 Ibid., Paragraph 5.

160 Ibid., Paragraph 7.

161 Alfred H. A. Soons, "The Background of Article 247 of the UN Convention on the Law of the Sea (UNCLOS)", 9; Florian H.Th. Wegelein, *Marine Scientific Research: The Operation and Status of Research Vessels and Other Platforms in International Law*, 313; Alexander Proelss, ed. *United Nations Convention on the Law of the Sea: A Commentary*, 1670–1673.

162 Alfred H. A. Soons, "The Background of Article 247 of the UN Convention on the Law of the Sea (UNCLOS)", 9.

163 Myron H. Nordquist et al., eds., *United Nations Convention on the Law of the Sea, 1982: A Commentary (Vol. IV)*, 524. It is the viewpoint of the Virginia Commentary that "ambiguous actions", such as abstention during the vote of the decision concerned, nonparticipation in the vote, or absence from the meeting at which the decision was taken, might still establish an approval in the meaning of this provision "in light of all the concurrent

of the project in whichever form. It is beyond the scope of the current study to adjudge which approach is better and more practicable. The international organization concerned, or more accurately its member States, have the discretion to decide the detailed mechanism to implement Article 247.

It is submitted that with regard to operational oceanographic activities that qualify as marine scientific research, the international organizations concerned can make use of the flexibility provided by Article 247 by, for example, setting up a detailed mechanism to implement this provision. When such a mechanism is in place, activities undertaken by or under the auspices of the international organization concerned can be carried out in areas under the jurisdiction of a coastal State under less stringent requirements.

7.4.1.3 Interim Conclusions

In sum, the application of the UNCLOS marine scientific research regime to certain operational oceanographic activities may encounter some implementation problems, especially considering the devices that are frequently used for this purpose. However, it is argued that these problems can be alleviated to a certain degree by resorting to the flexibility of the UNCLOS marine scientific research regime. So as to balance coastal States' authorization over foreign marine scientific research projects, the Convention provides for different ways through which the researching State can be more actively involved in the process of obtaining the consent from the coastal State. The relevant provisions of the Part XIII regime establish a two-way communication process for obtaining the consent as opposed to a one-way process as manifested in the provisions under Articles 246 and 248. Articles 242(2) and 243 respectively set up the obligation for the coastal State to provide "a reasonable opportunity" to obtain certain information and to "create favourable conditions" for the conduct of certain marine scientific research projects. It is submitted that for operational oceanographic activities that fall under the scope of these provisions, the provisions can be read as providing some leverage to the researching State to persuade the coastal State to grant its consent in the two-way communication mentioned above. The researching State or competent international organization may also enter into cooperative agreements with the coastal State concerning the collection of certain data (pursuant to Articles 242(2) and 243) in areas under the jurisdiction of the coastal State and to agree upon simpler

circumstance". Besides, where the coastal State is not a member of the organization – but has a bilateral agreement with it – clearly it cannot express any position by means of a vote in the decision-making process.

clearance procedures than the requirements of obtaining prior consent under Articles 245, 246, and 248.

Besides, Article 247 also provides a viable way to create simplified procedures if operational oceanographic activities were to be regarded as marine scientific research. International organizations concerned may use the flexibility provided by Article 247.

7.4.2 *Article 58 of UNCLOS and Operational Oceanography*

Depending on their function, some operational oceanographic activities may constitute "other internationally lawful uses of the sea related to" the freedoms of navigation, overflight, and of the laying of submarine cables and pipelines under Article 58(1) of the Convention. According to this provision, the undertaking of such activities forms part of the freedoms enjoyed by other States in the EEZ of a coastal State.[164] It is to be noted that the exercise of these freedoms is not without restrictions. Paragraph 3 of the same article provides that:

> [i]n exercising their rights and performing their duties under this Convention in the exclusive economic zone, States shall have due regard to the rights and duties of the coastal State and shall comply with the laws and regulations adopted by the coastal State in accordance with the provisions of this Convention and other rules of international law in so far as they are not incompatible with this Part.

The latter requirement concerning the compliance with the laws and regulations adopted by the coastal State indicates that the rights and duties to be observed by other States in the EEZ of the coastal State not only arise from the Convention but also national laws and regulations "adopted […] in accordance with the provisions of [UNCLOS]".[165] In this respect, States that carry out operational oceanographic activities that fall under the scope of Article 58(1) shall ensure that the undertaking of these activities do not violate the domestic laws and regulations of the coastal State, in particular those adopted by the coastal State for the exercise of its sovereign rights and jurisdiction in accordance with UNCLOS.

This provision also contains an obligation of due regard. A similar obligation of due regard is included in Article 56(2).[166] The content of the due regard

---

164 UNCLOS, Article 58(1).

165 Alexander Proelss, ed. *United Nations Convention on the Law of the Sea: A Commentary*, 456.

166 UNCLOS, Article 56(2). This provision stipulates that "[i]n exercising its rights and performing its duties under this Convention in the exclusive economic zone, the coastal State shall have due regard to the rights and duties of other States […]".

obligation, "rights and duties" protected by this obligation, and how the obligation is to be invoked, have been discussed in Chapter 3.3.2.3 of this study. It is argued that the scope of the rights and duties protected by the due regard obligation is considerably wide – such rights and duties are not limited to those mentioned in Articles 56(1) or 58(1).[167] Besides, as suggested by relevant case law, to fulfil this obligation, in cases where a conflict arises or may arise, the States concerned are required to engage in consultation with each other and properly balance the interests that may be involved.[168] Elements that should be taken into account during the consultation and the balancing exercise include:

> the nature of the rights held [...], their importance, the extent of the anticipated impairment, the nature and importance of the activities contemplated [...], and the availability of alternative approaches.[169]

The States concerned have the discretion to decide the approaches to fulfilling this obligation.[170] Such approaches include the conclusion of special agreements and the establishment of cooperative arrangements. The application of these requirements to operational oceanographic activities will be discussed in Section 7.5 of this chapter.

7.4.3 *Article 59 of UNCLOS and Operational Oceanography*

Article 59 is to be invoked when the rights or jurisdiction over the activity at issue falls neither at the hand of the coastal State under Article 56(1) nor other States under 58(1). According to Article 59, in cases where a conflict in relation to unattributed rights or jurisdiction arises between the interests of the coastal States and any other States:

---

167 Shotaro Hamamoto, "The Genesis of the 'Due Regard' Obligations in the United Nations Convention on the Law of the Sea", 7–24.

168 Annex VII Arbitral Tribunal of UNCLOS, *Chagos Marine Protected Area Arbitration (Mauritius v. United Kingdom)*, para.534.

169 Ibid., para.519.

170 ITLOS, *Dispute concerning delimitation of the maritime boundary between Bangladesh and Myanmar in the Bay of Bengal (Bangladesh/Myanmar)*, paras.475–476; Annex VII Arbitral Tribunal of UNCLOS, *Bay of Bengal Maritime Boundary Arbitration between Bangladesh and India*, paras.507–508. See also Mathias Forteau, "The Legal Nature and Content of 'Due Regard' Obligations in Recent International Case Law", 34. For a fuller discussion on this matter, see Chapter 3.3.2.3 of this study.

> the conflict should be resolved on the basis of equity and in the light of all relevant circumstances, taking into account the respective importance of the interests involved to the parties as well as to the international community as a whole.[171]

This provision indicates that to resolve potential conflict, a balancing test, which is based on equity and in the light of all relevant circumstances, is required.[172] In the context of the current discussion, for operational oceanographic activities falling under Article 59, in cases where a conflict arises, a balancing test should be carried out. Such a balancing test can be performed either by an international judicial body or by the States involved in the conflict themselves. In the latter case, it is argued that the States concerned are normally required to consult with each other and take into account different interests that may be involved.[173]

Article 59 does not define the scope of interests that should be considered in the balancing test. Because this article is intended to be a back-up clause for Articles 56 and 58,[174] and in light of the broad wording used in this provision – "all relevant circumstances" – the interests at play in the balancing test are not confined to those involved in Articles 56(1) or 58(1).[175] This observation will be further addressed in Section 7.5 below.

7.4.4 *Interim Conclusions and Some Additional Observations*

In sum, the UNCLOS Part XIII regime applies to operational oceanographic activities: 1) that constitute marine scientific research, and 2) that qualify as "scientific research" and at the same time involve the use or deployment of installations or equipment. An application of this regime to certain operational oceanographic activities brings about some challenges. It is argued that these challenges can be resolved by using the flexibility of the Part XIII regime. Options for using such flexibility are contained particularly in Articles 242, 243 and 247. These articles provide a legal basis to create simplified procedures in cases where operational oceanographic activities fall under the regulatory scope of the Part XIII regime. The creation of the simplified procedures is to take place through negotiations or consultations between the coastal State and the researching State(s).

---

171 UNCLOS, Article 59.

172 See Chapter 3.3.2.4 of this book.

173 See Chapter 3.3.2.4 of this book.

174 Alexander Proelss, ed. *United Nations Convention on the Law of the Sea: A Commentary*, 460.

175 See Chapter 3.3.2.4 of this book.

For operational oceanographic activities that constitute "other internationally lawful uses of the sea related to" the freedoms under Article 58(1), the researching State shall comply with the laws and regulations adopted by the coastal State in accordance with the provisions of UNCLOS and have due regard to the rights and duties of the coastal State. To fulfil the due regard obligation, in cases where a conflict arises or may arise, the States concerned are required to engage in consultation with each other and properly balance the interests that may be involved.

Article 59 may also have a role to play with regard to the regulation of operational oceanographic activities. For activities that fall under the scope of Article 59, in cases where a conflict arises, the conflict is to be resolved by performing a balancing test on the basis of equity and in the light of all the relevant circumstances. The balancing test can be performed either by an international judicial body or by the States involved in the conflict themselves. In the latter case, the States concerned are normally required to consult with each other and take into account different interests that may be involved.

In this context, it seems that the application of the Part XIII regime, Article 58, and Article 59 to operational oceanographic activities would point to the same direction – when a conflict arises or may arise, the States concerned are obliged to consult with each other. Hopefully, cooperative agreements or practical arrangements can be established as a result of successful consultations. It is noted that the analysis in this section only applies to the situations where the legal classification of operational oceanographic activity has been discerned and is without controversy. There are still instances where the legal classification of the activity concerned remains uncertain or controversial, in particular when the activity serves multiple purposes. Arguably, (potential) conflicts arising from the undertaking of this kind of activities can best be resolved in an appropriate intergovernmental setting, with sufficient and effective consultations and negotiations.[176]

---

176 Part XV of UNCLOS may also have a role to play in the resolution of conflicts arising from the conduct of operational oceanographic activities where the legal classification of the activities is unclear or controversial. However, two observations need to be made in this respect. First, to invoke the compulsory dispute settlement mechanism under Part XV, there has to be a dispute. In some instances, there might be controversies over the existence of a dispute. Second, the willingness of States concerned to submit a potential dispute concerning operational oceanographic activities to an international court or tribunal is minimal, especially considering "the minor nature of the violation" versus the cost of international judicial or arbitral proceedings, and the scope of the exceptions to mandatory jurisdiction under Articles 297 and 298. See Natalie Klein, *Dispute Settlement in the UN Convention on the Law of the Sea* (Cambridge University Press, 2005), 123, 125.

Although the Part XIII regime, Article 58, and Article 59 would all require the States concerned to consult with each other when conflicts arise, it is argued that under each kind of legal classification, the guiding principles for the consultation vary. For operational oceanographic activities that fall under the competence of either the coastal State or other States, it is the reciprocal due regard obligation that requires the States concerned to negotiate and consult with each other. Relevant international case law concerning the due regard obligation provides the guidance as to when and how the obligation is to be fulfilled to some extent. For operational oceanographic activities that constitute marine scientific research, it is submitted that the substantive provisions set out in Part XIII of UNCLOS provide detailed mechanisms to fulfil the due regard obligation. However, for operational oceanographic activities that fall under Article 59 of the Convention and those activities of which the legal classification remains controversial, the inspiration that can be drawn from the Convention and other sources (including international case law) on the consultation process is limited.

Besides, arguably in different scenarios, elements that should be taken into account in the consultations and the value to be attached to each element may vary. For instance, when the operational oceanographic activity at issue qualifies as marine scientific research, in the consultations, the interests of other States are not to override the coastal State jurisdiction over marine scientific research. However, in cases where the operational oceanographic activity at issue falls under Article 59 or the legal classification of the activity remains controversial, presumably, the interests of all States involved are to be balanced on an equal footing in the consultations.

Implications of these observations will be elaborated upon in the subsequent section in the analysis of future regulatory options for operational oceanographic activities.

7.5 Future Regulatory Options for Operational Oceanography

Building upon the discussion in the preceding sections, this section examines the options for regulating operational oceanographic activities and the considerations that could be taken into account during the process of consultations.

7.5.1 *Possible Forms and Mechanisms of Consultations*

Depending on the different legal classification of operational oceanographic activities, the consultations can be considered as an implementation of the Part XIII regime, Article 58, or Article 59. The States concerned may also choose to engage in consultations without deciding on the relevance of specific provisions when the legal classification of the activities at issue remains controversial. This is the case for the discussions leading to the adoption of the IOC Argo Guidelines and WMO Resolution 45 (Cg-18). The IOC Argo Guidelines do not address the legal classification of the activities concerned at all.[177] WMO Resolution 45 (Cg-18) expressly stated that the activities concerned "are not covered by UNCLOS Part XIII on marine scientific research".[178] However, it did not address the relevance of Article 58 or 59. By stating that the activities concerned "can consequently be freely operated in the EEZs",[179] the resolution can be regarded either as an implementation of Article 58, or an outcome arising from the resolution of (potential) conflicts under Article 59.

In addition, States also have the discretion to choose to enter into bilateral consultations or multilateral consultations. As discussed in the IOC/ABE-LOS meetings, delegations have agreed that for the deployment of floats and surface drifting buoys in the EEZs, there is no need for IOC/ABE-LOS to establish a specific set of guidelines because such deployment should be considered within the framework of bilateral cooperation and agreements.[180] In contrast, the IOC Argo Guidelines are the result of multilateral negotiations. Compared to bilateral arrangements, entering into multilateral agreements or guidelines with the potentially affected coastal States can secure widespread consent for operational oceanographic activities that are conducted under global projects. However, establishing bilateral agreements might be less time consuming. States concerned can, in light of the relevant circumstances, choose the more suitable form of cooperation.

7.5.2 *Elements to be Considered during the Consultations*

As to the elements to be taken into account during the consultations, with regard to operational oceanographic activities that fall either under Article 56(1) or 58(1), as required by the due regard obligation, relevant case law

177 "Guidelines for the Implementation of Resolution XX–6 of the IOC Assembly Regarding the Deployment of Profiling Floats in the High Seas within the Framework of the Argo Programme", Resolution EC-XLI.4. Some States consider the guidelines as an implementation of Article 247 of UNCLOS, while others consider it as a separate practical arrangement that exists in isolation from the Part XIII regime. For a fuller discussion on this matter, see Chapter 4.3.2.2 of this study.

178 "Abridged Final Report of the Eighteenth session of World Meteorological Congress", Doc. WMO - No.1236, at p. 149.

179 Ibid.

180 "Report of the Ninth Session of IOC/ABE-LOS", Doc. IOC/ABE-LOS IX/3 Rev., at pp. 8–9. For more information on this matter, see Chapter 4.3.2.1 of this study.

indicates that the balancing test shall proceed with "all possible consideration",[181] and take into account "the nature of the rights held [...], their importance, the extent of the anticipated impairment, the nature and importance of the activities contemplated [...], and the availability of alternative approaches".[182] It is argued that these elements are closely related to two aspects of operational oceanographic activities: the function of the activity, and data that are collected.

The function of activities is linked to "the nature and importance of the activities" concerned, and "the nature of the rights" involved and "their importance". As discussed in Section 7.2.1 of this chapter, the function of operational oceanographic activities is determined primarily by observational requirements identified by States, either through intergovernmental organizations or under various conventions. In this regard, the obligations of States in relation to the undertaking of certain operational oceanographic activities as provided by other parts of UNCLOS, for instance, Part XII on the protection of the marine environment,[183] can be taken into account in the negotiations as incentives to catalyze cooperation and the establishment of agreements. The obligations of States under other international legal instruments, including the obligation under UNFCCC to promote and cooperate in research and systematic observation related to the climate system[184] and the obligation under CBD to identify and monitor components of biological diversity important for its conservation and sustainable use[185] can also be used for the said purposes. Both the due regard obligation and the resolution of conflicts pertaining to unattributed rights and jurisdiction under Article 59 require that, in performing the balancing test, "all possible considerations" should be taken into account.[186] It is argued that the obligations of States under other parts of UNCLOS and other international conventions can be among such considerations.

Besides, the implications drawn from the Assessment Frameworks under the London Convention and London Protocol on the determination of the existence of "proper scientific attributes" (Chapter 5.4) and the Judgment of

181 ITLOS, *The M/V Virginia G Case (Panama v. Guinea-Bissau)*, para.347.

182 Annex VII Arbitral Tribunal of UNCLOS, *Chagos Marine Protected Area Arbitration (Mauritius v. United Kingdom)*, para.519.

183 For instance, Article 204(1) provides that "States shall, consistent with the rights of other States, endeavour, as far as practicable, directly or through the competent international organizations, to observe, measure, evaluate and analyse, by recognized scientific methods, the risks or effects of pollution of the marine environment". UNCLOS, Article 204(1).

184 UNFCCC, Article 4(1)(g).

185 CBD, Article 7.

186 See Chapters 3.3.2.3 and 3.3.2.4 of this book.

the ICJ on the *Whaling in the Antarctic* case on the identification of purpose of scientific research (Chapter 5.5) may be considered in the balancing test as well.

The element of "the extent of the anticipated impairment" brought about by the activities referred to in *Chagos Marine Protected Area Arbitration* can be related to the data that are collected by the activities at issue. Bateman has observed that an essential criterion that the coastal State would consider when determining whether the collection of a specific type of ocean data in its EEZ should be under its jurisdiction is the potential economic value and utility of the data to the coastal State.[187] Based on the conclusions drawn in Chapter 4 of this book on State practice,[188] and also considering the political willingness stemming from practical considerations, presumably coastal States' considerations pertaining to the data to be collected include 1) whether the data on the variables have a bearing on the exploration and exploitation of natural resources, 2) whether it is closely linked to the maritime security of the coastal States concerned, and 3) whether it can serve common interests.

For operational oceanographic activities that fall under Article 59 or those the legal classification of which remains controversial, arguably the observations made above can also apply. Apart from these observations, some further inspirations can be drawn from existing international instruments that result from negotiations, *i.e.*, the IOC Argo Guidelines and WMO Resolution 45 (Cg-18).

Both instruments focus on the collection of data on a specific set of variables. Such practice indicates that States prefer initiating negotiations that

187 Sam Bateman, "Hydrographic Surveying in the EEZ: Differences and Overlaps with Marine Scientific Research", *Marine Policy* 29, no. 2 (2005): 172. A similar observation is provided by Wegelein, who submitted that from a coastal State perspective, two elements of ocean data collection activities are of great importance – one being the objective of the activity and the other being the method or technology used as they might have potential implications for the national interests of the State. See Florian H.Th. Wegelein, *Marine Scientific Research: The Operation and Status of Research Vessels and Other Platforms in International Law*, 37.

188 It has been concluded in Chapter 4 of this book that "[r]elevant practice indicates that whether States are willing to establish practical arrangements depends on two major factors. The first factor is whether the States concerned share common interests that are pertinent to marine scientific research, or more broadly to ocean data collection. [...] The second factor concerns the objects and purposes of and the means and methods to conduct the ocean data collection activities concerned. States are more likely to reach agreements on cooperation in less sensitive fields of research. As indicated by the discussion under the IOC/ABE-LOS sub-group on the collection of oceanographic data, whether States are willing to enter into practical arrangements also depends on the means that are used for ocean data collection, and the type of data that are to be collected by the activity".

focus on specific variables. The adoption of the instruments, which indicates that the negotiations have been successful, shows that States are more willing to cooperate in operational oceanography that centers around the measurement of variables covered by the two instruments. Apart from the variables covered by the two instruments, IOC/ABE-LOS has agreed upon the definition of "oceanographic data" covered by its sub-group on the collection of oceanographic data.[189] According to the definition, oceanographic data "refers to variables and parameters listed in the annex, which is an integral part of these Guidelines that qualify the characteristics of the ocean in time and in space"; while "variables and parameters" include pressure, sea level, sea level pressure, currents, wind speed and direction, temperature, conductivity/salinity, CO_2, Oxygen concentration, partial pressure of CO_2.[190] It was also agreed that the list might be updated on a regular basis.[191] The fact that the delegations agreed upon this definition of oceanographic data indicates that States are more willing to cooperate on the collection of data pertinent to these variables and parameters.

In light of the above analysis, for operational oceanographic activities to be conducted in areas under the jurisdiction of a coastal State, it is an essential task for States to identify variables that have the potential to serve common interests and at the same time do not unjustifiably interfere with the coastal State's economic and security interests and to raise awareness of the benefits that can be delivered by the collection of such variables.

Potentially, confidence among States can be built upon existing cooperative mechanisms which facilitate the undertaking of certain operational oceanographic activities. Accordingly, the list of variables covered can be expanded. A typical example is provided by the Argo project. As mentioned above, at first, the Argo project limits its function to the collection of data on ocean temperature, salinity, and oxygen, since it was the agreement reached among the stakeholders by then. However, several decades later, the project is now expanding its mission to cover biogeochemical measurements, which are more sensitive variables when observed in the EEZ of a coastal State.

Besides, when the negotiations are to take place, international organizations such as IOC and WMO, and arguably the International Maritime Organization (IMO), can be used as platforms for the negotiations. The international organization that provides such a platform would influence the focus

---

189 For more information on this sub-group, see Chapter 4.3.2.1 of this study.

190 "Report of the Seventh Session of IOC/ABE-LOS", Doc. IOC/ABE-LOS VII/3, at p. 5.

191 Ibid.

of negotiations and potentially the relevant outcomes because each international organization has its own mandates.[192]

7.6 Conclusions

In conclusion, opinions differ as to the legal classification of activities under the notion of "operational oceanography". Based on the conclusions drawn in the previous chapters, this chapter looks at pertinent UNCLOS provisions to discern the legal classification of operational oceanography. It is submitted that depending on the function of the activity, operational oceanographic activities may have different legal classification. An operational oceanography activity may qualify as marine scientific research if it is undertaken with a scientific hypothesis. It may constitute "other internationally lawful uses of the sea" under Article 58 if it is, for instance, conducted to ensure the safety of navigation, overflight or of the laying of submarine cables and pipelines. When it fulfils none of these purposes, it may fall under the scope of Article 59 concerning unattributed rights and jurisdiction. Besides, given that operational oceanography activities usually serve multiple purposes, the legal classification of them may give rise to controversies.

Based on the legal classification of each kind of operational oceanographic activity, this chapter respectively looks at the results of applying the pertinent rules to it.

For operational oceanographic activities that constitute marine scientific research and that involve the use or deployment of "scientific research" installations and equipment, the application of the Part XIII regime to them potentially leads to some challenges, including 1) the difficulty of fully implementing prior consent requirements, and 2) the risk of impeding the development of marine science and timely provision of operational services. These challenges can be resolved to a certain degree by using the flexibility of the UNCLOS Part XIII regime. Relevant provisions of Part XIII establish a two-way communication process for obtaining the consent from the coastal State for undertaking certain marine scientific research projects as opposed to a one-way process as manifested in the provisions under Articles 246 and 248. For operational oceanographic activities that fall under the scope of these provisions, it is submitted that Articles 242(2) and 243 can be read as providing some leverage to the researching State to persuade the coastal State to grant

192 See Section 7.3.1 of the current chapter.

its consent in the two-way communication mentioned above. The researching State or competent international organization may also enter into cooperative agreements with the coastal State concerning the collection of certain data (pursuant to Articles 242(2) and 243) in areas under the jurisdiction of the coastal State and to agree upon simpler clearance procedures than the requirements of obtaining prior consent under Articles 245, 246, and 248. Besides, for operational oceanographic activities that qualify marine scientific research, the international organizations concerned can make use of the flexibility provided by Article 247 by, for example, setting up a detailed mechanism to implement this provision. When such a mechanism is in place, activities undertaken by or under the auspices of the international organization concerned can be carried out in areas under the jurisdiction of a coastal State under less stringent requirements.

As to operational oceanographic activities that fall under the scope of Article 58(1), according to relevant international case law, when a conflict arises or may arise, the due regard obligation requires the States concerned to carry out a balancing test. To perform such a test, the States concerned are required to engage in consultation with each other and properly balance the interests that may be involved.

For operational oceanographic activities that fall under Article 59 concerning unattributed rights and jurisdiction in the EEZ of a coastal State, in cases where a conflict arises, the States concerned are under an obligation to perform a balancing test "on the basis of equity and in the light of all the relevant circumstances". Similarly, when the test is performed by the States concerned themselves, the States are considered to be required to consult with each other so as to take all the necessary circumstances and interests into account.

Therefore, although different rules apply to different kinds of operational oceanographic activities, the application of such rules points in the same direction – States concerned should engage in consultation to resolve conflict. Hopefully, cooperative agreements or practical arrangements can be established as a result of successful consultations. Entering into such arrangements also helps to resolve conflicts arising from cases where the legal classification of an operational oceanographic activity remains unclear or controversial.

For purposes of the agreements mentioned above, States may choose to leave the legal classification of the activity concerned undefined. As shown by the relevant negotiations leading to the adoption of the IOC Argo Guidelines, this choice has the advantage of accommodating divergent positions on the legal classification of the activities concerned and opting for a more pragmatic approach in addressing more substantive issues pertaining to the regulation of operational oceanographic activities. Besides, depending on specific circumstances, consultations can take place bilaterally or multilaterally. In the latter scenario, international organizations such as IOC, WMO and IMO can provide the platform for negotiations.

In negotiating such agreements, it is better to focus on the variables concerned. States are more willing to enter into agreements for the measurement of variables that are less sensitive for the coastal States, and those that can deliver benefits which can be enjoyed by the community as a whole. Besides, the obligations of States under other provisions of UNCLOS, for example on the protection of the marine environment, and under other international instruments, such as UNFCCC, CBD, and the Sendai Framework for Disaster Risk Reduction, can be taken into account in the consultations and be used as incentives to facilitate cooperation.

To conclude, the legal classification of operational oceanographic activities may vary. For some operational oceanographic activities, their legal classification may be unclear or controversial. Moreover, the application of pertinent UNCLOS provisions, especially Articles 245, 246, and 248, leads to some challenges. Nevertheless, the author submits that UNCLOS, including its Part XIII regime, is still adequate for addressing the legal issues raised by operational oceanography.

CHAPTER 8

Concluding Remarks

8.1 Introduction

The emergence of new forms and methods of ocean data collection has raised important legal issues, particularly with regard to the legal classification of the activities concerned and the relationship between such activities and marine scientific research in the context of UNCLOS. States hold different opinions on the said issues, notably because of the lack of a generally accepted definition of the term "marine scientific research". Another reason for the existence of different opinions is that other ocean data collection activities are not clearly distinguished from marine scientific research and not separately regulated in detail by the Convention. Since UNCLOS was drafted with a view to settling "all issues relating to the law of the sea",[1] the regulation of "modern" ocean data collection activities and the resolution of any potential conflicts arising from the divergent opinions on this matter presumably need to be based on the pertinent provisions of the Convention. The above background information provides the context to the overarching question of the present research:

> To what extent do UNCLOS and its marine scientific research regime regulate "modern" ocean data collection activities, and through which regulatory arrangements might any gaps for regulation in the Convention be filled?

This research question results in several sub-questions:

1. What is the scope of regulation of the UNCLOS marine scientific research regime, *i.e.* what is the meaning of the term "marine scientific research" in the context of UNCLOS?
2. What are the rules that apply to different types of ocean data collection activities under UNCLOS in light of current developments, and how are they implemented in practice?
3. What are the limits and strengths of UNCLOS and its marine scientific research regime in regulating different types of "modern" ocean data collection activities?

1 UNCLOS, Preamble, 1st preambular Paragraph.

 | DOI:10.1163/9789004508590_009

3.1 Are there any regulatory gaps for UNCLOS and its marine scientific research regime in regulating different types of "modern" ocean data collection activities?

3.2 What options exist within UNCLOS to fill such regulatory gaps, and what are the implications of these options? Do relevant subsequent practice of States and rules contained in other international conventions provide any guidance in this respect?

To answer these questions, the present research is divided into six substantive chapters that roughly constitute two parts. The first part (Chapters 2 to 5) answers the first two sub-questions above. The second part (Chapters 6 and 7) contextualizes the observations made in the first part and carries out two specific case studies in order to answer the third sub-question of the research. This concluding chapter will, therefore, reflect on the key findings of these two parts and offer some final observations concerning the main research question of the present research.

8.2 Approach to Interpreting Relevant Treaty Provisions

As indicated in Chapter 1.3 of this book, before addressing the substantive research questions, it is necessary to determine the intention of the parties to UNCLOS concerning whether the interpretation of relevant UNCLOS provisions should follow the developments that occurred after the adoption of the Convention. To determine the approach to be adopted for treaty interpretation for the present research, Chapter 2 investigates the nature of UNCLOS as a "living instrument" (Chapter 2.5) and the object and purpose of the Convention (Chapter 2.6). It is submitted that these two elements indicate that the Convention has the ability to self-adapt to new circumstances to ensure contemporary relevance. Among others, interpretation of relevant treaty provisions is an indispensable means to keep the Convention in pace with recent developments. In other words, interpretation of relevant UNCLOS provisions cannot be isolated from developments that have occurred or will occur after the conclusion of the Convention. Otherwise, the Convention would soon become obsolete.

This being said, it is also noted that so as not to jeopardize "the coherence and uniformity of substance" of the Convention,[2] not all UNCLOS provisions are intended to change over time. Some provisions of the Convention are

2 Bernard H. Oxman, "Tools for Change: The Amendment Procedure", 197–198.

precise and definite to ensure the integrity and stability of the Convention, such as the provisions for the allocation of jurisdiction. In contrast, other provisions are left open for future developments in order to stand the test of time. In the context of the present study, since the term "marine scientific research" and phrases pertinent to the legal classification of ocean data collection activities have been left undefined, a natural assumption would be that the interpretation of relevant provisions, in particular, the term "marine scientific research", falls into the second category, and thus needs to incorporate subsequent developments.

To test the validity of the foregoing assumption, Chapter 2 looks at the drafting history of the definition of the term "marine scientific research" and observes that the omission of the definition of the term was an intentional choice (Chapter 2.3). This choice suggests that States intended to leave the definitional issue to future developments, through subsequent agreements and practice. This submission is attested by the inclusion of Article 251 in the Convention.[3] It is argued that by this provision, the drafters of UNCLOS advocate that States establish the nature and implications of marine scientific research on the basis of the practical experiences they have accumulated since the adoption of the Convention, at a time when they acquire a better understanding of this kind of activities and at a time when there is a consensus on what the term "marine scientific research" should mean. As such, a conclusion is warranted that the parties to UNCLOS intend to give the term "marine scientific research" a meaning that is capable of changing.

Chapter 2 also assesses whether the meaning of the term "marine scientific research" is indeed capable of including new developments, or in the words of the ICJ, whether it is a generic term, and concludes that this term has an evolutionary meaning that can adapt to the changing circumstances (Chapter 2.4).

The above discussion leads to the conclusion that the parties to UNCLOS intend to refer the meaning of the term "marine scientific research" to subsequent developments. Additionally, so as to give effect to the nature of the Convention as a "living instrument" and its object and purpose, relevant treaty provisions on ocean data collection are also to be interpreted in light of changing circumstances. A direct implication of such conclusions is that the interpretation of the term "marine scientific research" and relevant treaty provisions on ocean data collection should take into consideration new developments that occur after the adoption of the Convention. Interpretative elements such

3 This provision sets up an obligation for States to "seek to promote […] the establishment of general criteria and guidelines to assist States in ascertaining the nature and implications of marine scientific research".

as "the ordinary meaning" and "relevant rules of international law" under VCLT should be the ones that exist at the time of interpretation.

After determining the approach to be adopted when interpreting relevant UNCLOS provisions, Chapters 3 to 5 set out to address the first two sub-questions of this research, concerning 1) the scope of regulation of the UNCLOS marine scientific research regime, *i.e.*, the nature of and criteria for marine scientific research under the Convention, and 2) the rules to be applied to different types of ocean data collection activities under UNCLOS and their implementation in practice.

8.3 The Nature of and Criteria for Maine Scientific Research under UNCLOS

To discern the nature of and criteria for marine scientific research under UNCLOS, Chapters 3 to 5 respectively examine 1) the text of UNCLOS, 2) relevant subsequent practice of States that sheds light on understanding the meaning of the term "marine scientific research", and 3) other international treaties that have a bearing on the said matter. The pertinent discussion indicates the answer to the first sub-question of the present research.

Although UNCLOS does not define the term "marine scientific research", it is observed that the text of the Convention provides some useful hints for determining the scope of activities covered by this term. Relevant UNCLOS provisions set out the minimum requirement for constituting marine scientific research under the Convention. As minimum requirements, marine scientific research in the context of UNCLOS has to contribute to the furtherance of knowledge of the marine environment and display some scientific attributes. However, the Convention does not require marine scientific research activities to be conducted exclusively for scientific purposes – such activities may also serve commercial ends. In other words, marine scientific research can potentially serve multiple ends, and one of such ends shall be scientific. Some of the hints are supported by other relevant international conventions and subsequent developments of these conventions. Relevant practice also indicates that at present, States have not yet established an agreement on the definition of the term "marine scientific research" in the context of UNCLOS through State practice.

8.3.1 *The Minimum Requirement(s) for Constituting Marine Scientific Research*

As a minimum requirement for constituting marine scientific research under UNCLOS, the activity concerned should serve to increase knowledge of the marine environment. This observation is supported by the ordinary meaning of the term (Chapter 3.2.1), proposals made during UNCLOS III on the definition of the term (Chapter 3.2.1) and most notably the relevant UNCLOS provisions (Chapters 3.2.2 and 3.2.3). As an indication of such a purpose, the activity should have some scientific attributes. UNCLOS provisions provide indications for determining the existence of scientific attributes. To be more specific, the general principle under Article 240 of UNCLOS concerning the use of scientific methods and means indicates that to constitute marine scientific research, there needs to be a scientific hypothesis. Besides, the obligation to share research results and knowledge under Article 244 is another major aspect of scientific attributes. Because these provisions apply to marine scientific research at the same time, the two criteria are considered to be accumulative – an ocean data collection activity needs to satisfy both criteria to constitute marine scientific research.

These requirements are also contained in the legal instruments on marine geoengineering adopted under the framework of the London Convention and the London Protocol, which introduce the notions of "legitimate scientific research" and "specific marine scientific research" (Chapter 5.4.1). These legal instruments provide that to fall under these notions, the activity at issue shall have "proper scientific attributes" and set out the criteria for determining the existence of "proper scientific attributes". It is argued that some of these criteria reinforce the observations made above concerning the interpretation of UNCLOS provisions, such as the requirement of the existence of a scientific hypothesis, the use of appropriate research methodology, and the commitment to publish data and results.

A phrase that is closely linked to the term "marine scientific research" is included in ICRW – "for purposes of scientific research". The criteria for this phrase have been addressed by the ICJ in the *Whaling in the Antarctic* case (Chapter 5.5.2). The Court observed that the parties concerned agreed that scientific research should proceed on the basis of a certain question, which could take the form of a hypothesis.[4] This supports the current author's interpretation of the requirement of "scientific methods" under Article 240(b) of UNCLOS. However, the parties disagreed on the level of specificity required of such a hypothesis, and the Court did not express its view on this matter.[5] As discussed in Chapter 3 of this research, UNCLOS provisions do not shed much light on this issue either. Therefore, notably, it remained a controversial issue.

4 ICJ, *Whaling in the Antarctic (Australia v. Japan: New Zealand intervening)*, Judgment, para.77.
5 Ibid.

8.3.2 *Marine Scientific Research May Also Serve Commercial Purposes*

Although marine scientific research activities have to be conducted with scientific purposes, it is also observed that the Convention does not require such activities to be conducted exclusively for scientific purposes.

8.3.2.1 Pure and Applied Marine Scientific Research and Article 246 of UNCLOS

Ocean data collection activities that are undertaken exclusively for the furtherance of scientific knowledge of the marine environment are often termed as "pure" marine scientific research, as opposed to "applied" marine scientific research. As suggested by Article 246 of UNCLOS and the drafting history of the UNCLOS marine scientific research regime, marine scientific research under UNCLOS is not limited to pure marine scientific research (Chapter 3.2.4.1). Article 246(5)(a) of the Convention indicates that marine scientific research project can also be "of direct significance for the exploration and exploitation of natural resources".[6] By including this phrase, especially the qualifier "direct", in Article 246(5), the Convention recognizes that marine scientific research can be carried out with a view to the commercial utilization of the research objects (Chapter 3.2.4.3). This is because a marine scientific research project that is not conducted with such a view cannot be considered being "of direct significance for the exploration and exploitation of natural resources". If all marine scientific research under UNCLOS must be carried out without a commercial view, no research project may fall under Article 246(5)(a), and this provision will become obsolete.

The observation that marine scientific research may be conducted with commercial purposes is reinforced by relevant provisions of the Nagoya Protocol (Chapter 5.2). Article 8(a) of the Nagoya Protocol indicates that research on genetic resources may serve commercial and non-commercial purposes.

8.3.2.2 Marine Scientific Research Not Purely Serving Commercial Purposes

The conclusion that marine scientific research can be conducted with commercial purposes does not mean that marine scientific research is to be conducted purely for commercial purposes. First, all activities qualifying as marine scientific research under UNCLOS should meet the minimum requirement – they should serve the purpose of increasing scientific knowledge of the marine environment (Section 8.3.1). Second, ocean data collection activities serving

6 UNCLOS, Article 246(5)(a).

purely commercial purposes are to be considered "exploration", "exploitation" (Chapter 3.3.2.1.1) or "prospecting" (Chapter 3.3.4.1.1) under UNCLOS.

Article 56(1) of UNCLOS suggests that marine scientific research is different from 1) ocean data collection activities conducted "for the purpose of exploring and exploiting, conserving and managing the natural resources", and 2) those "for the economic exploitation and exploration of the zone".[7] Different sets of rights and obligations are set forth by the relevant provisions of UNCLOS for these activities respectively.[8] As suggested by the definitions contained the ISA Regulations, both the terms "exploitation" and "exploration" refer to research and analytical activities purely for commercial purposes.

Another kind of activity that is distinguished from marine scientific research by the Convention is prospecting. Different sets of rules have been established for marine scientific research and prospecting by the Convention and the ISA Regulations.[9] According to the definition given by the ISA Regulations, similar to exploration and exploitation, prospecting is also carried out purely for commercial purposes.

Since marine scientific research is distinct from the activities mentioned above and also bearing in mind that marine scientific research can be "of direct significance for" exploration and exploitation,[10] the conclusion is warranted that marine scientific research activities are not conducted with the sole intention to achieve commercial gains.

8.3.3 *The Lack of Subsequent Agreement on the Scope of Marine Scientific Research under UNCLOS*

Considering the effect of Article 251 of UNCLOS that advocates that States establish the nature and implications of marine scientific research after the adoption of the Convention (Chapter 2.3), Chapter 4 examines the relevant subsequent practice to identify whether States have established an agreement on the definition of the term "marine scientific research" through State practice or whether there is a tendency towards the establishment of such an agreement. As shown by the national legislation and policies on marine scientific research of several countries (Chapter 4.2) and viewpoints expressed by States in various international fora (Chapter 4.3), no agreement on the definition of

7 Ibid., Article 56(1).

8 The substantive rules for exploration and exploitation of natural resources are set out in Articles 62–73, while those for marine scientific research are set out in Articles 246–254 of the Convention.

9 Prospecting in the Area is regulated by Part II of the ISA Regulations, while marine scientific research in the Area is regulated by Article 143 and Part XIII of UNCLOS.

10 UNCLOS, Article 246(5)(a).

the term "marine scientific research" has been established therefrom. In some cases, States have taken different views on the scope of activities covered by the UNCLOS marine scientific research regime.

This being said, WMO Resolution 45 (Cg-18) excludes certain WMO meteorological observing activities from the scope of regulation of the UNCLOS marine scientific research regime (Chapter 4.3.4). The adoption of this resolution indicates that a significant number of States consider the activities concerned do not constitute marine scientific research under UNCLOS. Although this resolution may not be considered as a subsequent agreement between the parties to UNCLOS regarding the interpretation of the term "marine scientific research" in the meaning of Article 31(3)(a) of VCLT, potentially the Resolution will play a significant role in influencing State practice on this matter.

8.4 The Legal Framework(s) for Different Kinds of Ocean Data Collection Activities

The pertinent discussion in Chapters 3 to 5 lays the ground for answering the second sub-question of this research:

> What are the rules that apply to different types of ocean data collection activities under UNCLOS in light of current developments, and how are they implemented in practice?

As to the first part of the question, the Convention distinguishes several kinds of ocean data collection activities from marine scientific research and prescribes different sets of rules for different uses of the sea in different maritime zones. The legal classification of different ocean data collection activities primarily depends on the function or purpose of the activities. A fuller explanation of this conclusion is provided in Section 8.4.1.

As indicated by the substantive analysis, in some instances the Convention does not provide sufficient indications for distinguishing one ocean data collection activity from another. As a result, the legal classification of some activities may be unclear or controversial. With this in mind, Chapters 4 and 5 respectively focus on the subsequent practice of States and other international conventions pertaining to ocean data collection to demonstrate how ocean data collection activities are regulated, when the legal classification of the activities concerned is unclear or is not explicitly defined, and offer the answer to the second part of the above-mentioned question. It is submitted that an examination of the regulation of the said activities reveals the implementation of relevant UNCLOS provisions, such as ones on due regard obligations. Observations made in this regard are included in Sections 8.4.2 and 8.4.3.

8.4.1 *The Regulation of Different Kinds of Ocean Data Collection Activities under UNCLOS*

From the substantive rules set forth for different ocean data collection activities in each of the maritime zones contained in UNCLOS, the Convention distinguishes several kinds of activities from marine scientific research (Section 8.4.1.1). The problem of legal classification is most acute for activities conducted in the EEZ of a coastal State, mainly because in this zone, the Convention prescribes the most diversified rights and obligations for the States concerned. It is argued that the provisions under the UNCLOS EEZ regime provide a good basis for resolving the conflict that may arise from the legal classification and the regulation of ocean data collection activities (Section 8.4.1.2).

8.4.1.1 Rules to be Applied to Ocean Data Collection Activities that Are Distinct from Marine Scientific Research

8.4.1.1.1 *Activities Having a Direct Bearing on Passage*

Under the regimes of the territorial sea and archipelagic waters, relevant provisions make a distinction between research and survey activities on the one hand and innocent passage on the other (Chapter 3.3.1). According to Article 19(2) UNCLOS, the passage is no longer innocent if the foreign ship engages in any activity that does not have a direct bearing on passage. Among others, research and survey activities are listed as examples of activities that are not allowed during such passage.[11] Arguably, the innocent passage of a ship inevitably requires the collection of ocean data for the purpose of ensuring the safe passage of the ship itself. Therefore, ocean data collection activities which serve solely such an end are not to be considered as research or survey activities, and hence are different from marine scientific research.

8.4.1.1.2 *Prospecting, Exploration and Exploitation*

As reiterated in Section 8.3.2.2, prospecting, exploration and exploitation are distinct from marine scientific research in the sense that the former three kinds of activities are carried out purely for commercial purposes whereas marine scientific research is not. The finding that exploration and exploitation are distinct from marine scientific research is also supported by the relevant

11 Ibid., Article 19(2).

provisions on the continental shelf. Different sets of rules are formulated for the activities concerned (Chapter 3.3.3).

However, the distinction is not always easy to make in practice considering especially that marine scientific research can be "of *direct* significance for the exploration and exploitation of natural resources".[12]

8.4.1.1.3 *"Other Internationally Lawful Uses of the Sea Related to" the Freedoms under Article 58(1) of UNCLOS*

An ocean data collection activity may also fall under "other internationally lawful uses of the sea related to [the] freedoms [of navigation and overflight and of the laying of submarine cables and pipelines], and compatible with the other provisions of [UNCLOS]" under Article 58 of UNCLOS.[13] It is submitted that ocean data collection activities falling under this provision mainly include those that form an integral part of navigation, overflight, and the laying of submarine cables and pipelines. For instance, in the EEZ, for a ship collecting ocean data that are required for the safe passage of the ship itself, the data collection activity involved falls under "other internationally lawful uses of the sea related to" navigation.[14] When such data are collected not (or not only) for the safe navigation of the ship itself, but serve the purpose of, for instance, weather forecasting, "the situation becomes somewhat different".[15] However, as noted in WMO Resolution 45 (Cg-18), certain types of marine meteorological observations activities that contribute to weather forecasting are not covered by the UNCLOS marine scientific research regime. Potentially, these activities could qualify as "other internationally lawful uses of the sea related to" navigation.[16]

However, it is not hard to imagine that given the open-ended wording of this phrase, different interpretations exist concerning the scope of activities covered by it.

8.4.1.1.4 *Activities Falling under Article 59 of UNCLOS*

Apart from the cases mentioned above, in the EEZ of a coastal State, an ocean data collection activity may fall under Article 59 of the Convention concerning unattributed rights and jurisdiction. Article 59 itself does not contain many indications as to the scope of the activities covered by it. Rather, it suggests

---

12 Emphasis added. Ibid., Article 246(5)(a).

13 Ibid., Article 58(1).

14 When such activities are carried out in the territorial sea or archipelagic waters of a coastal State, they form a part of innocent passage of the ship.

15 Alfred H. A. Soons, *Marine Scientific Research and the Law of the Sea*, 149.

16 Another possibility is that when undertaken in the EEZ, such activities fall under Article 59 in relation to unattributed rights and jurisdiction.

that potentially certain uses of the sea, including ocean data collection, are not addressed by other provisions of the Convention. Where a conflict arises under such circumstances, the conflict should be resolved in accordance with Article 59.

8.4.1.1.5 *Observations on the Benchmark for Distinguishing Different Kinds of Ocean Data Collection Activities under UNCLOS*

Based on the discussion above, it is concluded that the benchmark for the legal classification of ocean data collection activities is the function or purpose of the activities. If an ocean data collection activity is conducted purely with a view to commercial gains, it should be considered as prospecting, exploration or exploitation. If an ocean data collection activity is conducted to ensure safe navigation, it can be considered either as part of the innocent passage of the ship in the territorial sea or through the archipelagic waters of a coastal State or as "other internationally lawful uses of the sea related to" the freedom of navigation in the EEZ, depending on the use of the data collected. Ocean data collection activities falling under "other internationally lawful uses of the sea related to" the freedoms mentioned in Article 58(1) also include those that form an integral part of navigation, overflight, and the laying of submarine cables and pipelines. Such activities do not constitute marine scientific research either, because different sets of rules apply. It may also be the case that an ocean data collection activity, when carried out in the EEZ of a coastal State, falls under the meaning of Article 59 concerning unattributed rights and jurisdiction. The legal classification of such an activity is different from marine scientific research and the situations noted above.

This being said, the legal classification of ocean data collection activities may give rise to different opinions, considering the fact that many relevant provisions of the Convention have been drafted in an open-ended manner, incorporating divergent interpretations. The complexity of the legal classification can also be attributed to the fact that ocean data collection activities can be conducted for multiple purposes, serving various ends. Because the distinguishing benchmark for different kinds of ocean data collection activities is the function or purpose of the activity, the legal classification of an ocean data collection activity that serves multiple purposes may be controversial or unclear.

8.4.1.2 Reciprocal Due Regard Obligations and the Basis for Resolving Conflicts Regarding the Attribution of Rights and Jurisdiction in the EEZ

The problem of legal classification is the most acute for activities conducted in the EEZ of a coastal State. It is argued that the provisions under the UNCLOS

EEZ regime provide a good basis for resolving the conflict that arises or may arise from the legal classification and the regulation of ocean data collection activities. Most notably, when rights over a certain ocean data collection activity are granted to either the coastal State or a third State, the exercise of such rights shall have due regard to the rights and duties of the other State concerned (Chapter 3.3.2.3). For unattributed rights in the EEZ, the relevant conflict shall be resolved according to the guideline contained in Article 59 of the Convention (Chapter 3.3.2.4). As required by both the reciprocal due regard obligation and the provision under Article 59, when a conflict arises or may arise from the conduct of an ocean data collection activity in the EEZ of a coastal State, the States concerned are required to carry out a balancing test taking into consideration the interests involved. When the balancing test is carried out by the States concerned themselves, the States need to enter into consultation with each other. This applies not only to cases where the rights and jurisdiction over the activity concerned fall under either the coastal State or other States, but also to the case where the jurisdiction has not been attributed by the Convention at all. Arguably, it may also apply in cases where the legal classification of the ocean data collection activities remains unclear or controversial.

8.4.2 *The Regulation of Different Kinds of Ocean Data Collection Activities in Practice*

Subsequent State practice concerning ocean data collection activities is examined in the present research (Chapter 4). Such an examination not only purports to identify whether States have established an agreement on the scope of marine scientific research or if there is a tendency to such an end (Section 8.3.3), but also tries to assess how the relevant UNCLOS provisions on ocean data collection are implemented in practice, even if the legal classification of the activity at issue remains controversial or undefined. Such practice is relevant for the current research in shedding light on the interpretation and implementation of legal terms under UNCLOS, such as the due regard obligation.

On this note, the current author observes that despite the absence of an agreement on the scope of marine scientific research and on the legal classification of certain ocean data collection activities, the operation of the UNCLOS marine scientific research regime and the Convention as a whole with respect to ocean data collection is generally in good shape. Practice shows that States are willing to enter into practical arrangements (multilateral and bilateral) for the regulation of certain ocean data collection activities even if they differ on the legal classification of the activities concerned. The IOC Argo Guidelines is a typical example of such practical arrangements (Chapter 4.3.2.2). Most of the existing arrangements on the said matter are concerned, at least partly, with the EEZ. Where the EEZ is concerned, the establishment of such practical arrangements can be considered as 1) the fulfilment of the due regard obligation under Article 56(2) or 58(3), or 2) the implementation of Article 59 concerning unattributed rights.

Relevant practice also indicates that the willingness of States to establish practical arrangements primarily depends on two factors: first, whether the States concerned share common interests in the undertaking of the activity at issue and, second, the sensitivity of the activity – States are more likely to enter into practical arrangements in less sensitive fields of research. In assessing the sensitivity of an activity, the objects of the research, purposes of the research, and the means and methods to conduct the activity are the elements to be considered. It is submitted that these factors may play a vital role when the States concerned are to fulfil the due regard obligation or implement Article 59 – these factors can be taken into account in the balancing test required.

8.4.3 *The Regulation of Different Kinds of Ocean Data Collection Activities under Other International Conventions*

International conventions apart from UNCLOS that are pertinent to the regulation of ocean data collection are also discussed (Chapter 5). These conventions not only assist in interpreting UNCLOS provisions, including the nature of and criteria for marine scientific research (Section 8.3), but also show how ocean data collection activities are regulated under legal instruments that have received wide-ranging support in cases where the legal classification of the activities concerned is unclear or undefined (Chapter 5.1). An examination of the pertinent rights and obligations set forth by these conventions and the implications drawn from such an examination help to identify the appropriate legal framework for a specific ocean data collection activity.

For instance, provisions of CBD and its Nagoya Protocol (Chapter 5.2) concerning prior informed consent, mutually agreed terms, and the special considerations to be given to access to genetic resources for non-commercial research purposes, suggest that similar to the UNCLOS marine scientific research regime, when the sovereignty or jurisdiction of the coastal State is affected by the activity at issue, the two regimes tend to lean towards the side of the coastal State; whereas when the activity is conducted without commercial intent, both regimes advocate the coastal State to create simplified or less stringent requirements for the researching State.

Under UNFCCC (Chapter 5.3), an obligation is created for the Contracting Parties to promote and cooperate in "research" and "systematic observation". An analysis of relevant practice indicates that potentially, an ocean data collection activity which is considered as "observation" in the context of UNFCCC also constitutes "marine scientific research" in the context of UNCLOS. In this regard, Contracting Parties' obligation to promote and cooperate in systematic observation under Article 4 of UNFCCC can be used as an incentive for the States concerned to enter into cooperative arrangements for certain ocean data collection activities when the legal classification of the activity at issue remains controversial, or when it is preferred to leave the legal classification of the activity undefined. Such an obligation can be taken into account in the balancing test as a fulfilment of the due regard obligation or as an implementation of Article 59 of UNCLOS.

8.5 Limits and Strengths of UNCLOS and Its Marine Scientific Research Regime in Regulating "Modern" Ocean Data Collection Activities

On the basis of the parameters set out in Chapters 3 to 5, Chapters 6 and 7 respectively take *in situ* access to marine genetic resources and operational oceanographic activities as examples to assess the strengths and limits of UNCLOS and its marine scientific research regime in regulating "modern" ocean data collection activities.

8.5.1 *Legal Regulation of* In Situ *Access to Marine Genetic Resources in Areas beyond National Jurisdiction*

Chapter 6 focuses on *in situ* access to marine genetic resources in areas beyond national jurisdiction. The legal regulation of such activities gives rise to divergent opinions and has been under discussion during the UN BBNJ process. *In situ* access to marine genetic resources can be viewed as ocean data collection in the sense that the said resources are not sampled for purposes of collecting the samples *per se*, but for extracting the genetic information therefrom for subsequent research and development.

In situ access to marine genetic resources is mostly conducted by researchers to gain a better understanding of the biodiversity of the marine environment (Chapter 6.2.1). In such case, the related activities fall squarely under the scope of marine scientific research, to which the UNCLOS Part XIII regime applies.

In other instances, *in situ* access to the said resources are undertaken for both scientific and commercial purposes (Chapter 6.2.1). For instance, marine genetic resources are sometimes collected and analyzed as part of scientific research projects, which involve partnerships between research institutes and industries. It is submitted that these activities are not to be considered as "prospecting" or "exploration" under UNCLOS, because these notions refer to activities that are carried out purely for commercial purposes. It is the view of the current author that such activities qualify as marine scientific research under UNCLOS. As discussed in Chapter 3, marine scientific research may also include commercial ends. Besides, the said activities meet the minimum criterion for marine scientific research – they have scientific attributes (Chapter 6.3).

Considering the features of activities concerning marine genetic resources (Chapter 6.2.2), it is argued that marine genetic resources can hardly be sampled purely for commercial purposes because, at the time of sampling, the commercial value of the resources is unknown. However, potentially in the future with the development of biotechnology and the accumulation of knowledge and research experiences, the level of interests in the commercial value of marine genetic resources will increase. As a result, hypothetically, *in situ* access to such resources may be conducted purely for commercial purposes and thus may amount to prospecting under UNCLOS (Chapter 6.3).[17]

An application of the UNCLOS marine scientific research regime to *in situ* access to marine genetic resources in areas beyond national jurisdiction leads to the following observations. These observations are related to the most contentious issues during the current UN BBNJ negotiations – the arrangement for access to marine genetic resources (Chapter 6.4.1) and options for the sharing of benefits arising from the utilization of such resources (Chapter 6.4.2).

In terms of the first issue, according to pertinent UNCLOS provisions, all States and competent international organizations enjoy the right to freely access *in situ* marine genetic resources in areas beyond national jurisdiction subject to certain obligations. For instance, access to marine genetic resources should be conducted with "appropriate scientific methods and means"[18] and be subject to the obligations of environmental protection. Besides, States or competent international organizations that carry out *in situ* access to marine genetic resources would be obliged to publish and disseminate information on the proposed activities and their objectives "through appropriate channels".[19] It is submitted that these channels could be decided during the upcoming negotiations. Lastly, *in situ* access to marine genetic resources by States Parties in the Area should follow the procedural obligations set out in Article 143(3) of UNCLOS.

17 In the view of the current author, such activities do not qualify as exploration under UNCLOS, as the threshold of the level of certainty to achieve commercial gains of exploration can hardly met.

18 UNCLOS, Article 240(b).

19 Ibid., Article 244(1).

As regards the second issue, the UNCLOS marine scientific research regime, or more specifically Article 244 of the Convention, provides the legal basis for establishing non-monetary benefit-sharing obligations. It is suggested that a clearing-house mechanism be established as a means of non-monetary benefit sharing. The mechanism can also serve as a useful tool to conserve biodiversity and preserve the marine environment in areas beyond national jurisdiction by avoiding duplicated or unnecessary visits. It may also reduce research gaps between developed and developing States, and foster research.

However, the application of the UNCLOS marine scientific research regime to activities concerning marine genetic resources is not free of problems. In particular, the requirement of open publication of information, data and research results leads to some concerns as to the interests in developing patents on the basis of marine genetic resources. It has been suggested that this concern could be addressed by allowing an embargo period to keep the information and data private for a certain period.

Because at the moment *in situ* access to marine genetic resources is to be considered as marine scientific research, it is suggested that provisions regarding access and benefit sharing of the new instrument be based on the UNCLOS marine scientific research regime. To address the hypothetical situation in which the related activities may qualify as prospecting in the future, an international organization can be designated in the new instrument to review the development of biotechnology and the knowledge of marine genetic resources in areas beyond national jurisdiction. If the organization considers the relevant information suffices in proving that the sampling activities may be conducted for prospecting, the organization may draft guidelines to regulate sampling of marine genetic resources for prospecting (Chapter 6.4).

Based on the preceding analysis, it is submitted that UNCLOS and its marine scientific research regime provide the legal basis for the classification of *in situ* access to marine genetic resources – at the moment the related activities are to be considered marine scientific research under UNCLOS, and hypothetically, some of such activities may amount to prospecting in the future. By applying relevant UNCLOS provisions to the related activities, several useful implications are drawn in terms of the arrangement for access and benefit sharing of marine genetic resources in areas beyond national jurisdiction. However, admittedly, the application is not free of problems. As mentioned above, the requirement of open publication under the UNCLOS marine scientific research regime may be incompatible with some activities concerning marine genetic resources when sampling results need to be kept confidential (for a certain period of time). Besides, when access to marine genetic resources amounts to prospecting in the future, there might be a legal vacuum in the Convention because the provisions on prospecting as contained in UNCLOS and the ISA Regulations on prospecting are drafted with mineral resources in mind. These can be considered as the limits or regulatory gaps of UNCLOS and its marine scientific research regime in regulating access to marine genetic resources in areas beyond national jurisdiction. It is the viewpoint of the current author that the current UN BBNJ negotiation process is an excellent opportunity for States to agree upon some mechanisms to fill such gaps and to include the mechanisms agreed upon in the new instrument.

8.5.2 *Legal Regulation of Operational Oceanography*

Chapter 7 focuses on the issue of operational oceanography. The notion of "operational oceanography" refers to a group of activities that share the same features in relation to 1) the function of the activities, 2) the data that are collected, 3) the manner in which data are collected, 4) tools and platforms that are deployed to collect data, and 5) data availability and open publication (Chapter 7.2.1). Unlike Chapter 6, which addresses the legal issues raised by activities conducted in areas beyond national jurisdiction, this chapter mainly focuses on the legal issues raised by operational oceanography that is conducted in areas under national jurisdiction, in particular, in the EEZ of a coastal State. The reason is that it is in such areas that the undertaking of operational oceanographic activities might lead to controversies or conflicts (Chapter 7.1).

It is submitted that not all operational oceanographic activities have the same legal classification under UNCLOS (Chapter 7.3). As concluded in Chapter 3 to 5, the decisive factor in the legal classification is the purpose or function of the activity. This conclusion is attested by a comparison of the IOC Argo Guidelines and WMO Resolution 45 (Cg-18). An operational oceanographic activity may qualify as marine scientific research if it is undertaken with a scientific hypothesis (Chapter 7.3.3.1). The UNCLOS marine scientific research regime also applies to operational oceanographic activities that are not "marine scientific research", but rather "scientific research" activities that involve the use and deployment of installations and equipment (Chapter 7.4.1). An operational oceanographic activity may constitute "other internationally lawful uses of the sea related to [the] freedoms" under Article 58(1) if, for instance, it is conducted to ensure the safety of navigation, overflight or of the laying of submarine cables and pipelines (Chapter 7.3.3.2). When it fulfils none of these purposes, it may fall under Article 59 concerning unattributed rights and jurisdiction (Chapter 7.3.3.3). As such, operational oceanographic activities can be roughly divided into three kinds, depending on their legal classification.

For each kind of operational oceanographic activities, the chapter looks at the results of applying the respective pertinent rules to them (Chapter 7.4). For operational oceanographic activities that qualify as marine scientific research or that involve the use and deployment of scientific research installations and equipment, the application of the Part XIII regime to them potentially leads to some challenges (Chapter 7.4.1.1). These challenges include the difficulty of fully implementing prior consent requirements and the risk of impeding the development of marine science and the timely provision of operational services. It is submitted that these challenges can be resolved to a certain degree by using the flexibility embedded in the UNCLOS marine scientific research regime (Chapter 7.4.1.2). The flexibility is provided by, among others, Articles 242, 243 and 247 of the Convention. These provisions provide options for the States concerned to enter into practical arrangements and agree upon simplified procedures to obtain the consent from the coastal State for future research projects. These provisions also establish a two-way communication process for obtaining the consent from the coastal State concerning the undertaking of certain marine scientific research projects. Relying on these provisions, the researching States can be more actively involved in the process of seeking for the consent from the coastal State.

For operational oceanographic activities that constitute "other internationally lawful uses of the sea related to" the freedoms pursuant to Article 58(1), the due regard obligation requires the researching State to carry out a balancing test and enter into consultation with the coastal State (Chapter 7.4.2). For operational oceanographic activities that fall under Article 59, in cases where a conflict arises, the States concerned shall also perform a balancing test "on the basis of equity and in the light of all the relevant circumstances" (Chapter 7.4.3). When the test is performed by the States concerned themselves, the States are considered to be required to consult with each other to take all the necessary circumstances and interests into account.

Therefore, although different rules apply to different kinds of operational oceanographic activities, the application of these rules points to the same direction – States concerned should engage in consultation with each other when a conflict arises or may arise and potentially enter into practical arrangements to resolve the conflict (Chapter 7.4.4).

Considering the uncertainties of clearly identifying the existence of a scientific hypothesis and whether an activity can be considered as "related to" the freedoms mentioned in Article 58(1), the legal classification of certain operational oceanographic activities may give rise to controversies (Chapter 7.4.4). The fact that operational oceanographic activities usually serve multiple purposes further adds to the complexity of legal classification. It is argued that, in such cases, States may also establish practical arrangements by opting to leave the legal classification of the activities undefined. Arguably this is the case of the IOC Argo Guidelines and WMO Resolution 45 (Cg-18). Depending on specific circumstances, consultations for the establishment of practical arrangements on operational oceanographic activities can take place bilaterally or multilaterally (Chapter 7.5.1). In the latter case, international organizations such as IOC, WMO, IMO can provide the platforms for consultation.

Several implications for consultations concerning the establishment of practical arrangements are drawn from relevant case law that deals with the content of due regard obligations and from existing practical arrangements that address legal issues raised by operational oceanographic activities (Chapter 7.5). In negotiating such practical arrangements, it is better to focus on the variables concerned. States are more willing to enter into agreements for the measurement of variables that are less sensitive for the coastal State, and those that have the potential to serve common interests. Besides, the willingness of States to enter into arrangements also depends on the function of the activities concerned. In this respect, the obligations of States under other provisions of UNCLOS, such as those on the protection of the marine environment, and under other international instruments, such as UNFCCC, CBD, and the Sendai Framework for Disaster Risk Reduction, can be taken into account in the negotiations and used as incentives to facilitate cooperation.

To conclude, the legal classification of operational oceanography may vary depending on the function it serves and the data that are collected. For some operational oceanographic activities, their legal classification may be controversial. Besides, for operational oceanographic activities that constitute marine scientific research, the application of pertinent UNCLOS provisions, in particular the consent regime, leads to some challenges. Nevertheless, the author submits that UNCLOS, including its marine scientific research regime, is still viable in addressing the legal issues raised by operational oceanography.

8.5.3 *Conclusions*

The substantive analysis carried out in the two case studies provides answers to the third sub-question of this research:

What are the limits and strengths of UNCLOS and its marine scientific research regime in regulating different types of "modern" ocean data collection activities?

- Are there any regulatory gaps for UNCLOS and its marine scientific research regime in regulating different types of "modern" ocean data collection activities?
- What options exist within UNCLOS to fill such regulatory gaps, and what are the implications of these options? Do relevant subsequent practice of States and rules contained in other international conventions provide any guidance in this respect?

There are mainly two types of limits or regulatory gaps of UNCLOS and its marine scientific research regime. It is submitted that these gaps can be filled by the relevant provisions of UNCLOS or by the establishment of practical arrangements drawing implications from the relevant State practice and other international conventions.

First, the Convention sometimes falls short in distinguishing different kinds of ocean data collection activities. Although relevant UNCLOS provisions indicate that for purposes of legal classification, the function or purpose of the activities is the decisive factor, the Convention does not sufficiently address the legal classification of activities that serve multiple purposes. Besides, the open-ended wording of the pertinent provisions entails that the scope of activities covered by different treaty phrases can be subject to different interpretations and thus gives rise to potential conflicts. This limit of the Convention is manifested, for instance, in the legal classification of operational oceanographic activities. It is controversial what kinds of operational oceanographic activities constitute "other internationally lawful uses of the sea" related to the freedoms under Article 58(1) and what activities fall under Article 59 concerning unattributed rights and jurisdiction in the EEZ of a coastal State. For assessing whether an operational oceanographic activity qualifies as marine scientific research, the Convention does not provide sufficient guidance in determining the existence of a scientific hypothesis, which is a requirement implied by Article 240(b).

The relevant State practice indicates that States may enter into cooperative arrangements with each other even in cases where the legal classification of the activities is unclear or controversial. When divergent positions exist on the legal classification of the activity at issue, States may choose to leave the legal classification undefined. Besides, as indicated by the application of different rules to different kinds of operational oceanographic activities, the application leads to similar results – a balancing test needs to be carried out to balance the various interests involved, and when the test is performed by the States concerned themselves, in cases where a conflict arises or may arise, these States are required to enter into consultation with each other and hopefully establish practical arrangements on the regulation of the activities in question. Therefore, it is argued that the gaps referred to concerning the legal classification of ocean data collection activities above can be compensated by the establishment of practical arrangements. The relevant case law, the practice of States concerning ocean data collection and other international conventions provide useful implications as to the form of such arrangements and elements to be considered during consultations towards the establishment of such arrangements.

Second, in some instances, UNCLOS and its marine scientific research regime do not provide sufficient rules for regulating some new forms of ocean data collection activities, and in some other instances, the application of relevant UNCLOS provisions would lead to challenges. For instance, as demonstrated by the case study on access to marine genetic resources in areas beyond national jurisdiction, the Convention does not explicitly address issues on the legal regulation of *in situ* access to marine genetic resources in the Area that amounts to prospecting in the future.[20] Besides, for *in situ* access to marine genetic resources that is subject to the regulation of the UNCLOS marine scientific research regime, the requirement of open publication may be incompatible with some activities concerning marine genetic resources when sampling results need to be kept confidential (for a certain period of time). It is argued that the current UN BBNJ negotiation process is an excellent opportunity for States to agree upon some mechanisms to fill such gaps.

Another instance is provided by the regulation of operational oceanographic activities that constitute marine scientific research or that involve the use or deployment of "scientific research" installations and equipment, the application of the Part XIII regime to them potentially leads to some challenges, including 1) the difficulty of fully implementing prior consent requirements, and 2) the risk of impeding the development of marine science and timely provision of operational services.

It is submitted that these challenges can be resolved to a certain degree by using the flexibility of the UNCLOS Part XIII regime as contained in Articles 242, 243 and 247. Articles 242 and 243 establish a two-way communication process for obtaining the consent from the coastal State as opposed to a one-way process as manifested in the provisions under Articles 246 and 248. For operational oceanographic activities that fall under the scope of these provisions, it is submitted that Articles 242(2) and 243 can be interpreted as providing some leverage to the researching State to persuade the coastal State to grant its consent in the two-way communication mentioned above. The researching State or competent international organization may also enter into cooperative agreements with the coastal State concerning the collection of certain data (pursuant to Articles 242(2) and 243) in areas under the jurisdiction of the coastal State and agree upon simpler clearance procedures than the requirements of obtaining prior consent under Articles 245, 246, and 248. Besides, for operational oceanographic activities that qualify as marine scientific research,

20 As discussed in Chapter 6.4.1 of this study, it remains unclear which regime applies. If it is the principle of the freedom of the high seas that applies, there is no need to regulate the said activities.

the international organizations concerned can make use of the flexibility provided by Article 247 by, for example, setting up a detailed mechanism to implement this provision. When such a mechanism is in place, activities undertaken by or under the auspices of the international organization concerned can be carried out in areas under the jurisdiction of a coastal State under less stringent requirements.

8.6 Final Remarks and Some Observations on Future Developments

The answers to the three sub-questions lead to the fundamental conclusion of this study, that although different opinions exist on the legal classification of some specific ocean data collection activities and challenges exist in implementing certain substantive provisions, UNCLOS and its marine scientific research regime still provide a general legal framework for regulating new forms of ocean data collection activities.

Although not spelt out in sufficient detail, the text of UNCLOS provides useful indications for the legal classification of ocean data collection activities. The relevant subsequent practice of States and rules of other conventions on the regulation of ocean data collection activities have contributed to clarifying some uncertainties or ambiguities contained in UNCLOS in relation to the legal classification of ocean data collection activities, in particular the nature of and criteria for marine scientific research. Further, an analysis of subsequent practice of States also indicates that States may and do enter into practical arrangements with each other for ocean data collection activities even when the legal classification of the activities remains unclear or when the States concerned prefer to leave the legal classification of the activities undefined.

Admittedly, in some instances, the application of certain UNCLOS provisions to some "modern" ocean data collection activities would lead to several problems. It is argued that such problems can be resolved by using the flexibility of the Convention and its marine scientific research regime. In other instances, the problems can be addressed by the establishment of practical arrangements drawing inspirations from relevant subsequent practice of States or rules of other international conventions. In addition, the ongoing UN BBNJ process provides an excellent opportunity to resolve potential incompatibilities raised by the application of some UNCLOS provisions to activities concerning marine genetic resources in areas beyond national jurisdiction.

Since the present research selects access to marine genetic resources and operational oceanography as examples to illustrate the strengths and limits of

UNCLOS and its marine scientific research regime in regulating modern ocean data collection activities, the substantive analysis and findings are put in the context of these two kinds of activities. In a broader context and for the regulation of "modern" ocean data collection activities in general, the study ends with some comments on the options for future developments and possible research.

It is noted that legal uncertainties of the relevant UNCLOS provisions on ocean data collection activities and the relationship between some ocean data collection activities and marine scientific research can also be clarified by resort to the dispute settlement mechanism under Part XV of UNCLOS. International courts and tribunals play a vital role in providing authoritative guidance on the interpretation of ambiguous treaty provisions.[21] This is no less true for UNCLOS and its marine scientific research regime. As pointed out by Boyle, the fact that no cases have so far been submitted to an international court or tribunal concerning marine scientific research "tells us little about disputes on the subject" – it does not mean there is no conflicts at all.[22]

The reasons that the parties to UNCLOS have not made use of dispute settlement mechanism under Part XV of the Convention in resolving disputes on marine scientific research may be two-fold. First, potentially, disputes arising out of Part XIII of the Convention have been settled without resort to an international court or tribunal.[23] The willingness of States concerned to submit a potential dispute concerning ocean data collection activities to an international court or tribunal may be minimal, especially considering "the minor nature of the violation" versus the cost of international judicial or arbitral proceedings.[24] Second, such disputes may have been avoided altogether because Part XV of UNCLOS excludes some important legal issues from the compulsory jurisdiction over disputes concerning marine scientific research.[25]

Considering these reasons, the potential of parties to UNCLOS resorting to Part XV of the Convention to resolve disputes arising from the undertaking of "modern" ocean data collection activities remains to be seen. This is also a field that warrants further study and research.

---

21 James Harrison, "Judicial Law-Making and the Developing Order of the Oceans", 286–287.

22 Alan Boyle, "Forum Shopping for UNCLOS Disputes Relating to Marine Scientific Research", in *Law, Science & Ocean Management*, edited (Brill Nijhoff, 2007), 522.

23 Such disputes might have been resolved through negotiation or the establishment of practical arrangement.

24 Natalie Klein, *Dispute Settlement in the UN Convention on the Law of the Sea*, 123, 125.

25 UNCLOS, Article 297(2). See also Alan Boyle, "Forum Shopping for UNCLOS Disputes Relating to Marine Scientific Research", 522–523; Natalie Klein, *Dispute Settlement in the UN Convention on the Law of the Sea*, 125.

Apart from the dispute settlement mechanism under Part XV of UNCLOS, as argued above, negotiations and establishment of practical arrangements are essential for the resolution of any (potential) disputes arising from the conduct and regulation of "modern" ocean data collection activities. In its Resolution on oceans and the law of the sea of 2017, the UN General Assembly decided to proclaim the United Nations Decade of Ocean Science for Sustainable Development for the 10-year period beginning on 1 January 2021.[26] As stated in the report of the twentieth meeting of the UN Informal Consultative Process on the theme of ocean science and the official website of the United Nations Decade of Ocean Science for Sustainable Development, "the Decade will be an important opportunity to address gaps in ocean science, increase knowledge, improve synergies and support the sustainable conservation and management of marine resources".[27]

In this regard, it is submitted that the Decade provides a good opportunity for States to initiate negotiations of practical agreements on ocean data collection activities. Because the implementation plan of the Decade is prepared by IOC "in consultation with Member States, specialized agencies, funds, programmes and bodies of the United Nations, as well as other intergovernmental organizations, non-governmental organizations and relevant stakeholders",[28] the practical arrangements agreed upon in such a framework is more likely to be based on the consideration of all the interests involved and acceptable to a broader scope of States.

26 "UNGA Resolution on oceans and the law of the sea of 4 January 2018", UN Doc. A/RES/72/73, para.292.

27 "Report on the work of the United Nations Open-ended Informal Consultative Process on Oceans and the Law of the Sea at its twentieth meeting", UN Doc. A/74/119, 2019, paras.7, 19, 22. See also the official website of UNESCO, "United Nations Decade of Ocean Science for Sustainable Development (2021–2030)", available at https://en.unesco.org/ocean-decade.

28 "UNGA Resolution on oceans and the law of the sea of 10 December 2019", UN Doc. A/RES/74/19, para.302.

Summary

Scientific advances and technological developments in recent decades drive transformative changes in how, where and by whom, ocean data collection activities can be conducted. These advances present opportunities to enhance knowledge and deliver benefits. However, they also bring new challenges for the applicable legal regime, particularly where the legal classification of the activities concerned is unclear. As "a constitution for the oceans", UNCLOS aims at settling "all issues relating to the law of the sea", including the ones concerning ocean data collection. Nevertheless, in several instances, UNCLOS provisions do not provide sufficient indications as to the legal classification of certain ocean data collection activities. A prominent example is provided by marine scientific research. The general regime regarding marine scientific research is contained, particularly, in Part XIII of the Convention. Although the Convention includes a whole part on marine scientific research, it does not contain a definition of the term "marine scientific research". As a result, the scope of activities covered by the term "marine scientific research", and hence the scope of regulation of the UNCLOS marine scientific research regime, remain unclear or controversial. This has led to different opinions on the relationship between some specific ocean data collection activities and marine scientific research. The problem of legal classification of ocean data collection activities becomes even more complicated along with the technological advances in ocean data collection methods and means.

This book therefore seeks to identify the appropriate legal framework(s) for "modern" ocean data collection activities. The main research question of this research is formulated as:

> To what extent do UNCLOS and its marine scientific research regime regulate "modern" ocean data collection activities, and through which regulatory arrangements might any gaps for regulation in the Convention be filled?

To answer the research question, the present research is divided into six substantive chapters that constitute two parts. The first part (Chapters 2 to 5) sets out the legal framework for the regulation of ocean data collection activities and assesses how the framework has operated. In the process, UNCLOS provisions pertinent to the regulation of ocean data collection activities, subsequent practice of States concerning ocean data collection, and rules contained in other international conventions concerning ocean data collection are examined. Special attention has been paid to the criteria for the legal classification of various forms of ocean data collection activities and the implications for their regulation. The second part (Chapters 6 and 7) contextualizes the observations made in the first part and carries out two specific case studies to examine the strengths and limits of UNCLOS and its marine scientific research regime in regulating certain "modern" ocean data collection activities.

Before the analysis of substantive UNCLOS provisions, the research first looks at the nature of UNCLOS as a "living instrument", the object and purpose of the Convention, the drafting history of the definition of the term "marine scientific research" and the nature of the term "marine scientific research" as a generic term, and observes that the interpretation of the term "marine scientific research" and relevant UNCLOS provisions on ocean data collection should take into consideration new developments that occur after the adoption of the Convention.

Although UNCLOS does not define the term "marine scientific research", the text of the Convention sets out the minimum requirement for constituting marine scientific research under UNCLOS. To constitute marine scientific research in the context of UNCLOS, an ocean data collection activity has to contribute to the furtherance of knowledge of the marine environment and display some scientific attributes – there has to be a hypothesis. However, the Convention does not require marine scientific research activities to be conducted *exclusively* for scientific purposes – such activities may also serve commercial ends. In other words, marine scientific research can potentially serve multiple ends, and one of such ends shall be scientific.

According to the substantive rules set forth for different ocean data collection activities in each of the maritime zones contained in UNCLOS, the Convention distinguishes several kinds of activities from marine scientific research, for instance, activities having a direct bearing on passage, prospecting, exploration and exploitation, "other internationally lawful uses of the sea related to" the freedoms of navigation and overflight and of the laying of submarine cables and pipelines under Article 58 of UNCLOS, and activities falling under Article 59 of UNCLOS. The legal classification of different ocean data collection activities primarily depends on the function or purpose of the activities. However, as indicated by the substantive analysis, in some instances, the Convention does not provide sufficient indications for distinguishing one ocean data collection activity from another. As a result, the legal classification of some activities may be unclear or controversial.

The problem of legal classification is most acute for ocean data collection activities conducted in the EEZ of a coastal State. It is argued that the provisions under the UNCLOS EEZ regime provide a good basis for resolving the conflict that arises or may arise from the legal classification and the regulation of ocean data collection activities. Most notably, when rights over a certain ocean data collection activity are granted to either the coastal State or a third State, the exercise of such rights shall have due regard to the rights and duties of the other State concerned. For unattributed rights in the EEZ, when a conflict arises, the conflict shall be resolved according to the guideline contained in Article 59 of the Convention. As required by both the reciprocal due regard obligation and the provision under Article 59 concerning the resolution of conflicts regarding unattributed rights and jurisdiction, when a conflict arises or may arise from the conduct of an ocean data collection activity in the EEZ of a coastal State, the States concerned are required to carry out a balancing test taking into consideration the interests involved. When the balancing test is carried out by the States concerned themselves, the States need to enter into consultation with each other.

Relevant State practice and international conventions other than UNCLOS show how ocean data collection activities are regulated in a way that is accepted by States in cases where the relationship between the ocean data collection activities concerned and marine scientific research is undefined. Besides, these sources provide useful guidance on interpreting legal terms that are pertinent to the regulation of ocean data collection activities, such as the "due regard" provision contained in UNCLOS.

In practice, States are willing to enter into practical arrangements with each other to solve practical problems in the field of ocean data collection even if they hold different positions on the legal classification of the activities concerned. Examples of such practical arrangements include the Argo Guidelines and bilateral or multilateral cooperative arrangements on the regulation of oceanographic data collection activities involving the use of floats and surface drifting buoys and the deployment of XBTs by ships of opportunity in EEZs. This could be attributed to the flexibility of the Convention, especially the provisions providing the due regard obligations, the basis for the resolution of conflicts concerning unattributed rights in the EEZ of a coastal States, and the obligation of promoting international cooperation and creating favorable conditions for marine scientific research.

The relevant practice also indicates that the willingness of States to establish practical arrangements primarily depends on two factors: first, whether the States concerned share common interests in the undertaking of the activity at issue; second, the sensitivity of the activity – States are more likely to enter into practical arrangements in less sensitive fields of research. In assessing the sensitivity of an activity, the objects of the research, purposes of the research, and the means and methods to conduct the activity are the elements to be considered. These factors may play a vital role when the States concerned are to fulfil the due regard obligation or implement Article 59 – these factors can be taken into account in the balancing test required.

Relevant provisions of CBD and the Nagoya Protocol also indicate the objects and purposes of the ocean data collection activity in question play a vital role in the balancing test: when the sovereignty or jurisdiction of the coastal State is affected by the activity at issue, both the UNCLOS marine scientific research regime and CBD tend to lean towards the side of the coastal State; whereas when the activity is conducted without commercial intent, both regimes advocate the coastal State to create simplified or less stringent requirements for the researching State.

Besides, in the balancing test, the obligations of States under other conventions pertaining to ocean data collection may be considered. For instance, the obligation of States to promote and cooperate in systematic observation under Article 4 of UNFCCC can be used as an incentive for the States concerned to enter into cooperative arrangements for certain ocean data collection activities when the legal classification of the activity at issue remains controversial, or when the States concerned prefer to leave the legal classification of the activity undefined.

On the basis of the observations above, the present research takes *in situ* access to marine genetic resources in areas beyond national jurisdiction and operational oceanographic activities in the EEZ of a coastal State as examples to assess the strengths and limits of UNCLOS and its marine scientific research regime in regulating new uses in the field of ocean data collection. In the process, focus is placed on ascertaining the legal implications of these "modern" ocean data collection activities and discussing the appropriate legal framework(s) applicable to them.

At the moment, *in situ* access to marine genetic resources in areas beyond national jurisdiction is conducted for scientific purposes or for both scientific and commercial purposes. Considering the purpose of such activities, which is the essential element in ascertaining the legal classification of ocean data collection activities under UNCLOS, *in situ* access to marine genetic resources in areas beyond national jurisdiction falls under the scope of marine scientific research and hence the UNCLOS marine scientific research regime applies. By applying the UNCLOS marine scientific research regime to the mentioned activities, several implications for establishing the arrangements for access to marine genetic resources in areas beyond national jurisdiction, and the mechanisms for the sharing of benefits arising from the utilization of such resources result.

However, the application of the UNCLOS marine scientific research regime to activities concerning marine genetic resources is not free of problems. In particular, the Convention does not (explicitly) address issues on the legal regulation of *in situ* access to marine genetic resources in the Area that hypothetically amounts to prospecting in the future (when the activity is purely conducted for commercial purposes) – it remains unclear which regime applies: the regime of the high seas or the regime of the Area. Besides, the requirement of open publication of information, data and research results leads to some concerns as to the interests in developing patents on the basis of marine genetic resources. It has been suggested that such concerns could be addressed by allowing an embargo period to keep the information and data private for a certain period.

As to operational oceanographic activities, the legal classification of these activities may vary depending on the function it serves and the data that are collected – when undertaken in the EEZ of a coastal State, it may qualify as marine scientific research if it is undertaken with a scientific hypothesis; it may constitute "other internationally lawful uses of the sea related to [the] freedoms" under Article 58(1) if, for instance, it is conducted to ensure the safety of navigation, overflight or of the laying of submarine cables and pipelines; it may also fall under Article 59 concerning unattributed rights and jurisdiction. Although different rules apply to different kinds of operational oceanographic activities, the application of these rules points to the same direction – States concerned should engage in consultation with each other when a conflict arises or may arise and potentially enter into practical arrangements to resolve the conflict.

For some operational oceanographic activities, their legal classification may be controversial. In such cases, States may also establish practical arrangements by opting to leave the legal classification of the activities undefined. Arguably this is the case of the IOC Argo Guidelines and WMO Resolution 45 (Cg-18). Depending on specific circumstances, negotiations concerning the establishment of practical arrangements on operational oceanographic activities can take place bilaterally or multilaterally. In the latter case, international organizations such as IOC, WMO, IMO can provide the platform for the negotiations. Several implications for negotiations concerning the establishment of practical arrangements can be drawn from relevant case law that deals with the content of due regard obligations and the existing practical arrangements that address the legal issues raised by operational oceanographic activities.

It is submitted that there are mainly two types of limits or regulatory gaps of UNCLOS and its marine scientific research regime. First, the Convention sometimes falls short in distinguishing different kinds of ocean data collection activities and, second, in some instances, UNCLOS and its marine scientific research regime do not provide sufficient rules for regulating some new forms of ocean data collection activities, and in some other instances, the application of relevant UNCLOS provisions would lead to challenges. It is submitted that these gaps can be filled by resorting to the flexibility provided by the relevant provisions of UNCLOS or by the establishment of practical arrangements drawing implications from the relevant State practice and other international conventions.

In sum, although different opinions exist on the legal classification of some specific ocean data collection activities and challenges exist in implementing certain substantive provisions, UNCLOS and its marine scientific research regime to a large extent still provide an appropriate legal framework for regulating new forms of ocean data collection activities.

Bibliography

Books

Abate, Randall S, ed. *Climate Change Impacts on Ocean and Coastal Law: US and International Perspectives*: Oxford University Press, 2014.

Buga, Irina. *Modification of Treaties by Subsequent Practice*. Oxford University Press, 2018.

Churchill, R. R., and A. V. Lowe. *The Law of the Sea*. Manchester University Press, 1999.

Creswell, John W. *Qualitative Inquiry and Research Design: Choosing Among Five Approaches*. Sage Publications, 2007.

De Arechaga, Eduardo Jimenez. *International Law in the Past Third of a Century*. Martinus Nijhoff, 1978.

Dörr, Oliver, and Kirsten Schmalenbach, eds. *Vienna Convention on the Law of Treaties: A Commentary (Second Edition)*: Springer, 2018.

Eckardt, Regine. *Meaning Change in Grammaticalization: An Enquiry into Semantic Reanalysis*. Oxford University Press, 2006.

Glowka, Lyle, Francoise Burhenne-Guilmin, and Hugh Synge. *A Guide to the Convention on Biological Diversity*. IUCN, 1994.

Gorina-Ysern, Montserrat. "Principles of International Law of the Sea Governing Coastal State Access to Marine Scientific Research Results." University of New South Wales, 1995.

Gorina-Ysern, Montserrat. *An International Regime for Marine Scientific Research*. Brill-Nijhoff, 2003.

H. Nordquist, Myron, Rosenne Shabtai, Yankov Alexander, and Grandy Neal R., eds. *United Nations Convention on the Law of the Sea, 1982: A Commentary (Vol. III)*. Dordrecht: Martinus Nijhoff Publishers, 1991.

H. Nordquist, Myron, Rosenne Shabtai, Yankov Alexander, and Grandy Neal R., eds. *United Nations Convention on the Law of the Sea, 1982: A Commentary (Vol. IV)*. Dordrecht: Martinus Nijhoff Publishers, 1991.

H.Th. Wegelein, Florian. *Marine Scientific Research: The Operation and Status of Research Vessels and Other Platforms in International Law*. Martinus Nijhoff Publishers, 2005.

Haomiao, Du. *An International Legal Framework for Geoengineering: Managing the Risks of an Emerging Technology*. Routledge, 2017.

Harrison, James. *Making the Law of the Sea: A Study in the Development of International Law*. Cambridge: Cambridge University Press, 2011.

Jennings, Robert, and Arthur Watts, eds. *Oppenheim's International Law: Volume 1 Peace (9th Edition)*: Oxford University Press, 2008.

Klein, Natalie. *Dispute Settlement in the UN Convention on the Law of the Sea*. Cambridge University Press, 2005.

Leary, David Kenneth. *International Law and the Genetic Resources of the Deep Sea*. Brill, 2006.

Lyons, John. *Semantics: 1*. Cambridge University Press, 1977.

Merkouris, Panos. *Article 31(3)(c) VCLT and the Principle of Systemic Integration: Normative Shadows in Plato's Cave*. Brill, 2015.

Morgera, Elisa, Elsa Tsioumani, and Matthias Buck. *Unraveling the Nagoya Protocol: A Commentary on the Nagoya Protocol on Access and Benefit-Sharing to the Convention on Biological Diversity*. Martinus Nijhoff Publishers, 2014.

Mossop, Joanna. *The Continental Shelf Beyond 200 Nautical Miles: Rights and Responsibilities*. Oxford University Press, 2016.

Odgaard, Liselotte. *Maritime Security between China and Southeast Asia: Conflict and Cooperation in the Making of Regional Order*. Routledge, 2017.

Orrego Vicuña, Francisco. *The Exclusive Economic Zone: Regime and Legal Nature under International Law*. Cambridge University Press, 1989.

Proelss, Alexander, ed. *United Nations Convention on the Law of the Sea: A Commentary*. edited by Alexander Proelss: C.H. Beck; Hart; Nomos, 2017.

Rothwell, Donald R, and Tim Stephens. *The International Law of the Sea (2nd edition)*. Hart Publishing, 2016.

Sea, United Nations Office for Ocean Affairs and the Law of the. *National Legislation, Regulations and Supplementary Documents on Marine Scientific Research in Areas Under National Jurisdiction*. 1989.

Sinclair, Ian McTaggart. *The Vienna Convention on the Law of Treaties*. Manchester University Press, 1984.

Soons, Alfred H. A. *Marine Scientific Research and the Law of the Sea*. Kluwer Law and Taxation Publishers, 1982.

Sørensen, Max. *Le problème dit du droit intertemporel dans l'ordre international*. 1973.

Talley, Lynne D, George L Pickard, William J Emery, and James H Swift. *Descriptive Physical Oceanography: An Introduction (Sixth Edition)*. Academic Press, 2011.

Tanaka, Yoshifumi. *The International Law of the Sea*. Second ed.: Cambridge University Press, 2015.

UN/DOALOS. *Marine Scientific Research: Legislative History of Article 246 of the United Nations Convention on the Law of the Sea*. New York: United Nations Publication, 1994.

Venzke, Ingo. *How Interpretation Makes International Law: On Semantic Change and Normative Twists*. Oxford University Press, 2012.

Villiger, Mark Eugen. *Commentary on the 1969 Vienna Convention on the Law of Treaties*. Brill, 2008.

Walker, George K. *Definitions for the Law of the Sea: Terms Not Defined by the 1982 Convention*. Leiden: Brill, 2011.

Wyatt, Julian. *Intertemporal Linguistics in International Law: Beyond Contemporaneous and Evolutionary Treaty Interpretation*. Hart Publishing, 2019.

Book Contributions, Journal Articles and Research Papers

Agnihotri, Kamlesh Kumar, and Sunil Kumar Agarwal. "Legal Aspects of Marine Scientific Research in Exclusive Economic Zones: Implications of the Impeccable Incident." *Maritime Affairs: Journal of the National Maritime Foundation of India* 5, no. 2 (2009): 135–150.

Allen, Craig H. "Protecting the Oceanic Gardens of Eden: International Law Issues in Deep-Sea Vent Resource Conservation and Management." *Georgetown International Environmental Law Review* 13 (2001): 563–660.

Andreone, Gemma. "The Exclusive Economic Zone." In *The Oxford Handbook of the Law of the Sea*, edited by Donald Rothwell, Alex Oude Elferink, Karen Scott and Tim Stephens, 159–180, 2015.

Apostle, Richard, Tsafrir Gazit, and Marcus Haward. "Ocean Tracking and Marine Species Protection in Australia and Canada: Science, Technology, and Knowledge Brokering." *Ocean Development & International Law* 47, no. 4 (2016): 368–377.

Arato, Julian. "Subsequent Practice and Evolutive Interpretation: Techniques of Treaty Interpretation over Time and Their Diverse Consequences." *The Law & Practice of International Courts and Tribunals* 9, no. 3 (2010): 443–494.

Arico, Salvatore, and Charlotte Salpin. "Bioprospecting of Genetic Resources in the Deep Seabed: Scientific, Legal and Policy Aspects." 2005.

Barnes, Richard. "The Continuing Vitality of UNCLOS." In *Law of the Sea: UNCLOS as a living treaty*, edited by Jill Barrett and Richard Barnes, 459–489. London: The British Institute of International and Comparative Law, 2016.

Barrett, Jill. "The UN Convention on the Law of the Sea: a "Living" Treaty?". In *Law of the Sea: UNCLOS as a living treaty*, edited by Jill Barrett and Richard Barnes, 3–37. London: The British Institute of International and Comparative Law, 2016.

Bateman, Sam. "Hydrographic Surveying in the EEZ: Differences and Overlaps with Marine Scientific Research." *Marine Policy* 29, no. 2 (2005): 163–174.

Beckman, Robert, and Tara Davenport. "The EEZ Regime: Reflections after 30 Years." Paper presented at the 2012 LOSI-KIOST Conference on Securing the Ocean for the Next Generation, 2012.

Bernhardt, Rudolf. "Evolutive Treaty Interpretation, Especially of the European Convention on Human Rights." *German YB Int'l L.* 42 (1999): 11.

Bethlehem, Daniel. "The Secret Life of International Law." *Cambridge Journal of International and Comparative Law* 1 (2012): 23–36.

Bianchi, Andrea. "Textual Interpretation and (International) Law Reading: The Myth of (in)Determinacy and the Genealogy of Meaning." In *Making Transnational Law Work in the Global Economy: Essays in Honour of Detlev Vagts*, edited by Pieter H. F. Bekker, Rudolf Dolzer and Michael Waibel, 34–56: Cambridge University Press, 2010.

Bianchi, Andrea. "The Game of Interpretation in International Law." In *Interpretation in International Law*, edited by Andrea Bianchi, Daniel Peat and Matthew Windsor, 34–58: Oxford University Press, 2015.

Birnie, Patricia. "Law of the Sea and Ocean Resources: Implications for Marine Scientific Research." *The International Journal of Marine and Coastal Law* 10 (1995): 229–251.

Boehme, Lars, K Kovacs, C Lydersen, OA Nøst, Martin Biuw, JB Charrassin, F Roquet, C Guinet, Michael Meredith, and Keith Nicholls. "Biologging in the global ocean observing system." Paper presented at the OceanObs 09: Sustained Ocean Observations and Information for Society (Vol. 2), Venice, Italy, 21–25 September 2009, I, 2010.

Bork, Katharina, Johannes Karstensen, Martin Visbeck, and Andreas Zimmermann. "The Legal Regulation of Floats and Gliders - In Quest of a New Regime?". *Ocean Development & International Law* 39, no. 3 (2008): 298–328.

Boyle, Alan. "Further Development of the Law of the Sea Convention: Mechanisms for Change." *International & Comparative Law Quarterly* 54, no. 3 (2005): 563–584.

Boyle, Alan. "Forum Shopping for UNCLOS Disputes Relating to Marine Scientific Research." In *Law, Science & Ocean Management*, 519–540: Brill Nijhoff, 2007.

Boyle, Alan. "Law of the Sea Perspectives on Climate Change." In *The 1982 Law of the Sea Convention at 30*, edited by David Freestone, 157–164: Brill Nijhoff, 2013.

Broggiato, Arianna, Thomas Vanagt, Laura E Lallier, Marcel Jaspars, Geoff Burton, and Dominic Muyldermans. "Mare Geneticum: Balancing Governance of Marine Genetic Resources in International Waters." *The International Journal of Marine and Coastal Law* 33, no. 1 (2018): 3–33.

Brown, ED. "The Exclusive Economic Zone: Criteria and Machinery for the Resolution of International Conflicts between Different Users of the EEZ." *Maritime Policy and Management* 4, no. 6 (1977): 325–350.

Buck, Matthias, and Clare Hamilton. "The Nagoya Protocol on Access to Genetic Resources and the Fair and Equitable Sharing of Benefits Arising from Their Utilization to the Convention on Biological Diversity." *Review of European Community & International Environmental Law* 20, no. 1 (2011): 47–61.

Buffard, Isabelle, and Karl Zemanek. "The "Object and Purpose" of a Treaty: An Enigma?". *Austrian Review of International and European Law* 3 (1998): 311–343.

Caflisch, Lucius, and Jacques Piccard. "The Legal Regime of Marine Scientific Research and the Third United Nations Conference on the Law of the Sea." *Ocean Development & International Law* 4 (1977): 297–342.

Castañeda, Jorge G. "Negotiations on the Exclusive Economic Zone at the Third United Nations Conference on the Law of the Sea." In *Essays in International Law in Honour of Judge Manfred Lachs*, edited by Jerzy Makarczyk: Martinus Nijhoff Publishers, 1984.

Chege Kamau, Evanson, "Access-Related Issues", *IUCN Information Papers for the Intersessional Workshop on Marine Genetic Resources,* 2013.

Chircop, Aldo. "Advances in Ocean Knowledge and Skill: Implications for the MSR Regime." In *Law, Science & Ocean Management*, edited by Myron Nordquist, Ronán Long, Tomas Heidar and John Norton Moore, 575–616: Brill, 2007.

Churchill, Robin. "The 1982 United Nations Convention on the Law of the Sea." In *The Oxford Handbook of the Law of the Sea*, edited by Donald Rothwell, Alex Oude Elferink, Karen Scott and Tim Stephens, 24–45: Oxford University Press, 2015.

Crema, Luigi. "Subsequent Agreements and Subsequent Practice within and outside the Vienna Convention." In *Treaties and Subsequent Practice*, edited by Georg Nolte, 13–28: Oxford University Press, 2013.

Crnićgrotić, Vesna. "Object and Purpose of Treaties in the Vienna Convention on the Law of Treaties." *Asian Yearbook of International Law* (1997): 141–174.

de La Fayette, Louise Angélique. "A New Regime for the Conservation and Sustainable Use of Marine Biodiversity and Genetic Resources Beyond the Limits of National Jurisdiction." *The International Journal of Marine and Coastal Law* 24, no. 2 (2009): 221–280.

Dedeurwaerdere, Tom, Arianna Broggiato, Selim Louafi, Eric W Welch, and Fulya Batur. "Governing Global Scientific Research Commons under the Nagoya Protocol." In *The 2010 Nagoya Protocol on Access and Benefit-Sharing in Perspective*, edited by Elisa Morgera, Matthias Buck and Elsa Tsioumani, 389–421: Brill Nijhoff, 2013.

Dupuy, Pierre-Marie. "Evolutionary Interpretation of Treaties: Between Memory and Prophecy." In *The Law of Treaties Beyond the Vienna Convention*, edited by Enzo Cannizzaro, 123–137: Oxford University Press, 2011.

Fife, Rolf Einar. "Obligations of 'Due Regard' in the Exclusive Economic Zone: Their Context, Purpose and State Practice." *The International Journal of Marine and Coastal Law* 34, no. 1 (2019): 43–55.

Fitzmaurice, Gerald G. "Law and Procedure of the International Court of Justice: Treaty Interpretation and Certain Other Treaty Points." *British Yearbook of International Law* 28 (1951): 1–28.

Fitzmaurice, Malgosia. "Interpretation of Human Rights Treaties." In *The Oxford Handbook of International Human Rights Law*, edited by Dinah Shelton, 739–771: Oxford University Press, 2013.

Fitzmaurice, Malgosia. "The Practical Working of the Law of Treaties." In *International law (Fourth Edition)*, edited by Malcolm D. Evans, 166–197: Oxford University Press, 2014.

Forteau, Mathias. "The Legal Nature and Content of 'Due Regard' Obligations in Recent International Case Law." *The International Journal of Marine and Coastal Law* 34, no. 1 (2019): 25–42.

Franckx, Erik. ""Reasonable Bond" in the Practice of the International Tribunal for the Law of the Sea." *California Western International Law Journal* 32 (2001): 303.

Franssen, Herman T. "Developing Country Views of Sea Law and Marine Science." In *Freedom of Oceanic Research: A Study Conducted by the Center for Marine Affairs of the Scripps Institute of Oceanography University of California, San Diego*, edited by Warren S. Wooster. New York: Crane, Russak & Company, Inc., 1973.

Freestone, David, and Alex Oude Elferink. "Flexibility and Innovation in the Law of the Sea: Will the LOS Convention Amendment Procedures Ever Be Used?". In *Stability and Change in the Law of the Sea: The Role of the LOS Convention*, edited by Alex Oude Elferink, 169–222: Martinus Nijhoff Publishers, 2005.

French, Duncan. "Treaty Interpretation and the Incorporation of Extraneous Legal Rules." *International & Comparative Law Quarterly* 55, no. 2 (2006): 281–314.

Gelman, Susan A, and Twila Tardif. "A Cross-Linguistic Comparison of Generic Noun Phrases in English and Mandarin." *Cognition* 66, no. 3 (1998): 215–248.

Glowka, Lyle. "The Deepest of Ironies: Genetic Resources, Marine Scientific Research, and the Area." *Ocean Yearbook Online* 12, no. 1 (1996): 154–178.

Glowka, Lyle. "Evolving Perspectives on the International Seabed Area's Genetic Resources: Fifteen Years After the 'Deepest of Ironies'." In *Law, Technology and Science for Oceans in Globalisation: IUU Fishing, Oil Pollution, Bioprospecting, Outer Continental Shelf*, edited by Davor Vidas, 397–420: Brill, 2010.

Gomez, Edgardo D. "Marine Scientific Research in the South China Sea and Environmental Security." *Ocean Development & International Law* 32, no. 2 (Apr 2001): 205–211.

Goodman, Camille. "Rights, Obligations, Prohibitions: A Practical Guide to Understanding Judicial Decisions on Coastal State Jurisdiction over Living Resources in the Exclusive Economic Zone." *The International Journal of Marine and Coastal Law* 33, no. 3 (2018): 558–584.

Gorina-Ysern, Montserrat. "Marine Scientific Research: Overview of Major Issues, Programmes and Their Objectives." In *Routledge Handbook of Ocean Resources and Management*, edited by Hance D Smith, Juan Luis Suárez de Vivero and Tundi S Agardy, 127–142: Routledge, 2015.

Gougenheim, André. "Oceanography and Hydrography—Basic Research and Descriptive Oceanography." *The International Hydrographic Review* (1965).

Gragl, Paul. "Marine Scientific Research." In *The IMLI Manual on International Maritime Law: Volume I: The Law of the Sea*, edited by David Attard, Malgosia Fitzmaurice and Norman A Martínez Gutiérrez, 396–430: OUP Oxford, 2014.

Greiber, Thomas. "Access and Benefit Sharing in Relation to Marine Genetic Resources from Areas Beyond National Jurisdiction: A Possible Way Forward." *Bonn: IUCN (BfN-Skripten, no. 301)* (2011).

Greiber, Thomas. "Meaning and Scope", *IUCN Information Papers for the Intersessional Workshop on Marine Genetic Resources*, 2013.

Guilfoyle, Douglas. "The High Seas." In *The Oxford Handbook of the Law of the Sea*, edited by Donald Rothwell, Alex Oude Elferink, Karen Scott and Tim Stephens, 203–225, 2015.

Hamamoto, Shotaro. "The Genesis of the 'Due Regard' Obligations in the United Nations Convention on the Law of the Sea." *The International Journal of Marine and Coastal Law* 34, no. 1 (2019): 7–24.

Harcourt, Rob, Ana Micaela Martins Sequeira, Xuelei Zhang, Fabien Roquet, Kosei Komatsu, Michelle Heupel, Clive Reginald McMahon, Frederick Gilbert Whoriskey, Mark Meekan, and Gemma Carroll. "Animal-borne telemetry: an integral component of the ocean observing toolkit." *Frontiers in Marine Science* 6 (2019): 326.

Harden-Davies, Harriet. "The Regulation of Marine Scientific Research: Addressing Challenges, Advancing Knowledge." In *Routledge Handbook of Maritime Regulation and Enforcement*, edited by Robin M Warner and Stuart Kaye, 212–230: Routledge, 2016.

Harrison, James. "Judicial Law-Making and the Developing Order of the Oceans." *The International Journal of Marine and Coastal Law* 22, no. 2 (2007): 283–302.

Helmersen, Sondre Torp. "Evolutive Treaty Interpretation: Legality, Semantics and Distinctions." *European Journal of Legal Studies* 6 (2013): 161–188.

Higgins, Rosalyn. "Time and the Law: International Perspectives on An Old Problem." *International & Comparative Law Quarterly* 46, no. 3 (1997): 501–520.

Higgins, Rosalyn. "A Babel of Judicial Voices? Ruminations from the Bench." *International & Comparative Law Quarterly* 55, no. 4 (2006): 791–804.

Hofmann, Tobias, and Alexander Proelss. "The Operation of Gliders Under the International Law of the Sea." *Ocean Development & International Law* (2015): 167–187.

Ishii, Yurika. "The 'Due Regard' Obligation and the Peaceful and Economic Uses of the EEZ other than Fisheries." *The International Journal of Marine and Coastal Law* 34, no. 1 (2019): 73–88.

Jørem, Ane, and Morten Walløe Tvedt. "Bioprospecting in the High Seas: Existing Rights and Obligations in View of A New Legal Regime for Marine Areas Beyond National Jurisdiction." *The International Journal of Marine and Coastal Law* 29, no. 2 (2014): 321–343.

Juniper, Kim, "Technological, Environmental, Social and Economic Aspects", IUCN *Information Papers for the Intersessional Workshop on Marine Genetic Resources,* 2013.

Kaikobad, Kaiyan Homi. "Non Consensual Aerial Surveillance in the Airspace over the Exclusive Economic Zone for Military and Defence Purposes." In *International Law and Power: Perspectives on Legal Order and Justice: Essays in Honour of Colin Warbrick*, edited by Kaiyan Homi Kaikobad and Michael Bohlander, 513–572: Brill Nijhoff, 2009.

Kaye, Stuart. "Marine Scientific Research and Military Survey: Law and State Practice." In *UN Convention on the Law of the Sea and the South China Sea*, edited by Shicun Wu, Mark Valencia and Nong Hong, 85–104: Ashgate Publishing, 2015.

Kirchner, Andree. "Bioprospecting, Marine Scientific Research and the Patentability of Genetic Resources." In *Serving the rule of international maritime law: essays in honour of Professor David Joseph Attard*, edited by Norman A Martínez Gutiérrez, 119–128. London: Routledge, 2009.

Kraska, James, Guillermo Ortuño Crespo, and David W Johnston. "Bio-logging of marine migratory species in the law of the sea." *Marine Policy* 51 (2015): 394–400.

Linderfalk, Ulf. "Doing the Right Thing for the Right Reason – Why Dynamic or Static Approaches Should be Taken in the Interpretation of Treaties." *International Community Law Review* 10, no. 2 (2008): 109–141.

Linderfalk, Ulf. "Who Are 'The Parties'? Article 31, Paragraph 3(c) of the 1969 Vienna Convention and the 'Principle of Systemic Integration' Revisited." *Netherlands International Law Review* 55, no. 3 (2008): 343–364.

Lodge, Michael W. "International Seabed Authority's Regulations on Prospecting and Exploration for Polymetallic Nodules in the Area." *Journal of Energy & Natural Resources Law* 20, no. 3 (2002): 270–295.

Long, Ronán. "Regulating Marine Scientific Research in the European Union: It Takes More Than Two to Tango." In *The Law of the Sea Convention: US Accession and Globalisation*, edited by Alfred H. A. Soons, Hak-so Kim, Myron H. Nordquist and John Norton Moore, 428–491: Martinus Nijhoff Publishers, 2012.

Marquet, Clément. "Prospective Linguistics and Trade: The Art of the Deal." In *Evolutionary Interpretation and International Law*, edited by Georges Abi-Saab, Kenneth Keith, Gabrielle Marceau and Clément Marquet, 195–204: Bloomsbury Publishing, 2019.

McIntyre, Trevor. "Trends in tagging of marine mammals: a review of marine mammal biologging studies." *African Journal of Marine Science* 36, no. 4 (2014): 409–422.

McLachlan, Campbell. "The Principle of Systemic Integration and Article 31(3)(c) of the Vienna Convention." *International & Comparative Law Quarterly* 54, no. 2 (2005): 279–320.

McLaughlin, Richard J. "UNCLOS and the Growing Use of Electronic Tagged Marine Animals as Autonomous Ocean Profilers." In *Governing Ocean Resources - New Challenges and Emerging Regimes: A Tribute to Judge Choon-Ho Park*, edited by Jon

M. Dyke, Sherry P. Broder, Seokwoo Lee and Jin-Hyun Paik, 489–501. Leiden, The Netherlands Martinus Nijhoff Publishers, 2013.

McLaughlin, Richard J. "Bio-Logging as Marine Scientific Research Under the Law of the Sea: A Commentary Responding to James Kraska, Guillermo Ortuño Crespo, David W. Johnston, Bio-Logging of Marine Migratory Species in the Law of the Sea, Marine Policy 51 (2015) 394–400." *Marine Policy* 60 (2015): 178–181.

Merkouris, Panos. "(Inter)Temporal Considerations in the Interpretative Process of the VCLT: Do Treaties Endure, Perdure or Exdure?". *Netherlands Yearbook of International Law* 45 (2015): 121–156.

Merrie, Andrew, Daniel C. Dunn, Marc Metian, Andre M. Boustany, Yoshinobu Takei, Alex Oude Elferink, Yoshitaka Ota, Villy Christensen, Patrick N. Halpin, and Henrik Österblom. "An ocean of surprises – Trends in human use, unexpected dynamics and governance challenges in areas beyond national jurisdiction." *Global Environmental Change* 27 (2014): 19–31.

Nolte, Georg. "Subsequent Agreements and Subsequent Practice of States Outside of Judicial or Quasi-judicial Proceedings - Report 3 for the ILC Study Group on Treaties over Time." In *Treaties and Subsequent Practice*, edited by Georg Nolte, 307–386: Oxford University Press, 2013.

Nowlin Jr, Worth D, and Thomas C Malone. "Research and GOOS." *Marine Technology Society Journal* 37, no. 3 (2003): 42–46.

Oliva, Maria Julia. "The Implications of the Nagoya Protocol for the Ethical Sourcing of Biodiversity." In *The 2010 Nagoya Protocol on Access and Benefit-sharing in Perspective*, edited by Elisa Morgera, Matthias Buck and Elsa Tsioumani, 369–387: Brill Nijhoff, 2013.

Oude Elferink, Alex G. "Reviewing the Implementation of the LOS Convention: the Role of the United Nations Assembly and the Meeting of States Parties." In *Oceans Management in the 21st Century: Institutional Frameworks and Responses*, edited by Alex G. Oude Elferink and Donald R. Rothwell, 295–302. Leiden: Martinus Nijhoff Publishers, 2004.

Oude Elferink, Alex G. "The Regime of the Area: Delineating the Scope of Application of the Common Heritage Principle and Freedom of the High Seas." *The International Journal of Marine and Coastal Law* 22, no. 1 (2007): 143–176.

Oxman, Bernard H. "An Analysis of the Exclusive Economic Zone as Formulated in the Informal Composite Negotiating Text." In *Law of the Sea: State practice in Zones of Special Jurisdiction - proceedings [of the] Law of the Sea Institute [of the] thirteenth annual conference, co-sponsored by the Center for Economic and Social Studies of the Third World, Mexico City, October 15–18, 1979, Mexico City, Mexico*, edited by Thomas A. Clingan, 57–78, 1979.

Oxman, Bernard H. "Tools for Change: The Amendment Procedure." Paper presented at the Proceedings of the Twentieth Anniversary Commemoration of the Opening for Signature of the UNCLOS, New York, 2003.

Palchetti, Paolo. "Interpreting "Generic Terms": Between Respect for the Parties' Original Intention and the Identification of the Ordinary Meaning." In *International Courts and the Development of International Law*, edited by Nerina Boschiero, Tullio Scovazzi, Cesare Pitea and Chiara Ragni, 91–105: Springer, 2013.

Pfirter, Frida Armas. "The Management of Seabed Living Resources in "the Area" under UNCLOS." *Revista electrónica de estudios internacionales (REEI)*, no. 11 (2006): 1.

Plesmann, Wolf, and Volker Röben. "Marine Scientific Research: State Practice versus Law of the Sea?". In *Law of the Sea at the Crossroads: The Continuing Search for a Universally Accepted Régime*, edited by Rüdiger Wolfrum, 373–392. Berlin: Duncker & Humboldt, 1991.

Press, Anthony. "Science in the Court! The Role of Science in 'Whaling in the Antarctic'." In *Whaling in the Antarctic: the ICJ Judgment and its Implications*, edited by Malgosia Fitzmaurice and Dai Tamada, 346–386: Brill Nijhoff, 2016.

Prezas, Ioannis. "Foreign Military Activities in the Exclusive Economic Zone: Remarks on the Applicability and Scope of the Reciprocal 'Due Regard' Duties of Coastal and Third States." *The International Journal of Marine and Coastal Law* 34, no. 1 (2019): 97–116.

Proelss, Alexander. "International Legal Challenges Concerning Marine Scientific Research in the Era of Climate Change." Paper presented at the Securing the Ocean for the Next Generation: Papers from the Law of the Sea Institute, UC Berkeley–Korea Institute of Ocean Science and Technology Conference, Seoul, Korea, 2012.

Proelss, Alexander. "The Law on the Exclusive Economic Zone in Perspective: Legal Status and Resolution of User Conflicts Revisited." *Ocean Yearbook* 26 (2012): 87–112.

Rayfuse, Rosemary. "Climate Change and the Law of the Sea." In *International Law in the Era of Climate Change*, edited by Rosemary Rayfuse and Shirley V. Scott, 147–174: Edward Elgar Publishing, 2012.

Redgwell, Catherine. "The Never Ending Story: the Role of GAIRS in UNCLOS Implementation in the Offshore Energy Sector." In *Law of the Sea: UNCLOS as a living treaty*, edited by Jill Barrett and Richard Barnes, 167–186. London: British Institute of International and Comparative Law, 2016.

Reiter, Nils, and Anette Frank. "Identifying Generic Noun Phrases." Paper presented at the Proceedings of the 48th Annual Meeting of the Association for Computational Linguistics, 2010.

Roach, J. Ashley. "Defining Scientific Research: Marine Data Collection." In *Law, Science & Ocean Management*, edited by Myron Nordquist, Ronán Long, Tomas Heidar and John Norton Moore, 541–574: Brill, 2007.

Rummel-Bulska, Iwona. "Law of the Sea and Meteorological and Oceanographic Observations from Ocean Areas." In *International Marine Environmental Law: Institutions, Implementation and Innovations*, edited by Andree Kirchner, 61–67: Kluwer Law International, 2003.

Rutz, Christian, and Graeme C. Hays. "New Frontiers in Biologging Science." The Royal Society London, 2009.

Ryder, Peter. "A possible migration from marine scientific research to operational oceanography in the context of the United Nations Convention on the Law of the Sea (UNCLOS)." *Elsevier Oceanography Series* 69 (2003): 25–35.

Salpin, Charlotte. "The Law of the Sea: A before and an after Nagoya." In *The 2010 Nagoya Protocol on Access and Benefit-Sharing in Perspective: Implications for International Law and Implementation Challenges*, edited by Elisa Morgera, Matthias Buck and Elsa Tsioumani, 149–183: Brill Nijhoff, 2012.

Salpin, Charlotte, Vita Onwuasoanya, Marie Bourrel, and Alison Swaddling. "Marine Scientific Research in Pacific Small Island Developing States." *Marine Policy* 95 (2018): 363–371.

Sands, Philippe. "Sustainable Development: Treaty, Custom and the Cross-Fertilization of International Law." In *International Law and Sustainable Development: Past Achievements and Future Challenges*, edited by Alan Boyle and David Freestone, 39–60: Oxford University Press, 1999.

Satyawan, IA. "Scientific Cooperation to Respond Climate Change in the South China Sea: The Study of Tides and Sea Level Change." Paper presented at the IOP Conference Series: Earth and Environmental Science, 2018.

Scott, Shirley V. "The LOS Convention as A Constitutional Regime for the Oceans." In *Stability and Change in the Law of the Sea: The Role of the LOS Convention*, edited by Alex Oude Elferink, 9–38: Martinus Nijhoff Publishers, 2005.

Scovazzi, Tullio. "The Concept of Common Heritage of Mankind and the Genetic Resources of the Seabed Beyond the Limits of National Jurisdiction." *Agenda Internacional* 14, no. 25 (2007): 11–24.

Scovazzi, Tullio. "Is the UN Convention on the Law of the Sea the Legal Framework for All Activities in the Sea? The Case of Bioprospecting." In *Law, Technology and Science for Oceans in Globalisation: IUU Fishing, Oil Pollution, Bioprospecting, Outer Continental Shelf*, edited by Davor Vidas, 307–318: Brill, 2010.

Scovazzi, Tullio. "'Due Regard' Obligations, with Particular Emphasis on Fisheries in the Exclusive Economic Zone." *The International Journal of Marine and Coastal Law* 34, no. 1 (2019): 56–72.

Sefrioui, Sarra. "Adapting to Sea Level Rise: A Law of the Sea Perspective." In *The Future of the Law of the Sea*, edited by Gemma Andreone, 3–22: Springer, 2017.

Shearer, Ivan. "Oceans Management Challenges for the Law of the Sea in the First Decade of the 21st Century." In *Ocean Management in the 21st Century: Institutional Frameworks and Responses*, edited by Alex Oude Elferink and Donald Rothwell, 1–18: Brill, 2004.

Shimmield, Graham, "Extent and Types of Research, Uses and Applications", *IUCN Information Papers for the Intersessional Workshop on Marine Genetic Resources*, 2013.

Smith, Shawn R., Gaël Alory, Axel Andersson, William Asher, Alex Baker, David I. Berry, Kyla Drushka, Darin Figurskey, Eric Freeman, Paul Holthus, Tim Jickells, Henry Kleta, Elizabeth C. Kent, Nicolas Kolodziejczyk, Martin Kramp, Zoe Loh, Paul Poli, Ute Schuster, Emma Steventon, Sebastiaan Swart, Oksana Tarasova, Loic Petit de la Villéon, and Nadya Vinogradova-Shiffer. "Ship-Based Contributions to Global Ocean, Weather, and Climate Observing Systems." *Frontiers in Marine Science* 6, no. 434 (2019-August-02 2019).

Song, Yann-Huei. "The South China Sea Workshop Process and Taiwan's Participation." *Ocean Development & International Law* 41, no. 3 (2010): 253–269.

Soons, Alfred H. A. "Marine Scientific Research Provisions in the Convention on the Law of the Sea: Issues of Interpretation." In *The UN Convention on the Law of the Sea: Impact and Implementation*, edited by ED Brown and RR Churchill, 365–372. Honolulu: The Law of the Sea Institute, William S. Richardson School of Law, University of Hawaii, 1987.

Soons, Alfred H. A. "The Developing Regime of Marine Scientific Research: Recent European Experience and State Practice." In *New Developments in Marine Science and Technology: Economic, Legal and Political Aspects of Change*, edited by LM Alexander, S Allen and LC Hanson, 43, 1988.

Soons, Alfred H. A. "Regulation of Marine Scientific Research by the European Community and Its Member States." *Ocean Development & International Law* 23, no. 2–3 (1992): 259–277.

Soons, Alfred H. A. "The Background of Article 247 of the UN Convention on the Law of the Sea (UNCLOS)." In *Procedure for the Application of Article 247 of the United Nations Convention on the Law of the Sea by the Intergovernmental Oceanographic Commission of UNESCO*, edited by UNESCO/IOC/LAW OF THE SEA (IOC/LOS). Paris, 2007.

Soons, Alfred H. A. "The Impact of Technological Developments on the International Legal Regime of Marine Scientific Research." In *30 Years after the Signature of the United Nations Convention on the Law of the Sea: the Protection of the Environment and the Future of the Law of the Sea*, edited by Marta Ribeiro, 329–330: Coimbra Editora, 2014.

Stephens, Tim. "Warming Waters and Souring Seas: Climate Change and Ocean Acidification." In *The Oxford Handbook of the Law of the Sea*, edited by Donald Rothwell, Alex Oude Elferink, Karen Scott and Tim Stephens, 777–798, 2015.

Stephens, Tim, and Donald Rothwell. "Marine Scientific Research." In *The Oxford Handbook of the Law of the Sea*, edited by Donald Rothwell, Alex Oude Elferink, Karen Scott and Tim Stephens, 559–581: Oxford University Press, 2015.

Tanaka, Yoshifumi. "Obligation to Co-Operate in Marine Scientific Research and the Conservation of Marine Living Resources." *Zeitschrift fur Auslaendisches Oeffentliches Recht und Voelkerrecht* 65, no. 4 (2005): 937–965.

Telesetsky, Anastasia, Donald K Anton, and Timo Koivurova. "ICJ's Decision in Australia v. Japan: Giving up the Spear or Refining the Scientific Design?". *Ocean Development & International Law* 45, no. 4 (2014): 328–340.

Testa, David. "Coastal State Regulation of Bunkering and Ship-to-Ship (STS) Oil Transfer Operations in the EEZ: An Analysis of State Practice and of Coastal State Jurisdiction Under the LOSC." *Ocean Development & International Law* 50, no. 4 (2019): 363–386.

Thirlway, Hugh. "The Law and Procedure of the International Court of Justice 1960–1989: Part One." *British Yearbook of International Law* 60, no. 1 (1989): 1–157.

Thirlway, Hugh. "The Law and Procedure of the International Court of Justice 1960–1989: Part Three." *British Yearbook of International Law* 62, no. 1 (1991): 1–76.

Treves, Tullio. "The General Assembly and the Meeting of States Parties in the Implementation of the LOS Convention." In *Stability and Change in the Law of the Sea: The Role of the LOS Convention*, edited by Alex G. Oude Elferink, 55–74. Leiden: Martinus Nijhoff Publishers, 2005.

Treves, Tullio. "The Development of the Law of the Sea since the Adoption of the UN Convention on the Law of the Sea: Achievements and Challenges for the Future." In *Law, Technology and Science for Oceans in Globalisation: IUU Fishing, Oil Pollution, Bioprospecting, Outer Continental Shelf*, edited by Davor Vidas, 41–58: Brill Nijhoff, 2010.

Treves, Tullio. "Coastal States' Rights in the Maritime Areas under UNCLOS." *Brazilian Journal of International Law* 12 (2015): 39–48.

Treves, Tullio. "The International Tribunal for the Law of the Sea and the Rule of Law." In *The Contribution of the International Tribunal for the Law of the Sea to the Rule of Law: 1996–2016*, edited by ITLOS, 69–76: Brill-Nijhoff, 2018.

Tvedt, Morten Walløe, and Ane E Jørem. "Bioprospecting in the High Seas: Regulatory Options for Benefit Sharing." *The Journal of World Intellectual Property* 16, no. 3–4 (2013): 150–167.

Verlaan, Philomene. "Geo-engineering, the Law of the Sea, and Climate Change." *Carbon & Climate Law Review* 3, no. 4 (2009): 446–458.

Verlaan, Philomène. "Marine Scientific Research: Its Potential Contribution to Achieving Responsible High Seas Governance." *The International Journal of Marine and Coastal Law* 27, no. 4 (2012): 805–812.

Verlaan, Philomène A. "Current Legal Developments: Intergovernmental Oceanographic Commission of the United Nations Educational, Scientific and Cultural Organization (IOC/UNESCO)." *The International Journal of Marine and Coastal Law* 24 (2009).

Verlaan, Philomène A. "Current Legal Developments: London Convention and London Protocol." *The International Journal of Marine and Coastal Law* 26, no. 1 (2011): 185–194.

Vierros, Marjo, Gwenaëlle Hamon, David Leary, Salvatore Arico, and Catherine Monagle. "An Update on Marine Genetic Resources: Scientific Research, Commercial Uses and a Database on Marine Bioprospecting." Paper presented at the side event of the eighth meeting of United Nations Informal Consultative Process on Oceans and the Law of the Sea, 2007.

Warner, Robin M. "Protecting the Diversity of the Depths: Environmental Regulation of Bioprospecting and Marine Scientific Research beyond National Jurisdiction." *Ocean Yearbook*, no. 22 (2008): 411–443.

Wood, Michael. "Reflections on the United Nations Convention on the Law of the Sea: a Living Instrument." In *Law of the Sea: UNCLOS as a living treaty*, edited by Jill Barrett and Richard Barnes, LXXVII–LXXXII. London: British Institute of International and Comparative Law, 2016.

Wyatt, Julian. "Using Intertemporal Linguistics to Resolve the Problem at the Origin and Core of the Evolutionary Interpretation Debate." In *Evolutionary Interpretation and International Law*, edited by Georges Abi-Saab, Kenneth Keith, Gabrielle Marceau and Clément Marquet, 47–56: Bloomsbury Publishing, 2019.

Yanai, Shunji. "The Contribution of the Tribunal to the Progressive Development of International Law." In *The Contribution of the International Tribunal for the Law of the Sea to the Rule of Law: 1996–2016*, edited by ITLOS, 79–82: Brill-Nijhoff, 2018.

You, Kijun. "The Law and Practice Relating to Marine Scientific Research in Northeast Asia ". In *The Law of the Sea Convention: US Accession and Globalisation*, edited by Alfred H. A. Soons, Hak-so Kim, Myron H. Nordquist and John Norton Moore: Martinus Nijhoff Publishers, 2012.

Yu, Chuxiao. "Implications of the UNCLOS Marine Scientific Research Regime for the Current Negotiations on Access and Benefit Sharing of Marine Genetic Resources in Areas Beyond National Jurisdiction." *Ocean Development & International Law* 51, no. 1 (2020): 2–18.

Reports and Summary Record of Diplomatic Meetings

"Abridged Final Report of the Eighteenth session of World Meteorological Congress", Doc. WMO - No.1236, 2019.

Benefit-Sharing, Ad Hoc Open-Ended Working Group on Access and, "Report of A Workshop on Access and Benefit-Sharing in Non-Commercial Biodiversity Research", UNEP/CBD/WG-ABS/7/INF/6, 2009.

"Chair's streamlined non-paper on elements of a draft text of an international legally-binding instrument under the United Nations Convention on the Law of the Sea on the conservation and sustainable use of marine biological diversity of areas beyond national jurisdiction", 2017.

"Evolving Capabilities of the Argo Global Array of Profiling Floats - Information Document", Doc. IOC/INF-1344, 2017.

Group, Biogeochemical-Argo Planning, "The Scientific Rationale, Design and Implementation Plan for a Biogeochemical-Argo Float Array", 2016.

J. Tirpak, Elizabeth, "Practices of States in the Fields of Marine Scientific Research and Transfer of Marine Technology: An Update of the 2005 Analysis of Member State Responses to Questionnaire No. 3", Doc. IOC/ABE-LOS VIII/8, Paris, 2008.

Kantai, Tallash, Jennifer Bansard, Tasha Goldberg, Katarina Hovden, and Asterios Tsioumanis, "Summary of the Third Session of the Intergovernmental Conference (IGC) on the Conservation and Sustainable Use of Marine Biodiversity of Areas Beyond National Jurisdiction: 19–30 August 2019", *IISD - Earth Negotiations Bulletin.*

Koskenniemi, Martti, "Fragmentation of International Law: Difficulties Arising from the Diversification and Expansion of International Law (Report of the Study Group of the International Law Commission)", UN Doc. A/CN.4/L.682, 2006.

Morgera, Elisa, Asheline Appleton, Daniela Diz, and Asterios Tsioumanis, "BBNJ IGC-1 Highlights: Wednesday, 12 September 2018", *IISD - Earth Negotiations Bulletin.*

Morgera, Elisa, Asheline Appleton, Daniela Diz, and Asterios Tsioumanis, "Summary of the First Session of the Intergovernmental Conference on an International Legally Binding Instrument under the UN Convention on the Law of the Sea on the Conservation and Sustainable Use of Marine Biodiversity of Areas Beyond National Jurisdiction: 4–17 September 2018", *IISD - Earth Negotiations Bulletin.*

Morgera, Elisa, Asheline Appleton, Tallash Kantai, and Asterios Tsioumanis, "Summary of the Fourth Session of the Preparatory Committee on Marine Biodiversity beyond Areas of National Jurisdiction: 10–21 July 2017".

Morgera, Elisa, Asheline Appleton, Tallash Kantai, and Asterios Tsioumanis, "Summary of the Third Session of the Preparatory Committee on Marine Biodiversity beyond Areas of National Jurisdiction: 27 March – 7 April 2017".

Morgera, Elisa, Daniela Diz, Tallash Kantai, and Asterios Tsioumanis, "Summary of the Second Session of the Preparatory Committee on Marine Biodiversity beyond Areas of National Jurisdiction: 26 August – 9 September 2016".

"Ocean Fertilization: Report of the Legal and Intersessional Correspondence Group", LC 30/4, 2008.

"Ocean Fertilization: Report of the Working Group on Ocean Fertilization", LC 30/WP.6, 2008.

"Practices of States in the Fields of Marine Scientific Research and Transfer of Marine Technology: An Analysis of Responses to ABE-LOS Questionnaire No. 3", 2009.

"Progress Report on the Implementation of the Programmes of Work on the Biological Diversity of Inland Water Ecosystems, Marine and Coastal Biological Diversity, and Forest Biological Diversity (DECISIONS IV/4, IV/5, IV/7)", Doc. UNEP/CBD/COP/5/INF/7, 2000.

"PSIDS Submission to the Second Meeting of the Preparatory Committee for the Development of an international legally binding instrument under the United Nations Convention on the Law of the Sea on the conservation and sustainable use of marine biological diversity of areas beyond national jurisdiction (BBNJ Prep-Com) (August 2016)".

Pugh, David. "Criteria and Guidelines for Ascertaining the Nature and Implications of Marine Scientific Research (IOC/ABE-LOS I/7)." In *First Meeting of the Advisory Body of Experts on the Law of the Sea* (*ABE-LOS*). Paris, 2001.

"Report by GPO on "the Argo Project" Developments", Doc. IOC/ABE-LOS I/10, 2001.

"Report of the Chairman of the Third Committee: Extract from the Official Records of the Third United Nations Conference on the Law of the Sea, Volume XIV (Summary Records, Plenary, General Committee, First and Third Committees, as well as Documents of the Conference, Resumed Ninth Session)", Doc. A/CONF.62/L.61, 1980.

"Report of the Eighth Session of IOC/ABE-LOS", Doc. IOC/ABE-LOS VIII/3, 2008.

"Report of the Fifth Session of IOC/ABE-LOS", Doc. IOC/ABE-LOS V/3, 2005.

"Report of the Forty-first Session of the Executive Council of IOC", Doc. IOC/EC-XLI/3, 2008.

"Report of the fourteenth Meeting of States Parties to UNCLOS", Doc. SPLOS/119, 2004.

"Report of the Fourth Session of IOC/ABE-LOS", Doc. IOC/ABE-LOS IV/3, 2004.

"Report of the International Law Commission (Fifty-eighth session)", Doc. A/61/10, 2006.

"Report of the International Law Commission (Seventieth session)", Doc. A/73/10, 2018.

"Report of the International Law Commission covering the work of its eighth session - Extract from the Yearbook of the International Law Commission: 1956, vol. II", Doc. A/3159, 1956.

"Report of the International Law Commission on the second part of its seventeenth session and on its eighteenth session", Doc. A/CN.4/SER.A/1966/Add.1, 1967.

"Report of the Ninth Session of IOC/ABE-LOS", Doc. IOC/ABE-LOS IX/3 Rev., 2009.

"Report of the Preparatory Committee established by General Assembly resolution 69/292: Development of an international legally binding instrument under the United Nations Convention on the Law of the Sea on the conservation and sustainable use of marine biological diversity of areas beyond national jurisdiction", UN Doc. A/AC.287/2017/PC.4/2, 2017.

"Report of the Secretary-General on oceans and the law of the sea of 4 March 2004", UN Doc. A/59/62.

"Report of the Secretary-General on oceans and the law of the sea of 12 March 2007", UN Doc. A/62/66.

"Report of the Seventh Session of IOC/ABE-LOS", Doc. IOC/ABE-LOS VII/3, 2007.

"Report of the Sixth Session of IOC/ABE-LOS", Doc. IOC/ABE-LOS VI/3, 2006.

"Report of the Thirtieth Meeting of the Scientific Group of the London Convention and the First Meeting of the Scientific Group of the London Protocol", LC/SG 30/14, 2007.

"Report of the Thirty-First Meeting of the Scientific Group of the London Convention and the Second Meeting of the Scientific Group of the London Protocol", LC/SG 31/16, 2008.

"Report of the Thirty-Ninth Session of the Executive Council of IOC", Doc. IOC/EC-XXXIX/3, 2006.

"Report of the Twenty-Fifth Session of the Assembly of IOC", Doc. IOC-XXV/3, 2009.

"Report of the Twenty-Ninth Consultative Meeting and the Second Meeting of Contracting Parties", Doc. LC 29/17, 2007.

"Report of the Twenty-Second Session of the Assembly", Doc. IOC-XXII/3, 2003.

"Report of the Working Group on Ocean Fertilization", LC/SG 31/WP.3/Rev.1, 2008.

"Report on the work of the United Nations Open-ended Informal Consultative Process on Oceans and the Law of the Sea at its eighth meeting ", UN Doc. A/62/169, 2007.

"Report on the work of the United Nations Open-ended Informal Consultative Process on Oceans and the Law of the Sea at its fifth meeting", UN Doc. A/59/122, 2004.

"Report on the work of the United Nations Open-ended Informal Consultative Process on Oceans and the Law of the Sea at its twentieth meeting", UN Doc. A/74/119, 2019.

"Revised draft text of an agreement under the United Nations Convention on the Law of the Sea on the conservation and sustainable use of marine biological diversity of areas beyond national jurisdiction - Note by the President", Doc. A/CONF.232/2020/3, 2019.

Ryder, Peter, "Marine Scientific Research and Operational Oceanography in the Context of the UN Convention on the Law of the Sea", Doc. IOC-WMO-UNEP/I-GOOS-VI/10, 2003.

"Statement of Concern regarding iron fertilization of the oceans to sequester CO2", LC-LP.1/Circ.14, 2007.

"Study of the Relationship between the Convention on Biological Diversity and the United Nations Convention on the Law of the Sea with Regard to the Conservation and Sustainable Use of Genetic Resources on the Deep Seabed (Decision II/10 of the Conference of the Parties to the Convention on Biological Diversity)", UN Doc. UNEP/CBD/SBSTTA/8/INF/3/Rev.1, 2003.

"Summary Record of the 46th meeting of the Third Committee: Extract from the Official Records of the Third United Nations Conference on the Law of the Sea, Volume XIV (Summary Records, Plenary, General Committee, First and Third Committees, as well as Documents of the Conference, Resumed Ninth Session)", Doc. A/CONF.62/C.3/SR.46, 1980.

"Technical Report on Scoping of Operational Oceanography", Doc. IOC/INF-1291, 2012.

"Technical Workshop Enhancing Ocean Observations and Research, and the Free Exchange of Data, to Foster Services for the Safety of Life and Property: Final Report", Geneva, Switzerland, 2019.

"Textual proposals submitted by delegations by 20 February 2020, for consideration at the fourth session of the Intergovernmental conference on an international legally binding instrument under the United Nations Convention on the Law of the Sea on the conservation and sustainable use of marine biological diversity of areas beyond national jurisdiction (the Conference), in response to the invitation by the President of the Conference in her Note of 18 November 2019 (A/CONF.232/2020/3)", 2020.

Wallace, Doug, Cliff Law, Philip Boyd, Yves Collos, Peter Croot, Ken Denman, Phoebe Lam, Ulf Riebesell, Shigenobu Takeda, and Phil Williamson, "Ocean Fertilization: A Scientific Summary for Policy Makers", Doc. IOC/BRO/2010/2, Paris, 2010.

Cases

Aegean Sea Continental Shelf (Greece v. Turkey), (1978).

Bay of Bengal Maritime Boundary Arbitration between Bangladesh and India, (2014).

Case concerning Land Reclamation by Singapore in and around the Straits of Johor (Malaysia v. Singapore), Provisional Measures, (2003).

Chagos Marine Protected Area Arbitration (Mauritius v. United Kingdom), (2015).

China - Measures Affecting Trading Rights and Distribution Services for Certain Publications and Audiovisual Entertainment Products, (2009).

Dispute concerning delimitation of the maritime boundary between Bangladesh and Myanmar in the Bay of Bengal (Bangladesh/Myanmar), (2012).

Dispute Concerning Delimitation of the Maritime Boundary between Ghana and Côte d'Ivoire in the Atlantic Ocean (Ghana/Côte d'Ivoire), (2017).

Dispute Regarding Navigational and Related Rights (Costa Rica v. Nicaragua), (2009).

The 'Enrica Lexie' Incident (Italy v. India), (2020).

Gabčíkovo-Nagymaros Project (Hungary/Slovakia), (1997).

Iron Rhine Arbitration (Belgium/Netherlands), (2005).

Kasikili/Sedudu Island (Botswana/Namibia), (1999).

Legal Consequences for States of the Continued Presence of South Africa in Namibia (South West Africa) notwithstanding Security Council Resolution 276 (1970), (1971).

The M/T "San Padre Pio" Case (Switzerland v. Nigeria), Provisional Measures, (2019).

The M/V "SAIGA" (No. 2) Case (Saint Vincent and the Grenadines v. Guinea), (1999).

The M/V Virginia G Case (Panama v. Guinea-Bissau), (2014).

The MOX Plant Case (Ireland v. United Kingdom), Provisional Measures, (2001).

Request for an Advisory Opinion submitted by the Sub-Regional Fisheries Commission (SRFC), (2015).

Rights of Nationals of the United States of America in Morocco (France v. United States of America), (1952).
Territorial and Maritime Dispute (Nicaragua V. Colombia), (2012).
United States - Import Prohibition of Certain Shrimp and Shrimp Products, (1998).
Whaling in the Antarctic (Australia v. Japan: New Zealand intervening), (2014).

International Agreements

Convention for the Protection of the Marine Environment of the North-East Atlantic, 1992.
Convention of the World Meteorological Organization, 1947.
Convention on Biological Diversity, 1992.
Convention on the Continental Shelf, 1958.
Convention on the Prevention of Marine Pollution by Dumping of Wastes and Other Matter, 1972.
International Convention on the Regulation of Whaling, 1946.
Kyoto Protocol to the United Nations Framework Convention on Climate Change, 1997.
Nagoya Protocol on Access to Genetic Resources and the Fair and Equitable Sharing of Benefits Arising from Their Utilization to the Convention on Biological Diversity, 2010.
Paris Agreement, 2015.
Protocol to the Convention on the Prevention of Marine Pollution by Dumping of Wastes and Other Matter, 1996.
International Seabed Authority (ISA). *Regulations on Prospecting and Exploration for Cobalt-rich Ferromanganese Crusts in the Area*, 2012.
International Seabed Authority (ISA). *Regulations on Prospecting and Exploration for Polymetallic Nodules in the Area*, 2013.
International Seabed Authority (ISA). *Regulations on Prospecting and Exploration for Polymetallic Sulphides in the Area*, 2010.
United Nations Convention on the Law of the Sea, 1982.
United Nations Framework Convention on Climate Change, 1992.
Vienna Convention on the Law of Treaties, 1969.

Policy and Decisions of International Organizations

(ILC), International Law Commission, "Draft conclusions on subsequent agreements and subsequent practice in relation to the interpretation of treaties and commentaries thereto", *Report of the International Law Commission, Seventieth session*, Doc. A/73/10, 2018.
Council, IOC Executive, "Evolving Capabilities of the Argo Global Array of Profiling Floats", Decision IOC/EC-LI/4.8, 2018.

Draft [Practical] Guidelines of IOC, within the Context of UNCLOS, for the Collection of Oceanographic Data by Specific Means, IOC/ABE-LOS VII/7, 2007.

Draft Convention on the Legal Status of Ocean Data Acquisition Systems, Aids and Devices (ODAS): Second Revision, 1993.

"The Global Observing System for Climate: Implementation Needs", Publication No. GCOS 200 (GOOS-214), 2016.

"Guidelines for the Implementation of Resolution XX-6 of the IOC Assembly Regarding the Deployment of Profiling Floats in the High Seas within the Framework of the Argo Programme", Resolution EC-XLI.4, 2008.

IOC, "Strengthening and Streamlining GOOS", IOC Resolution XXVI-8, 2011.

IOC, "The Global Ocean Observing System 2030 Strategy", IOC Brochure 2019–5 (IOC/BRO/2019/5 rev.), Paris, 2019.

"IOC Assembly Resolution on the Argo Project", IOC/Resolution XX-6, 1999.

Observing, The Task Team for an Integrated Framework for Sustained Ocean, "A Framework for Ocean Observing", Doc. IOC/INF-1284, 2012.a

OSPAR Code of Conduct for Responsible Marine Research in the Deep Seas and High Seas of the OSPAR Maritime Area, Source: OSPAR 08/24/1, Annex 6, 2008.

Procedure for the Application of Article 247 of UNCLOS by the Intergovernmental Oceanographic Commission of UNESCO, 2005.

"Resolution LC-LP.1 (2008) on the Regulation of Ocean Fertilization".

"Resolution LC-LP.2 (2010) on the Assessment Framework for Scientific Research Involving Ocean Fertilization".

"Resolution LP.4(8) on the Amendment to the London Protocol to Regulate the Placement of Matter for Ocean Fertilization and Other Marine Geoengineering Engineering Activities", 2013.

"Resolution on Whaling under Special Permit", Doc. Resolution 2014–5, 2014.

Sea, United Nations Office for Ocean Affairs and the Law of the, "Marine Scientific Research: A Guide to the Implementation of the Relevant Provisions of the United Nations Convention on the Law of the Sea", New York, 1991.

UN/DOALOS, "Marine Scientific Research: A Revised Guide to the Implementation of the Relevant Provisions of the United Nations Convention on the Law of the Sea", New York, 2010.

"UNGA Resolution on "Development of an international legally-binding instrument under the United Nations Convention on the Law of the Sea on the conservation and sustainable use of marine biological diversity of areas beyond national jurisdiction" of 19 June 2015", UN Doc. A/RES/69/292.

"UNGA Resolution on "International legally binding instrument under the United Nations Convention on the Law of the Sea on the conservation and sustainable use of marine biological diversity of areas beyond national jurisdiction" of 24 December 2017", UN Doc. A/RES/72/249.

"UNGA Resolution on "Third United Nations Conference on the Law of the Sea" of 14 December 1983", UN Doc. A/RES/38/59.

"UNGA Resolution on oceans and the law of the sea of 4 January 2018", UN Doc. A/RES/72/73.

"UNGA Resolution on oceans and the law of the sea of 10 December 2019", UN Doc. A/RES/74/19.

"UNGA Resolution on oceans and the law of the sea of 17 March 2011", UN Doc. A/RES/65/37.

"UNGA Resolution on the law of the sea of 19 December 1994", UN Doc. A/RES/49/28.

Miscellaneous

Linderfalk, Ulf. "Discussing the Evolutionary Interpretation of Treaties." *EJIL: Talk!* (December 16, 2014). https://www.ejiltalk.org/discussing-the-evolutionary-interpretation-of-treaties/.

Nelson, Dolliver. "Exclusive Economic Zone." In *Max Planck Encyclopedia of Public International Law* [*MPEPIL*], 2008.

Treves, Tullio. "Marine Scientific Research." In *Max Planck Encyclopedia of Public International Law* [*MPEPIL*], 2008.

Index

www.ingramcontent.com/pod-product-compliance
Lightning Source LLC
Chambersburg PA
CBHW071229230926
51849CB00001B/62